BRITAIN

At Your Leisure

Produced by the Publishing Division of The Automobile Association

Contents

Roy Johnstone – former editor of *Choice*, the monthly retirement planning magazine: also former editor of *Travelling* magazine and author of several books, including one on leisure.

Tony Lycholat – fitness specialist, British Amateur Athletics Board coach and British Association of Weight Lifting Associations teacher; honours degree in human movement; lecturer and author of several books on various keep-fit aspects.

Margaret Mason – former editor, now consultant editor of *Yours*, the monthly consumer newspaper published by Help the Aged; specialised subjects include pensions and housing.

John Ruler – travel journalist for 25 years and member of British Guild of Travel Writers; regular contributor to a number of newspapers and journals.

Bill Tadd – former financial editor of *Choice* magazine and co-author of a handbook on retirement; also course leader of the Pre-Retirement Association's retirement planning holidays.

Dr Eric Trimmer – general practitioner for 40 years, author of many general and scientific medical books; former editorial director of *Medical Tribune*; contributor to numerous medical and consumer publications.

Consultant Editor: Roy Johnstone

Walks and Tours prepared by the Home Routes Research and Development Unit of The Automobile Association.

Mapping produced by the Cartographic Department, The Automobile Association. Regional maps based upon Ordnance Survey maps with the permission of the Controller of Her Majesty's Stationery Office.
Crown copyright reserved.
© The Automobile Association 1988

Filmset by Avonset, Midsomer Norton, Bath.
Printed and bound by Purnell Book Production Ltd.
Member of BPCC plc.

The contents of this publication are believed correct at the time of printing. Nevertheless, the publishers cannot accept responsibility for errors or omissions, or for changes in details given.

© The Automobile Association 1988

Produced and published by The Automobile Association, Fanum House, Basingstoke, Hampshire RG21 2EA.

AA reference 53497.

THE WEST COUNTRY

June Lewis – a frequent lecturer and broadcaster on the history and culture of the West Country; well-known playwright and author, a Cotswold Warden and the official town historian of Fairford.

SOUTH & SOUTH EAST ENGLAND

Myrrhine Raikes – has worked in publishing for many years, and has lived in the South and South East all her life.

CENTRAL ENGLAND & EAST ANGLIA

Roland Smith – Head of Information Services for Peak National Park. Author of several books on Britain's countryside and regular contributor to magazines.

THE NORTH COUNTRY

Carol Bond – former Marketing and Publicity Officer for Northumbria Tourist Board; has lived in the North of England all her life and contributes to AA publications.

SCOTLAND

Ross Finlay – well-known writer on the Scottish countryside. Contributor to several books published by the AA.

WALES

Peter Allen – has travelled extensively throughout Wales, where he has lived all his life. He has written several books, as well as articles on wildlife in Wales.

Introduction

A poor life this if, full of care,
We have no time to stand and stare.

W.H. Davies had it about right when he
declared that the world would be a poor
place if people were so pre-occupied with
work and worries or a combination of the
two that they had no time to relax and
enjoy even the simplest pleasures of life.

Of course, things have changed since
WHD penned that popular verse. More
and more people are being given the
option of early retirement with quite
handsome pay-offs in some cases. Add, in
even more instances, a healthy level of
savings, a home that these days, in some
parts of the country at least, seems to
appreciate in value by the minute, plus
the prospect of a meaningful occupational
pension – and it is clear that many people
(and the number is growing all the time)
have the resources to enjoy their later
years as never before.

That is not all. People are healthier and,
helped in part by the advances in medical
science and technology, are living and
remaining active longer. As for leisure
opportunities and things to do, the sky is
the limit; there are even those who are
taking that literally and are trying their
hand at flying, hot-air ballooning and
hang-gliding. Age simply is not a barrier
any more.

This book is designed for the over-50s,
whether you are already retired or still
looking forward to that day.

Handled properly, retirement should be
the happiest phase of life but, it has to be
said, for many the sudden transition from
a rigid nine-to-five routine over 40 years
or more to a carefree existence of doing
precisely what you want, when you want
comes as a bit of a shock to the system and
can take a while to get used to. The key is
to prepare well ahead and this book,

compiled by a team of experts, provides a mine of invaluable advice and information.

It anticipates the pitfalls and the problems that cause the most concern: in particular good health and financial security – the very cornerstones of successful and happy retirement. Get these right and you are ready to enjoy your precious leisure time to the full.

But perhaps you are, or think you will be, at a loss as to how to keep occupied. If so, you are by no means alone: many people are so busy earning a living they do not have time for outside interests or for any exercise other than the occasional swim on holiday. The sections on hobbies and sport and recreation should point you in the right direction and, frankly, it is never too late to start.

As for holidays, there has never been a wider choice to suit all pockets and preferences – like taking a break from the cold and miserable British winter for a start. Once you are no longer accountable

to a work commitment or restricted by family ties, there's every good reason for spending some of the chilly months in a warm climate. And, as the holiday section of this book shows, it need not cost a fortune. Chances are it will cost no more than staying at home.

Finally, in the comprehensive Gazetteer section of the book, places of interest are listed alphabetically, region by region. There is also a selection of walks and drives. All have been chosen for leisurely enjoyment, with the accent on leisure. And remember: when time is your own you can go to places midweek or outside the peak season, and avoid the crowds and the hassle (and when you are out with grandchildren, a long ice cream queue can cause needless hassle!).

This book will prepare you for a real welcome to the wonderful world of leisure – and help you enjoy the happiest days of your life.

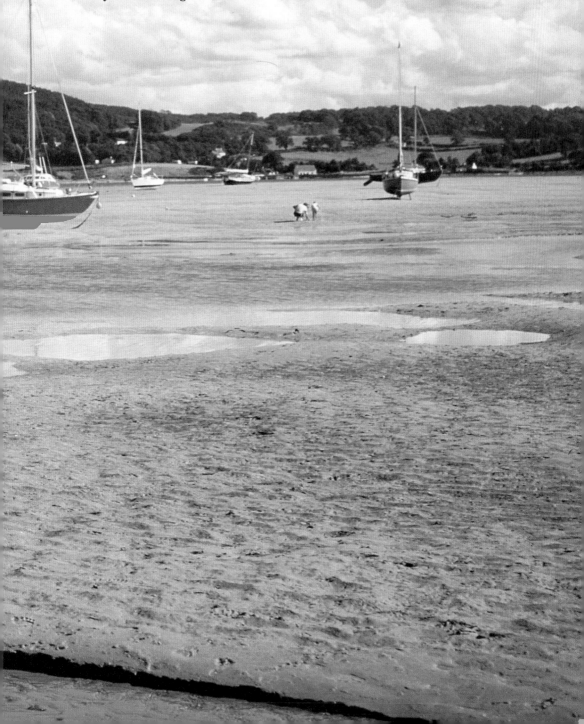

Health for leisure

In order to realise what is meant by good health it is necessary to come to terms with some of the less joyful aspects of living, perhaps discovering unsuspected personal limitations that may have resulted from any number of influences over the years. Such a confrontation need not be as traumatic or devastating as it sounds — even in later years — and the understanding it gives allows steps to be taken against or around problems which might otherwise prove restrictive.

Cases in point
Three particular cases of people who successfully adapted their retirement plans after finding that they were not as fit as they imagined are instructive.

The first, a woman of 55, looked forward to getting the garden into shape, but when she came to it she first suffered a minor injury then fractured a wrist. Her doctor diagnosed osteoporosis — the brittle bones of middle age and later — and she had to change her plans by working out a completely different kind of gardening.

A patient who looked forward to spending much more time on the golf course had trouble with his knee and was forced to limit his sporting activities to 18 holes maximum in any one day. Another, who had planned plenty of hill walking, experienced chest pains after a brisk pull up a steepish slope, and was diagnosed as suffering from angina. He had to make

considerable changes in the way he organised his life.

All these ailments arose in one way or another from damage caused by the individual's previous lifestyle – and all were combated to the extent that impairment of their leisure-time enjoyment became minimal.

Contributory to the gardener's problem was a lack of calcium-rich foods in previous years, because she had avoided milk, cheese and the like in order to keep her weight down. Following the fracture her doctor put her on a calcium-rich but non-fattening diet – skimmed milk and low-fat cheese, a calcium supplement and magnesium tablets. He also planned graduated exercise schedules for her, and prescribed some hormone replacement therapy.

In contrast, the golfer had developed osteoarthritic knees. His doctor advised a weight-reduction programme – alcohol-free beer and no second helpings, together with a firm 'pass' at the sweet trolley – and in six months' time he was able to manage 27 holes. The hill walker was lucky, although he did not think so at the time. After tests his heart specialist told him that giving up smoking might help. The advice was taken and the angina stopped interfering with his hill walking.

All in the mind
All three had experienced a warning, done something about it and preserved most of their leisure fitness, but physical ailments are not the only ones that can put a drag on life in later years. This was discovered by a middle-aged woman who was appalled at what was happening to her body, and tried to resist it. A friend suggested that she should dress more in tune with her years, but she refused to go along with

Drugs and driving
Driving under the influence of drugs is as much an offence as when impaired by alcohol – and many of those who commit such 'medical' transgressions do so because they have not been informed that the medication which they have been prescribed has side effects. Preparations to be wary of are listed here.

All tranquillisers. Perhaps the most popular of these is Diazepam, which is prescribed mostly as Valium. Anyone taking this sort of drug should allow a 36-hour 'wash-out' period before attempting to drive.

Travel-sickness pills. Most of these, particularly the antihistamine type such as Dramamine, have a sedating effect – especially after the smallest alcoholic drink. Non-antihistamine remedies, notably those containing hyoscine, often affect eyesight. Travel-sickness pills are for passengers only.

Sleeping pills. These can have an appreciable sedative effect on the system for anything up to 12 hours after being taken.
Some of the blood-pressure medications are also sedative in their action, and sufferers should always check with their doctors that it is safe to drive while taking them.
Anyone who is taking one of the anti-convulsive drugs, particularly phenobarbitone, should not even consider getting into the driving seat of any vehicle.

this and bought more and more expensive 'young' clothes, determined to keep up with her daughter. Then one day she overheard someone referring to her as mutton dressed as lamb.

She was mortified, and almost overnight became a voluntary prisoner in her own home – afraid of the ridicule that she had, in a way, courted. Needless to say, her middle-aged leisure opportunities plummeted, a situation made all the worse by the fact that her appearance meant everything to her.

She had nothing else to make life worthwhile, and one day became so desperate that she phoned the Samaritans. The story has a happy ending, for she eventually released herself from her self-imposed jail sentence and began to enjoy life again. Now she finds satisfaction in helping others by doing a stint on the Samaritans' switchboard.

Fitness to drive

These four people all had one considerable asset in that they could drive – and were allowed to, although the tranquillisers prescribed to the last-mentioned case put her off the road for three months (see panel). However, drivers who develop symptoms and signs of illness that might affect their ability to control a vehicle are duty bound to report their problem to the DVLC, and may be taken off the road.

A medical diagnosis of epilepsy will mean immediate disqualification, for some time at least, and other illnesses – such as diabetes, stroke illness, heart attack, various neurological disorders and disabling severe arthritis – should be notified at once to the licensing authorities and the relevant insurance company. A doctor's or a specialist's report is vital – particularly in cases of eye diseases like glaucoma or cataract, which may or may not exclude the victim from driving. A regular two-yearly sight test is advisable anyway.

The law states that, once a driver reaches the age of 70, he or she must annually produce a doctor's certificate to prove that they are sufficiently fit to handle a motor vehicle. The examination will probably be charged for, but that is money well spent if it keeps the driver and other road users from harm.

Fitness to drive does not necessarily mean fitness in general, for a seriously disabled person who can walk only a very short distance might be perfectly safe behind the wheel – and eligible for the monthly non-taxable Mobility Allowance and free road tax.

People vary tremendously as age advances where safety behind the wheel is concerned, and some 80-year-olds are more reliable than many people of 18. But there is no room for complacency, and full use should be made of glasses and hearing aids; driving in difficult road conditions should be avoided altogether. It is often the case that a spouse in the passenger seat will notice slower-than-safe reflexes more readily than a stranger, and their observations should always be heeded. A practical tip for senior citizens who fall foul of a moving traffic offence is to make sure that they appear in court with medical confirmation of continuing fitness to drive. This could go a long way to persuading the Bench not to impose a driving test order.

Eating for health

Twentieth-century people tend to think that nutritional deficiency is a thing of the past, but by no means is that the complete case. Many over-55s experience abnormal tiredness, irritability and the sort of rheumaticky symptoms to which doctors cannot really put a name, and increasingly nutritionists are looking to vitamin and mineral deficiency in their search for a cause. Modern eating habits provide plenty of all the basic nutritional building blocks – protein, carbohydrate and fat – but today's methods of food production seem to have created a vitamin and mineral 'famine'. Some imbalances, including the type of malnutrition that results in obesity, can be rectified, but the problems are not always so clear cut.

Quite new in nutritional circles is the concept of micronutrients, important food minerals that are present in tiny quantities and which are often removed by modern food-production techniques and overcooking in the kitchen. The result may be a shortage in the body of selenium, zinc or magnesium which over-55s should consider taking in the form of dietary supplements.

Modern medical thought is coming around to the idea that a special diet for the over-55s is a good notion, and high on the list of priorities to promote health and fitness is a change in eating habits for anyone who is overweight. The problem is working out what 'overweight' means, since the old quick-reference tables using different 'frame sizes' are totally unscientific and from a health point of view quite useless. For a start, it is impossible for individuals to judge their own frame sizes with any accuracy, so the height–weight computation is likely to be miles out. Also, the tables are based on data worked out by a life-insurance company in the 1930s – a curious yardstick of health for men and women 50 years on.

However, a better method is at hand, based on painstaking research by modern nutritionists. Known as the 'Body Mass Index', it is a series of 'code' numbers based on a height–weight calculation in which height (in centimetres) multiplied by itself is divided into body weight (in kilos). The result will be a long number – like ·002173 – but the zeros and everything else bar the first two figures are irrelevant. Those two are most important and represent the current state of fitness. Anything over 25 indicates obesity that is having an effect on the health of the individual being tested. From 25–30 is low-risk obesity; 30–34 is moderate risk and over 40 is high risk – and none of this is guesswork.

How to slim
The theory is easy – those who use more

energy than they absorb will lose weight – but the practice is fraught with difficulties caused by the fact that people differ enormously in the efficiency with which they use food and store fat. This means that individuals must be careful to choose a diet that suits their particular constitution, or they may well be wasting a lot of time and effort. Nutritionists, doctors – and even the local library – can help.

Over the last few years various important committees of learned people have been pondering over whether or not modern food makes people ill as well as obese. However, food is big business and many of the conclusions drawn by these impressive-sounding bodies are confusing, but beneath all the verbiage is a simple, clear three-part plan for healthier eating.

- *Cut fat consumption by 25 per cent (by eating less saturated fats)*
- *Reduce sugar intake by 50 per cent*
- *Increase dietary fibre by 33 per cent (mostly by eating more wholewheat cereals, fruit and vegetables)*

Anyone with a Body Mass Index of over 25 needs to lose weight, but it is important that any diet is kept in balance with this three-part plan. Most women tend to eat less than 1500 calories a day in a reducing diet, but men can often slim quite well on 2000. More calories can be allowed by someone who exercises than by one who is sedentary. Ferreting out the fat needs thought, for a great deal is hidden. For instance, a nice lean steak can be substantially fatty, as is all meat except chicken. Fats used for spreading and cooking are easily identified and eliminated, but what of milk and cheese? Neither should be omitted altogether since

Healthy eating for the over-50s: less fat and sugar, more fibre, minerals and vitamins

Regular physical activity will make up for years behind a desk – and can even be fun

they are staple foods, but they can be replaced by skimmed or semi-skimmed milk and fat-reduced cheese. Biscuits, cakes, pies, luncheon meats, sausages and similar foods are all fat heavy.

Fat reductions made with this list in mind will reduce substantially calorie intake and put the slimmer well on the way to a fitter Body Mass Index. The BMI magic figure also gives a clue as to how long it will take to get below that 25 ideal. Numbers from 25-30 indicate three months of dieting, 31-35 six months and over 35 as much as a year.

Dieting is not particularly difficult so long as it is accepted that some long-established tastes may have to change, sometimes not that drastically. A simple transition from full-fat milk to skimmed milk will cut fat intake by 14 per cent, which is well on the way to the 25 per cent recommended – and even compromising with semi-skimmed milk will show a reduction of 7 per cent. But changing from butter to margarine saves nothing, since in most cases their calorie content is identical. The answer, in this case, is to switch to a low-fat spread.

While the intake of all fat-rich foods is reduced, that of high-fibre vegetables, salads and cereal products should be increased.

Good fat . . . bad fat

It has been seen that part of the route back to fitness lies in sensible eating and attention to the magic figures of the Body Mass Index, both of which require particular vigilance with regard to the amount of fat ingested. This is actually more complex than it seems, for the nutritional surveys from which the three-part plan for healthier eating were formulated made a distinction between two kinds of fat – saturated and unsaturated – stating that a diet should not have more than 15 per cent of its calories coming from the former.

Both these terms have crept into the language from the science laboratory, and are chemical descriptions of the way in which carbon and hydrogen atoms are linked together in the molecular structure of fats in food. Basically, saturated fats are solid at room temperature, and include animal products such as suet and butter. Unsaturated fat products, like cooking oils and some margarines, are softer at room temperature and many remain liquid unless frozen.

Understanding the difference between the two, and their effect on health, requires the acceptance of the concept that essential fats are part of a health-giving diet. This is not the contradiction to previous statements that it sounds, and arises from the work of Professor Sinclair, the first person to link diet and heart disease.

He did so by studying Eskimos who ate an enormously fatty diet, but who seldom died of coronary artery disease. Another oddity about these people was that they were prone to prolonged bleeding, because their blood took a long time to clot. Dr Sinclair 'went Eskimo' and after eating as they did for several months, found that he too developed prolonged bleeding. Subsequent research showed that the health-protective factor present in the marine oil that the Eskimos quaffed in such quantities was an unsaturated fat (fish have to keep their body fat liquid at freezing temperatures) which Sinclair termed essential, because the human body cannot make it. People have to eat it to get it – and the very interesting thing is that its absence increases the likelihood of artery disease and heart attacks.

The key to the secret of essential fat is that it prevents clotting – thus the Eskimos' prolonged bleeding – and, of course, a coronary thrombosis is a clot of blood.

But there is another character on this stage, one which in the popular mind is the villain. This is cholesterol, a cheesy-like substance that gets deposited in diseased arteries, sometimes blocking them. Too much cholesterol in the blood increases the risk of coronary thrombosis, stroke, high blood pressure and various forms of artery disease. But this is only part of the story, for the system actually needs cholesterol, because it is also an essential building block in the body's chemistry.

The enigma is rationalised by the realisation that there are several forms of cholesterol, some good and some bad. However, it is important that the balance is kept right by essential fatty acids like those eaten by the Eskimos thus preventing arteries fudging up and abnormal blood clots forming.

In the last 50 or so years the average person's diet has swung away from fish and its essential marine oil to foods which are high in saturated animal fats. It is thought that this has been a considerable factor in the present epidemic of heart and artery disease among the over-55s. It is obvious that the way to health involves the cutting down of fats, as the nutrition surveys suggest, but not all fats. Those from the sea are health protective and, if they cannot be eaten every other day, they should certainly be replaced with a dietary supplement.

Physical Fitness

Anybody who finds that everyday tasks like gardening and shopping have become more physically demanding with time should not dismiss the fact, since physiologists are agreed that, once past the age of 30, the body engages reverse gear and goes into what they term 'functional decline'.

Between the ages of 30 and 70, for example, work capacity decreases by up to 30 per cent, as does muscle mass and general flexibility. Nerve impulses travel more slowly and blood pressure rises, while bone mass decreases – especially in women – by around 25 per cent. The metabolic rate also falls by an average of 10 per cent.

These effects, along with associated decreases in kidney, lung, visual and hearing functions, can impair physical activity to the point where tasks and leisure activities which were once carried out with ease begin to assume Herculean proportions. But all is not gloom and doom, for while 'functional decline' is an irreversible part of getting older, only 50 per cent of the decrease in physiological functions is actually due to the ageing process itself. The other half is the product of disuse and can be countered through regular physical activity. This, in effect, slows down the rate of functional decline.

The idea is not new. In 5BC Hippocrates said: 'Speaking generally, all parts of the body which have a function, if used in moderation and exercised in labours to which each is accustomed, become thereby healthy and well-developed and age slowly; but if unused and left idle they become liable to disease, defective in growth and age quickly.' By accepting this it is easy to understand how the perpetually active person stays active, for in a sense their physiological age is less than their actual years. Research has revealed that men in their 70s who have remained physically active can 'outperform' inactive, sedentary men in their 20s when it comes to tests of physical fitness.

So the way to maintain as much physical prowess as possible, well into retirement years, is to take regular exercise – but in a careful and planned way. It should always be borne in mind that, although there are considerable benefits to regular exercise (see panel on page 12), inappropriate exertion can cause injury. All specialists recommend that an exercise prescription

---

First aid – mouth-to-mouth respiration

The rescuer should pinch the victim's nostrils, after checking their airway, take a deep breath, and 'seal' their mouth around that of the victim before blowing into his or her chest. Then the rescuer's mouth should be removed, whereupon the patient's chest will fall and air will whistle out like a sigh. If it does not, the victim's airways should again be checked, and mouth-to-mouth respiration repeated. If breathing does not resume spontaneously after four attempts, check for pulse – at the wrist, in the neck, or over the left side of the chest.

If the heart stops beating, chest compressions must be performed together with mouth-to-mouth ventilation. Place the heel of one hand along the line of the breastbone, two finger breadths above the junction of the rib margins at the bottom of the breastbone. Cover this hand with the heel of the other, fingers interlocked, and arms straight. Fifteen compressions, at the rate of 80 per minute should be followed by two mouth-to-mouth breaths. Compressions should be stopped once the pulse returns. Continue mouth-to-mouth ventilation until natural breathing is restored.

First aid – clearing the airway

Too often people die unnecessarily because something has stopped the vital passage of air from mouth to lungs. The obstruction could be something as simple as dislodged dentures, a blood clot in the mouth, or a swallowed tongue; it can be removed by positioning the victim so that the neck is extended, then pulling the lower jaw forward (and open) with the thumb in order to sweep the forefinger of the other hand inside the mouth, thus removing the block. Mouth-to-mouth respiration should be applied if the victim has stopped breathing.

First aid – how to staunch blood loss

Forget about finding pressure points and using a tourniquet, because the best way to stop bleeding is to apply firm, constant pressure over the place from which it seems to be coming. There is no need to remove clothing in order to find the exact point, for the priority is to improvise a pad and keep the pressure on until skilled first-aid help arrives . . . or until the blood flow seems to have stopped. The pad can be made from a rolled scarf, a hat, folded newspapers, or anything of a similar nature.

Assessing the effort
A reliable way of ensuring that exercise is pitched at the correct intensity is for the subject to monitor his or her heart, which during aerobics should be operating at about 60 per cent of its maximum potential.

Maximum heart rate decreases with the years, and can be predicted by subtracting the subject's age in years from 220.

For example, the predicted maximum heart rate of a 50-year-old is arrived at by subtracting 50 from 220, giving the answer 170 beats per minute. Sixty per cent of the maximum is found by multiplying by 0.6 – thus, in this case,

170 bpm × 0.6 = 102 bpm.

Heart rate is counted by monitoring the pulse, either at the wrist on the thumb side, or by feeling with the fingers only of one hand at a point on the neck just below the jaw bone. Whichever method is used, the number of beats in six seconds is counted and a zero is added to this figure to give the number of beats per minute. Remember that the first beat counted is zero, the next is one . . . and so on.

How exercise helps
Apart from the more obvious benefits, regular exercise has been shown to develop stronger joints and joint structures, help prevent osteoporosis (thinning bones), improve the subject's shape and appearance and assist blood flow to the skin. First-hand reports also indicate increased energy levels and a general feeling of well-being and satisfaction.

Researchers who have concentrated on the psychological benefits of regular exercise have shown improvements in confidence, self image – and even memory.

should begin with a detailed evaluation of current health and fitness, and an appraisal of personal medical history. Such assessments are more and more commonly being provided by private health-care organisations, while simple fitness tests are often conducted by health clubs, with medical clearance from the subject's GP.

In the past, it has always been considered best to take medical advice before starting a scheme of exercise. However, the Health Education Authority and the Sports Council say this is totally unnecessary for the great majority, including older people. If you stick to the basic rule of starting gently and building up slowly over the weeks, and always avoid doing anything uncomfortable, you should be fine. But if you are worried in any way, then seek a medical opinion before starting out.

Muscles, heart and lungs
Fitness has many components but, in formulating a campaign of exercise, it is common to consider aerobics (efficiency of the heart and lungs); muscular strength and endurance; and general joint flexibility. To those major health-related items can be added such skill-related aspects as agility, balance and co-ordination.

All such components are important contributors to full enjoyment of life. Strength and endurance facilitate lifting, moving and carrying; flexibility allows a full range of body movement and the skill-related functions allow effective execution of complex co-ordination patterns.

However, they take second place to aerobic fitness, the exercises which help reduce the risk of heart disease and cardiovascular problems in general, reduce the level of harmful cholesterol in the blood and assist in the management of high blood pressure and obesity.

The 'classic' aerobic activities include brisk walking, jogging, dancing, cycling and swimming, but even these will prove ineffective unless they are carried out for long enough, at a sufficient intensity, and on a regular and progressive basis.

Effective aerobic exercise is continuous and makes the subject comfortably out of breath for at least 10 minutes. It is repeated in equally spaced bouts – say, three times a week – and as fitness develops the sessions are gradually increased in extent until after several weeks they each take some 20 minutes. The starting point should be whatever can be managed in the very first stages, and may well be less than 10 minutes. Irrespective of that, the subject should persevere – keeping the intensity of exercise low (see panel above) – whilst gradually extending the exercise period until the target time is reached.

Slow, safe and sure
Exercise for other components of fitness should be similarly progressive, the golden rule being never to attempt too much too soon. The body will soon react to over exertion and, at the least sign of dizziness, nausea, unsteadiness, pains or tightness in the chest, or disturbed breathing, the subject should cut back on the intensity and duration of exercise – and seek specialist advice.

Untoward stiffness or fatigue in the limbs following exertion is another warning to reduce exercise and re-assess personal limitations. Everybody is different, and each individual should work at his or her own pace. It is also important when exercising to develop a technique that prevents injury.

Forced or bounced movements should be avoided, as well as straining and breath-holding positions which can raise the blood pressure. Clothes must be comfortable, and each bout should begin at very low intensity, with joints and limbs being taken through the ranges of movement until they are 'warmed up' and ready for greater exertion. 'Cooling down' is also important, with the intensity of exercising being tapered down gradually to light stretching and relaxation. A successful session should leave the subject refreshed and relaxed, not exhausted!

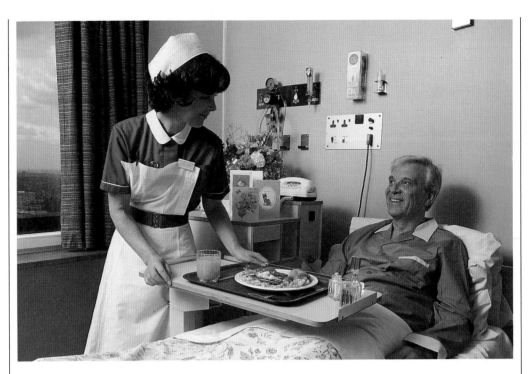

Checks and screening

Until now, the major emphasis of this feature, has been on regaining health and fitness through self-help, and henceforth maintaining both at a satisfactory level. However, for such a programme to be properly effective it should include a good monitoring system, and there can be none better than regular check-ups by the professionals.

The simplest screening can be handled by a GP or practice nurse and involves blood-pressure testing and weighing. More detailed examinations by various private organisations include blood tests – checking for cholesterol, for instance – so that anyone at special risk can be quickly identified and set on a healthier and safer course.

A medical truth that is slowly beginning to dawn on people is that nobody is younger than their arteries. When they become diseased, these vital rivers of life can cause a host of problems: heart attacks and strokes; blindness in uncontrolled diabetics and muscular degeneration;

Regular screening – either a simple GP's check-up or a more detailed examination – will give early warning of any ailment

the agony of claudication, and even impotence.

Looking after the arteries should be a preoccupation of the over-55s. Smoking is out, and proper nutrition is essential. Regular screening will spot uncontrolled diabetes, which destroys arteries, in time for something to be done about it.

Prevention is better than cure, and the sooner an ailment is diagnosed the better are the chances of a complete cure. Worrying symptoms (some of which are identified below) should never be ignored, but taken straight to a concerned doctor.

By following the basic rules of sensible eating, exercise, self-assessment and regular contact with their local GP and health organisations, the over-55s can achieve and maintain a level of fitness that will enable them to get the very best from their well-deserved years of retired leisure.

Private health insurance
Various independent schemes are available – most of them covering consultant referral and hospital charges. It is also possible to insure against being off work with a policy that will make various cash payments towards loss of earnings and domestic bills.

Policies should always be read most carefully before any agreement is signed, and a particular check should be made to ensure that any exclusions are acceptable – especially if age-related. Any

doubts can usually be settled by the Citizens Advice Bureau or a local GP.

Anyone who before retirement age has become a member of a private-health insurance or provident scheme should have no trouble in continuing membership, but arranging it for the first time after retirement is trickier. Private Patients Plan (PPP), however, offers one such package (details from PPP, PPP House, Upperton Road, Eastbourne, East Sussex BN21 1LH; (0323) 401505).

Worrying symptoms –
- Unexplained weight loss
- Cough – coughing up of sputum, especially blood
- Chest pain on exertion, or breathlessness
- Any unexplained change in appetite or bowel habit
- Any blood loss from any part of the body
- Any lump or sore that will not heal

A comfortable living

RETIREMENT from work does not mean retirement from life. The world goes on, and to succeed in it requires just as much effort as might previously have been devoted to a job or business.

A prime objective must be to maintain the standard of living that a lifetime of work has earned – to protect assets and secure an income that will permit the realisation of opportunities that are waiting to be grasped as soon as the habit of 2,000 hours spent every year at office desk or factory bench has been broken.

Lower retirement ages, redundancy and superior health care mean that most people will spend far more of their lives in retirement, and the earlier they start planning, the better.

The first step is to assess how much of a gap will exist between full-time earnings and retirement income. Current outgoings should be matched against expenditure in retirement (see panel on page 16). It is then possible to calculate the effect retirement will have on personal finances, but first it is necessary to know about any entitlements that may be due.

There are three prime requirements for a state pension, and the claimant must:
- Have reached state retirement pension age, 65 (man) 60 (woman),
- Have genuinely retired from full-time work,
- Have made sufficient National Insurance contributions.

The DHSS keeps records of contributions, and will supply details to use with the table in their leaflet NP.32 (*Your Retirement Pension*). This will show whether full pension entitlement applies – and, if not, what proportion can be expected. It is not possible to fill old gaps with lump-sum payments, but recent shortfalls can sometimes be made good – although at current contribution rates, not at those which applied when the deficiency arose. Entitlements that can also be claimed include:

- Extra pension for a spouse
- Additional pension (SERPS)
- Graduated pension
- Christmas bonus
- Age addition (at 80)

About pensions

Retirement income will be made up of several components – the occupational pension, state benefits and any incomings arising from investments and savings. These are added together and the total is taken from present earnings to discover what any shortfall is likely to be. Details regarding the form of occupational pension which applies will be forthcoming from employers or their pensions managers, and are needed to work out an idea of how much can be expected. Probably, it will be calculated on a sixtieth or eightieth of pensionable salary for each year of pensionable service. Pensionable salary could be that received at retirement, an average over the last three or five years – even an average of the three highest-paid consecutive years. 'Salary' can mean basic salary, or salary plus overtime payments, bonuses and commissions.

Pensionable service is the number of years during which the employee has been covered by the pension scheme. Once the

The Budget

Income	Working	Retired	Expenditure	Working	Retired	Expenditure	Working	Retired
Gross salary			Pension cons			Car tax		
Occupational pen			Nat Ins cons			Car maint		
State pension (inc. SERPS & grad)			Tax			House repairs		
			Rates (inc water)			Decorations		
Personal pen			Mortgage			Holidays		
Building Society int			Home insurance			TV/video rental		
Bank dep int			Car insurance			TV licence		
Nat Savings int			Other insurance			Theatre/cinema		
Dividends			Phone			Hobbies		
Other interest			Electricity			Drink		
Part time work			Gas			Tobacco		
Any other income			Clothes			Postage		
			Dry cleaning			Subscriptions		
			Household food			Charities		
			Eating out			Papers/books		
			Fares			Other expdtr		
Totals			Petrol			Totals		

number of pensionable years is known, along with the way the calculations have been worked out, it is possible to work out what pension should be forthcoming.

The inflation-proofed state pension is added to the projected retirement income (DHSS leaflet NI.196 gives current benefit rates), but it must be borne in mind that a man does not qualify for this until aged 65, and a woman until 60. That just leaves the addition of any other income, including that from investments and savings, to give a figure to match against actual income at work. Then it is time to measure the relative outgoings.

In retirement these will be less, for contributions to occupational pensions and National Insurance will no longer be made, income tax will be less (see panel) and there will be no more outlay on travel to work. However, bills for heating and lighting at home may go up.

Extra pension for a spouse is payable to a man of 65, even though his wife may not be 60. When she reaches 60 this becomes hers, and she may choose whether to take it or any state pension she has acquired through her own full contributions (reduced rate 'small stamp' contributions do not count). If she is younger than 60 and still working, the extra pension earned by her husband will be wiped out if her earnings reach a certain level.

A further state pensions pitfall is the Earnings Rule. Retired people are allowed to earn part-time but, if their wages rise above a certain level the pension diminishes and may eventually be extinguished altogether. DHSS leaflet NI.196 also gives current earnings rules.

Withdrawal of pension can be deferred for a maximum of five years, and will increase in value by 7½ per cent for each. That percentage is added to the pension at the time it is taken, not when the decision is made to defer. Men of 70 and women of 65 are entitled to the state basic pension, without deduction, regardless of earnings.

SERPS – State Earnings Related Pension Scheme – is to be phased out, but will continue unchanged for people who reach retirement age in this century. It gives better pensions to higher earners, who have paid for it with higher National Insurance contributions. It will reach its peak value in 1998, 20 years after it started, but nine years after it began it was paying more than £20 a week to those whose earnings had been at the top level. Those in 'contracted-out' employment will not benefit from SERPS, but are covered by a guaranteed minimum pension.

Taxing answers

Age Allowance At 65 single people and married couples (when one of them reaches 65) receive a higher allowance to set against income before tax. Higher incomes will diminish that allowance, but not below the level of the personal amount that everyone can set against income. The age allowance rises further at 80.

Income Tax State pensions, except the invalidity pension, are taxable (although tax is normally paid only if tax liability exceeds personal allowance). Former employers deduct tax from occupational pensions. Income from investment or savings is also taxable, but in most cases this is deducted at source. Dividends and interest from shares and unit trusts are paid after tax deduction. Anybody not liable for tax can reclaim it, but it is not possible to recover composite-rate tax deducted at source from interest on bank and building society deposits.

Capital Gains Tax This applies to any asset which may be disposed of at a profit, with the exception of the subject's principal private residence: cars, government stocks, gifts between husband and wife, endowment policies, personal equity plans and small personal possessions also escape. Before liability is assessed, allowance is made for inflation. On top of this is an exemption limit.

Inheritance Tax This problem is really for heirs, but their burden can be eased and professional advice should be taken from an accountant or independent financial adviser. Anyone who feels that this tax does not concern them should tot up the value of their house, furniture, car, savings and investment, then compare the total with the current exemption limit.

The graduated-pension scheme which operated for 14 years from 1961 gave units – which change in value – in exchange for contributions. The maximum number of units anyone can have amassed is 86 for a man and 72 for a woman. Basic pension, SERPS, guaranteed-minimum pension and graduated-pension are all protected against inflation and rise each April to match prices. Christmas bonus and age addition are not, however, and are tiny.

If, once all the calculations have been done, the difference between disposable income in retirement and at work presents a pretty bleak picture, there is much that can be done.

Remedies for shortfalls

Additional Voluntary Contributions (AVCs) provide a means for 'topping up' pensions. The maximum investment is 15 per cent of earnings. Tax relief is given on the contributions, and higher-rate taxpayers get greater advantage. The 15 per cent of earnings allowed to be used in this tax-beneficial way includes pensions' contributions deducted at source. So, if the employer is already putting 5 per cent of the employee's salary into the pension scheme, the investor may add only 10 per cent. Various free-standing AVC schemes are run by financial institutions, but the overall investment limit remains at 15 per cent. For self-employed people the limit is 17½ per cent, and they are also allowed to go back six years to take up the tax advantages for the whole of that time. Under Inland Revenue rules it is not permissible to earn a pension that exceeds two-thirds of the final salary, so AVCs should be geared accordingly.

It pays to invest for growth rather than income when building retirement finances, but it is a mistake to become over-invested. Stocks, unit and investment trusts can go down and anyone who has not retained sufficient capital outside investment which can be withdrawn at short notice may have to sell their stock at a loss to meet a sudden cash need. Sound and sensible investment will rise again if given a chance, and should be left sitting tight while contingency interest-earning deposit funds are tapped to cover the crisis. Working people who invest for income pay tax on it at their top rate, but investing for growth is designed to increase capital, and capital-gains tax is far less onerous (see panel). At retirement, when income-tax liabilities are lower and allowances greater, capital can be converted as needed into high-income investments or interest-bearing deposits.

Personal Equity Plans (PEPS) give a tax incentive to investment in British industry. From £240 to £2,400 a year – £20 to £200 by monthly instalment – may be paid into these schemes and, provided it is kept there for a further year, and the dividends are re-invested, both income and gain are free from tax for that 12 months and all following years. At the end of 12 months it is permissible to start another PEP. The state of the Stock Market and British industry are crucial to such plans, and they should not be embarked on with a short-term view. Various schemes are offered by the banks and other money managers.

Professional advice

Some advisers, such as company-employed insurance salesmen, can proffer only one range of products. Others, like bank managers, are obliged to put the customer's interests first when making recommendations. Independent advisers earn their living by commissions from insurance companies, unit-trust managers and the like. Unfortunately, the levels of commission are not uniform, and insurance companies pay the higher rates. So how is it possible to evaluate the adviser and the advice?

The first thing to assess is whether the adviser has asked for all the information he needs to recommend a package. Details might include lifestyle and outgoings, mortgage, rates and how much is spent on holidays and hobbies, as well as general finance such as pensions, savings and earnings. An adviser can give suitable advice only when he or she knows the client – and that means a personal

---

Lump sums

It is possible to take up to one and a half times the final salary from a pension as a tax-free lump sum (three-eighths for each year of pensionable service), but to achieve the maximum requires 40 years in the scheme. Generally, a man of 65 will lose £1 from his pension for every £9 cash he takes, while women at 60 lose £1 for £11.

Factors to consider are: an inflation-proofed pension carries a life-time guarantee of value, and none of it should be given up lightly. However, most pensions are sure to diminish in value, and the lump sum offers a chance to remedy that by investment.

Financial Services Act

Under the Securities and Investment Board, regulatory bodies are responsible for overseeing those who give advice, or make financial arrangements for clients. Operation without authorisation is illegal.

Competence, solvency and adequate professional indemnity insurance are principal requirements for authorisation, and an industry-wide compensation scheme is planned to give private investors complete cover up to £30,000 and 90 per cent of the next £20,000, should an authorised person – or firm – holding investors' money, go into liquidation.

Compensation does not cover the normal risks of investment. According to the SIB, its existence no more removes the need for investors to be careful with their money than the existence of the Highway Code removes the need to look before crossing the road!

Timeshare can provide comfortable holidays in glorious settings

interview, not a questionnaire. Terms of business should be set out in writing, and the adviser should be able to commit himself to likely earnings from his recommendations. In addition, he should explain fully the reasons for the advice he is giving, and have references.

All advice given should also be in writing, and include a tax computation showing what sum is likely to be received, and how much tax will be owed. Also, it is important to avoid the danger of being over-invested, so the person being advised must work out whether the package

offered will cause this to happen. A general rule is not to tie up more than 60 per cent of capital in investments.

The Financial Intermediaries, Managers and Brokers Regulatory Association (FIMBRA) will supply the names of authorised financial advisers in any particular locality, and it is always possible to check the standing of an adviser with the appropriate regulatory body (see panel).

Bricks and mortar

Sound advice is necessary before any lump sum is taken from a pension to settle debts. For instance, it is often a mistake to pay off a mortgage because – unless the house is sold to buy another, or home improvements are made – the householder will not get a similarly tax-beneficial loan. If that amount of capital is available, it is better to invest it elsewhere. Building societies and banks are often prepared to re-schedule mortgages over an extended period to reduce monthly repayments, thus enhancing income – and it is even possible to negotiate payment of interest only, leaving the capital loan to be repaid eventually from the householder's estate.

A home is probably the ordinary person's biggest asset, but the capital is locked in it. However, if it is sold and a lesser property is bought, some of that capital will become available – but there are other ways of using your home to raise income later in life.

Home-income plans provide capital, by way of a mortgage, with which to buy an annuity. The age limit is generally 69, and the older the applicant, the better the

---

Further help

DHSS Leaflets Unit, PO Box 21, Stanmore, Middlesex HA7 1AY. Publications: *Earning extra pension by cancelling your retirement (NI.92); Married women – your national insurance position (NI.1); National insurance contribution rates (NI.208); National insurance for self-employed people (NI.41); Retirement benefits for married women (NP.32B); Retiring? (FB.6); Your retirement pension (NP.32); Your retirement pension if you are widowed or divorced (NP.32A).*

These and other booklets are also obtainable from local DHSS offices.

Home-income plans:
Hinton and Wild (Home Plans) Ltd, 374-378 Ewell Road, Surbiton, Surrey KT6 7BB (01-390 8166).

Investment:
The Stock Exchange, Public Affairs Department, London EC2N 1HP (01-588 2355)

Unit Trust Association, Buckingham House, 6-7 Buckingham Street, London WC2N 6BU (01-930 4241) Publications: *Everything you need to know about unit trusts; Explaining unit trusts.*
Association of Investment Trust Companies, 16 Finsbury Circus, London EC2M 7JJ (01-588 5347). Publications: *More for your money; How to make it.*

Pensions:
Company Pensions Information Centre, 7 Old Park Lane, London W1Y 3LJ (01-493 4757). Publications: *How to understand your pension scheme; How a pension fund works; What pension terms mean; How changing job affects your pension.*
(For these booklets send 9in×7in sae.)

Regulatory bodies:
FIMBRA, 22 Great Tower Street, London EC3R 5AQ (01-929 2711)

Securities and Investments Board, 3 Royal Exchange Buildings, Cornhill, London EC3V 3NL (01-283 2474)
The Life Assurance and Unit Trust Regulatory Organisation (LAUTRO), Aldermary House, Queen Street, London EC4N 1TP (01-248 4477)
The Securities Association, Stock Exchange, London EC2N 1HP (01-588 2355)

Recommended reading
Tax Saving Guide, Consumers' Association, London
The Daily Mail Income Tax Guide, Associated Magazines, London
The Macmillan Handbook for Retirement, Macmillan Reference Books, London
The Which? Book of Money, Consumers' Association, London
The Which? Book of Saving and Investing, Consumers' Association, London
Using Your Home as Capital, Age Concern, Mitcham, Surrey

annuity. Part is used to pay interest on the mortgage, the remainder comes in as income, but nothing is paid off the capital loan during the householder's lifetime. The debt is finally discharged from the estate, and the property, of course, provides the security. Residents who have adopted such a scheme have the unfettered right to occupy the house for the whole of their lives, and it remains their property. Also, their heirs may choose whether to keep the house and pay off the mortgage, or sell it to settle the debt.

Under reversion schemes the house is sold, although the residents have the right to live in it for their lifetimes. It is generally possible to obtain a higher income from such arrangements because there is no mortgage interest to repay, but the property cannot be willed to heirs. Some schemes do not insist that capital is used to buy an annuity, but allow the recipient to do what they wish with it. Property-reversion schemes lack appeal for many since, once they are agreed, the residents have no interest in the equity and cannot benefit from future appreciation.

Investing in leisure

Many people use some of their severance pay to buy holiday retreats. Holiday homes add up to money well spent – provided the owners are content to return to the same spot year after year. For people who prefer the freedom of open dates and the open road, buying a caravan to tow behind the car – or even a motorised one – may well be the answer.

There are plenty of advertisers offering homes around the Mediterranean, and some will even provide English solicitors to scrutinise the deeds – although prospective purchasers would be wiser to choose their own from firms specialising in overseas sales. The complexities of buying overseas need not be a problem; the Federation of Overseas Property Developers, Agents and Consultants (FOPDAC – see panel below) produces a pack which explains the legal position in clear and concise terms.

Some villa owners take out leasing arrangements with the intention of paying for their holiday homes in a few years. When not using the residence themselves, the owners put it into the hands of local agents and derive an income from sub-letting that could be around £90 a week.

A good option for those interested in Timeshare is to go for a British development which has links overseas, so that the option is left open to swap weeks for a vacation abroad. Such an arrangement offers the best of both worlds – property that is close enough to keep an eye on, and more opportunities for weeks in the sun at other times. The two main Timeshare networks are Resorts Condominium International (RCI) and Interval International, both of which exchange facilities with thousands of developments in 55 countries.

The Villa Owners Club acts as the main UK agents for the scheme, and also provides discounts on flights, car hire and other holiday expenses.

Even in this country it is possible to have a holiday home or cottage and get others to pay for it. For instance, a caravan on the south coast could well realise £100 a week during the peak summer season, and £60 at other times. Most new caravans on commercial sites are let out at double these figures, but owners rely on the site proprietors to arrange bookings that help offset high rents of around £600 a year.

Perhaps the major leisure purchase outside a holiday home is private transport, and this should be chosen with care and an eye to its future use. There can be a world of difference between a model needed to tow a caravan and a runabout for shopping and pleasure. A hatchback scores in the small car stakes where a lot of luggage is to be carried.

Before trading a car in, it is wise to try all the dealers in the area, and never to accept the first price offered. The recommended route is via a reputable garage, arranging an AA inspection and report before purchase.

Buying a holiday home
There are seven golden rules to be followed when buying a holiday home here or abroad.
- Never sign anything or hand over money until the small print has been read and understood
- Never proceed with a major investment without proper legal advice. The Law Society can help with lawyers who are able to check overseas property documents
- Check the development and accommodation personally, making sure that the buildings are structurally sound. If on a site, inspect the leisure facilities
- Bear in mind the cost of travelling to and from a holiday retreat. In mid-summer the fares will be at peak levels
- Ignore offers of large discounts or gifts for an immediate decision and take time to think things over. Never be rushed into any transaction
- After-care and maintenance. Check quality of after-care and maintenance, and any charges involved
- Never feel guilty about saying no

Addresses
British Property Timeshare Association, Westminster Bank Chambers, Market Hill, Sudbury, Suffolk CO10 6EN
Caravan Club, East Grinstead House, East Grinstead, West Sussex RH19 1UA
FOPDAC, 15-19 Kingsway, London WC28 6UU
Interval International, 57-61 Mortimer Street, London W1N 7ID
RCI Europe Ltd, Parnell House, 19/28 Wilton Road, London SW1V 1LW
Villa Owners Club Ltd, Rutland Chambers, High Street, Newmarket, Suffolk CB8 8LX

At home and away

LIKE all decisions made by retired people, the question of whether to move or stay put should not be taken hurriedly. Firstly, they should ask themselves why they have not moved before. It could be that they like the area, or because they have lived there most of their lives and made friends with the neighbours – or simply that they have never seen another house or locality that suits them better.

On the surface these are strong reasons for continuing to live in the same place, but they may change under closer examination. Perhaps the area was suitable because it was near work, and the house ideal for children who have since gone. All these and many more factors must be carefully weighed up, not forgetting to include the financial benefits that might be achieved by moving to a smaller house. It is also a time for honesty, and self-questioning about the ability to make new friends easily. Gregarious couples who are content with one another's company, or loners should find no social problems in moving – but people who form deeper relationships could be in difficulty.

Whether to move or not is a decision that should be made well in advance of retirement, so that there is ample time to choose a new location. Also, the bright side is not always the best aspect to view, so that long-sought-after seaside cottage should be looked at in December or January, rather than the balmy days of summer.

A reason for moving that can go sadly wrong is to be near the children and grandchildren for,if the younger family is forced to move for any reason, the older couple or individual could be left very lonely in unfamiliar surroundings.

Another mistake is for the retired householder to move to a smaller property as a plan for old age, for he or she probably has 20 or more active years ahead and can easily enjoy a large house with spare rooms for visitors, space to lay out a train set and a garden to work in. There will be opportunity enough to change later, if necessary, by which time the larger house will have acquired comparatively greater value that can be converted into a tax-free capital gain.

Many people harbour a life-long hankering to live in the country or on the coast, but there are many disadvantages hidden among these pastoral attractions. Locations should be chosen with care, with a particular weather-eye cocked at the prevailing climate. Information on rainfall, snow, temperatures and hours of sunshine is provided by local meteorological offices and the London Weather Centre. A mistake can be costly, for people who trade down and then change their mind might find they cannot afford to move back.

More than 400,000 Britons have their state pensions paid to them abroad where they have found a warm, sunny existence in which heating, lighting and clothes are not the onerous expense they can be at home. Climate is unlikely to change, but cost of living advantages cannot be relied on – all countries are victims of inflation.

There is no difficulty in having a state pension paid abroad, but whether this will be supplemented by the increases that protect it against inflation depends on whether or not the country concerned has a reciprocal agreement with the UK. EEC nations do, but the increases protect only against British inflation – not against that in the country chosen for retirement. Information about agreements with other countries is available from the DHSS Overseas Branch, Newcastle-upon-Tyne, NE98 1XY.

The National Health Service, sometimes much maligned, is nonetheless there to care for people in need. Its equivalent is rarely found abroad and, though most foreign countries likely to attract the retiring Briton have high standards of medical care, the cost should be considered. Reciprocal health schemes exist with some (again, the DHSS should be consulted) but this will not provide the cover enjoyed by British tourists making short-term trips abroad. Extra insurance is advisable, preferably with a British company so that it is possible to read and understand the small print. Some companies impose a maximum age limit above which they will not offer insurance. Others charge higher premiums for the over-65s.

Dreams of slipping abroad to avoid the taxman's clutches are futile and, at best, overseas residents exchange a known devil for one which is unknown . If they spend 183 days in Britain – whether successive or as a result of numerous visits – in one tax year, they become liable for UK tax. If they live in Spain, for example, for 182 days in one year, their income (including a wife's, whether or not she has spent the same amount of time there) becomes liable to Spanish tax.

It is possible to be regarded as resident in two countries at the same time, but luckily there are agreements to eliminate the iniquity of double taxation. Inland Revenue offices will supply details as to which countries have such arrangements with the UK, and copies of them may be bought from HM Stationery Office. They tend to vary in form from country to country. To establish non-residence in the UK the 'emigrant' must provide proof that he or she does not intend to return to the country for more than an average of three months in each tax year. Selling a home here and buying one abroad is good evidence, but if other UK accommodation is available and used for even the briefest

Pros and Cons		
A smaller house	**Coast and country**	**A foreign country**
For	**For**	**For**
Possible acquisition of capital	Less pollution	More sunshine and warmth
Lower maintenance costs, rates	(noise and atmospheric)	Possibly lower living costs
etc	Less crime	Healthier existence
Less cleaning work	More leisurely existence	
Smaller garden	Lower cost of living	**Against**
Against	**Against**	Even greater distance from
Large houses appreciate faster	Fewer facilities (transport etc)	friends and relatives
Less room for visitors and	Fewer entertainments	Uncertainty of fluctuating
hobbies	Loss of old friends	currency values
Feeling of lack of space	Expense of extra travel to visit	Language problems
Smaller garden	family, etc	Health-care problems

period, the 'emigrant' will be regarded as still resident in this country. The type of property concerned might be a flat rented by a spouse. It is even more complicated to establish domicile abroad – which is particularly important where Inheritance Tax is concerned – and may not be a wise move anyway. Lawyers or tax experts from both countries must be retained to advise on the pros and cons of residence and domicile.

People set on retiring abroad should plan well ahead, try to learn enough of the language to get by on and make several visits at different times of the year before taking the final decision.

Buying an overseas property requires even more care than purchasing a house in Britain. Ideally, a lawyer with experience in such matters should be found in this country to instruct a local lawyer abroad.

The market in homes built specifically for the retired has changed dramatically during the last 10 years or so. Builders and developers have realised that the picture of a pensioner huddled over two coals in a grate does not apply to those retiring with substantial occupational pensions and lump-sum opportunities.

Sheltered homes have sprouted up across the country, although – it must be admitted – there is far more development of this nature in the south and south-east than in the north. A young 65-year-old eagerly anticipating the joys of retirement may well be right to disregard the sheltered home, but it should be kept in mind as an option to be considered later.

'Sheltered' can be read as 'protected', and such complexes of flats, bungalows and houses are designed with the safety and security of the older person in mind. They also help residents to preserve an independent way of life, incorporating taps that are easy to turn, even with arthritic hands, and electric points positioned to

avoid undue bending. Incidentally, do-it-yourself enthusiasts determined to remain in their present homes can do a great deal along these lines – although electrical modifications should be left to those qualified to handle them. Sheltered communities also have wardens or nurses to keep an unobtrusive eye on residents, and to be handy in case of emergency. Alarms are normally fitted in every room.

There are many exciting projects on drawing boards, or in the process of development. Facilities including community centres, bowling greens, swimming pools, sub-post offices and a marina are planned for some, and incorporated in others is full nursing care and even a nursing home. Also, harking back to retirement in the sun, developers are casting their eyes towards the Mediterranean.

Over 150 developers specialise in various forms of sheltered accommodation, and there are many others concentrating on more traditional dwellings. The New Homes Marketing Board in London can provide up to date information on both types (see panel), but they prefer enquiries about sheltered housing to be made by letter.

On a completely different level altogether are park homes, which are pre-constructed and transported to the chosen site – where they cease to move. They are less expensive than bricks and mortar, but mortgages are not available on them – though tax-deductible hire-purchase often is. Interest rates are always much higher, and loans are generally repayable in 10 years.

Also, it is usual to pay a fee to the site operator, who will probably be entitled to a commission of 10 per cent if the home is later sold. As to future financial implications, while traditional buildings tend to increase in value, mobile homes go the other way and depreciate.

Further help

Home for Life, Concept House, 193 Three Bridges Road, Crawley, Sussex RH10 1LG (0293 552751)
National Federation of Housing Associations, 175 Gray's Inn Road, London WC1X 8SY (01-278 6571)
New Homes Marketing Board, 82 New Cavendish Street, London W1M 8AD (01-935 7464 for normal developments, 01-580 5588 for sheltered developments)
Weather Centre, 284 High Holborn, London WC1V 7BX (01-836 4311)

Retiring abroad?
DHSS Overseas Branch, Newcastle-upon-Tyne NE98 1YX (pension and health agreements)

For health insurance abroad:
Exeter Hospital Aid Society, 5-7 Palace Gate, Exeter EX1 1VE (0392 75361)
Federation of Overseas Property Developers, Agents and Consultants, International House, 15-19 Kingsway, London WC2B 6UU (01-891 5444)
Inland Revenue, Somerset House, London WC2R 1LB (01-438 6622)
Kent Insurance and Securities Services, PO Box 30, Ashford, Kent TN24 9YY
HM Stationery Office, 49 High Holborn, London WC1V 6HB (01-211 5656)

Useful reading
Buying and Selling Your Home, Law Society, London

Double Taxation Relief (IR6), Inland Revenue, London
Mobile Homes (Booklet 16), Department of Environment, London
Nationwide Building Society Survey of regional property prices, London
Overseas Property Guide, Daily Telegraph Publications, London
Residents and non-residents liability to tax in the UK (IR20), Inland Revenue, London
Shared Ownership (Booklet 13) Department of the Environment, London
The Macmillan Handbook for Retirement, Macmillan Reference Books, London.
Which? Way to Buy, Sell and Move House, Consumers' Association, London

Forging new friendships

MANY people look forward to retirement and plan ahead to realise long-cherished dreams and ambitions. All sorts of latent talents which have been held in check through pressures of work are free to be developed, and there are years ahead to renew friendships, visit favourite places and do all the things that in the past have had to be put aside.

For some couples this is the time of their lives when they are able to enjoy leisurely days together, longer and perhaps more frequent holidays and a chance to recreate the closeness of earlier years once the children have flown the nest. However, not everyone can feel so optimistic or well-prepared, and single people who have relied on colleagues at work for friendship may find themselves suddenly at a loss. Others might be alone through the death of a partner, or late divorce.

For them the years ahead can seem like a yawning chasm, without a framework. Many are frightened by the recent loss of status, particularly former executives used to deference and company perks – free petrol, for instance, and someone to put it into the car. In fact, no matter how well- or ill-prepared people may be, on retirement most will have to adjust to a completely different set of circumstances in which there is less income, more leisure, and former colleagues are absent. It is then that the need to make new contacts becomes vitally important, especially for those who are alone.

But how are friends made? People who live alone often complain that they have spoken to nobody for days, but what they mean is that no one has broken the ice and spoken to them first. Some people can stand at a bus stop and strike up a conversation, while others might shrink back in horror at such presumption. However, a person with friends is in turn a friend, and part of that pleasant status is the conscientious maintaining of contact. If someone has promised to ring and doesn't, a friend will pick up the 'phone and find out what has happened. Promises to keep in touch with former colleagues must be honoured too – but unheralded visits on days known to be busy for an acquaintance are not a good idea. Re-establishing lost contact can be done by asking ex-workmates round for coffee or out for a drink – or even by giving a retirement anniversary party if too many months have gone by.

Newcomers to a district can strike up friendships by contacting a local charity or organisation and suggesting that they

Helping at the village fête – an ideal way to meet friends in a new or familiar area

hold an event in their homes. The relevant committee will circulate the date among supporters, the householder can drop in a few cards at local newsagents – and on the day he or she could well be inundated by hosts of friendly local faces.

A tendency for people to think back to their 'roots' when growing older is used to advantage in many places to provide first-hand information in Life History projects, in which schoolchildren, middle-aged and retired people work together researching local history and collecting old photographs, postcards and mementoes.

Another route away from loneliness is to rediscover long-lost relations by researching the family tree. The starting point for this fascinating and instructive enterprise could be an old photograph with a date and place, a birth certificate or – best of all – a family Bible. From such small beginnings it is possible to follow leads and clues all over the country in search of church records and registers, and branches of the family whose existence had never before been suspected. Such an interest can also lead to far-flung colonial offshoots, who are likely to be both amazed and delighted to discover their 'new' relative from the 'old country'. The Society of Genealogists (see panel on page 41) can help once a start has been made – preferably with at least one set of great-grandparents – and its library is open to non-members for a daily fee of £7.50.

There is always something to be done in the community – particularly in pre-school playgroups and services for the disabled and frail elderly – and volunteers are eagerly embraced. The WRVS are at the forefront in this field, not only in

providing Meals on Wheels, but also in their escort and book services for the housebound. Books on Wheels should appeal to anyone who loves reading and likes to share their enthusiasm. Volunteers need to be fairly strong, with preferably a hatchback car to stash away the heavy volumes and cassettes. Unlike the hurried visits made by Meals on Wheels, Books on Wheels' deliverers are encouraged to sit and talk with the borrowers.

Summoning the initiative to join a group takes courage in the first instance, but it may well lead to new friends and an improved social life. Local libraries will always provide a wealth of information on activities in the area. Keen gardeners might consider a horticultural society, not just for the annual flower show and cheap fertiliser, but also so they can join visits to world-famous gardens in the company of like-minded people. Enthusiasts for the open-air life should volunteer for work on archaeological digs, canal restoration projects and in countryside conservation. Their services will be gratefully received. Anyone keen on giving time to charities could find rewarding work in one of their shops, or as a driver perhaps, and the headquarters of such organisations often need accountants, typists and book-keepers. Friends of local hospitals always welcome drivers who are prepared to use their cars for patients and visitors.

More options
Good listeners are perpetually sought after by the Samaritans, and anyone with legal or consumer skills should knock at the local Citizens Advice Bureau. Hospital Broadcasting Services are run by volunteers who may well find a slot for the experienced viewpoint – or how about editing local news on to a tape for the visually handicapped? There are plenty of opportunities – though perhaps more in some places than others – for contributing valuable work to the community while making a wide circle of good friends, so nobody has to be isolated or feel useless.

Adult Education can sound forbidding for anyone who hated sitting still at school, but the advantages are numerous. Becoming fluent in a foreign language will add another dimension to holidays abroad, and stashing up exam results will certainly earn the respect of the grandchildren. Cooking can become an absorbing and essential skill for men who are on their own, while car-maintenance classes have given plenty of women greater bargaining power at the garage.

Such classes are not just ways in which to fill the winter evenings, for they can lead to weekends away and study courses at some of the country's many adult residential colleges – at prices that most people can afford. More expensive – but

Opportunities abound to develop talents that pressures on time may have held in check

held in the more luxurious Embassy hotels – are Leisure Learning weekends, which cover all sorts of subjects from art, opera and photography to taking a look at yesterday's world.

Anyone who is good with a needle or interested in history and the arts might consider joining the Guild of Embroiderers, which has 138 branches throughout the country and arranges holidays touring homes, castles and museums in Britain and overseas. Other types of arts organisations encourage the development of hitherto unsuspected talent, and extra hands are always needed to help run craft fairs or organise workshop sessions.

In ways no other mid-life generation has known before, the over-55s of today have the chance to remain active, involved and venturesome, using to the full an acquired capacity for enjoyment that few youngsters can ever know. Also – and this is not a point to take lightly – they have the chance to see things and make friends in the leisurely fashion of a sadly bygone age, for they can make visits to sports complexes, stately homes and other attractions in the uncrowded luxury of off-peak times.

While everybody else is tied down to desk, bench or computer terminal, the retired are able to meet and enjoy life in a graceful manner reminiscent of days when there were fewer people around and the pace of living was more sensible – days when firm friendships were cemented in relative peace.

Pastimes, hobbies and sport

PEOPLE in full-time employment spend around two-thirds of their daytime hours at work (not including overtime) plus various amounts of time travelling between work and home. Some, in an idle moment, may have wondered what they could do with all that time if 'set free' – and sooner or later that will no longer be a hypothetical issue, but the stark reality which stares everybody in the face the day they retire.

At first the novelty of the situation lulls many into thinking that all is sweetness and light – no more rush-hour travel, a lie-in to whatever time they choose, then maybe an afternoon's drive finishing up at a roadside restaurant for a cream tea. But the chances are that anyone who approaches retirement as one long holiday will be bored within a few weeks and itching to get back to work. The trouble is, of course, that there is no longer a job to go back to.

That is the first point to take into account – retirement is not an extended version of the annual vacation. Rather, it is a complete change of lifestyle. Of course, there are some people who cannot wait to get shot of what they term the 'daily grind' – and others who are perfectly

happy to do little more than lounge around the house and potter in the garden after a leisurely read of the papers.

Many, on the other hand, need either to carry on working or find activities and interests that are mentally demanding or physically challenging – or both. Sadly, there are also those who completely let themselves go, and who – through an almost total lack of stimulation – slowly vegetate away. They seem to become old before their time, in stark contrast to those who lead active lives and who look and act as if they are at least 10 years younger.

Ideally, one should think about how to keep occupied in retirement a long time before the event.

Danger of disruption

Married people especially should talk it over long and hard, for the retirement of one partner can disrupt the routine of the other and cause a strain on the relationship. If a wife has already spent a number of years in a domestic rather than a work environment, she will have built up a wide circle of friends with whom she comes into regular contact.

With an eye on her weight and her health, it is also quite probable that she has a light lunch or none at all, preferring a more substantial supper later in the company of her husband. Suddenly having her other half at home all day can throw her cosy routine completely out of kilter. She may feel duty bound to prepare a full mid-day meal, and even forgo some of her weekly outings and pleasures to keep him company. Many wives actually experience feelings of guilt in such circumstances.

In extreme cases, especially if the husband is content to mooch around the house doing nothing in particular, she can find him getting under her feet when attending to the housework.

Such a scenario is unfortunately rather common and scarcely conducive to domestic happiness – particularly if the wife becomes increasingly inhibited. Perhaps she and her friends have been in the habit of getting together for a natter over a cuppa in each other's houses occasionally. It would be a pity if she stopped joining in because she felt uncomfortable at the thought of enjoying herself while her spouse was at home on his own – or because she felt she could no longer invite her lady friends into her home.

Keeping busy

The key to keeping occupied in retirement is to plan ahead – and, say the experts, the emphasis should be on variety and balance. In other words, activities should exercise both the mind and the body, and range from the serious to the frivolous. Some can be done alone, some with a spouse and others with a group.

Sound advice is given by the National Westminster Bank in its guide, *Countdown to Retirement* (Hutchinson Benham), which urges that arrangements should be sufficiently flexible for there always to be time 'for the odd job or impulse, or just for enjoyable idling'. It continues that a properly formulated plan 'saves you from drifting, and so wasting the precious leisure you have worked a lifetime to gain'.

Anyone in doubt as to whether they have sufficient basic interests to fill much more than a day or two a week should recall particular accomplishments in the past. For instance, a one-time draughtsman might try sketching for pleasure, while someone clever with their hands may find that they have it in them to shine at craftwork.

But care should be taken not to turn an interest into an obsession, though the planning ahead should never stop.

Popular activities

According to social surveys (Gallup Poll), watching television and listening to the radio are the favourite leisure activities of some 60 per cent of 60 to 75-year-olds – rising to 70 per cent among the over-80s. Next comes reading – enjoyed by half of those quizzed, and by women more than men.

Gardening is seemingly more of a male pursuit and comes third on the list – though, like travel, its appeal markedly diminishes among the late 70s and 80s.

Surprisingly, perhaps, cooking for pleasure increases in popularity after the age of 70; other hobbies, however, keep about a quarter of over-60s busy right through to when they are 80.

According to a MORI survey, the things that people do more often in retirement are (in order of extra frequency): watching television; reading books and magazines; listening to the radio; visiting relatives; calling on friends; gardening; voluntary or charity work; DIY; taking a vacation in Britain; playing sport; watching sporting events; and holidaying abroad.

Things that are done less often are: going out for a drink; attending a dance or social function; visiting the cinema and theatre; and booking for a concert.

Togetherness is important in any relationship, but that is not the same thing as pursuing identical hobbies in each other's company every minute of the day. Providing there is some common ground, it is healthy that partners have special interests of their own – and both the time and opportunity to pursue them. Recognising one's own needs and those of a partner should be an essential element of everybody's retirement planning. Clearly, it also makes sense to think positively about how to fill all those extra leisure hours in ways that will give maximum satisfaction and enjoyment.

Something to do

People who feel that they have no special interests should think back to the days before work and family commitments began to make inroads on their leisure. It is just possible that some almost forgotten hobby can be rekindled to good effect. Also, it is never too late to set out on a voyage of discovery, trying this and that just for the heck of it. Everybody has to begin somewhere, and more experienced class- or club-mates can be a great help when it comes to developing a skill or talent that has fired the imagination. There is no need to stay with one subject, and every area has plenty of opportunities to try others – the public library is the gateway to many.

In the garden

As might be expected, two of the most common retirement pursuits are very much home-oriented – gardening and do-it-yourself. Where the garden is concerned, what inspires so many is the thought that if they can achieve a pleasing enough result by merely working on it every other weekend and on weekday evenings, then what could be done when a great deal more time is lavished on it? Gardening can be anything from the creation of a pleasant place to sit or wander to a full-blown hobby and provider of cheap, fresh fruit and vegetables, scrumptious summer salads and the ingredients for home wine-making – another absorbing pastime. Newcomers to a district should be able to contact the local gardening club through the library or by writing to the Royal Horticultural Society, 80 Vincent Square, London SW1P 2PE.

Nor does it have to become a chore with the years, for gradual redesigning will make things easier to manage and maintain. The lawns, for instance, can be increased at the expense of some of the flower beds – power mowing is not nearly as backbreaking as digging and weeding.

Keen DIY types can have a field day indoors, but they too might turn their attention to the open air and produce that long-wanted patio and barbecue, decorative arches and screening, floodlights, a pond – even a swimming pool. Constructing a shed-cum-workshop – power-connected and insulated – is a possibility which would provide a permanent base for hobbies and, if sited in the right spot, peace and quiet from the neighbours.

Boats and boating

There are a number of other hobbies which overlap – painting and frame-making, for instance, and boating – an occupation that can be absorbing all year round. Summer can be spent cruising, and there is always ongoing maintenance to cope with, not to mention refits and tinkering with the engine. Some die-hards

say they have no time for anything else. Building or part-building a boat is well within the realms of possibility, and given the heat-retention properties of modern materials there is no reason why winter voyaging – especially inland – should not be enjoyed. Canals are prone to icing up, but a steel narrowboat with an ice-breaking hull would have no problem.

Altogether, including rivers, there are some 3,000 miles of waterways waiting to be explored in Britain, but it can be an expensive hobby. Things to take into account include the annual mooring, licence and insurance fees, not to mention the purchase price and subsequent maintenance costs. However, some of the expense can be recouped by hiring the craft out for a few weeks in high season, though it will be necessary to inform the insurers and appropriate licensing authorities of such an intention.

Stalls and stories
Many people have been both surprised and delighted to find their hobby suddenly earning them pin-money. This has especially been the case with those who, out of curiosity or simply for a day out, have taken to putting their heads round the doors of local auctions and house-clearance sales. Several have ended up leasing stalls on a regular basis at antique and bric-à-brac markets – not especially for profit, but rather for fun and the opportunity it offers to meet new faces.

More popular still, judging by the number of specialist clubs and courses that exist around the country, is writing. The volume of editors' and publishers' rejection slips seems only to encourage budding novelists and journalists to increase their output. However, now and again an item is selected for publication and, when this

The pace of life on a narrowboat is leisurely, relaxing – and time-consuming

happens, the thrill of seeing one's work (and by-line) in print is usually far more important than the cheque.

Sometimes a real talent is unearthed – like the woman who won a readers' short-story competition in a national retirement planning magazine and has since had three romantic novels published by Mills and Boon.

More than a few people go through life wondering if they had chosen the right career, and whether they might have been cut out for something more enjoyable and fulfilling. From time to time during their working lives, many people day-dream of doing somebody else's job – particularly if it has glamour appeal. Retirement is the time to stop wondering and put substance to the day-dreaming. It may be easier than it seems.

Broadcasting at home
For example, people who pass a broadcasting audition might within a few weeks find themselves reading the news or handling a programme or two – on hospital radio, that is. However, HR is regarded as a tremendous training ground for the real thing, and promotes contact with all kinds of people – fellow enthusiasts in other studios, patients, hospital staff, and the outside world in general.

It is the sort of thing that can easily become a full-time interest, with time spent on dreaming up ideas, making the necessary interview arrangements, tape-recording, editing, scripting, choosing appropriate music and actually presenting the programme. Some of the more go-ahead organisations even have outside broadcast facilities for sports commentaries, live theatre shows and local events.

Some retired folk have become so proficient that tapes they send 'on spec' to local BBC and IBA radio stations frequently go out on air. These are usually of a newsy nature – and are paid for!

Thanks to the quite astonishing advances in the home-entertainment field it is even possible to make DIY TV programmes. Combined cameras and video recorders, lightweight and battery-powered, are becoming ever more versatile and sophisticated, and are easier to use than cine equipment. They also record sound and, unlike film, the pictures can be played back instantly through either the camera's viewfinder or a TV set. Couple the camera to a domestic video recorder, and an editing facility is created. Special graphics software packages enable animated 'films' to be made electronically.

The chances are that a talented television programme maker will quickly be entertaining an altogether larger audience than the family and neighbours. At least one hospital broadcasting set-up already has expanded into closed circuit television, and in time many areas could have their own local or community TV-cable channel.

Getting up steam

A childhood dream shared by many is to drive a steam railway locomotive, and privately preserved lines all over the country have made this a real possibility, thanks – ironically – to the demise of steam on BR. What is more, the refurbished engines are the very ones that hauled holiday expresses and so stirred the imagination in years gone by.

Aspiring 'engineers' have to go through much the same kind of apprenticeship as the footplatemen of yore – learning how everything works, carrying out cleaning and servicing, and proving competence as a fireman. But whereas these preliminaries could take half a lifetime or more in the old days, the system is not quite so protracted now. Nonetheless, written and practical exams have to be passed, with much emphasis on operational and public safety.

Many of the country's top tourist attractions – not only railways – depend on volunteer labour and expertise, from office work, catering and marketing to carpentry, bricklaying, welding and heavy engineering. In fact, there is scarcely a job skill that is not in demand by some charity or volunteer organisation somewhere.

Model activities

Model making from scratch or from kits is another absorbing and popular pastime – the more so if it works, for then the double pleasure of building it and putting it through its paces can be enjoyed. Radio-controlled aircraft, ships and cars are

---

Hobby help

To find out more about activities mentioned particularly in these pages, write to the following.

Adult Residential Education: **Adult Residential Colleges Association**, 19b De Montfort Street, Leicester LE1 7GE

Band Playing: **British Federation of Brass Bands**, 21 Woulds Court, Moira, Burton-on-Trent, Staffs DE12 6HB

Bird Watching: **Royal Society for the Protection of Birds**, The Lodge, Sandy, Beds SG19 2DL

Boating: **Inland Waterways Association**, 114 Regent's Park Road, London NW1 8UQ; **Royal Yachting Association**, Victoria Way, Woking, Surrey GU21 1EQ

Cinematography: **Institute of Amateur Cinematographers Ltd**, 63 Woodfield Lane, Ashtead, Surrey KT21 2BT

First Aid: **St John Ambulance Association and Brigade**, 1 Grosvenor Crescent, London SW1X 7EJ

Gardening: **National Society of Allotment and Leisure Gardeners Ltd**, 22 High Street, Flitwick, Beds MK45 1DT;

Royal Horticultural Society, Vincent Square, London SW1P 2PE

Hospital Broadcasting: **National Association of Hospital Broadcasting Organisations**, 5 Portreath Drive, Allestree, Derby DE3 2BJ

Model Making: **Historical Model Railway Society**, 21 St James Road, Harpenden, Herts AL5 4PB

Miniature Armoured Fighting Vehicle Association, 15 Berwick Avenue, Heaton Mersey, Stockport, Cheshire SK4 3AA

Model Railway Club, 4 Calshot Street, London N1 9AT

Society of Model and Experimental Engineers, Marshall House, 28 Wanless Road, London SE24

Society of Model Aeronautical Engineers Ltd, 47 Vaughan Way, Leicester LE1 4SE

Society of Model Shipwrights, 8 Alan Close, Dartford, Kent DA1 5AX

Motoring: **Guild of Experienced Motorists**, 1 East Grinstead House, East Grinstead, West Sussex RH19 1UF

Institute of Advanced Motorists, IAM House, 359–365 Chiswick High Road, London W4 4HS

RoSPA Advanced Drivers Association, Royal Society for the Prevention of Accidents, Cannon House, The Priory, Queensway, Birmingham B4 6BS

Railway Preservation: **Association of Railway Preservation Societies**, Sheringham Station, Sheringham, Norfolk NR26 8RA

For details of other national leisure-oriented organisations, refer to the *Book of Associations* in the reference section of the nearest public library.

In addition, there are two monthly magazines for the over-50s which regularly feature leisure: *Choice* (obtainable at leading newsagents), and *Saga* (available on subscription from Saga Holidays plc, Bouverie House, Middleburg Square, Folkestone, Kent CT20 1AZ). Another reading suggestion is *The Complete Guide To Retirement Planning* (on sale at leading newsagents).

great fun – and there is no shortage of clubs filled with like-minded soulmates.

As for model railways, these can range from a real steamer that can take passengers round the garden to the ubiquitous electric train set. An enthusiast at Sutton Coldfield, for example, has built a remarkable tableau featuring Birmingham New Street station and its environs, all in 00-gauge scale, in his back yard. From time to time he runs the whole thing to British Rail's actual timetable, and, as changes occur to the real city centre, he updates the model – truly a life-long hobby.

Occasionally he allows the public in for a peek – to the inconvenience of the local population, for so popular an event is it that every local street is chock-a-block with visitors' cars; not that anyone hears the charities, to whom all the proceeds are donated, complaining!

Making Music
Retirement is a golden opportunity to take up music, a rewarding but time-consuming pursuit that demands the luxury of constant attention. Age is no barrier to learning to play an instrument from scratch, especially where brass bands are concerned. Many run beginners' classes and will happily loan a spare instrument to start with (wind instruments can produce only one note at a time and are comparatively easy to learn). Moreover, it is not necessary to reach a high standard before joining the chosen band in public performances, for there are three levels of competence, each one of which has a part to play. According to those who have given it a try, joining a band can be lots of fun and an excellent way to make new friends.

Strictly for the birds
Few people with time on their hands can resist watching the antics of man's feathered friends from the kitchen or lounge window and, once bitten, it is not long before they start putting out food and water with the express purpose of attracting more species. From that point on, as thousands have found, it is a short step to joining the Royal Society for the Protection of Birds (RSPB), even for people who have no intention of becoming serious students.

Membership, designed to make an absorbing pastime even more interesting, includes a free quarterly colour magazine, free admission to most of the 116 RSPB reserves and access to lively members' groups, conferences and meetings featuring well-known speakers. Joining fees are reduced for retired people.

In contrast, the highspot in the lives of a growing number of retirees is to be summoned to the headquarters of the Open University at Milton Keynes and be presented with a degree – but more about that later.

Learning at leisure
Prospectuses for day and evening classes, which are run by most local authorities at reasonable cost, can usually be found in libraries and the area Adult Education Institute. Also in the library will be contact numbers and addresses for various

Bird watching is an absorbing pastime – the RSPB can advise beginners

Open University

People who spend part of their leisure time studying with the Open University are in good company, numbering about 100,000 students every year. Age and infirmity are no barriers: a 92-year-old has successfully obtained a degree; so has a 65-year-old Scot who – paralysed from the neck down by multiple sclerosis –

worked on a typewriter which he operated by blowing and sucking into a tube.

There are five basic menus available – BA degree, higher degree, professional diploma (or training or updating), community education and personal interest – and long and short courses designed to increase knowledge in subjects of particular interest to the

student.

Previous qualifications are not necessary, and there are no entrance exams.

One of the community-education subjects is, by coincidence, on planning retirement. For details of the programmes available, write to: Enquiry Office, The Open University, PO Box 71, Milton Keynes MK7 6AG.

specialist-interest groups – photographers, artists, writers, musicians, bee-keepers and many more.

It is quite usual for classes to exist in 100 or more subjects, and the Open University runs home-study degree courses supplemented by a summer residential school. Where appropriate the OU provides students with audio cassettes or records as well as textual material, and considerable use is made of radio and television – though often in 'unsocial' hours. Enrolment is twice yearly, and fees vary according to subject.

The University of the Third Age consists of groups of retired, redundant or unemployed people who meet to study subjects of mutual interest. These groups are set up by local initiative, and the 'U3A' headquarters in London will be able

to confirm or otherwise that a group exists in any particular locality – or advise on establishing one.

Universities and polytechnics frequently conduct evening courses for the public – often with the Workers' Educational Association, which itself organises talks and demonstrations. The local WEA number will be found in the telephone directory, or at the library.

The National Extension College provides a wide range of correspondence courses, including studies for GCSE and 'A' level examinations. There are many other organisations offering correspondence courses too, information about which is available from the Council for the Accreditation of Correspondence Colleges.

The Field Studies Council has centres in various parts of the country where it runs

Colleges and courses

Holiday courses

Leisure Learning (Embassy Hotels), 107 Station Street, Burton-on-Trent DE14 1BZ

Galleon Art Holidays, Units 40/41, Temple Farm Industrial Estate, Southend SS2 5RZ (0702 617900)

Ladbroke Hotels, Millbuck House, Clarendon Road, Watford WD1 1DN

PRA Retirement Holiday Courses, 78 Capel Road, East Barnet EN4 8JF (01-449 4506)

Riviera Breaks, Carlton Chambers, Vaughan Parade, Torquay TQ2 5JG (0803 27428)

SAGA Holidays plc, Bouverie House, Middleburg Square, Folkestone, Kent CT20 1AZ (0303 47000)

Savoy Continental School of Cookery, Crossways, Whalley Road, Padiham, nr Burnley BB12 8JR (0282 72423)

Trust House Forte, 24–30 New Street, Aylesbury HP20 2NW (0227 462618)

Residential courses

Cookery at the Grange, The Grange, Beckington, Bath BA3 6TD (0373 830607)

Field Studies Council, Preston Montford, Montford Bridge, Shrewsbury SY4 1HW (0743 850674)

Retirement Preparation Services, 19 Undine Street, Tooting, London SW17 8PP (01-767 3225)

The Centre for Heraldic and Genealogical Research, Northgate, Canterbury CT1 1BA

The Earnley Concourse, Earnley, Chichester PO20 7JL (0243 670392)

Study

Council for the Accreditation of Correspondence Colleges, 27 Marylebone Road, London NW1 5JS (01-935 5391)

National Extension College, 18 Brooklands Avenue, Cambridge CB2 2HM (0223 316644)

Open University, PO Box 71, Milton Keynes MK7 6AG (0908 74066)

University of the Third Age (U3A), 6 Parkside Gardens, London SW19 5EY

University of Stirling, Pathfoot Building, The University, Stirling FK9 4LA

Workers' Educational Association, Temple House, 9 Upper Berkeley Street, London W1H 8BY (01-402 5608)

Holiday learning

'Interest' weeks and weekends run by various holiday centres are listed in brochures available from travel agents. A selection of typical offers follows.

Butlin's: bowls, dancing, keep fit

Pontin's: gardening, bridge, bowls, 'bless 'em all' (spirit of

the '40s), model making, country music, brass bands, dancing

Riviera Breaks: activity holidays centred around Torbay, including natural history, dinghy sailing, moorland exploration

Warner: Burns night, old-time and sequence dancing, old-time music hall, traditional jazz, cookery, darts

Leisure Learning (Embassy Hotels): country photography, folklore, literature, music, Royal Doulton weekend

Ladbroke: ballooning, health and beauty, living history, bridge, word games, walking and rambling, snooker

Trust House Forte: clay-pigeon shooting, fly fishing, painting, antique collecting, wine appreciation

Outside information

Historic Houses Association, 38 Ebury Street, London SW1W 0LU (01-730 9419)

Ramblers' Association, 1–5 Wandsworth Road, London SW8 2XX (01-582 6878)

The Council for British Archaeology, 112 Kennington Road, London SE11 6RE (01-582 0494)

The National Trust, 36 Queen Anne's Gate, London SW1H 9AS (01-222 9251)

The Royal Society for the Protection of Birds, The Lodge, Sandy, Beds SG19 2DL (0767 80551)

weekend and week-long courses in subjects such as natural history, geology, painting and drawing, botany, history, architecture and much more.

Other residential courses in such subjects as music, literature, food and wine, languages and arts and crafts are held by the Earnley Concourse, and generally last from two to four days. The University of Stirling runs summer schools in non-academic subjects such as calligraphy, folk dancing, knitting, spinning and gardening, and people living in other university towns might find that similar opportunities exist near them.

Specialist courses of wide and bewildering variety are also available, and they are not necessarily designed exclusively with experts in mind. Anyone who is interested in their family history should contact The Centre for Heraldic and Genealogical Research, which runs residential courses at Allington Castle, near Maidstone, Kent. Galleon Art Holidays provide painting instruction for beginners and accomplished artists in various parts of the country, and a set-up known as Cookery at the Grange runs culinary courses of between five days and four weeks. The Savoy Continental School of Cookery week-end gourmet classes offer the attractive propsect of eating well and learning at the same time. These examples are just three of literally thousands that are available.

Retirement offers a golden opportunity to discover Britain's historic houses. Saltram House in Plympton is one of the properties preserved by the National Trust

Out and about

Britain's historic and scenic heritage is famous throughout the world, but surprisingly few Britons find time to enjoy it. Retired people, however, have a golden opportunity to discover everything the nation has to offer, from mountains, moors and waterfalls to castles, canals and stately homes. Anyone embarking on such explorations should take out annual membership of the National Trust, as this will give them free entry to the hundreds of houses, gardens and other attractions in the care of that august body. A similar arrangement can be made with the Historic Houses Association, which has some 260 properties.

Archaeology enthusiasts, or anyone who wants to have a try at this absorbing pastime, will find that local societies are always on the lookout for volunteers (a list of such groups is held by the Council for British Archaeology). Conservation groups of all types welcome help – skilled or unskilled – and the Ramblers' Association in particular needs people to walk footpaths, build and repair stiles and erect signposts. It has 250 local groups, and membership fees are reduced for retired people.

Paid and unpaid work
Anybody looking for post-retirement work to keep them active rather than make them rich should contact the Retired Executives Action Clearing House at 89 Southwark Street, London SE1 0HD. This organisation aims to prevent the waste of talent by redirecting retired management towards organisations which need business and professional skills, but cannot afford them.

Unpaid posts in charity and other voluntary bodies can be obtained by applying direct, or enquiring at the Citizens Advice Bureau. Useful addresses for people seeking salaried part- or full-time employment:

Employment Fellowship and Buretire, Wensley House, Bell Common, Epping, Essex CM16 4DY

Executive Standby Ltd, 51 The London Wool & Fruit Exchange, Brushfield Street, London E1 6EU

Forty-plus Career Development Centre, High Holborn House, 49-51 Bedford Row, London WC1V 6RL

Inter Executives UK Ltd, Chancery House, 53-64 Chancery Lane, London W2A 1QU

National Advisory Centre on Careers for Women, Drayton House, Gordon Street, London WC1H 0AY

Over Forty Association for Women Workers, 120-122 Cromwell Road, London SW7

Over Sixties Employment Bureau, Age Concern, 186 Crampton Street, London SE17

Part Time Careers Ltd, 10 Golden Square, London W1R 3AF.

Carry on working

Another way to fill leisure time in retirement is to carry on working, a choice adopted by a surprising number of people in their 60s and 70s. This may seem at variance with the popular concept of retirement as something that is experienced after 40 to 50 years of earning a living, but the retirees concerned will argue that nothing else but work can give them anywhere near the same level of stimulation, challenge, fulfilment and pleasure.

Put that way, who can argue that this vision of retirement is any less valid than roses around the front door, putting one's feet up and living the life of leisure in the usual sense of the word? Some, on the other hand, go for the compromise – part-time work in a week devoted mainly to recreational interests. Others work on because they are not yet ready to retire, or – quite bluntly – because they need the money. Then there are those who freely give their time and services to charities and voluntary organisations, and the 'self-employed' who by accident or design have turned hobbies into lucrative pastimes or second careers.

Not all companies by any means insist that someone reaching retirement age should 'call it a day' there and then; many firms find mature employees and senior citizens tend to be more reliable and industrious on the whole than other age groups.

However, becoming re-employed is unlikely to produce a duplication of the position, duties, responsibilities and remuneration package enjoyed in the last job. A consultancy might be offered if certain experience and special skills are in demand, but it should come as no surprise if the new duties include very routine, ordinary or menial tasks.

It is up to the individual to accept or reject a position, depending on how much they need the money or – in the absence of a hobby, interest or company during the day – on whether there is no other opportunity to keep occupied.

Some people, it seems, just happen to be in the right place at the right time – like a Harpenden man of 65 who had reluctantly retired as an accountant and a week later was asked by the joint managing director of a local business if he knew of a retired bank manager who would be prepared to take on the company's credit control. He put himself forward, was given the job and has reaped the benefits of health and satisfaction as well as money.

Giving a hand

It is astonishing what a friendly, familiar face and a chat can do for the morale of someone who is spending a protracted spell in hospital. It can actually aid recovery, which might mean an earlier return home. Unhappily, all too many patients have no family or friends to visit them.

Undoubtedly, more people would go out of their way to call on those less fortunate than themselves (whether in hospital or confined through illness, disability or age to their own homes) if they were aware of the problem – and providing they had the time to give.

People in retirement have that time – and many are already giving such comfort, in addition to helping out with shopping, changing library books, driving invalids to their clubs or places of treatment and even delivering their meals.

Others do their bit for support groups by helping with appeals, jumble sales and administrative duties. A bonus for participants is that many such local bodies stage social events during the year.

Of course, the ill and infirm are not the only ones in need of a leg up. Neglected children, battered wives, victims of crime and people in gaol are also deserving causes.

People interested in being involved with this kind of activity can make a start by getting in touch with local organisations and finding out which have openings for the kind of help they would most like to give.

Enquiries can also be made to the Citizens Advice Bureau, the old people's welfare council, the local authority's social services department, churches, the Samaritans, the British Legion, the league of friends at the nearest hospital, Mencap, and the Women's Royal Voluntary Service (which also counts males among its members, incidentally).

For good measure, all branches of the St John Ambulance Brigade run regular first-aid courses – knowledge that could save a life.

The corner shop
By tradition, working in retirement is buying a corner shop and living over it. The stimulation of running a business cannot be denied, but it can be very risky. A better idea is to take on a franchise, particularly for an early retiree in his or her 50s. In this way, all the stimulation of running a business can be enjoyed, but the risk is reduced by two thirds.

Initial costs might be greater for, in addition to start-up capital, the franchiser's licence fee has to be found – and a percentage of the profit or gross income handed over. But the advantages include expert help at the initial stages, and the bonus of being able to trade under the name of a well-known, established company.

Pitfalls await the unwary, but these are well mapped in a comprehensive information pack obtainable from the British Franchise Association, 75a Bell Street, Henley-on-Thames, Oxon RG9 2BD.

The Association – which binds member franchisers to a code of ethics – also has an arbitration scheme for use in cases of dispute, and will even advise on the credentials and trustworthiness of franchisers who are not members.

Latent talent

When a former transport supervisor who took up woodwork and carpentry on retirement discovered skills he never knew he possessed, he and his wife – a keen member of the WI – transformed their home and garage into a mini-production line to turn out a range of soft toys, dolls' houses, sledges, bird feeders and collages. Everything they make is sold for charity.

Another case study concerns an engineer whose company pension was nothing to write home about and who lacked the wherewithal to start up his own business. He found a job without prospects, then out of the blue a professional institution he belonged to nominated him to advise and help enquirers with engineering problems. He eventually became a self-employed consultant working from home and said goodbye to money problems while finding stimulus and mental satisfaction in solving all manner of awkward posers for clients.

A woman from Edinburgh who yearned to go back to work after just four weeks in retirement answered a Scottish Tourist Board advertisement and was accepted for training – which proved very hard going. She persevered, passed four exam papers and a practical test, and was finally let loose on international tourists visiting Scotland. The only thing missing from her life is the time to be bored.

Another Scottish retiree who planned to spend his leisure time quietly gardening, wood carving and writing suddenly found that his professional knowledge of ship repairing and dry docks was in demand. As a result, he became a part-time consultant and – at others' expense – has been flown to Algeria, the Gulf, Hong Kong, Kowloon, the United States and Indonesia.

A north London woman who felt a desperate need to be wanted after the death of her husband got to hear that her local hospital was looking for outside help in its ward for young disabled people. She now assists twice a week and has become totally absorbed in the care of people who are worse off than herself.

Another London woman successfully obtained a degree from the Open University and applied for a research assistant post. At the interview she was told that age was irrelevant, because the important thing was to appoint the right candidate. Her previous experience with medical and para-medical personnel won the day, even though one of the main tasks was to set up a computer database – something she had never done before, but quickly learned. She now attends conferences at home and abroad and can afford holidays in Australia and America with family and friends. However, she is the first to admit that she went after the Open University degree to help get back to work.

Others have found themselves in a second career virtually by accident – like a former aviation technical sales manager who, back in the late 1950s gave up motor racing because of family commitments and turned his hand to making model aircraft instead. Also interested in photography, he began to experiment with equipping his radio-controlled models with a 35mm camera. After much trial and error, he succeeded – and, with one thing leading to another, his aerial photography hobby has today become big business. Like the others, he is having the time of his life working rather than relaxing in retirement.

Games and Pastimes

Many people will remember those not-so-distant days when the dining table was an important focus of family life – not only at meal times, but also when it doubled as the venue for a variety of family entertainments on long winter evenings. That was, of course, before the small screen started its invasion of the home some three decades ago, relegating snakes and ladders, ludo, Chinese chequers and playing cards to musty exile in favour of television's more passive and less social attractions.

Cards and Boards

Of course, the real enthusiasts have never stopped – for instance, no chess players let their concentration falter for the news, and a rubber of bridge takes precedence over a quiz show any day. But for the not so dedicated, the enormous range of games and pastimes available is worth review, since in most cases they offer a wealth of

Scrabble is a sociable way of exercising the mind – and those with a competitive streak can aim for the National Championships!

entertainment for the outlay of just a few pounds.

As well as the new games which are brought onto the market every year in a blaze of publicity, there are plenty of traditional forms with histories locked in the mists of antiquity. A version of backgammon was certainly played in Roman times, and its forerunner – a dice and board game – was found in excavations at Ur, dating back to 3000BC.

Another winner in the longevity stakes is chess, which originated in India as an army game. In ancient times it was played by four people, two using red and the other two black, just like the suits in modern playing cards. The game has retained such popularity that it is easy to find a partner in most areas by consulting the local library notice board. Alternatively, most clubs are registered with the British Chess Federation.

In recent years Trivial Pursuits has knocked other commercial board games out of the running, perhaps because it is reputed to be a favourite in royal circles. Another popular one is entitled Capital Adventure, which was awarded the Best Quiz Game title at London's Toy Fair in 1987. It has elements of Monopoly, Trivial Pursuits and Travel GO, in that by answering quiz questions correctly the player earns money to pay for 'travel' worldwide.

Scrabble, favourite game of crossword addicts, was invented in 1931 but remained untrademarked until after 1948. In the last 40 years it has become a great family favourite, and Travel Scrabble has whiled away many dreary delays at

airports the world over. The British National Scrabble championships were instituted in 1971 and are open to everyone.

Games from the past

Back to ancient history, the East lays claim to the very first playing cards – but, whereas the Chinese say they were invented by one of the Emperor's concubines, in India a wily maharajah's wife is supposed to have thought them up to stop her husband from pulling his beard. Whatever the truth, cards arrived in Europe at the time of Marco Polo's travels, and reached their peak of popularity in the 19th century when fortunes were won or lost on a turn. Whist, in vogue then and still played in many clubs, began life as Triumph – from which derives the word 'trump' for a special suit. Nowadays whist drives are popular ways of raising money for charities, the 'donations' being admission charges and prizes the largesse of local traders.

Beggar-your-neighbour, Snap and Rummy help children to accept winning and losing with good grace, and for two adults there are endless amusements in such time-honoured games as Cribbage and Bezique. Cribbage was supposedly invented by the 17th-century dramatist Sir John Suckling, who probably based it on a less sophisticated game called Noddy. Certainly, the wooden board and pegs have survived for centuries.

The heavyweight of all card games, and perhaps the most skilful, is Bridge. The English Bridge Union, at 15b High Street, Thame, Oxfordshire OX9 2BZ, organises the English national championships and can be joined for a small annual membership fee. An enjoyable way for players to pick up hints is to read the columnist Freddie North whose *Bridge with Aunt Agatha* and *Aunt Agatha Plays Tournament* offer helpful advice spiced with wit. They are published by Faber and should be in most local libraries. Gyles Brandreth's *Card Players' Omnibus* (Willow Books) will settle disputes over rules relating to other games.

Playing chess

Chess is played in every country of the world, and is a universal form of communication that transcends language, religion and culture.

Wartime refugees from the eastern European countries found that – even though they could not speak the language of their new homes – they could open many doors simply by following the ivory armies. Small wonder that so many Polish expatriates are such excellent players.

Chess has even been played by letter and radio, between ship and shore and across continents. Modern dimensions to such long-distance games include the use of telephone and Telex networks, computers – even ground-to-space communication systems.

Closer to home, nearly every locality has its clubs, many of which meet in surprising venues including cafés, pubs and similarly unlikely places.

A nationwide list of registered clubs is published by the British Chess Federation, 9A Grand Parade, St Leonards-on-Sea, Sussex TN38 0DD, which also represents Britain in international events.

Two of many good books on the subject are, for beginners, *Instant Chess* by David Levy and Kevin O'Connell and, for the more advanced player, *My Best Games of Chess*, by Laszlo Szabo (both published by Pergamon).

A word on Scrabble

Scrabble is an excellent medium through which to forge new friendships and closer partnerships – perhaps as good as chess, if not quite so widespread.

A particular widower discovered this after advertising in the local press for players to form a club. He placed the advertisement because he was at a total loss after losing his wife – and the result was gratifying.

Some 20 members signed up within days, and eventually he became a regional organiser for Scrabble championships in the West Country.

More importantly, he found a new life partner and was also given the opportunity to join the world championships in America. From tiny acorns mighty oaks do grow . . .

Application forms for the British National Scrabble Championships are issued by the Scrabble Club Co-ordinator from 42 Elthiron Road, London SW6 4DW. Also available is an invaluable list of permissible two-letter words, to defuse those end-of-game arguments.

Applications for the national championships are accepted from individuals as well as club members.

On stage

With life today relegating too many people to just 'stand and stare' rather than participating, there is an enormous pleasure in taking up amateur dramatics or choral singing. Local drama groups always need extra hands to sell tickets, work backstage, and help with make-up, costumes, lighting and amplifiers, as well as treading the boards!

The British Theatre Association, Regent's College, Inner Circle, Regent's Park, London NW1 4NW, has the largest theatre library in the world. It also gives advice on setting up amateur groups, runs training courses in performance and technical skills and arranges visits to theatres in and around London. Annual membership is available. Those with musical leanings should contact the Amateur Music Association, Medlock School, Waldeson Road, Manchester M13 9UR, where advisors will put them in touch with local musical societies. Many such parochial groups also advertise in public libraries. Practice is easy since tapes of gentle piano or full orchestra are available for use in the car, bath or anywhere else. Professionals have been using them for years and a good range is offered by the 'Music Minus One' series.

Take your partners

Cecil Sharp recognised the value of England's rich folk-music dance and song

---

Try something new

A great mistake is to put off something just because it is unfamiliar. Retirement offers the chance to try new avenues of leisure enjoyment, and most clubs and societies welcome new blood.

Bowls is, perhaps, the fastest-growing sport – indoors and out – and there are bound to be facilities at the local green for hiring woods and overshoes for a 'try-out' – not to mention plenty of free advice. Golf is another sport which can be taken up in later years. Membership of a club is not essential, since there are plenty of municipal and private courses which offer playing facilities on payment of a green fee. The Sports Council can give details about the governing bodies of any sport which appeals.

Gardeners new to a district can contact the Royal Horticultural Society to find the local club, and the evergreen popularity of bridge means that club details will certainly be posted in the library. There are scrabble clubs all over the country too – often run by retired people – and chess, of course, has its full quota of societies.

Useful addresses: **The Sports Council**, 16 Upper Woburn Place, London WC1H 0QP (01-388 1277); **The Royal Horticultural Society**, 80 Vincent Square, London SW1P 2PE.

heritage when he toured country districts at the beginning of this century, recording the traditional songs and customs of centuries. His remarkable collection is preserved in the Library of the English Folk Dance and Song Society at Cecil Sharp House, Regent's Park Road, London NW1 7AY and is enjoyed by thousands of people through a nationwide network of clubs, concerts, ceilidhs and festivals. Folk and barn dances are also held weekly at Cecil Sharp House, which is open to the general public for a small admission fee. Individual and joint membership are available with reductions for retired people.

Similarly, there is the Royal Scottish Country Dance Society at 12 Coates Crescent, Edinburgh, which has affiliated branches and groups all over the world and, for those who prefer a stronger beat, most local dance studios hold sessions for beginners in ballroom, Latin-American, disco and sequence dancing. Many local councils and holiday hotels also hold tea dances.

Best feet forward

Many dance clubs and societies have competitions which – whilst not obligatory – can add an extra edge to the participants' enjoyment and encourage a healthy self-interest in physical fitness.

For instance, a couple who took up Latin-American competition dancing after their retirement found that the rhythm made them want to get on to the floor the minute the band struck up.

They felt that it kept them young, and if the exercise involved in two afternoon and four evening sessions every week is anything to go by, they were probably right.

Social dancing with like-minded people is certainly a good way to make friends, and the options became even wider with the travel and opportunities of the competition circuit.

Also, there is no excuse for life-long non-dancers not to participate, because it is never too late to learn. The British Council of Ballroom Dancing at 87 Parkhurst Road, London N1 0LP holds full details of local schools.

Lectures and talks

Amongst various groups which tour the country with informative and interesting talks is the National Association of Decorative and Fine Art Societies, whose headquarters are at 38 Ebury Street, London SW1W 0LV. Its 200 or so member societies, scattered nationwide, plan programmes of monthly lectures, visits to museums, art galleries and stately homes. Annual membership is offered and details of local branches can usually be found in public libraries. Information regarding similar groups is to be found there too, as well as in local parish magazines and newsletters.

Sporting chances

Following a vigorous Sports Council campaign in 1983, more and more adults of retirement age and older have taken up a variety of sports and recreational activities, many of them returning to pursuits which gave them pleasure at school or university.

Physical activity, after all, is certainly not just for the young. The benefits of regular exercise for the older population are well documented and a lifetime of keeping active can leave a 60-year-old in rude health and with the physical prowess of a sedentary person half the age. As well as improving fitness levels, regular sport and recreation provide the mental challenge of learning new skills, assist the formation of new friendships and social contacts and – above all – increase the ability to really enjoy new-found freedom.

Partly because of the Sports Council's campaign, the choices are vast and encompass activities – at various levels of expertise – ranging from archery to gliding, swimming and yoga. However, an essential precursor to choosing which sport to follow is a thorough medical check-up to make sure that all is well. This is particularly important for someone who has not taken part in regular physical activity for a number of years or who has specific medical problems relating to the heart, cardio-vascular system in general, or certain joints or muscles. Specialist guidance should also be sought by anyone suffering from over-tiredness, dizziness, chest pains or disturbed breathing upon mild exertion. Generally speaking, though, reasonably healthy people are recommended by the Sports Council to start their activity programme as soon as possible.

There is no reason why only one pursuit

New Horizons

A young charity called New Horizons is offering cash incentives of up to £5,000 to bodies which are creating innovative community projects by using the skills and experience of mature members. There must be at least 10 people in each group, half of whom must be 60 or over. The main objective is to harness the creative energies, talents and knowledge of those in retirement.

Schemes so far helped by New Horizons have included a 20-strong orchestra from Esher, Surrey, which performs popular classics of the 1930s at local day centres, and at blind and over-60s clubs; an angling club for the retired (with its own exclusive stretch of water) at Copthorne, in Sussex; a heritage centre and museum on the Isle of Wight; and a nature trail around the city of Lichfield, in Staffordshire.

For details, write to the New Horizons Trust at Premier House, 10 Greycoat Place, London SW1P 1SB.

should be chosen, although the first should be something that does not require a high level of physical fitness – depending upon the fitness level initially. Dress should be comfortable and appropriate for both the activity in question and prevailing weather conditions. For instance, jogging shoes are needed for running, and loose fitting garments that allow full freedom of movement are ideal. Whatever else, the clothes should be warm. Exercise in climatic extremes of hot or cold should be avoided, and activities should be started gently. The time and intensity taken in pursuing a chosen sport can be gradually increased as the weeks go by, and as levels of fitness and dexterity improve.

Above all, each individual should proceed at his or her own pace and stop at the least sign of untoward discomfort or pain. Having stopped, no attempt should be made to resume the activity until specialist advice has been sought.

A few options

The following suggestions include common sports and recreational activities that are generally available, but the list is by no means exhaustive. Some activities require specialist equipment or facilities – like sailing for example – while others may demand only reasonable health and time. Regional Sports Councils will be able to advise on the full extent of activities available in particular areas, and likewise the governing bodies of particular pursuits. Local authorities, adult education institutes and similar groups can be just as helpful. Many run activity sessions specifically for mature people. Public libraries are good sources of addresses and contact numbers and the local sports centre or health club will also provide good leads.

Organised action

Some hotels – and even cruise lines – offer activity holidays too, where the first-timer can attempt all manner of challenges from horse-riding to cross-country ski-ing. Travel agents can usually advise on these. The Sports Council information desk can be contacted on 01-388 1277 and will provide telephone numbers and contact addresses of regional sports councils, as well as those of the governing bodies of the various sports.

Archery is suitable for virtually everyone, including the disabled, and can be pursued both inside and out of doors. Equipment varies from the simple to the sophisticated and can initially be hired from most clubs or recreation centres. It requires a high level of skill and upper-body strength but does little for aerobic – heart and lung – fitness.

Badminton, a very sociable game which can be played to varying standards, is a good general fitness activity. Courts and

Jogging, a popular keep-fit activity, is a good way to exercise alone or in company

clubs can be found in church halls and sports centres all over the country and the only equipment generally required is good shoes and a racket, which can often be hired. Some clubs specify the wearing of all-white clothing.

Bowls is played indoors and out, and most towns have facilities provided by the local authorities. Many villages also have their own greens, and seaside resorts usually have several. Woods can be hired from clubs, and flat-soled shoes are the only other essentials – although some clubs have definite rules on clothing. This is a very sociable activity, but perhaps not sufficiently demanding to improve greatly a player's fitness level.

Cycling can be leisurely or highly competitive, but either way it is an excellent aerobic activity which scores high in the 'getting-fit' stakes. A good bike and alert road sense are essentials, plus see-and-be-seen clothing which affords good weather protection. There is nothing to prevent individuals or couples going their own two-wheeled ways, but also to be considered are cycling clubs which regularly organise tours, routes and races in age groupings.

Jogging, perhaps the most popular fitness activity of recent years, offers excellent health benefits, is easy to do and at the basic level requires very little specialist equipment other than an appropriate pair of shoes from the local sports shop. A tracksuit might also be considered. Numerous jogging groups exist, and thousands of events are organised each year, from short fun runs of a couple of miles to full marathons and beyond. All properly organised races are run in age groupings.

With time on your side, walking the dog can become an enjoyable day's outing

A good walk

Walking is a marvellous way of getting to grips with the countryside and far better than just skimming through it by car – although ideally a family outing combines the two. Dogs have made walkers out of many an armchair slouch, but children are far more stimulating companions. Whether grandchildren or youngsters belonging to friends, they are open to an early interest in conservation and ready to be encouraged in the appreciation of flowers, trees and birds – in fact the wealth of rural Britain seen through experienced eyes. Opportunity abounds, since in England and Wales there are some 120,000 miles of footpaths, bridleways and green lanes, many in areas of outstanding beauty.

Walking out

The Ramblers' Association exists not only to help people walk the footpaths of Britain – it positively encourages them to do so and is always grateful for helping hands when it comes to stile mending, undergrowth clearance and similar maintenance.

A large number of local groups exists under the loose administration of the Association itself, which is based at 1/5 Wandsworth Road, London SW8 2XX, and can be joined for an annual fee.

Joint-membership arrangements are available, and there are reductions for retired people. Members receive a yearbook which contains bed-and-breakfast addresses and lists of shops from which the right clothing and footwear may be bought at discount prices.

Details on walking in Scotland are available from the Scottish Rights of Way Society, 32 Rutland Square, Edinburgh EH1 2BW.

Added extras

Tennis is another sociable sport which can be played at various levels, both indoors and out. Local authority facilities are cheapest – although the most crowded – and proficient players may consider the club scene. Many courts have specific rules regarding clothing, and the obvious essentials are a racket and good shoes.

Swimming is one of the most complete 'whole-body' fitness activities available, being great for the heart and lungs, and very good for improving muscular strength, endurance and flexibility. Local pools organise lessons for beginners, sessions for style improvement and usually have associated clubs which organise competitions in groups of similar ages.

A Taste of retirement

The Pre-Retirement Association (PRA), a government-supported charity (see panel on page 32), runs week-long retirement holiday courses every year in spring and autumn at Pontin's South Devon holiday centre. The aim is to help people plan their retirement in advance, and as well as independent financial advice and counselling on state and occupational pensions and health, the programme covers a wide range of hobbies and leisure pursuits including gardening, bridge, golf, tennis, home decorating, DIY, macramé, art, car maintenance, photography, public speaking, skin and hair care, and flower arranging. Evenings offer a choice of dancing the night away or illustrated talks on subjects ranging from English inn signs to journeys through China.

At Sion College in London the Retirement Preparation Service of the PRA provides one-day seminars, and at Stanford Hall in Leicestershire there are three-day residential courses. SAGA Holidays have week-long courses at Dundee University.

These are just a few organised activities with which the mature sportsman or woman might become involved, but there are many others. Traditional sports like soccer, netball, rugby, hockey and similar games all offer scope for the older adult, particularly someone who was a keen follower or player in previous years. Not that performing on the pitch or court is the only avenue by any means, for experienced linesmen, umpires, referees and coaches are always in great demand too. Then there is the ever-present need for people to run the club. The options are many, varied and well within the grasp of retired people.

Other activities that might be enjoyable 'firsts' could include gliding, water ski-ing, sailing on yacht or board . . . an endless list of challenges that were once too time consuming to be considered and which are loaded with immense potential for satisfaction and enjoyment.

Age is no excuse for sitting in front of the television and vegetating. Bear in mind that Sir Francis Chichester was 65 when he sailed single-handed round the world.

Off-peak fitness

Health clubs are often short of custom during the working day, and it is well worth the while of anyone who is interested in using such facilities to find out if special rates apply during off-peak hours.

A wide variety of keep-fit opportunities is always offered, and there is generally an excellent social scene too – not to mention plenty of room for veteran-team organisers, officials and participants.

Anyone who has led an active life before retirement and wants to stay in trim should find everything they need in such clubs, on both the social and sporting levels.

Physical definitions

Carefully structured physical activity with the aim of improving fitness is 'exercise'. Physical activity with definite rules and a competitive goal may be considered as 'sport', and 'recreation' can include physical activity which is not necessarily structured or geared towards competition – playing ball with the grandchildren, or pushing the pram round the park, for instance.

Naturally, there is some overlap between these broad definitions. Jogging may be exercise if it is in accordance with a specific training programme, or recreation if pursued at whim for lone and individual pleasure. Then again, it can be a sport in which competitors battle for supremacy over various mileages and terrains. Interestingly, road racing in the veterans category (men of 40-plus, women 35-plus) is on the increase, helped by veteran competitions up to world-championship level. All major sports organise competitions in age-group categories, and once years have been taken into account the most unlikely candidates can turn out to be world beaters.

The Age Well project

London's Hammersmith and Fulham Council is one of the most forward-thinking boroughs when it comes to providing exercise and activity facilities for the 50-plus age group.

Two years ago it began the Age Well project – a scheme designed to introduce senior citizens to local exercise, sport and recreation facilities.

The project has been immensely successful, with the swimming and other water sessions proving particularly popular – especially with arthritis sufferers. Equally strong followings were attracted to the bowls, table-tennis, dance, yoga and weight-training classes.

In summer the programme involves more outdoor activities, including walks and rambles (with picnics along the way), and the 'regulars' help organise trips and social events. Housebound and disabled people are encouraged to join in, since Age Well organises transport to and from meeting points and activity centres. Other local authorities run similar schemes, and it is always worth checking to find out what is available in any particular area – especially for newcomers. Also, if a scheme does not exist, there is an obvious need for organised pressure to start one!

Useful addresses
British Trust for Conservation Volunteers, 36 St Mary's Street, Wallingford OX10 0EV
Council for British Archaeology, 112 Kennington Road, London SE11 6RE
Dateline, 23 Abingdon Road, London W8 6AH
Leisure Learning (Embassy Hotels), 107 Station Street, Burton-upon-Trent DE14 1BZ
Society of Genealogists, 14 Charterhouse Buildings, London EC1M 7BA

Guild of Embroiderers, Hampton Court Palace, East Molesey, Surrey KT8 9AU
Historical Association, 59A Kennington Park Road, London SE11 4JH
Inland Waterways Association, 114 Regents Park Road, London NW1 8UQ
Talking Newspaper Association UK, 90 High Street, Heathfield, East Sussex TN21 8JB
National Institute of Continuing Adult Education, 19B De Montfort Street,

Leicester LE1 7GE
National Trust, 36 Queen Anne's Gate, London SW1H 9AS
Pre-school Playgroups Association, Alford House, Aveline Street, London SE11 5DH
Royal Horticultural Society, Vincent Square, London SW1P 2PE.
Samaritans, 17 Uxbridge Road, Slough, Berkshire SL1 1SN
WRVS, 234-244 Stockwell Road, London SW9 9SP

Holidays

AT long last the travel trade has recognised the existence of the so-called 'Grey Revolution', that large and youthful body of senior citizens who have time on their hands, and both the money and inclination to enjoy it by exploring overseas.

That the holiday industry has taken so long to cotton on is surprising, since an easy extrapolation of statistics indicates that by the year 2000 every fourth European will be aged 65 or over. Add to that august number the mid-50s retirees, and the potential demand for foreign breaks is staggering.

Already the market is being eagerly sought and wooed, which is good news for mature globetrotters because that should mean plenty of special offers and discount deals aimed specifically at them – not to mention holidays and tours organised to suit their particular needs. Currently, the most publicised arrangement geared to the over-55s – and in one instance, the over-50s – is the long-stay, off-peak, winter sunshine holiday with tempting offers of accommodation for less than two pounds sterling a day. These undoubted bargains are quick profit earners for the travel companies and need closer examination. For instance, it is wise to check that the resort, hotel and weather are suitable: not too noisy or too quiet, nor too hot or cold, depending on requirements.

Medical facilities, which vary enormously in standard, must also be

considered. So must methods of drawing cash or a pension while abroad, personal preferences in diet, and the availability of essential drugs and medicines. Eating is not so much of a problem, since many authorities maintain that local produce, if washed and prepared properly, is far more beneficial than the imported, pseudo-international type of menu served at many tourist hotels. The moral there is to forget the hotel and go self-catering.

A comparatively new development that is likely to grow is the health resort. Spain has one at Lago Jardin, where the water is claimed to have recognised therapeutic benefits, and the nearby centre of Torrevieja – near Alicante – offers a range of conventional sports and entertainment too.

All this makes sense for, while increasing age takes its toll and the style of holiday often remains fundamentally the same, some customers are looking for something altogether different.

While many are happy to be with people of their own age, enjoying the social whirl and an even more hectic nightlife, others prefer a quieter, more sedate existence.

Others look upon retirement not so much as a chance to relax in the sun, but more as an opportunity to travel – perhaps on an adventure or activity holiday at home or abroad, or visiting places at a leisurely pace, independently or through an arranged cruise or coach trip. Frequently, culture, heritage, museums, cathedrals and historic places are high on the list of priorities.

Additionally – and figures confirm this – there are those who go in for winter

Activity & hobby breaks

There is hardly a hobby or interest that is not catered for in Britain by some form of holiday or short break.

To begin with, just one establishment offers activities associated with antiquarian books, archaeology, archery, bird watching, bridge, dressmaking and soft tailoring, fencing, flower arranging, patchwork and video filming. Should none of these summer-long offerings at Millfield School, in the heart of the Somerset countryside, appeal, there are more than 100 others to choose from – including many sports and recreations, and a retirement course.

In recent years a number of educational establishments have flung open their doors and offered facilities to the public at large. Also, hotel groups such as the Ladbroke and Embassy chains arrange a variety of weekend diversions at some of their establishments.

Just how wide the choice is can be gleaned from appropriate publications issued by the national tourist organisations, including the English Tourist Board's *Activity & Hobby Holidays*.

The bonus of meeting like-minded people and making new friends is an essential aspect of these schemes.

---

sports, husky-dog sledging and climbing in the Himalayas – living testimony to George Burns' immortal lines: 'We can't help getting older; the only trick is to avoid getting old.' That homily is fine in theory, but it neglects to mention the need for good medical insurance – including air ambulance repatriation cover. Broken bones overseas might easily break the bank.

Insurance experts suggest that holidaymakers should do only that which they are capable of doing at home, though how they square ski-ing with a saunter on Bournemouth beach is difficult to imagine. The best ploy is to pick a holiday within known personal capabilities, first establishing whether or not it involves physical effort, travelling long distances, or suits the personality and temperament of the holidaymaker.

Too many breaks are ruined by wrong selection, and one of the great advantages of retirement is that there is plenty of time to sit down and assess the pace of a holiday, solve any queries well in advance and make good use of information from a variety of sources, including tourist offices.

Retirement allows plenty of time to practise your swing and improve your handicap

Holidays in Britain

Most advice relates to holidaying in Britain, which is still the majority choice of the over-55s, who are in the ideal position to enjoy considerable gains. Off-peak holidays – the so-called mini-breaks – are particularly appealing, including special-interest and activity weekends that can be financially very attractive. They can also be adjusted in many cases to include weekdays.

It is probable that in recent years nothing on the leisure scene has changed more dramatically than the *Hi-de-Hi* image of holiday camps. Many have become self-catering, others offer half-board or full-board terms – and almost all have shopping facilities on site. Millions of pounds have been spent by companies like Butlin's on updating the accommodation – some to a real luxury standard – and introducing special-interest weeks, dancing festivals, and so on. Again, these are often subject to off-season offers.

Hotel groups, universities, schools and other centres of learning all feature weekend and week-long activity and hobby holidays, partly solving the stubborn problem of providing for the single older person – perhaps widowed, even divorced, retired from a busy life and becoming

Coaches and canals
Coach tour brochures are stocked by most high-street travel agents, or the operating companies can be contacted direct. Among the leading companies are:

Excelsior Holidays Ltd, 22 Sea Road, Boscombe, Bournemouth BH5 1DD; **Glenton Tours**, 114 Peckham Rye, London SE15 4JE; **Golden Rail Holidays**, Ryedale Building, 60 Piccadilly, York YO1 1YX; **National Coach Holidays**, George House,

George Street, Wakefield, West Yorkshire WF1 1LY; **Wallace Arnold Tours**, 8 Park Lane, Croydon, Surrey CR0 1JA.

For Saga Holidays' advice and brochures, telephone free of charge 0800 300600, or write to **Saga Holidays plc**, Bouverie House, Middleburg Square, Folkestone, Kent CT20 1AZ.

As far as inland waterway holidays are concerned, firms offering craft for hire are far too numerous to be listed here. However, there are five booking agencies:

Blakes Holidays Ltd, Wroxham, Norfolk NR12 8DH (06053 3221); **Blue Riband Club**, Weltonfield Farm, Welton, Daventry, Northants NN11 5LG (0327 842282); **Boat Enquiries Ltd**, 41–43 Botley Road, Oxford OX2 0PT (0865 727288/725333); **Hoseasons Boating Holidays**, Sunway House, Lowestoft, Suffolk NR32 3LT (0502 62211); **UK Waterways Holidays Ltd**, Penn Place, Rickmansworth, Herts WD3 1EU (0923 770040/778231).

---

increasingly bored, or simply too shy to indulge in a more extrovert holiday. A common interest is a good leveller of personalities and backgrounds. Some companies specialise in catering for the single holidaymaker.

Long gone are the days when newspapers and specialist property publications had to be bought for details and addresses of holiday accommodation in the UK. Today, many vacations in Britain are arranged in exactly the same way as Continental breaks – by collecting brochures from a high street travel agent and, after browsing through them at leisure, making a booking.

Despite the unpredictability of the weather, almost two-thirds of holidays lasting more than four nights taken by the British are spent in their own country. The most popular tourist regions by far are the west – including the Scilly Isles – followed by the south of England, which also takes in the Isle of Wight. The busiest weeks, dictated in many cases by when the nation's schools break up, are in July and August.

Here, immediately, is an excellent reason why retired people have an advantage, for by taking their breaks in June and September they can avoid the peak prices and the big crowds who are 'chained' to the school holidays. They also score on day trips, because they are not

obliged to limit their outings to weekends and public holidays. Also, they can take their time when sampling sights and attractions and – given the more relaxed atmosphere – enjoy them so much more, even with lively grandchildren in tow!

For complete freedom it is hard to beat caravanning. True, a brand-new outfit will cost around £6,000, but if used several times a year it will prove a really cheap form of holiday accommodation. There is no problem about roughing it either, for the modern caravan has a host of creature comforts including efficient insulation, double glazing, gas cooker, hot water, central heating, a shower and a flushing loo – all very civilised.

On the road
Around one in ten UK holidays are organised coach tours, and it is not difficult to work out why they are so popular with older people.

To begin with, the children are married or old enough to do their own thing, so there is no longer any need to opt for sea, sand and resorts where the youngsters can disco the night away. In any case, lolling on the beach is hardly the kind of activity that appeals to the active retired. They prefer to be out and about, exploring and soaking up new experiences. After all, they probably have a lot of sightseeing to

---

Nightline to Scotland
It is not widely known, but there are British rail-tour holidays which – like the coach companies – concentrate on majestic scenery. These mini-breaks depart from London on Friday nights, have pick-up points at St Albans, Leicester and Derby, and return mid-evening the following Monday or early on Tuesday, depending on the itinerary chosen.

The Highlander, for example, heads through the night to Scotland's north coast, wending its way through the magnificent Grampians and Cairngorms just as its well-rested passengers are waking. After that, rail or coach transportation is provided to

the scenic delights of John o'Groats, the Queen Mother's Castle of Mey, the natural splendours between Inverness and the Kyle of Lochalsh, the Isle of Skye, a whisky distillery and the pretty coastal route between the Tay and Forth bridges.

The other train, the West Highlander, visits Fort William, Oban, the islands of Mull and Iona – then behind a steam loco ventures to Mallaig over what many consider to be Britain's most scenic rail journey.

Enquiries and bookings should be directed to Intercity Scottish Land Cruises, 104 Birmingham Road, Lichfield, Staffs WS14 9BW.

Training the car
Someone who lives in the south and is planning a motoring holiday in Scotland is not compelled to drive the length of England to get there, for British Rail has a scheme that will cope.

Car and driver are loaded aboard at Euston Station in London, and after a good night's sleep the traveller wakes up in Carlisle, Edinburgh, Stirling, Aberdeen or Inverness, fit and ready for an early-morning start.

There is also a motorail service from Bristol to Edinburgh, and – for travellers who are bound west – from London (Paddington) to Penzance.

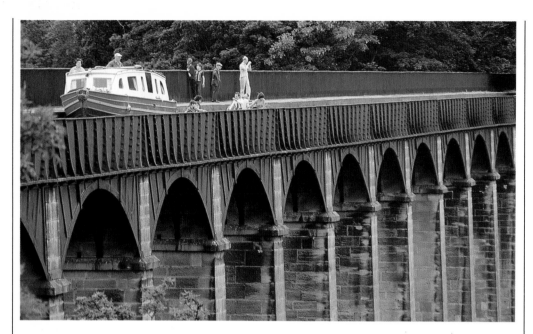

Britain's 3,000 miles of canals offer a unique viewpoint of the countryside

catch up on – even in their own country – and there are few better ways of doing that than by joining a coach party.

Broadly, there are two types of coach trip to choose from – a fixed destination that includes half- and full-day excursions in the area visited; or a tour in the real sense of a whistle-stop trip, with different stop-overs each night – apart from one or two places which take rather longer to view properly. Either way, the beauty of an organised programme is that, unlike on a motoring vacation, there are no worries about finding accommodation and so on at the end of the day. Indeed, relaxation is the byword – no driving, no parking problems and no chance of missing the attractions en route. Passengers are also seated higher than they would be in a car, which means they can see more. Also, given the gregarious nature of coach accommodation, this form of travel offers marvellous opportunities for meeting fresh faces and striking up new and often lasting friendships.

There is scarcely any part of Britain that is not on at least one coach company's itinerary, and the pick-up points for passengers are generally numerous and convenient.

Scenic routes, not unnaturally, are the most popular – north of the border in particular. Apparently, more and more people are heading for Scotland every year, and National Coach Holidays offer options there which include hotel rooms with baths and toilets *en suite* – and no single room supplements. By way of variation and to enable the visitor to spend as much time as possible touring, National and one or two other companies offer the choice of travelling to Scotland by rail before joining the coach. Tours of Wales, the Lake District, the Yorkshire Dales, the West Country and the New Forest are also very popular.

Rivers and canals

Backdoor England and Wales, espied from a slow-moving canal or river boat, is no less attractive. It is possible to travel by waterway from London to York, returning by a completely different route – not that anyone can expect to cover that kind of distance in just a week or a fortnight, but even at just 15 or 20 miles a day it is surprising how far it is possible to go. By choosing a 'ring', or circuit, return trips can be made along routes that never pass through the same stretch of countryside twice. One of the best known is the Cheshire ring, and in the south a popular 'roundabout' is formed by the River Thames and the Grand Union and Southern Oxford Canals. The most picturesque routes are arguably the Llangollen Canal and the waterway link between Leeds and Liverpool.

Hire craft are self-drive and fully

Driving documents
On any motoring holiday abroad it is important to make sure that all the important documentation is in order well before the start, including green card insurance for the car, driving licence and comprehensive AA 5-Star cover or its equivalent for the driver and passengers. Ferry bookings should also be in advance, especially for anyone going away in the peak season. Also, a car owner who intends to share out the driving should inform the insurance company, as they will consider the risk to be increased.

Driving can be considerably reduced by using European motorail services from Paris and Brussels, and the Channel ports of Calais and Boulogne. Enquiries and reservations should be directed to high street travel agents.

---

equipped, with comfortable beds, cooking facilities, hot water, central-heating systems, refrigerators, showers and loos. They are also comparatively easy to 'drive', and the mystique of lock and swing bridge operation is very soon fathomed. On the other hand there are always hotel boats where the work is done by others.

Motoring Abroad

Given the correct preparation – and there is no shortage of helpful advice from motoring organisations and ferry companies – there are considerable advantages in taking a car abroad, including the freedom to obey personal rather than imposed schedules.

The Scandinavian countries, especially Denmark, are good testing grounds for first timers to adapt to driving on the right, since the roads are generally good, there is far less traffic about and standards are high. Such holidays can be more costly than those on the immediate Continent, though they are cheaper out of season and come neatly packaged, with a good choice of accommodation, ranging from hotels to log cabins beside a lake.

An alternative is perhaps to try an off-season break closer to home in France or Belgium – of which there is a number available through travel agents – and then go for the big one in the summer, again avoiding the expensive high-season ferry fares. Whatever date is chosen, the traveller should at all costs avoid clashing with any Continental holidays, which can make driving horrific.

Highways and byways

For those to whom motoring abroad has become second nature, perhaps through business or past family holidays, retirement brings an additional blessing – the freedom to approach the ultimate destination in a leisurely fashion, avoiding major routes and tolls. Motorways are certainly the quickest way south to the French Riviera, Spain or Italy, but they are not always the shortest or easiest of routes. The same holds true for the main arterials into the Benelux countries, Austria and Switzerland.

The AA offers various non-motorway, scenic and other types of route through the Continent but, while these are often attractive and comparatively relaxing, they can be subject to seasonal delays. Another option is a mixture of toll and non-toll motorway routes, including sufficient easy motoring to lessen the overall strain of driving.

It is also possible to reduce considerably the amount of overseas driving necessary by taking a car ferry that docks further south – maybe even at Santander, where the route to southern Spain can be joined. Although more costly, it will prove less tiring and save an overnight stop. The same applies at the northern end, with the opportunity to save road miles by sailing from Harwich to Holland for Germany and Switzerland. A vigilant weather-eye for bargains from the ferry companies will pick up some mid-week and off-season offers, all money-saving and particularly suitable for those with time on their side. Discounts so advertised are usually in addition to reduced tariff rates, applicable to crossings at non-peak or less popular times. Regarding the crossing itself, the ferry boat should be used as a hotel – a chance to eat and sleep before the driving ahead.

Flower tours
The Dutch bulbfield tours regularly attract a third of a million British visitors every year between May and early June. The majority are older people and, despite the 'bargain basement' air fares to Amsterdam from many airports in the UK, the most popular inclusive programmes continue to be those that feature coach travel the whole way there and back.

Such trips normally last around four days, and usually include sightseeing in Amsterdam.

By coincidence, the province of Southern Holland – the tulip-growing centre – is in the west of the Netherlands, where one of the major attractions is the Keukenhof. This park is re-landscaped every year to offer new and kaleidoscopic arrays of tulips, crocuses, daffodils and hyacinths that never fail to be breathtaking. A little earlier in the season is the famous parade – a magnificent procession of flower-bedecked floats between Haarlem and Noordwijk.

Many of Britain's leading tour operators, among them Saga, Thomson, Time Off and Travelscene, offer package deals for these occasions. Dates of the major events and other information are available from the Netherlands Board for Tourism, 25/28 Buckingham Gate, London SW1E 6LD.

Coach travellers should ensure that the operator with whom they are travelling is a member of ABTA (Association of British Travel Agents), and carries the triangular 'bonded' sign of the Bus and Coach Council, or is a member of The Guild of British Coach Operators. This is the only way to protect the price of the holiday and to be sure that the required safety standards have been met.

Avoid peak periods and the ferry crossing makes a relaxing start to a holiday abroad

The French connection

One of the biggest growth areas in motoring breaks has been the *gîte*-based holiday. By definition, a *gîte* is reasonably priced self-catering accommodation – part or all of a house – almost invariably in the countryside, though sometimes within reach of the coast. They can be found on farms and in small villages, in remote places and clustered in rural groups, collected under one roof or as self-contained flats in the owner's house. All belong to the *Federation Nationale des Gîtes Rureaux de France*, and are classified by ears of corn. One ear signifies basic comfort, and three – the top – shows excellent appointment and situation, usually in an area of outstanding beauty, interest or recreational opportunity.

These classifications should be remembered when selecting from the numerous inclusive motoring holidays offering *gîte* accommodation. These can also be booked direct with *Gîtes de France Ltd*, 178 Piccadilly, London W1V 0AL. Their directory lists over 1,500 properties, so the choice is wide – but going independently may lose inclusive benefits gained through a package deal.

Holiday packages for motorists show considerable flair. Accommodation other than *gîtes* includes villas, campsites (either providing ready-erected tents, or with site charges included), country hotels at budget prices, chateaux hotels, caravans and holiday homes. Most ferry operators have their own inclusive programmes, and there are numerous companies specialising solely in villas or hotels. The best bet is to get a list of them through the French Government Tourist Office, 178 Piccadilly, London W1V 0AL.

Variations on a theme

It should be remembered that the *gîte* system is not peculiar to France, and other countries – Belgium among them, with properties in the Ardennes in particular – offer similar self-catering accommodation. Details can be obtained from firms specialising in the regions, and from tourist offices.

Farmhouse holidays, with a motoring content, are also an attractive proposition available throughout Europe and in Scandinavia.

A novel way to explore Spain is through the *paradores* – a fascinating collection of ancient castles, medieval monasteries, country mansions and city palaces that have been restored as tourist accommodation. The most atmospheric are found inland, being situated in places of scenic interest; those on the coast are much more like modern hotels. The Portuguese system of *pousadas* is similar, and both feature in motoring deals – although they can also be individually booked in advance, and paid for with vouchers provided.

Anyone doubtful about taking their own car abroad should consider one of the many fly-drive schemes that are available through holiday companies and also feature *paradores* and *pousadas*. Winter is a sensible time for holidays in Spain and Portugal, as the weather then is warm but not uncomfortable.

The ocean wave

Soon a motoring vacation on the Continent – or at least the start of one – will be about as eventful as travelling on the London Underground. Perhaps progress should not be hindered, but many will rue the day should the Channel tunnel ring the death knell for the car ferries – particularly those romantics who still regard the sea crossing as something rather special, and whose holidays really do start at any of the UK gateway ports to mainland Europe and Scandinavia.

Retired people and anyone else with time on their hands are even more likely to feel this way, since they can actually enjoy ferry travel by planning their schedules to avoid the crowds and traffic jams, while the majority are obliged to hop across the water in the busiest and most expensive weeks of the year. In peak periods, crossings are cheaper during midweek or late at night. Recent years have shown the Sally Line route between Ramsgate and Dunkirk to be the least expensive choice, irrespective of destination, although that estimation assumes that the traveller has taken accommodation and meals en route.

For people more interested in cutting back miles at the wheel than the cost of the journey, the following list shows the shortest ways from five UK cities to some of the most popular motoring holiday areas in mainland Europe. Road mileages and sailing times, including the minimum required check-in period, are shown in brackets – though confirmation that these are still current should be sought at the time of booking.

Faro, Portugal/Malaga, Spain/Tossa de Mar, Spain: via Plymouth – Santander (25hr) from Birmingham (845m, 795m 697m respectively), Bristol (770m, 720m, 622m), Glasgow (1,135m, 1,085m, 987m), London (860m, 810m, 712m), Manchester (930m, 880m, 782m). **Freiburg, Germany:** via Felixstowe – Zeebrugge (5¾hr) from Birmingham (567m), Bristol (611m); via Hull – Rotterdam (16hr) from Glasgow (656m), Manchester (506m); via Dover – Ostend (4hr) from London (481m).

Geneva, Switzerland: via Portsmouth – Le Havre (6¼hr) from Birmingham (594m), Bristol (544m); via Hull – Rotterdam (16hr) from Glasgow (776m), Manchester (626m); via Newhaven – Dieppe (5hr) from London (509m).

Nice, France: via Portsmouth – Le Havre (6¼hr) from Birmingham (850m), Bristol (800m), via Newhaven – Dieppe (5hr) from Glasgow (1,173m), London (765m), Manchester (971m). **Paris, France:** via Portsmouth – Le Havre (6¼hr) from Birmingham (270m), Bristol (220m), Glasgow (575m), Manchester (365m); via Newhaven – Dieppe (5hr) from London (185m).

Quimper, Brittany: via Plymouth – Roscoff (7hr) from Birmingham (263m), Bristol (188m), Glasgow (553m), London (278m), Manchester (348m).

Rome, Italy: via Felixstowe – Zeebrugge (5¾hr) from Birmingham (1,180m); via Portsmouth – Le Havre (6¼hr) from Bristol (1,103m); via Hull – Zeebrugge (15hr) from Glasgow (1,263m), Manchester (1,113m); via Newhaven – Dieppe (5hr) from London (1,063m).

Venice, Italy: via Portsmouth – Le Havre (6¼hr) from Birmingham (957m), Bristol (907m); via Hull – Rotterdam (16hr) from Glasgow (1,045m), Manchester (895m); via Newhaven – Dieppe (5hr) from London (872m).

Options and deals offered by the ferry companies are endless, so the first step in any holiday plan should be the amassing of all available brochures from Brittany Ferries, DFDS, Hoverspeed (hovercraft), North Sea Ferries, Olau Line, P&O European, Sally Line, Sealink British Ferries, the European-based Sealink operations, and Truckline. Scandinavian services are operated by Danish Seaways, Fred Olsen and Norway Line. Never be afraid to shop around.

Alternative car-ferry routes to those already mentioned are (sailing times in brackets): Dover – Calais (35min by hovercraft, 1¼hr by ferry), Dover – Boulogne (40min by hovercraft, 1hr 40min by ferry), Dover – Zeebrugge (4¼hr), Folkestone – Boulogne (1hr 50min), Harwich – Hook of Holland (6¾hr), Harwich – Hamburg (up to 21½hr), Poole – Cherbourg (4½hr), Portsmouth – Caen (5½hr), Portsmouth – Cherbourg (5hr), Portsmouth – St Malo (9hr), Sheerness – Flushing (up to 8½hr), Weymouth – Cherbourg (4hr). Car-ferry routes to Scandinavia are Harwich to Esbjerg in Denmark, Gothenburg in Sweden, Hirtshals in Denmark, Kristiansand and Oslo in Norway; and Newcastle-upon-Tyne to Bergen, Esbjerg and Gothenburg.

Channel Islands' car ferry crossings to Guernsey and Jersey are from Portsmouth and Weymouth.

The major ferry companies also sell fixed-location and on-the-move motoring holiday packages in various parts of Europe, featuring accommodation. Catalogues for these, and for ferry and hovercraft tariffs and schedules, are obtainable at high street travel agents.

Lakes and mountains

For many people the overseas holiday boom began with Switzerland – which is hardly surprising, since despite being one of Europe's smallest countries it offers scenery that is more impressive than most others. Austria, less sophisticated and certainly less costly, later vied for interest – though both Alpine regions slid in popularity when the cheap sunshine package deals appeared. Prices rose, and for some years both countries remained in the tourist doldrums.

Grindelwald, in the Lütschinen valley, is one of Switzerland's best-known resorts

music (though this is not always welcome) and often a non-smoking area. Some operators run tours for non-smokers only.

Also invaluable is the fact that many coach holidays have local departure points. Decisions regarding the choice of holiday should be based on the ease of reaching these, plus the quality and extent of the itinerary and the type of vehicle being offered. It can also be advantageous to look out for special reductions aimed at retired people, though these are usually limited to certain dates and hotels, and apply to only a few companies. Thomas Cook offers a discount to senior citizens booking its lakes and mountains air holidays.

Another aspect of Alpine holidays is activity – walking, tennis and golf, for instance. A forerunner in this type was Crystal Holidays, who wanted to encourage more youngsters. The company found instead that it was the older clientele who were snapping up the offers!

But their appeal has remained strong, and now most major companies offer a separate Alpine programme, often based on coach travel and mainly targeted at the popular resorts. In addition, a growing number of specialist companies is offering train, air, or self-drive holidays using the traveller's own car.

Where coach travel gains is that someone else does the driving, the splendid scenery may be savoured at leisure, and – compared with alternative means of travel – prices are cheaper. Additionally, modern coaches are often double-deckers that are well ventilated and have such creature comforts as reclining seats, a washroom and toilet, hot and cold soft drinks, on-board video and

Where to go

For commercial reasons, many programmes are based on the more popular regions. For instance, in Austria the main concentration is in the Tyrol area and the lakeland region of Salzkammergut. This is understandable, for the former includes Mayrhofen, Kitzbuhel, Seefeld and Westendorf, and the latter St Wolfgang, Fuschl and Zell am See – all well-established resorts. Equally, it is possible to find holidays in the more remote villages especially in the brochures of the specialist companies, or by seeking advice from the Austrian National Tourist Office, 30 St George Street, London W1R 0AL.

Another decision that has to be made is whether to go for a one-centre holiday – where the coach is merely the means of

---

Reduced travel

Rail travellers making their way independently of a holiday company should invest in a Rail Europ Senior Card, which is available at small cost to men over 65 and women aged 60 and over. It gives hefty reductions on standard fares in 18 European countries, but the holder must also have a British Rail Senior Citizen's Railcard. Available from BR Travel Centres or travel agents, the Rail Europ facility gives up to 50 per cent savings on rail travel in Belgium, Eire, Finland, France, Greece, Luxembourg, the Netherlands, Norway, Portugal, Spain, Sweden and on most Swiss railways, with up to 30 per cent off in Austria, Denmark, West Germany, Hungary, Italy and Yugoslavia.

Other concessions include up

to 30 per cent on sea crossings to the Continent between Dover and Ostend, or between Portsmouth and Le Havre when part of a through rail-and-sea journey.

Concessions may be obtainable without the Europ Card, but most foreign railways recommend getting one. An alternative is to use rail-rover tickets, such as the French Vacances Pass, which may prove even cheaper. Most national railways have offices in the UK.

Austria and Switzerland both have special-reduction schemes for senior citizens, and the Swiss Hotel Association produces a booklet which is available through the Swiss National Tourist Office, Swiss Centre, New Coventry Street, London W1V 8EE. Holland's Leisure Card is available for a

small sum from the Netherlands Board of Tourism, 25-28 Buckingham Gate, London W1R 6HB and gives healthy discounts for all ages.

A booklet entitled *Senior Citizens Travel in Germany* is issued by the German National Tourist Office, 61 Conduit Street, London W1R 0EN. In Scandinavia, Norway relies on the Fjord Pass for reduced accommodation rates, irrespective of age, and Denmark offers senior citizen rates at museums, and other attractions. Sweden makes concessions on local transport and entry to museums – more details from the local tourist offices. The domestic services of SAS in Sweden has special fares for passengers over 65, and in Denmark there is a standby fare for those aged 60 or over.

transport there and back – or an actual coach tour which stops at different resorts.

Switzerland gets less of a showing in the inclusive offers, but where it does feature the coverage includes resorts such as Grindelwald, Interlaken and Zermatt. More comprehensive choice is offered by the Swiss company Kuoni, which issues its own brochure but bases its holidays on air transit. Once in the country the traveller can choose from a wide selection of escorted coach holidays. Perhaps one of the most famous and romantic ways of reaching Switzerland is by the Orient Express.

Train travel in general is a superb way to see the country, and anyone exploring by this means from one base should be sure to make use of either the Swiss half-price travel card, or one of the holiday-coupon cards. Holidays of this type can be found through the Swiss Travel Service. Travel out of the main season, say in May or autumn, gives the opportunity of bargain offers; the only drawback is the weather, which can be chilly then.

Holidays at Italy's Lake Maggiore, Lake Como and Lake Garda, other than coach tours, are most likely to be based on air travel. Anyone who wants to avoid this should contact companies like Citalia (in the case of Italy), who run holidays by train.

Roving by rail

Train is certainly the best way to see many European countries, and Germany is no exception, with Bavaria and the Black Forest in particular boasting magnificent scenery. Inclusive rail holidays there are available through DER Travel Service. Also sometimes overlooked, though featured in tours by major coach companies such as Wallace Arnold, are Eastern European countries like Czechoslovakia and Hungary. Out-of-pocket prices are generally a lot less than in Alpine areas.

Just as price conscious is Yugoslavia, another country grouped under the Lakes and Mountains banner, with holidays generally centred on Kranjska Gora for the mountains or Lake Bled. Understandably, considering the distances involved, these are based on air travel – with optional coach offers laid on for those who wish them. Yugotours, like Phoenix Holidays, specialise in the area and offer a grand coach tour of Yugoslavia, Hungary and Austria.

Less well featured, but according to a major survey third among the top 10 countries the British would most like to visit, is Norway. Bergen is the gateway to the fjord district, and Voss offers similar scenery with the added attraction of Lake Vang. Strictly speaking it is not, however, a coach-travel country. Cars are more appropriate.

Summer packages

Although in recent years tour operators have made genuine attempts to describe accurately the resorts they feature – quiet, noisy, sand or pebbles – many older people still find it difficult to select a vacation from the bewildering variety offered in the brochures. The following hand-picked menu of holiday sunspots that provide the most sought-after ingredients – not too noisy but not too quiet either, a reasonably level terrain, and a good base for interesting excursions – should help.

Spain and the Balearic Islands

Costa Brava: Rosas is a fishing port backed by mountains, with most of its big holiday hotels fringing a wide, sandy beach outside the old community.

Costa Dorada: Sitges does not have too much high-rise development, though its interesting town centre can be somewhat congested. Weekends can be worse, as Barcelona is less than an hour away and the airport just 40 minutes. Pineda is a peaceful resort on a busy coast, with little entertainment itself, but it is only 2m from the attractions of Calella. It is reached by 1hr transfer from Barcelona Airport.

Costa Blanca: Javea has a pleasant harbour area and flattish landscape and is less hectic than Benidorm – which attracts more British than any other sunspot destination. Crowds aside, Benidorm has good beaches, bags of British-style entertainment, and – apart from areas like the old town – is flattish.

Costa de la Luz, the 'Coast of Light', extends to the Algarve border from

Train travel affords superb views of Switzerland's magnificent mountains

Algeciras and features the Hotel Tierra Mar at Matalascanas. Near by are the natural wildlife reserve and bird sanctuary of the Côte Donana, included in holidays by Spanish specialists Mundi Color and Saga.

Majorca: Puerto de Pollensa is an uncommercialised resort near Palma that is a favourite with the British – especially the older age group. Set in a bay with a background of green mountains, it has few skyscrapers but can be busy at lunchtime when the coaches call in. It is reached by a transfer of about 1hr from Palma Airport. Cala Fornells, a tiny fishing port on a small bay with rocky beaches, is only 1½m from Paguera and is reached by 45-min transfer from Palma Airport. Cala Millor has a long, sandy beach and offers sporting activities such as golf and tennis. It is reached by 1½-hr transfer. Formentor offers superb coastal scenery, with inland woodland and a fine luxury hotel that is well equipped for sporting activities.

Minorca: Santo Tomas is a quiet resort with a sandy beach, tennis club and a colourful collection of bars, shops and restaurants – though it has no real centre. Transfer time from the airport is 45 min.

Portugal

Algarve Coast: Montegordo lies 35m east of the airport at Faro and is very close to the Spanish border. The terrain is flat, and the skyline shows only a limited amount of high-rise development. The Vasco de Gama Hotel gives direct access to the vast beach, which gets crowded in the town area at peak times. Transfer from Faro takes 1hr 15 min. Vilamoura is a

Boats in the Marina at Capri are a delightful feature of this popular resort

purpose-built resort with a yachting marina and golf course. There is attractive countryside inland, and a suitable base might be the Hotel Dom Pedro. Transfer time from the airport is 30 min. Armacao de Pera – a residential development with a short tree-lined promenade – retains the look and atmosphere of an old village. Car drivers can visit Albufeira, which is 7m away, or motor 12m to Portimao. The 4-star Hotel Do Garbe was designed by its architect-artist owner, and is rated highly.

Estoril Coast: Estoril, close to Lisbon and 45 min from the airport, can be crowded – but the beaches and public gardens are good. Surprisingly, it has an English library and bridge club.

Costa Verde: Viana do Castelo is an interesting medieval town on the River Lima, but the only beach is rocky and 20 min from the centre. However, there is a sandy beach 2m across the river at Cabedelo.

Italy, Sardinia and Sicily

Venetian Riviera: Venice Lido, just a 15-min ferry trip across the lagoon, is an island that is hardly peaceful but offers good beaches, elegant shops, restaurants, villas, a casino and an 18-hole golf course in compensation. It is a good place to combine a beach holiday with sightseeing.

Liguria: Sestri Levante was originally a small fishing village and has retained an attractive waterfront facing two good bays. It is a useful base from which to explore by boat the Cinque Terre – a rocky stretch of coastline – and in its winding back streets are all manner of cafés and trattorie. Hotels should be chosen with care by anyone wishing to avoid too much climbing. Public transport includes local buses and a mainline railway, and the transfer time from Pisa Airport is 2hrs 30min. Alassio is a well-established resort with a wide sandy beach, café atmosphere and well-patronised shopping streets– but it can be a bit pricey, and has only a short season of settled weather. Transfer time from Nice Airport is about 3hrs.

Neapolitan Coast: Ravello, 1,000ft above sea level, is the 'jewel' of the Amalfi coast and is on the Grand Tour that was once an essential ingredient in the education of young English noblemen. Spectacular views abound, and some of the hotels are old palaces. Excursions can be made to Capri, Pompeii and Rome. Transfer time from Naples Airport – via Amalfi – is about 2hrs 45min.

Tuscany: Viareggio – a busy, flat resort with a good stretch of beach and municipal parkland – offers plenty of entertainment, cafés, gift shops and a quieter quarter at the north end. Good bus links exist with other Versilian resorts, there is a mainline railway station and the transfer time from Pisa Airport is 1hr. Marina di Pietrasanta lies halfway between Forte dei Marmi and Viareggio, and has a sandy beach set against pinewoods at the foot of the Apuanian Alps.

Central Adriatic: Pesaro is situated between two hills – a rarity on this coast of long flat stretches – and has a good beach of soft sand, about ¾m from the old town. It is quieter than the resorts to the north. Senigallia, with its bathing huts and umbrellas, was once regarded as the most organised beach on the Adriatic. However, it has plenty of history and a nearby wine region that can be visited. Public transport includes a town bus and mainline station. Ancona Airport is 45min away.

Sardinia: Baia Sardinia is said to be the prettiest and best-developed resort north of the famed Costa Smeralda. The beaches are sandy, the island generally flat, and the transfer time from Olbia Airport is 1hr.

Greece and the Greek Islands

Corfu: Arillas is a quietish, level resort on the north-west coast, with a sandy beach and mostly villa accommodation – although there are two small hotels as well. A car would be advantageous, though some local excursions are organised, in particular to Corfu Town some 24m away. Sidari, the northernmost village and 18m from Corfu Town, is in flat country and has a long sand and shingle beach. In the single main street are small hotels and lively little restaurants, and although central accommodation may be noisy, the evenings are generally quiet. Both resorts are around an hour or so coach ride from the airport.

Crete: Plakias is often said to be for naturalists, naturists and those looking for nothing more than a reasonable beach. Worthwhile walks can be enjoyed in the surrounding mountains, and the bird life is noted. Busy months are July and August.

Kos: Kardamena should be avoided in peak season, but at other times this mix of resort and Greek village is reckoned a good base for excursions. It is not 'pretty', but a meeting place for locals and ideal for the first-time visitor to Greece. The airport is 15min away, and Kos Town can be reached by local bus.

Rhodes: Rhodes Town – busy with huge numbers of hotels along pleasant tree-

One of the delights of Cyprus: a mouth-watering buffet at a Limassol hotel

lined avenues – has numerous shops and restaurants within strolling distance. There is plenty to see, and buses serve hotels a few miles out of town (away from the airport noise). This is a good base for excursions to Lindos, for example, a picture-postcard place that has become rather commercialised. Pefkos, 3m south by taxi, offers quiet apartment-type holidays which may appeal to those with cars.

Cyprus: Paralimni (Protoras) sometimes known as Fig Tree Bay, can be very quiet in the early spring. Kato Paphos is perhaps the prettiest part of this, the Paphos region. However, good beaches are generally scarce. The Troodos Mountains are ideal for keen walkers, and have good links to the coast. The main hotel is the Forest Park. At Droushia – a mountain village about 40min drive from Paphos – are self-catering apartments run by The Droushia Heights Hotel.

Malta: Sliema is very touristy, but useful for anyone who wants to be close to the shops, the rocky beaches and the promenade. St Julian's Bay is virtually a Sliema suburb, but less hectic and patronised more by the Maltese. Mellieha Bay, isolated on the northern coast and with a good bus service to Valletta, has a superb sandy beach near by but should be avoided during the main season. Marsascala is a large fishing village 7m south of Valletta, with the newish Jerma Palace Hotel. A good bus service operates to Valletta. Gozo – a quiet, green island off mainland Malta – offers Xlendi (which is pretty dead in winter), or Marsalforn, with its small sandy beach. A car is essential for getting about the island.

Yugoslavia

This country offers plenty of historical interest and some excellent scenery, but it tends to go in for holiday complexes (marked C), as well as hotels. Even a resort can almost be a complex, so it is important to check that any destination chosen really is suitable. Special hotels exist for the older holidaymaker, and there are good discounts for the over-55s.

Mainland: Ankaran (C); Baska Voda, Becici; Cavatat; Dubrovnik (lovely old walled town – for visitors with strong legs); Kastel Stari (C); Malinska (C); Makarska; Novigrad; Porec; Rabac; Rovinj; Split; Vodice; Zadar (C).

Islands: Bosava; Hvar and Korkula.

Cruising

Cruising tends to attract the older type of passenger, if for no other reason than that it is relaxing, timeless, and avoids such stressful situations as jet lag. Equally, being confined on ship means that fellow passengers are the only company available, which on a small vessel might easily produce strain. Also, anyone with mobility difficulties should think twice about such holidays, especially if there is a number of shore excursions which they will miss out on. Vessels catering for particular needs might not necessarily suit in other ways, so a lot of planning is required before a cruise is actually booked, and a long talk with a travel agent specialising in cruising is vital.

The trouble is that cruising took a tumble in the swing towards package holidays, and only now is it building up again. Some fine ships are available, and fly-cruise arrangements that take the passengers to their departure ports by air are proving particularly popular. However, the fall from favour caused a depletion of available expertise – though specialists like Paul Mundy Ltd, of 11 Quadrant Arcade, Regent Street, London W1R 5PB, can help. They have their own club, whose members and their companions get automatic discount on all standard cruises for a comparatively small, once-only lump-sum payment. Mundy's also have a standby scheme with the Cunard Line for even more savings on minimum rates. There is a registration fee payable, and the subscriber is allocated a cabin number anywhere on the ship eight weeks before sailing.

It should be said that discounts similar to those applied to the sunshine package deals can be found outside clubs. P&O offers savings on their Canberra programme and, though prospective travellers are required to be flexible with their timings and allocations, they stand to benefit by about one third off list price. It is always worth asking around, for

cruise ships want a full complement, just the same as hotels.

Ships like those in P&O's Princess Voyages' fleet have helped boost interest generally. There is an enormous choice on offer between cruises to the North Cape, Scandinavia and Russia, and winter sailings to North Africa, Madeira and the Canary Islands – some being available through well-known tour companies. It is also significant that the Norwegian coastal cruises have become more popular.

Another newcomer, and actually a new ship rather than a refurbished one, is the *Astor* – which should appeal to those looking for a smaller, well-equipped vessel. In addition there are inland cruises like those on the Rhine, Danube and Nile, which are occasionally discounted by tour companies. Theme cruises are another option, such as the well-known cultural tours operated by Swan Hellenic. This company has been known to offer some healthy standby rates, and give a discount for travellers willing to spend a month in the Med.

Long-haul Holidays

While it is headline-catching to say that British pensioners can now be spotted exploring the Aztec ruins or scrambling around Kashmir, some caution must be exercised with long distance travel. Flying is stressful, and one consultant has emphasised that anyone who under normal circumstances feels that sitting in one position without any sleep for up to 20 hours is not on should certainly forget long aircraft journeys.

Ways out, if financially possible, are

Life on board a cruise liner can be every bit as exciting as the ports of call

either to break the journey into stages, or travel first-class, and pay for more leg room. It should also be remembered that travellers normally need half the number in days to recover as the time zone change in hours, plus one if they are flying east, and minus one if they are travelling west. Translated, this means a couple of days to get over a journey to Miami, and more like three or four days on returning.

Once this has been accepted and personal health verified by a doctor, there is no reason why the older traveller should not enjoy the range of experience and good value for money that long-haul holidays give. Price-wise they are fast becoming comparable to those nearer home, due mainly to the competitiveness of hotel rates – especially in the Far East. Generally higher standards of service are another bonus.

Against these good points are high humidity, incidence of delayed flights and slowness at airports (of which India is an example), plus sudden changes of itineraries. All take their toll.

Where immunisation is listed as recommended rather than essential, medical experts advise that it should be done anyway. Malaria tablets must be taken when visiting malaria zones – and for some time after – and salt tablets or pre-salted water will help against sickness or tummy upsets, while preventing dehydration.

It is also wise to find a specialist tour company when planning a visit to far-flung places. Bales and Kuoni Travel are two, the latter's brochure lifting the lid on some hard facts of long-haul travel.

For many, visiting friends or relatives is the main motive for travelling great distances, though these have been outstripped – at least as far as Australia is concerned – by casual holidaymakers. Both groups benefit from their combined numbers, because the industry wishes to attract their custom by offering competitive packages that can often slot neatly in with a family visit.

The same applies to New Zealand, which is often tied in with Australia as a holiday destination. Anybody wanting to make their own arrangements should look out for special deals. The Australian Tourist Commission (Heathcoat House, 20 Savile Row, London W1X 1AE) or the New Zealand Government Tourist Office at New Zealand House, Haymarket, London SW1Y 4TQ can both help. There are also reunion flights, while Qantas operates an escorted-flight scheme aimed mainly at the elderly and those who may not have travelled abroad before. The escort actually travels with the passenger, helping sort out the sometimes puzzling aspects of air travel.

North America is increasingly being packaged, though programmes often allow travellers to create their own inclusive deals – for instance, by selecting an appropriate trans-Atlantic fare from the mass available (senior-citizen reductions exist on some charter flights), then using a variety of vouchers for accommodation and travel. This scheme benefits both the holidaymaker and people who are visiting relatives, by making arrangements as flexible as possible.

For good measure Amtrak – the rail system in the States – has various restricted offers.

Canada, which comes up trumps generally in what it offers senior citizens, has a large basic rail reduction for anyone over 60 – and the province of Ontario publishes a 34-page *Senior Citizens' Travel Guide*, listing dozens of attractions which can be visited free or at substantial discounts.

There are also senior citizens' air fares on North American domestic routes, but even those can be undercut by buying a VUSA fare or Flexipass before leaving Britain.

In Australia there are various discount schemes, including the Austrailpass, which are best discussed with a travel agent before departure. New Zealand offers a Travelpass, which covers train and ferry – again, advice should be sought from a professional.

Long-stay winter holidays
Long-stay winter holidays, with their annual crop of tempters – £2 a day and no fuel bills – began not as kindness on

Hours of Continental sunshine		
In this guide to average sunshine hours and temperatures around Europe, the first figures have been taken in January and the second between March and April.	**Algarve** (Portugal): 5.1 hours of sunshine and 58F (January); 8.8 and 67F (March to April). **Costa Blanca** (Spain): 5.8 and 61; 8.7 and 65. **Costa Brava** (Spain): 5 and 56; 7.4 and 65. **Costa del Sol** (Spain): 5.9 and 62; 7.8 and 69. **Cyprus**: 5.5 and	61; 8.2 and 68. **Gran Canaria**: 6 and 70; 9 and 74. **Lanzarote**: 5.9 and 68; 8.6 and 75. **Madeira**: 5.3 and 66; 5.6 and 67. **Majorca**: 5 and 57; 7.4 and 65. **Malta**: 5.6 and 58; 8.8 and 67. **Minorca**: 5 and 57; 7 and 67.

Even ever-popular Benidorm has its quieter attractions for the browsing tourist

behalf of the travel trade, but a wonderful way in which to keep bulk-booked hotels ticking over out of season. Mini-breaks were introduced in Britain for the same reason, and both have proved big money-spinners which, by the way, have greatly benefited the older holidaymaker.

Some of the cheapest offers are based on self-catering apartments and, provided these are near a good shopping centre or market, they can be fun that also makes good financial sense. However, people with weak stomachs or diet limitations should ensure that locally bought food is fresh and well cleaned before cooking. Those who are hotel-based may prefer to steer clear of the social life in winter, though it must be stressed that this varies considerably.

For certain is that many resorts, which discerning visitors would avoid like the plague in summer can seem like paradise out of season.

Weather, too, should be considered, for even the Med has a real winter. Spain's aptly named Costa del Sol (Coast of the Sun) enjoys temperatures of 60 degrees Fahrenheit or more during the day, even

Companies with special deals

The following companies either produce a separate brochure or include long-stay holidays that are geared to the more mature traveller in their main literature.

Saga Holidays: Book direct on Freephone 0800 300500, or for enquiries only on 0800 300600.
Age group: 60 or over; travelling companion can be 50 or over.
Coverage: six brochures (including the UK), covering some 20 countries worldwide, from six regional airports. Long-stay holidays in Spain (Costa del Sol, Costa Blanca, Costa Almeria, Costa del Azahar, Costa Brava, Costa de la Luz and Costa Dorada), Minorca, Majorca and the Canary Islands; also, the Algarve, Portugal, Cyprus and Malta.
Accommodation: hotels to self-catering.
Extra services: singles deals, a wide range of special-interest holidays, a Med Card Health scheme and group travel.

Horizon: Home from Home (bookable through ABTA travel agents).
Age Group: over-55.
Coverage: winter (November to April) brochure with flights from eight regional airports to Tenerife, Majorca, Spain – Costa Blanca, Costa del Sol and Costa Almeria (Mojacar) – and Cyprus.
Accommodation: hotels to self-catering.
Extra services: entertainer in many hotels, specialist reps, activity weeks, deals for singles and group travel.

Intasun: Golden Days (bookable through ABTA travel agents).
Age group: over-55.
Coverage: winter (October to April) with flights from 15 regional airports to Tenerife, Spain (Costa Dorada-Salou, Costa Blanca, Costa de Almeria, Costa del Sol), Portugal (Algarve), and Malta.
Accommodation: hotels to self-catering.
Extra services: own hosts and hostesses, often in the older age group themselves; singles and group deals and special interest offers.

Thomson: Young at Heart (bookable through travel agents).
Age group: over-55.
Coverage: winter (November to April) with flights from 10 regional airports to Spain (Costa Blanca, Costa de Almeria, Costa del Sol – plus excursions to Gibraltar), Majorca, Tenerife, the Algarve and Estoril coasts of Portugal, Tunisia and Malta.

Also offering long-stay deals are **Global** (Golden Circle for over 55s), **Cosmos** (for over-50s), **Enterprise** (now part of the huge Redwing group), and **Lancaster** (Good Companions). **Phoenix Holidays** and **Yugotours** offer senior citizens' reductions at selected Yugoslav hotels, and **Balkan Holidays** has an over-55s section for its Bulgarian Black Sea Holidays.

Footnote: *Long-stay holidays vary in extent considerably, with some of the longer ones tied into certain departure times and airports. So shop around, bearing in mind that it is sometimes possible to extend a short stay into a longer one by prior arrangement with the tour company.*

Holiday health insurance
There is no such thing as 'cheap' insurance that does all things for all people, because the policy holder only gets what he or she pays for. Policies should be read very carefully to make sure that they do what is wanted of them, and it is wise to consult the experts – the AA, an insurance broker, or travel agent – to find the best cover. For example, points to check by anyone seeking insurance for a fly-drive holiday are:
- Should the cover be for accident only (which is relatively cheap), or illness too – which is the most expensive?
- Will there be any reliance on reciprocal EEC arrangements for visitors to Europe? Anyone who wishes to use this system should consult the Department of Health (leaflet SA30) and complete the E111 application form. There are treatment limitations, and not all European countries participate in the scheme.
- It should be remembered that there is no reciprocal arrangement with the USA or other American countries, and medical care there is very expensive. Advice should be sought from the AA, or a travel agent.
- It is possible to insure against the cost of repatriation in the event of becoming seriously ill abroad, and further cover will ensure return shipment of the victim's vehicle in his or her absence.

in January and February. But evenings can be chilly, so it is worth finding out whether there is central heating. A good reason for choosing a hotel geared to the older age group is that staff and travel company reps are used to dealing with complaints and ailments associated with the more mature traveller.

For a more certain climate, the Canary Islands offer a virtually perpetual spring – though they are more expensive and rain can be expected round Puerto de la Cruz on Tenerife, a resort surrounded by banana groves and a lush collection of flowers and shrubs. A drier alternative is the southern coast, with its warped volcanic rocks, giant cacti and fig trees. Main centres are Playa de las Americas and Los Cristianos.

Sun is almost certain, too, on Lanzarote – an island of volcanic craters and extensive lava plains. Madeira, an island of flowers, might also fit the bill – and, though it may not be mentioned in the main long-stay brochures it is worth asking if an extended-visit deal can be arranged. Most firms, especially in the winter months, are prepared to stretch the traditional two to three week offers, some even promoting four weeks for the price of three.

Assessing your needs
But even good weather cannot make a holiday if the basic choice has been wrong and boredom, loneliness or irritation with a noisy crowd sets in. Every care must be taken to get things right.

Convenience, of course, counts for a lot – but so does cost – so the first step should be an examination of what the major tour companies offer, and for how much. Some produce more than one brochure, with vacations lasting from a week to anything up to 84 days.

Activities at hotel holidays range from dancing and bowls to bridge, rambling and photography. Golfers, too, are catered for, and the deciding factor may not be financial – for most long-stay holidays are within the same price bracket – but based on the diversions available.

Single rooms, with no extra supplement, are widely advertised at some hotels – though they may be cramped or lack a personal in-house phone. In such cases it is better to share a double room with a friend, or someone of the same sex selected by the holiday company.

Other drawbacks of long-stay holidays can be home sickness and family pressure, the inability to make friends when entertainment is not laid on, and monotonous food. Experts' assessments can be contradictory, with meals at the same hotel being variously described as awful and good, depending on personal preferences. An answer to hotel food problems is to eat out. In any event, an emergency fund should be built into the budget.

Major companies also cater for handicapped and infirm holidaymakers, provided that they are informed accordingly at the time of booking.

Health on holiday
Health generally, and treatment abroad, is another anxiety. While holiday companies have their own insurance cover, it is

Disabled travellers
Anyone who feels that they cannot take a holiday due to disability, impairment or any other factor which makes travelling difficult (even the need to look after a close relative) should write to the Holiday Care Service, 2 Old Bank Chambers, Station Road, Horley, Surrey RH6 9HW. This free consultancy is sponsored by the Association of British Travel Agents, whose holiday-care know-how provides help to anyone with problems which may not be covered by a relevant voluntary group. Also of use are two guides: *Holidays for Disabled People* and *Holidays and Travel Abroad; a guide for disabled people.* Published by RADAR (Royal Association for Disability and Rehabilitation), these guides are available from many bookshops.

Pensions
Someone who receives a UK retirement pension and is going abroad for *less* than three months does not need to tell their Social Security Office unless they are likely to need their pension paid abroad, or it depends upon their presence in Great Britain.

Anyone staying abroad *longer* than three months should contact their local Social Security Office to find out how their pension will be paid. At least *six weeks* should be allowed for arrangements to be made.

important to ensure that this is adequate and that the actual policy has been seen before departure. Anyone with misgivings should insure separately, especially if they have chosen somewhere fairly remote, which may necessitate an air-ambulance home.

Medical treatment generally is pretty good. Where the horror stories crop up is with dirty linen and inadequate nursing care, both of which arise from a clash of cultures – especially in parts of the southern Mediterranean, where traditionally the care of patients lies in the hands of their immediate family.

Such problems, according to medical consultants attached to top insurance companies, are usually confined to remote areas and occur less in the major cities and resorts. Portugal presents a few problems, but Spain not so much, due to the number of private clinics favoured by tourists. This is no reflection on the Spanish NHS hospitals – which provide good medical treatment – but is again due to the standard and style of nursing.

Weekend breaks

Not long ago the 'weekend break' was an experiment by a handful of British hotels who wanted to fill their empty rooms on the two nights a week that businessmen and sales reps were re-familiarising themselves with the interiors of their own homes.

The 'carrot' for the non-expense account general public included special low tariffs which, in addition to bed and breakfast, usually included an evening meal.

Little did the inventors realise that they had dreamed up what was to prove, and continues to be, one of Britain's major growth industries.

Just how sophisticated the whole business has become can be gauged not only from the sheer number of hotels that have jumped on the bandwagon, but also by the array of special activities that many lay on.

Short breaks in Paris, Brussels and Amsterdam are commonplace too – but then in these days of jet travel they are

less than an hour's flying time away. All in all, Messrs Boeing, Douglas, Lockheed and BAC have shrunk Europe to such a degree that the mini-holiday boom has already reached as far as Rome, Venice, Florence, Milan, Bologna, Genoa, Turin, Vienna, Budapest, Madrid and Munich. There are even 'long weekends' to New York! And Florida! Even California!

Richard Branson's Virgin Holidays offers short Broadway breaks and shopping trips to New York – complete with a discount card entitling the tripper to huge reductions at a number of clothing wholesalers – and two whole days of Miami sunshine. Even more amazingly, considering the distance, Hollywood and Golden Gate breaks in Los Angeles and San Francisco are available too.

Other airlines offer similar US deals.

Given that it has been shown that many retirees take more holidays each year than other age groups, it follows that a lot of over-60s are regular weekenders. Especially popular are Leisure Learning breaks at Embassy hotels. Canals, fine china, opera, wine, yesterday's world and vanishing Britain are just some of the subjects on the agenda. Saga Holidays, on the other hand, organise three-night bridge, dancing, whist, Scrabble and antique breaks among other interests for over-55s.

In addition, Danish Seaways' ferries sail to Esbjerg and back very cheaply in a vessel that could easily be mistaken for a mini cruise liner.

Failing that, there is always a half- or one-day excursion, or a short break on Concorde.

Prepare and enjoy

However, no matter what the holiday – long-haul, extended stay, the traditional week or fortnight, or weekend break – thorough preparation is highly recommended. A pre-trip medical is an excellent plan, and professional assistance an essential element in working out insurance cover and general finances. Not least, there should also be someone at home to keep an eye on the house.

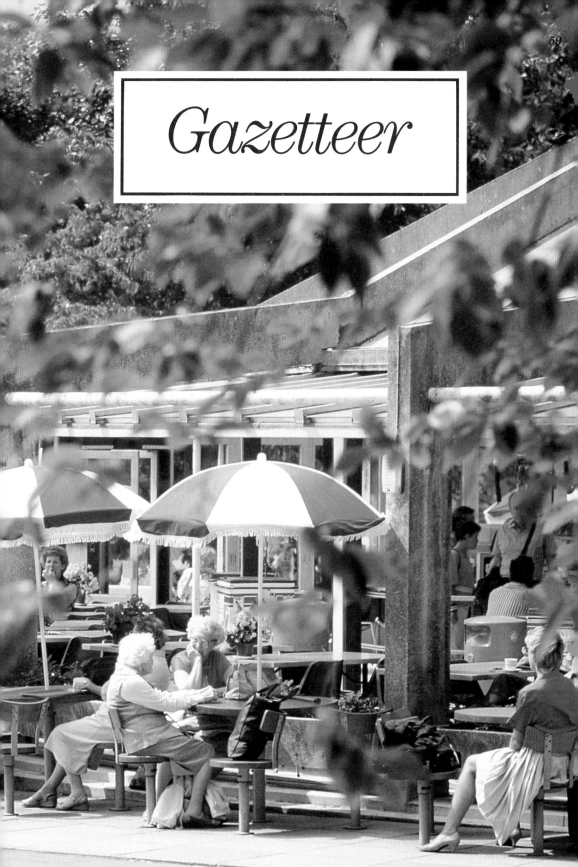

Gazetteer

In this Gazetteer places of interest throughout Britain have been selected by a team of writers who either live in or have long been associated with their area.

Written expressly for people able to enjoy Britain at their leisure – some of whom may feel a little less active than in former years – many entries include information on, for instance, ease of access to places of interest.

Opportunities to pause for rest and refreshment are also highlighted. Many places will be enjoyed by most younger people too and the four Walks within each region are designed to suit all the family.

The maps at the start of each area plot the routes of Walks and Motor Tours as well as marking every location in the Gazetteer. The map legend is given on page 60.

West Country

Scale: Approx 16 miles to 1 inch

Legend

Motorway	
Motorway under construction	
Primary route single carriageway	
Primary route dual carriageway	
Other A roads	
Motorway junction	
Motorway junction with limited entries or exits	
Town walks	
Tours	

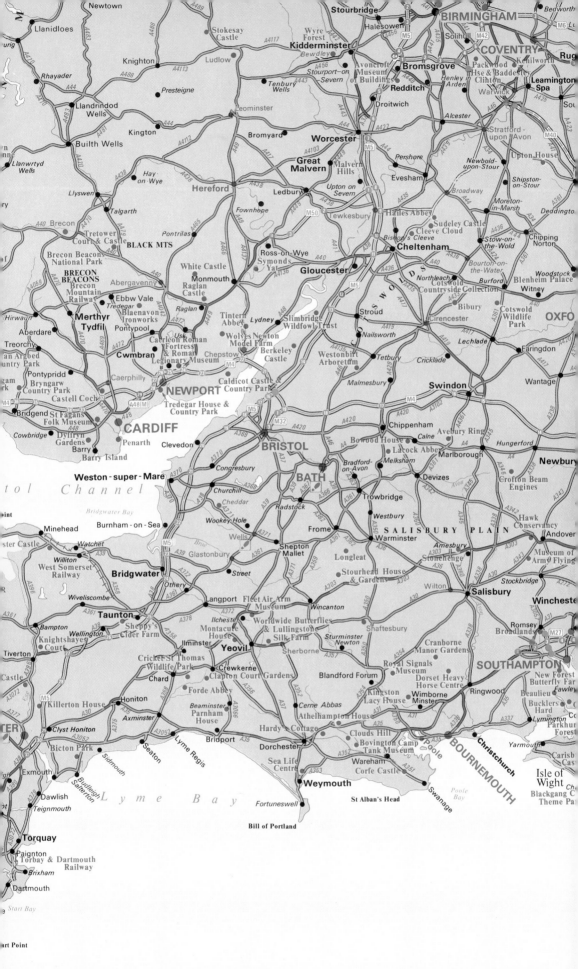

TOUR 1 58¾ MILES

Exmoor seascapes

In R D Blackmore's fiction, Oare Church was where Lorna Doone married John Ridd, and where she was shot by Carver Doone

The rolling uplands of Exmoor are a dominant feature of this tour, which also explores the switchback coastline, deep wooded combes, and heathery clifftops offering dramatic sea views.

The drive starts from the large hill-top village of Lynton. *Leave by the Lynmouth road and on the descent turn sharp left with the B3234. Continue the steep descent of Lynmouth Hill (1 in 4) to the small resort of Lynmouth – attractively situated at the mouth of the East and West Lyn rivers. Follow signs Minehead A39 and ascend Countisbury Hill (1 in 4).* One of the most famous hills in the West Country, it offers good sea views.

After the long climb to the hamlet of Countisbury the road emerges on to the northern extremity of Exmoor. Three miles farther the drive enters Somerset and shortly passes the turning to Oare (on the right). A short detour from here leads down to Oare Church, famous as the location of the wedding ceremony in Blackmore's *Lorna Doone.*

The main tour continues along the A39 for almost 6 miles and then makes the notorious twisting descent of Porlock Hill (1 in 4) to reach the village of Porlock. A

diversion to the left along the B3225 leads to the coast at Porlock Weir (1½ miles), with its small harbour. At Porlock go forward through the village with the Minehead road, and at the end keep left then turn right with the one-way system. Half a mile farther turn right on to an unclassified road, signed Horner and Luccombe, and proceed through the attractive Horner Valley.

In 1½ miles, at the crossroads, turn right, signed Dunkery Beacon. (Alternatively, keep forward to visit the delightful village of Luccombe – ½ mile – with its thatched cottages.) The main tour immediately ascends (1 in 5) and after ¾ mile it bears left in order to continue the long climb over the shoulder of Dunkery Hill. At the 1,453ft summit a footpath on the right leads to the AA Viewpoint on Dunkery Beacon, Exmoor's highest point and a popular destination for many.

There is an easy descent for 2¾ miles, after which turn right on to the Simonsbath road, B3224. Continue through undulating countryside for 3¾ miles before turning left on to an unclassified road, signed Winsford. This pleasant by-road later enters the valley of the River Exe to reach Winsford. At the telephone kiosk turn right (signed Molton), then bear left. After another 1½ miles meet the crossroads junction with the B3223. The road ahead leads to Tarr Steps, a medieval clapper bridge and Exmoor beauty spot on the River Barle.

The main route turns right on to the Lynton, Simonsbath road, B3223, and crosses Winsford Hill (1,405ft summit). Proceed through more open countryside and in 4 miles at the crossroads turn left. At the small Exmoor village of Simonsbath branch left with the B3358, signed Blackmoor Gate and Ilfracombe. Follow this moorland road to Challacombe and after a further 2¼ miles at the T-junction turn right on to the B3226. At Blackmoor Gate turn left then immediately right, A399, signed Combe Martin. Two miles farther turn right on to an unclassified road, signed Trentishoe and Hunter's Inn. In another 1¼ miles turn right again and later pass the car park for Holdstone Down (on the left), from where there are fine views. Almost a mile farther bear right (still signed Hunter's Inn) and descend to the beautifully situated Hunter's Inn.

Here turn left, signed Martinhoe, and ascend along a narrow by-road. At the top turn left again and continue to the hamlet of Martinhoe. Pass the church and in almost ½ mile branch left, signed Woody Bay Hotel, then take the next turning left. After the descent continue with signs Lynton via Toll Road, passing the Woody Bay Hotel – with impressive views across the Bristol Channel. Follow the narrow coast road and in 1¼ miles pass through a tollgate. Later go forward at the roundabout, entering the spectacular Valley of the Rocks, with its many jagged tors and rocky outcrops, before the return to Lynton.

TOUR 2 46 MILES

The land's end

Starting at Penzance, the drive visits the fishing villages of Newlyn and Mousehole, then veers inland and continues to Land's End. The coastal road to St Ives passes through rugged moorland interspersed with farms. Beyond St Ives Bay a detour is made to view St Michael's Mount.

The drive starts from Penzance, where a mild climate encourages exotic plants, and Regency buildings testify to long popularity.

Follow signs to Newlyn and Mousehole (A3077) alongside the harbour. Newlyn, a busy fishing port, became famous for its artist colony in the 19th century. Painters still live and work there.

From Newlyn, continue along the A3077. After crossing a bridge, turn left on to an unclassified road to Mousehole. With its granite houses and workmanlike harbour, the village has a flavour of traditional Cornwall. Drivers must take care, as the streets are narrow.

Turn left and drive to the harbour, then turn right and right again, signed Paul. This is the burial place of Dorothy Pentreath, one of the last people to speak the ancient Cornish language.

Go past the church (signed Land's End). In just over ½ mile turn left on to the B3315. After passing Sheffield, take the first turning left to Lamorna Cove. Later turn left to re-join the B3315 and continue for 3½ miles. At the T-junction, turn left. The road descends steeply, with a hairpin bend, then goes up to Treen. The tiny village stands near the end of a fortified headland known as Treen Castle.

Continue on the B3315 for ¾ mile, then turn left (unclassified) to Porthcurno. To the west of the good beach is the Minack Theatre, built in 1931 with an auditorium cut into the rock and a stage above the sea.

Re-join the B3315 and continue westwards. After 2 miles, turn left on to the A30 and drive for about ½ mile to Land's End. This is England's most westerly mainland point. On a fine day the Isles of Scilly are visible 28 miles away to the west.

Return along the A30, and reach Sennen. Leave Sennen on the A30. After 1¾ miles, turn left on to the B3306, signed St Just. After 3 miles turn left at the T-junction on to the A3071 and enter St Just. The old church has an ancient wall painting, an inscribed stone of the 5th century, and part of a 9th-century cross.

Continue along the B3306 to Morvah. About 1 mile south of the village, which lies on the edge of Penwith moorland, are Chûn Castle and Chûn Quoit, an Iron Age stone fort and a Neolithic chamber tomb.

Continue on the B3306 to Zennor and St Ives. Old houses and winding alleys cluster beneath the 120ft spire of the 15th-century church.

Leave St Ives on the A3074, signed Hayle. Pass Carbis Bay on the left and continue into Lelant on the River Hayle. At Lelant turn right and in ½ mile bear right at the mini-roundabout, signed Penzance, with the 'Cornucopia' on the left. At the next roundabout, take the third exit on to the A30, passing Canonstown and Crowlas. After a mile, at the next roundabout, take the second exit on to an unclassified road, signed Marazion. St Michael's Mount, with its splendid castle (NT) and priory, can be reached by boat from Marazion, or on foot along a causeway which is uncovered for three hours at low tide.

Return along the unclassified road, signed Penzance. Re-join the A30 at the roundabout at Longrock, and return to Penzance.

Dolly Pentreath, claimed to be the last Cornish-speaking person, lived in Mousehole village during the 18th century

The Museum of Wiltshire Folk Life is based at Avebury, in this superb 17th-century barn

many of the houses – evidence of expedient repairs before the ring was designated an ancient monument. The Alexander Keiller Museum, reached by way of the churchyard, houses an interesting collection of Neolithic finds from the area, including items from Windmill Hill (a mile north west), and Silbury Hill – a curious 130ft man-made mound about a mile south. Other exhibits come from the delightful little village itself.

BATH, Avon

Map Ref: ST7464

Industrial Heritage Centre,
Camden Works, Julian Rd

Open all year

Stairs make access to this interesting museum in the old Camden Works difficult for some people, but it should not be missed if at all possible. At the core of the collection is the entire stock-in-trade of Bowler's Victorian Brass Foundry, Engineering and Aerated Water Manufactory, displayed in such a way as to preserve the ethos of the original premises. Other permanent exhibitions include: the 'Story of Bath Stone', with a reconstructed mine face to illustrate the conditions in which miners worked to supply the stone which built Bath; and 'Bath Cabinet Making' – based mainly on the collection of the Keevil family, who were prominent cabinet makers of their day. Various temporary displays cover such subjects as local history, the grocery trade, the railway and crafts.

Museum of Costume,
Assembly Rooms

Open all year

A ticket giving admission to both this museum and the Roman Baths (see entry) is a good investment – and it is worthwhile making time to join one of the guided tours, which add the benefit of 'inside knowledge'. Guides explain the origin of the Assembly Rooms in which the museum is housed, imparting atmosphere to a collection of costumes which ranks amongst the largest and most comprehensive in the world. All aspects of dress – men's, women's and children's; royal, ceremonial and everyday; accessories, jewellery and underwear – are shown, along with a display of toys and dolls. Dating from the late 16th century to the present day, the exhibition concludes with a 'Dress of the Year' by a modern designer (*continues on page 66*).

ATHELHAMPTON HOUSE,
Dorset

Open spring to late summer; 1m E of Puddletown on A35. Map Ref: SY7694

This splendid medieval building, with its Great Hall and spectacular timber roof, stands on the site of King Athelstan's legendary palace and is regarded as one of the most outstanding houses of its time. A family home for the full 500 years of its history, nowadays it extends hospitality to visitors in the form of refreshments and souvenir-shopping opportunities. There are also some 10 acres of landscaped and river gardens in which to wander. A mile away is Puddletown, a Victorian estate village with a 17th-century church, which bridges the gap between old baronial house and 'new' settlement.

AVEBURY RING, Wiltshire

Open grassland; 6m W of Marlborough. Map Ref: SU1069

Avebury village settles back within the ancient ring of a massive prehistoric monument which is regarded as one of the most significant in Europe. The main road winds through three circles – two inners, one outer – which together encompass some 28 acres of grassland. A walk round the sarsens – gigantic stones hauled from the Marlborough Downs around 2300BC to mark out some form of open-air temple – appeals to all ages, although the less able may find themselves confined to flatter areas between the raised banks, or spectating from the comfort of the thatched Red Lion public house.

The village itself is a mixture of thatch, timber and weathered stone buildings, including a fine Elizabethan manor house (NT). The church, with its lovely lych gate, contains fragments of the ring stones in its fabric, as do

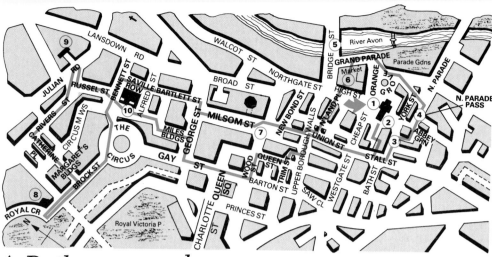

A Bath promenade

Although a Celtic and a Roman watering place, Bath is a true Georgian city, the creation of the local postmaster Ralph Allen and his architects, John Wood and son. The result is one of the finest planned townscapes in Britain. Many of Bath's loveliest streets, gay with window boxes and hanging baskets of flowers, are now pedestrian-only areas.

1 BATH ABBEY
The building of Bath Abbey is a story of continual checks and setbacks. The first Norman cathedral, replacing the Saxon abbey church, was gutted by fire in 1137, then abandoned until 1499 when Bishop Oliver King began work on the present structure. The Dissolution of the Monasteries in 1539 caused another interruption, but when Elizabeth I visited Bath in 1574, she urged them to complete the abbey. Even so, it was not until the 17th century that the nave was roofed, and then only with timber. The splendid stone fan vaulting dates from 1864.

2 PUMP ROOM AND ROMAN BATHS
In the elegant Pump Room, completed at the end of the 18th century, visitors to Bath gathered to taste the waters and to meet each other – a scene eloquently described by Jane Austen in *Northanger Abbey*. Coffee and afternoon tea are now served in these gracious surroundings, and music is provided by the Pump Room ensemble. The Roman Baths were lost to view for centuries, and the Great Bath was only re-discovered in 1878. Other small baths, cold plunges and the hypocaust room can also be seen, and the museum adjoining the baths contains a superb collection of Roman remains.

3 BURROWS TOY MUSEUM
This delightful little museum houses a staggering, international array of children's toys from the past three centuries.

4 SALLY LUNN'S HOUSE
Sally Lunn's House dates from 1482 and is reputedly the oldest inhabited house in Bath. Sally Lunn, who gave her name to the teacakes she made (which are still sold locally), lived here around 1680. Her house is, fittingly, a tea shop.

5 PULTENEY BRIDGE
The design of Pulteney Bridge, built by Robert Adam in 1770, was inspired by the famous Ponte Vecchio in Florence. It is the only bridge in England completely lined with shops on both sides.

6 GUILDHALL
Next door to the fine old covered market, the Guildhall, designed by Thomas Baldwin and completed in 1775, contains a magnificent Banqueting Hall, with walls and ceilings in Adam-style plasterwork.

7 MILSOM STREET
The grand stone buildings in this street were designed by John Wood the elder, and like Gay Street, it links the lower and upper parts of the city. Just off Milsom Street, the 18th-century Octagon building houses the museum of the Royal Photographic Society.

8 THE CIRCUS AND ROYAL CRESCENT
These two superb architectural compositions were created by John Wood the elder and his son, John Wood the younger. The father died in 1754, just as work was starting on The Circus, which he had planned as a perfect circle. No. 1 Royal Crescent, the house designed by John Wood the younger for his father-in-law Thomas Brock, has been meticulously restored by the Bath Preservation Trust.

9 CAMDEN WORKS MUSEUM
This fascinating museum preserves and displays the city's Victorian industrial heritage. J B Bowler was a small family firm of engineers and brass founders, with a profitable sideline in mineral waters.

10 ASSEMBLY ROOMS AND MUSEUM OF COSTUME
Completed in 1771 by John Wood the younger, these elegant reception rooms were known as the Upper Rooms to distinguish them from the earlier assembly rooms in North Parade (the Lower Rooms).

In the basement is the Museum of Costume, which covers the fashions of four centuries, from 1580.

PARKING; *Broad St, Manvers St, Walcot St*

OPENING TIMES:
Roman Baths & Pump Room: *open all year*
Burrows Toy Museum: *open all year*
Guildhall: *open all year Mon–Fri all day*
Octagon (National Centre of Photography): *open all year (closed Sun)*
1 Royal Crescent: *open summer only. Tue–Sat all day. Sun pm only*
Camden Works: *open all year. Summer Mon-Sun pm only. Winter weekends pm only*
Assembly Rooms and Museum of Costume: *open all year*

ROUTE DIRECTIONS
Start at Bath Abbey (1), then cross to the Pump Room and Roman Baths (2). Leave by Stall St, turn l, and l. again into York St to the Toy Museum (3). Continue along the street, then turn r. into Abbey St, leading to Abbey Grn, and l. into North Parade Pass, passing Sally Lunn's House (4). Turn l. along Terrace Walk (at the end of North Par), cross Orange Grove and keep r. along Grand Par. Ahead is Pulteney Br (5). Turn l. through the market. (On Sundays continue, turn l. into Bridge St, and l. again into High St for Guildhall). On the l. is the Guildhall (6). Cross High St to Northumberland Pl and walk through to Union St. Turn r. and cross Upper Borough Walls to go along Old Bond St into Milsom St (7). On the r. is the Octagon. At George St turn r, cross over and walk up Bartlett St and Saville Row to Bennett St. Turn l. and walk to The Circus. Leave The Circus along Brock St, which leads to the Royal Cres and the period house (8). Return to Margaret's Bldgs and turn l. to reach Catherine Pl. Turn r. along Rivers St, and at the end cross Julian Rd to the Camden Works Museum (9). Return to Bennett St via Russel St. Turn r. and cross over to the Assembly Rooms (10). On leaving, turn l, down the alleyway, then turn r, leading to Miles Bldgs. At George St, turn r, then l. down Gay St to Queen Sq. Turn l. along Wood St, r. down Queen St, l. into Trim St, then turn l. into Upper Borough Walls and turn r. into Union St for the return to the abbey.

Period room-settings from the Victorian age onwards make a fascinating series for anyone interested in the changing fashions of clothes and home furnishings through recent generations. Refreshments in summer and a shop in which to browse make this an ideal wet-weather stop.

Roman Baths

Open all year

Roman grandeur and Georgian grace, despite being centuries and civilisations apart, are both in Bath – a glorious, cream, stone-built city with streets beautified by baskets of flowers in summer, and a new interest round every corner. But of all the glories that are Bath, it is the baths themselves which hold the key to this city's eternal charm.

The Romans built their bathing establishment around the magical springs that gushed hot water out of the green valley of the Avon. The water – which never freezes and varies neither in temperature nor volume – still splashes, steaming and steady, over the iron-red stones in that ancient complex. The remains are remarkably complete in layout, but it is the Great Roman Bath – in whose vapoury surface are reflected the shapely pillars and balustrades surrounding it, and the stone splendour of the great abbey behind it – which is the focus of this stunning scene. In the precinct below on the site of their ancient temple are bold stone statements of Roman religion, with a sacrificial altar, tombstones, fierce carvings and votive offerings retrieved from the 'Sacred Spring'.

When you have left the underworld of the Romans, make time to sample sugar-encrusted Bath buns in the elegance of the Regency Pump Rooms, to the haunting strains of a string ensemble.

No.1 Royal Crescent

Open in summer

Bath is full of museums covering so many aspects of this most beautiful of British cities, but here the Bath Preservation Trust has realised its long-cherished aim to furnish a Georgian house in contemporary style. And what more splendid example than No.1 of John Wood the Younger's exquisite masterpiece, the Royal Crescent. Jane Austen's day seems that bit closer as you come across a quill pen on a desk – but today's cooks may find the kitchen more quaint than covetable.

BERKELEY CASTLE,
Gloucestershire

Open spring to late summer; off A38. Map Ref: ST6899

The name Berkeley is found in London's famous Square and across the Atlantic in Virginia and California, but in history it is known for the brutal murder of King Edward II. Both the cell of the ill-fated king and the dungeon are still awesome 660 years later – but there is much more to this noble, Severn Vale castle than the shameful shades of centuries past.

Berkeley's pink-grey stone is steeped in history. One of the most imposing feudal strongholds and one of the oldest inhabited castles in the West Country, the forbidding fortress has been turned by the Berkeleys over some 800 years into one of the stateliest family homes in the country. A guided tour takes about an hour, and there are lovely terraced gardens, a free-flight butterfly house, a picnic area and tearooms to keep the visitor occupied much longer. Make time to see the little Temple of Vaccinia – a picturesque thatched shed in the grounds – where Edward Jenner inoculated his first patients against smallpox. A museum devoted to Jenner's work is in the doctor's childhood home, 'The Chantry', in Berkeley itself.

BIBURY, Gloucestershire

Map Ref: SP1106

William Morris acclaimed Bibury as 'the most beautiful village in England', and judging by the number of visitors who come here throughout the year, it has lost none of its charm. The narrow, shallow River Coln is its prominent feature. It runs alongside the road behind a low stone wall until joined by an idle flow in front of the old weavers' cottages of Arlington Row – gables, chimneys and an irregular roofline etched against a dark, wooded bank. The water meadow opposite is alive with waterfowl and the footpath encircling it leads to Arlington Mill, now a folk museum. Next door is the Trout Farm, where visitors can feed or catch the trout for which Bibury is famed throughout the fresh-water angling world. The Swan Hotel, just over the bridge, is the local fisherman's haunt. A handful of shops and tearooms is scattered among the honey-stone cottages, but no other tourist trappings intrude. Visitors come here for tranquillity.

BICKLEIGH CASTLE, Devon

Open spring to autumn; off A396. Take A3072 from Bickleigh Bridge. Map Ref: SS9407

When approaching this castle by way of the pretty village of Bickleigh, tucked deep in a fold of the Exe Valley, you should allow sufficient time to wander at leisure among the thatched and whitewashed cottages, finding the water-mill which is now a centre where craftsmen can be seen practising age-old skills. This is a real pocket of the England that endured until comparatively recently, for at the neighbouring farm might be seen shire horses and oxen steadily working the land. There are many rare and traditional breeds among the animals there, and Devon country life at the turn of the century is captured in a museum collection.

Historic Bickleigh Castle is across the river. Some 900 years of domestic and national milestones are forged into this romantic moated home of the Earls of Devon, which has a gatehouse and small chapel dating from Norman times, an

Elizabethan bedroom, a Stuart farmhouse, an armoury and a guard room. A fascinating exhibition – including details of the legendary *Mary Rose*, and how Tudor maritime development was linked to the castle – is made even more interesting with a display of ship miniatures. Of all the exhibits, that of spies and prisoner-of-war escape tricks and gadgetry should not be missed, for it is the most complete collection of espionage and escapology equipment known to have survived from World War II.

BICTON PARK, Devon

Open spring to autumn; N of Budleigh Salterton, A376. Map Ref: SY0785

The entire family in all its ages is catered for here, where some 60 acres of classical gardens, landscaped by the designer of Versailles, are complemented by an extensive pinetum. Entertainments based on the themes of 'yesterday' include 'penny-in-the-slot' machines, magic-lantern shows and a countryside collection. A

'tomorrow' section has a space station and an extensive range of leisure facilities includes crazy golf, an adventure playground, a putting green and an assault course. Other favourite features are the narrow-gauge woodland railway and falconry displays. Refreshments, a picnic area and shops are also readily to hand.

BOURNEMOUTH, Dorset

Map Ref: SZ0991

Big Four Railway Museum, Dalkeith Hall, Dalkeith Steps

Open daily except Sun & Bank Hols. Access at rear of 81A Old Christchurch Rd

Bournemouth owed its rapid development at the end of the Victorian era to the coming of the railway. The resort is Thomas Hardy's 'Sandbourne', of which the great Dorset writer had Angel Clare say: 'a fashionable watering place, with its eastern and western stations, its piers, its groves of pines . . .'. It is fitting that a museum there should be devoted to railway memorabilia, where train

Classical gardens afford elegant respite from Bicton's more energetic attractions

enthusiasts are rewarded by finding one of the largest collections of old locomotive name and work plates in the country – as well as a good display of model trains and a working model railway.

Russell-Cotes Art Gallery & Museum, East Cliff

Open daily except Sun

Bournemouth has long been noted for its six miles of sandy beach, its pleasure-gardens and band music, its symphony orchestra and the balmy climate to which tired matrons and retired colonels traditionally resorted. That air of refined gentility still pervades the town, but it does not live in the past. Today, it is as popular a seaside town with the young as with their grandparents, featuring amusements and entertainments, and cultural and sporting events that offer a wide programme sweeping across the age and taste ranges.

The Russell-Cotes Museum at

East Cliff Hall fulfils a hankering for the weird and wonderful. Amongst the motley assortment of displays may be found Oriental art, butterfly and moth collections, an aquarium and a terrace exhibiting over 200 geological specimens. The Henry Irving collection will appeal to those interested in theatre.

BOURTON-ON-THE-WATER, Gloucestershire

Map Ref: SP1620

A tourist honeypot, Bourton-on-the-Water is included on every Cotswold tour and has learned to cater accordingly. The river, running under attractive low bridges alongside a broad green, is the outstanding natural feature of the village. Traditional stone cottages with steeply-pitched roofs and dormer windows, set deep between rose- and ivy-clad walls, are separated one from the other by shops and tearooms, bakeries and museums. There

Robert Adam designed Bowood's Orangery as part of a range added in the 18th century

can be few such villages in Britain, where so many attractions are packed in to such a short walking distance. A motor museum is centred on the old watermill, with a perfumery close by. Exotic butterflies and model railways are to be found in the High Street, and there is a trout farm by the large car park.

Two particular places of interest are so long established that they form part of the village fabric. Both were created by local men in their own gardens, and neither was intended to become a tourist attraction. Both are, however, and what is more they are the best of their kind in the world.

Perhaps the most famous is the Model Village, a Lilliputian Bourton-on-the-Water built from Cotswold stone in the garden of the Old New Inn. It delights grown-ups with its craftsmanship and detail, and enchants children with its scale – exactly one-ninth the size of the village itself.

The other is announced by flashes of scarlet, purple feathers and the mimicry of macaws, which beckon visitors across the little river to

Birdland, a garden where sugar-pink flamingoes pick their long-legged way across the lawns in front of Chardwar Manor. It was founded by the late Len Hill – the Penguin Millionaire – as home for some 600 different species from all over the world.

BOVINGTON CAMP TANK MUSEUM, near Wareham, Dorset

Open all year (closed 10 days Christmas & New Year); off A35. Map Ref: SY8389

Bovington is for boys – old, young and the not-so-young – for here are almost 200 armoured fighting vehicles dating from World War I and later. The mechanically minded will appreciate the cut-away Centurian tank, which reveals its internal workings. Also on show are displays of armaments, power plants and related equipment, together with working models and video shows in the museum theatre. There is a book shop too, and a self-service restaurant caters adequately for visitors. A large picnic area gives groups extra

freedom, and family, school and party tickets are offered at special prices. Servicemen are admitted free.

BOWOOD HOUSE, Wiltshire

Open spring to autumn; 2m W of Calne off A4. Map Ref: ST9770

Graciously Georgian, Bowood is a treasure house of paintings, sculpture, costumes, Victoriana and an elegant library designed by Robert Adam. Also open to view is the laboratory where Dr Jospeh Priestley discovered oxygen gas in 1774.

Grand though Bowood is, it is its grounds which command the most attention. From the formal gardens immediately around the house, the stroller is tempted to wander at leisure into the pleasure gardens. These were planted in mid-Victorian times and now comprise one of the country's best collections of trees and shrubs, including the loftiest Cedar of Lebanon and tallest poplar. One of the great pleasures is that the grass is kept mown, which makes walking the winding paths – shaded by massive oaks and

brilliant in season with the blossom of rhododendrons and azaleas – even more enjoyable. The whole is contained within some 100 acres of what is generally acclaimed as one of the finest parks in England – an 18th-century creation showing Capability Brown at his best. Leading from the central, elongated lake are romantic grottos and lively cascades – places to dream while younger members of the family expend their energy in the adventure playground. There are also refreshments and a picnic area, a shop and garden centre on site.

BRISTOL, Avon

Map Ref: ST5872

SS Great Britain, Great Western Dock, Gas Ferry Rd

Open daily. Map Ref: ST5872

The ancient city centre of Bristol is more newly-built than old-preserved, for – as many will recall – it was devastated in the blitzes of World War II. Post-war rebuilding of the commercial complexes, and a large immigrant population, have given a modern rhythm to the heart of this busy metropolis. But Bristol has always had a cosmopolitan air in its city streets, for it was a port long before it was a city. International trade was the seed from which it developed over a thousand years, and it was from here that explorers such as Cabot ventured to discover the New World before Bristol emigrants sailed to make a new life in it. Many of them would have sailed on *SS Great Britain*, Brunel's screw-propelled, ocean-going iron ship.

Revitalisation has now given new life to Bristol's dockland. Warehouses have been converted and refurbished to house a range of contemporary arts, and the Watershed complex comprises museums and a centre devoted to maritime heritage.

SS Great Britain is the centrepiece of the Great Western Dock, where visitors make their various ways to take pride in the grand old vessel's long and loyal service – and to appreciate her restoration. The first ship of her kind, she was launched in Bristol in 1843. Her career as a liner and cargo vessel was interrupted twice when she became a troopship for the Crimean War and the Indian Mutiny. Abandoned in the Falklands in 1886 to become a port store, she was towed back in 1970 and now, restored to

her former magnificence, is permanently berthed at the place of her birth.

Zoological Gardens, Clifton Down

Open daily. Map Ref: ST5774

Do you remember *Animal Magic*? That popular television series was filmed entirely at Bristol Zoo, with Johnny Morris talking to the animals. Many of those early friends are still around.

Founded on Clifton Down in 1836, it is the oldest zoo in provincial Britain and the fifth oldest in the world. Some of the magnificent trees were planted then, and the gardens – with their rare and exotic flora, beautiful rockeries and flower-filled beds between lawns and lake – make the zoo outstanding. As much attention is paid to spring and autumn colour as abundant summer.

It is difficult to envisage a more attractive setting for the 1,000 individual animals, including over 300 different species. Several recent features include a tropical house where you can walk among brilliant-plumaged birds, two penguin enclosures, a monkey house, reptile enclosures and an aquarium. The nocturnal house, where day and night are reversed, offers the opportunity to see nature's night-life. A self-service cafeteria, a waitress-service restaurant and a picnic area give visitors a choice of styles at their own feeding times!

BUCKFAST ABBEY, Devon

Open daily; off A38. Map Ref: SX7467

Buckfast village is overshadowed by its great abbey and grounds – and all who have known its history are awed by its restoration. A monastic stronghold for a thousand years, the abbey was successfully supported by Cistercians farming sheep on Dartmoor, until it was sacked at the Dissolution and became derelict. Ravaged and robbed over three centuries, it was in a sorry state when a handful of Benedictines planned to restore it to its original purpose. The minute workforce of just six monks who undertook the mammoth task completed the beautiful abbey church 30 years later. A tribute to their tenacity and faith, it stands today as the centrepiece of a full working monastic community.

Outstanding craftworks to be seen in the new church include the stained glass of the great east window and a magnificent mosaic pavement. Near by is the unusual House of Shells, which contains examples of shellwork in art and crafts form. Visitors are catered for with a licensed restaurant and shop.

BUDLEIGH SALTERTON,
Devon
See Bicton Park

BURFORD, Oxfordshire
See Cotswold Wildlife Park

CALNE, Wiltshire
See Bowood House

**CARNGLAZE SLATE
CAVERNS,** St Neot, Cornwall

Open spring & summer; off A38. Map Ref: SX1866

Cornish slate gives distinctive colour and texture to the roofscapes in this westerly point of the West Country. At Carnglaze slate has been quarried for 600 years, and the resulting caverns – one of which is some 300ft high – are a place of exploration for venturesome visitors seeking the underground lake. The more trepid will be satisfied with a look at the tramway which originally hauled the stone to the surface.

CHARD, Dorset
See Forde Abbey

**CHEDDAR CAVES &
MUSEUM,** Somerset

Open spring to late summer Gough's Cave open all year; off A371. Map Ref: ST4553

The great Cheddar Gorge in the Mendips is exciting from the moment you wind your way off the hills in dramatic descent along a road overhung with foliage between sheer rock walls. The scenery is spectacular – a prelude to the fantasia awaiting underground. Firstly, though, the world of tourism offers its array of amusements, souvenir shops and cafés, and a chance to see how Cheddar cheese is made. The custom-built demonstration unit, unhappily, has little resemblance to the old stone-flagged dairies and dark cheese-rooms which countryfolk will remember. Such a well-visited spot must, however, cater accordingly – and the commercialism is well confined.

Gough's Cave extends for about a quarter of a mile underground and has been described as the most beautiful in Britain. The entire system of caverns is a strange and awesome extravaganza in a secret world fashioned by primeval powers, where the colours and shapes of the stalagmites and stalactites play tricks on your imagination so that the weird becomes wondersome and the beautiful breathtaking. Skilful lighting enhances and exploits the underworld fantasy, but flights of fancy are leavened by excellent exhibitions and factual displays in the museum. Guided tours ensure that exploration is undertaken in relative comfort and sensible safety. There is ample opportunity for the more venturesome to undertake caving expeditions, and helmets, lamps and protective clothing are included in the price of the ticket. It is but prudent, unless you are a fully experienced caver, to join an organised group. Advice on this is available 'on site'.

**CIRENCESTER &
CORINIUM MUSEUM,**
Gloucestershire

Open daily. Map Ref: SP0201

Cirencester – Shakespeare's 'Cicester' – is the capital of the Cotswolds. As *Corinium* it was the second largest town in Roman Britain, and antiquities from that far-off age are displayed in the purpose-built museum as one of the finest collections in the kingdom. Full-scale reconstructions of a kitchen, dining room and mosaic craftsman's workshop recapture domestic and working life of the time, and there is a full and varied programme of associated activities.

Within walking distance is the largest parish church in Gloucestershire. Spacious and full of historical detail, it has an exquisite fan-vaulted and oriel-windowed south porch, built by the abbots of Cirencester as an office and used by the townsfolk as the town hall after the great abbey went the way of all powerful and profitable religious foundations at the Dissolution.

Abbey Grounds – the footpath entrance to which is behind the church – is an extensive lawn meadow with swans on the River Churn at its foot, and a gnarled old mulberry tree propped up beside the path. It is a pleasant place to wander away from the busy main streets.

Heading the other way from the museum, by way of Cecily Hill, the explorer soon finds Cirencester Park – which affords even more scope for walkers. The finest surviving example in England of pre-landscape planting, it was set out in geometrical avenues of 'rides' by the first Earl Bathurst and his friend Alexander Pope. A small, rusticated stone pavilion just inside the park, called Pope's Seat, is the bower in which the poet wrote of his plans for the park's 'open avenues, cut glades' . . . which are still there. The park also has a fine polo ground where the Prince of Wales often plays.

**CLAPTON COURT
GARDENS,** Somerset

Open all year; 3m SW of Crewkerne, B3165. Map Ref: ST4409

Gardeners, whether actively engaged on their own plots or simply admirers of others' toils, will enjoy the beauty at Clapton Court. There are many rare and unusual specimens among the shrubs and plants, and as the whole area is only about 10 acres, the expedition does not become onerous. Particularly colourful in spring and autumn, the gardens are a lovely mix of formal layout and natural woodland. Refreshments are available, and the plant centre is well stocked with a good variety of unusual species.

CLEEVE CLOUD,
Gloucestershire

Open countryside, fairly rugged walking; NE of Cheltenham, A46. Map Ref: SO9825

The attraction of Cleeve Cloud is that it is the highest point of the Cotswolds. It lies on the Cotswold Way long-distance footpath, which follows the westerly scarp line from Chipping Campden to Bath. It is way-marked and can be picked up close to The Rising Sun public house, alongside the A46.

The ascent from here is fairly gradual, but can be muddy in wet weather. A topograph in the heathery heights adds detail to the Winchcombe Valley below, and it comes as a bit of a surprise to learn that about a mile along the rocky outcrop is the actual 1,083ft summit, which appears as a broad plateau edging Cleeve Common.

The views are expansive, and in an evening memorable – for then the setting sun highlights the hill-edged western horizon, throwing into relief the misty blue of the Malverns, the Black Mountains and the Herefordshire uplands. Dawn walkers can thrill to the sound of hoof on turf as the Cheltenham racehorses exercise on the long gallops.

Cleeve Common is a natural amphitheatre in a bracing position. An 18-hole golf course covers much of it, and visitors are welcome to enjoy a round – plus the club's bar and restaurant facilities. Now that the YHA has opened its membership to all ages, the Youth Hostel here (the only one on the Cotswold Way), makes an ideal base from which to explore the rugged beauty of the escarpment.

CLOUDS HILL, Dorset

Open all year; 4m SW of Bere Regis off B3390. Map Ref: SY8290.

Literary lovers of romance will find a visit to this part of Dorset quite fascinating, for Clouds Hill was the home of T E Lawrence – but they have to be prepared for limitations, as only three rooms are open to the public. The remote tree-screened house on the hill a mile north of Bovington Camp (see page 68), was where Lawrence spent the last 12 years of his colourful life, and it still holds an aura of the enigmatic Welshman who lived, fought with and wrote about the Arabs. Lawrence's home life in secluded Dorset was a Spartan contrast to the extravagance of the Middle East he so loved. His effigy in Wareham Church shows him as history remembers – as Lawrence of Arabia, a different figure from the lone writer who ended his days in Hardy's Dorset.

Four miles distant is pretty Bere Regis, Thomas Hardy's 'Kingsbere-sub-Greenhill' in his novel *Tess of the D'Urbervilles.* In the church rest members of the Turberville family. Nearby Woodbury Hill was the fair site in *Far from the Madding Crowd.*

CORFE CASTLE, Dorset

Open early spring to autumn daily; in winter weekends only; on A351. Map Ref: SY9582

Corfe developed as a small town whose industry, commerce and buildings were all built on and with the Purbeck stone which is to be seen in so many Dorset churches and monuments. It has a most attractive town square, and a church with one of the finest towers in the kingdom. A model of the town and castle is set in a garden off the main street.

It is the dominant castle ruin, on its boldly-isolated summit, to which visitors are constantly drawn. A powerful statement of Norman power, it must have been a formidable fortress in its prime – and it is hauntingly

A Saxon stronghold stood at Corfe over a century before this Norman castle was built

romantic in its ruin. A river loops round the foot of the steep hill on which it stands, a bridge spans a deep moat on the town side, and the ruin itself picturesquely guards a natural gap in the Purbeck Hills. The Normans took over a Saxon predecessor, and it is their great wall (some four yards thick in places) which withstood the ravages of time and the Civil War. The massive King's Tower dates back 800 years. As excavations take place, a little more is revealed of the castle's long history each season.

Corfe Castle is certainly one of the ruins that Cromwell 'knocked about a bit'. In fact, knocking about even by Roundhead standards made little structural damage to this stronghold. It was being blown up by gunpowder that lifted the roof off to the skies. There are no complete rooms of a stately home to be seen, and nothing under cover remains. But the great walls and outlines have a majesty of their own, and

Shamrock, a River Tamar ketch-rigged barge, moored to the riverside quay at Cotehele

wandering among the ruins on a fine day makes a pleasant excursion – especially as there is a tea-garden by the entrance. From there you can ponder over a cup or two, wondering at the greatness of all that must once have been.

COTEHELE HOUSE (NT), Cornwall

Open spring to autumn, daylight in winter – garden only; 8m SW of Tavistock off A390. Map Ref: SX4269

Seekers after the romantic notion of a Cornish medieval house will find that Cotehele comes closer to that ideal than most, even granted the need for it to open its ancient doors to the public. Now under the care of the National Trust, the grey granite building holds centuries within its tapestry- and armour-filled rooms, additionally offering visitors the facilities for refreshment and the pleasure of walking through colour-filled terraced gardens. Sloping gently to the thickly-wooded Tamar Valley, the gardens lead to a water-powered corn mill – restored to

full working order – and to Cotehele's own quay, where there is a small museum of shipping.

COTSWOLD COUNTRYSIDE COLLECTION, Northleach, Gloucestershire

Open spring to autumn; off A429. Map Ref: SP1114

This award-winning museum is a clever combination in which a preserved 'model prison' built around 1789 by Sir Onesiphorus Paul has been used to house an extensive collection relating to agricultural history. The House of Correction, complete with magistrates' court and cells, contains vivid examples of an age when law and justice wore different coats. In contrast is the Lloyd-Baker collection of farming life, displayed in the prisoners' exercise yard. Demonstrations of various crafts, and a changing programme of visitor-participation activities, also bring new life to these old buildings at a crossroads on the edge of Northleach.

Northleach itself is a small market town built from the profits of the Cotswold wool trade, boasting many fine old buildings centred on a market square which has a splendid 'wool' church as its magnificent cornerstone.

COTSWOLD WILDLIFE PARK, Burford, Oxfordshire

Open daily; S of Burford, A361. Map Ref: SP2408

Rhinos roaming the grounds of a Cotswold manor is just one of the surprises offered by this wildlife park, near the old coaching town of Burford. Mammals and reptiles, winged wonders and water creatures plod and prance, slither and splash, strut and fly in spacious enclosures spread over some 200 acres of gardens and woodland. A narrow-gauge railway takes visitors on a gentle rumbling run around the main areas. Great spreading trees in the park are ideal for picnickers, and there is a restaurant. Elsewhere are found a brass-rubbing centre, pony rides, a playground, shops and a garden centre.

CRANBORNE MANOR GARDENS, Dorset

Gardens open Wed early spring to autumn, garden centre all year; on B3078. Map Ref: SU0513

Rupert Brooke immortalised Cranborne in one of his poems when he stayed at the Fleur-de-Lis inn. Red-brick and colour-washed buildings, cottages clustering round the village green and a medieval church rich in ancient murals make this most attractive village – on the edge of the rolling chalk uplands of Cranborne Chase – well worth a visit.

Cranborne Manor, close to the church, is a greystone Jacobean house which was once the Chase Court. It is not open to the public, but the 17th-century gardens sometimes are, and in summer present a picture of roses and geraniums, Italian statuary, silver foliage and herbs. An Elizabethan knot garden and river gardens are pleasant to walk among, and the garden centre has a lot to offer. This is a privately-owned property without tourist facilities or trappings.

CREWKERNE, Somerset
See Clapton Court Gardens

CRICKET ST THOMAS WILDLIFE PARK, Somerset

Open daily; off A30. Map Ref: ST3708

Television fans will recognise the fine old Georgian mansion of Cricket House as 'Grantleigh Manor' in TV's *To The Manor Born*. What the cameras do not show is the real life of the manor park, for here – in a sheltered valley below Windwhistle Ridge – is a landscape filled with wildlife from all over the world.

An aviary in the Orangery, sea lions in the lake and camels in the old cabbage gardens may not have been what the famous architect John Soane envisaged when he designed the manor 200 years ago, but so well integrated with its historic and landscaped background is the wildlife park that it ranks as one of the finest of its kind in the country. A woodland railway affords a leisurely means of viewing the more far-roaming animals.

A collection of Victorian dairy equipment, a museum of country life and a chance to see modern dairying methods are additional features. Also here is the National Heavy Horse Centre. A licensed restaurant, picnic area, shop and garden centre are open to visitors.

CROFTON BEAM ENGINES, Wiltshire

Open spring to autumn; 1½m SW of Gt Bedwyn. Map Ref: SU2662

Crofton is in a scenic village at the highest point of the Kennet and Avon Canal, and a destination to which steam-pumping-engine enthusiasts flock to see the oldest working steam engines in the world. Now fully restored, two beam engines which were once used to pump water up to the canal are occasionally put to work for public viewing. Visitors to the site will find refreshments, a picnic area and a shop to cater for their basic needs. A trip on a traditional narrow boat is a must during the programme of steam weekends, but for those who miss the schedule there is still the pleasure of a walk along the canal towpath to anticipate.

DARTINGTON GLASS CENTRE, Torrington, Devon
See Torrington.

DART VALLEY RAILWAY, Devon

Open summer; off A38 at Buckfastleigh. Map Ref: SX7466

Smoke clouds in sunlit skies and the pulsating throb of busy steel wheels on long steel tracks are nostalgic recollections of an age not long past, but sometimes as distant seeming as the dinosaurs. However, because the demise of steam trains is so recent, they have not yet been consigned to history and misty memory – and Buckfastleigh, an attractive mill town on the old coaching road between Exeter and Plymouth, still echoes in summer to their hiss and whistles.

The Dart Valley Railway was re-opened in 1969, seven years after it was officially axed in the great national rail closures. Now, resplendent in their original Great Western Railway chocolate and cream colours, the coaches once more offer all the atmosphere of their period. Both they and the railway have featured in many major films.

The railway's northern terminus, Buckfastleigh, was built in 1872 to serve the heavy Victorian industries that settled in and around this cobbled old town, in the limestone hills of South Devon. From Buckfastleigh the route winds through the tranquil woods of the lovely Dart Valley to Totnes. A round trip of 14 miles is offered, but it is also possible to make this short, nostalgic journey part of a longer modern one – now British Rail trains also stop at Totnes!

Rail enthusiasts are further catered for by a steam park, a store of GWR rolling stock, a model railway and a museum. Also to hand are a licensed restaurant, picnic area, shop, river walks and – if you still have the energy – a 196-step climb to admire wonderful views from Buckfastleigh Church. Go before dusk unless your nerves match your stamina, because legend tells of haunting sounds around the mausoleum. It is said that this tale inspired Conan Doyle while writing his famous *The Hound of the Baskervilles*.

DOBWALLS THEME PARK, Cornwall

Open spring to autumn; N of Dobwalls off A390. Map Ref: SX2165

The major feature of this pleasure park is the Forest Railway, an elaborate miniature steam line modelled on two sections of the great

Pretty, timeworn corner among the medieval residences of Cathedral Close, in Exeter

American railroads. In the course of one mile it emulates the Denver and Rio Grande route, then in another mile is based on the Union Pacific – complete with lakes and forests, dark tunnels and deep canyons, and the steepest gradient to be found on any miniature railway. Also here are a railway walk, an indoor railway museum, a restaurant, picnic and play areas, a shop, radio-controlled boats and the 'Hall of Memories'.

A permanent memorial to Archibald Thorburn – one of the country's leading bird painters – is an exhibition of his works, complete with photographs, letters and books.

DORSET HEAVY HORSE CENTRE, Dorset

Open daily spring to autumn; 1¼ m NW of Verwood off B3081. Map Ref: SU0709.

It is to see the majestic working-horse champions – the Shire, the Ardennes, the Percheron, the Clydesdale and the Suffolk Punch – that visitors beat a path to Brambles Farm, but good static displays of farm waggons and agricultural implements can be enjoyed too. Also,

demonstrations of harnessing, plaiting and driving appeal to anyone at all interested in the traditional world of real horse power. There are refreshments and a shop on the farm, and both family and party tickets are available.

DUNSTER CASTLE (NT), Somerset

Open spring to late summer; on A391. Map Ref: SS9943

Dunster Castle dominates this beautiful medieval village in the hilly Avill Valley, and visitors are well catered for, even though there are no obvious tourist intrusions to spoil the locality's natural charm. An octagonal Yarn Market on which the village is centred was where the community conducted its early trading, and the ancient bridge over which packhorses carried loads of 'Dunster' – the name given to the local cloth – still spans the river. At the end of Mill Lane is an original 17th-century watermill, where stone-ground flour can be bought.

The Norman castle, family seat of the Luttrells (to whom Dunster owes its preserved character), was given in trust to the nation in 1976. Set on a wooded hill above the village, it has oak-panelled halls, magnificent ceilings and many rare portraits among its treasures. Sub-tropical terraced gardens and a splendid gatehouse are features of the grounds.

DUNSTONE, Devon
See National Shire Horse Centre

EXETER MARITIME MUSEUM, Devon

Open daily. Approach via Alphington St and Haven Rd. Map Ref: SX9292

'Messing about in boats' on the river is a particular pleasure here, where a huge and international collection of craft can be seen under cover, ashore and afloat at the head of the Exeter Canal, on the south side of the city. Visitors are free to explore many of the 130 vessels exhibited in and around the old fish market and warehouses, once used as an authentic backdrop for the TV series *The Onedin Line*.

A ferry trip across the River Exe, between exhibition areas, adds an insight into boat-building in all its different forms. Comical little coracles and paper-thin dhows contrast dramatically with Brunel's *Bertha*, the world's oldest

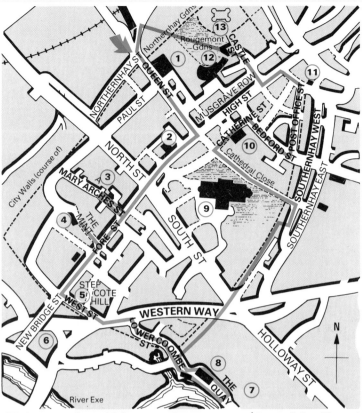

Rise of a Phoenix

A thriving city and excellent shopping centre, Exeter suffered devastating bomb damage in World War II, and as a result has a lot of modern building. However, many gems of the medieval and Georgian city have survived, and in several places old and new stands companionably side by side.

1 ROYAL ALBERT MEMORIAL MUSEUM AND ART GALLERY
Opened in 1868, this large Victorian-style building has 14 exhibition rooms covering a wide range of subjects and periods.

2 THE GUILDHALL
One of England's oldest municipal buildings, the Guildhall was rebuilt in 1330 on foundations that were possibly Saxon.

3 ST MARY ARCHES CHURCH
This is the only church in Devon to retain its double Norman nave arcade. The interior is spacious and has 16th- and 17th-century monuments.

4 ST NICHOLAS' PRIORY
Founded soon after the Norman Conquest, the priory is one of Exeter's most fascinating buildings. The entire west range, consisting of the guest rooms, has survived.

5 ST MARY STEPS CHURCH
Originally adjoining the west gate of the city, this church is set in a delightful corner of Exeter, next to Stepcote Hill – a steep, cobbled medieval street – and near several lovely Tudor houses.

6 MEDIEVAL EXE BRIDGE
The building of the new road system over the twin Exe bridges has made it possible to expose this substantial survival of the medieval city.

7 THE QUAY
Exeter has traded from here since Roman times, at first by river and since 1566 by canal – the first with pound locks to be built in England. At the water's edge stands the fish market, whilst near by is the Custom House.

8 MARITIME MUSEUM
Over 100 craft from all over the world can be seen here. Some are afloat in the canal basin, and may be boarded. Smaller craft are on display in two large warehouses.

9 EXETER CATHEDRAL AND CLOSE
The Cathedral Church of St Peter is still the city's centrepiece 600 years after its completion. The west front is adorned with exquisitely carved figures, while, inside, the 14th-century rib vaulting of the nave is breathtaking.

10 RUINS OF ST CATHERINE'S ALMSHOUSES
Founded in 1450 as a charity to take care of 13 poor men, these almshouses suffered bomb damage in 1942.

CITY WALLS
Early in the 3rd century the Romans improved the original earthen rampart round the city by building a massive stone wall, enclosing almost 100 acres.

11 UNDERGROUND PASSAGES
Exeter was privileged among medieval cities in having a supply of fresh spring water piped into it via a network of vaulted underground conduits. Part of the system – now dry of course – has been restored and is a fascinating place to explore.

12 ROUGEMONT HOUSE MUSEUM
This is Exeter's main collection of archaeological material. Most of the exhibits were found locally.

13 ROUGEMONT CASTLE AND GARDENS
All that survives of Exeter's Norman castle today is the restored gatehouse and what is known as Athelstan's Tower.

MARKET DAYS: *Mon & Fri*

PARKING: Mary Arches St, Paul St, Queen St

OPENING TIMES:
Royal Albert Memorial Museum and Art Gallery: open all year. *Tue – Sat*
Guildhall: open all year (except when in use). *Mon – Sat*
St Nicholas' Priory: open all year. *Tue – Sat*
Maritime Museum: open all year
Underground Passages: open all year. *Tue – Sat pm only*
Rougemont House Museum: open all year. *Mon – Sat*

ROUTE DIRECTIONS
Begin in Queen St at the Northernhay St junction. Walk along Queen St past the Museum (1) and turn r. into High St. Pass the Guildhall (2) and at the traffic lights continue into Fore St. Turn r. along Mary Arches St to the church (3) and return to Fore St. Continue down to The Mint, turn r. and walk up to St Nicholas' Priory (4). Return to Fore St and go down to the crossroads, turning l. into West St and St Mary Steps Church (5). Before crossing the dual carriageway, look r. for the old Br. (6). Cross, turning l. and r. into Lower Coombe St. Bear r. to the quay (7) and the Maritime Museum (8). On the return, turn r. by the Custom House to follow the path beside the city walls. Cross Western Way at the top and pass another section of city walls. Cross South St to reach another path beside the walls. Cross the car park, then turn r. and l. into Southernhay West. Turn l. after about 150yds into the Cathedral Close for the Cathedral (9), continuing to St Martin's Church. Turn r. here and continue into Catherine St, past the almshouses (10), then turn r. into Bedford St and l. past the Post Office into Post Office St, following the city walls. Turn l. at the end of the wall, cross a paved area, passing the entrance to the Underground Passages (11), then turn l. into High St. After about 50yds turn r. into Castle St and just before the top of the hill, turn l, through the gates into Rougemont Gdns, where the Museum (12) and the Castle (13) ruins are. Bear r. where the path forks and turn l. through the arch into Northernhay Gdns. Turn l. and walk downhill to the Queen St gate, then turn l into Queen St to complete the walk.

working steam boat, and a Danish ice-breaker; African rough dug-out canoes are shown alongside romantic Venetian gondolas; and flimsy rafts from the Pacific are next to the colourful craft of the Portuguese. Take a launch down the canal to enjoy the water at leisure, or if you feel more energetic, work your own way by hired small craft. Refreshments with a licensed bar and shop extend the facilities of this fascinating museum.

The Quay is but a short walk from the city centre, and by way of the cobbled and stepped Stepcote Hill – where the Exeter of old can be traced back to the time when it was a principal seaport.

EXMOOR NATIONAL PARK

Map Ref: SS7040 etc

This vast national park reaches north to the sea across Devon and Somerset, taking in the wooded steeps of Lynton and Porlock in its combe-cut and cliff-girded boundary. Sweeping east across rugged and bog-pocked moorland is a diverse patchwork of dense forest and open villages, remote farms and ancient tumuli, strange nameless stones and story-book valley bottoms. This is home to the red deer and the dun pony; it is a place for the walker, the pony-trekker, the motorist who enjoys quiet roadways, and the lover of outstanding natural beauty in its wildest forms.

FLAMBARD'S TRIPLE THEME PARK, Helston, Cornwall

Open spring to autumn. Map Ref: SW6726.

It is easy to understand why this leisure park is an award winner, catering as it does for all the family by providing all-weather facilities and three major attractions.

First comes Flambard's Victorian Village – life-size and complete with shops, carriages and the fashions of Victorian England. Then there is Britain in the Blitz, again life-size. Here a complete street has been reconstructed to illustrate life in war-torn British towns, stirring many memories (not all bad) and provoking questions from those who wonder how their elders survived.

Cornwall Aero Park, the old title from which the leisure park developed, spans the whole history of airflight from early 'planes to the Battle of Britain. Exhibits also include helicopters, a Concorde flight

deck and an SR2 simulator.

Special exhibitions, children's amusements and the lovely landscaped gardens in which the whole complex is set extend the attractions of Flambard's. Hilly Helston, on which the park is centred, has a small collection of its own local history in the Old Butter Market. The town's famous Floral (or Furry) Dance is held in May.

FLEET AIR ARM MUSEUM, Yeovilton, Somerset

Open daily; off A303. Map Ref: ST5422

The full title of the 'Fleet Air Arm Museum and Concorde 002' at the Royal Naval Air Station embraces the full range of this vast collection in Yeovilton. Aviation at sea is portrayed by 50 historic aircraft, models of ships and pictorial and graphic illustrations which trace developments from the early years to modern supersonic passenger flight. Exhibitions of Kamikaze attacks and the Falklands Campaign feature in the story of naval flying, and there is an aviation viewing area. Facilities also include refreshments, a shop and picnic area, parking for coaches and caravans, and a place where children can play safely.

FORDE ABBEY, Dorset

Open spring to autumn; SE of Chard off B3167. Map Ref: ST3505

Set in extensive grounds, of which rock and water gardens are a particular feature, this

lovely old country house had an earlier rôle as a Cistercian monastery. Cromwell's Attorney General converted it to lay use in the mid 17th century, and it has been a family home ever since. It has a shop, a garden centre and facilities for refreshments. Outstanding among the many treasures preserved here are five famous Mortlake tapestries. Woven in the early 18th century to fit the salon walls, they represent cartoons by Raphael.

GLASTONBURY ABBEY, Somerset

Open all year; on A39. Map Ref: ST4938

Glastonbury, the cradle of Christianity in Britain, lies under its ancient Tor in a mystical land of myth and mystery. Local legend links King Arthur and Avalon, Joseph of Arimathea and the Holy Thorn, as a circle of charms embracing the old town. Certainly, it grew up around the site of an ancient abbey and was a place of pilgrimage for many centuries. Echoes of its monastic past are perpetuated in such places as the old Pilgrims Hotel. Pre-Christian artefacts include finds from an Iron Age 'lake village' at Meare, now housed in the medieval abbey courthouse. The Abbey Barn, 100 years older than the courthouse, is the Somerset Rural Life Museum, and the Abbey Farmhouse gives an interesting insight into Victorian farm life, both in exhibition form and live in the farmyard.

Of Glastonbury Abbey itself, the well-preserved remains give some idea of its former greatness, and a superb model in the new museum in the medieval gatehouse adds missing detail. By far the best fragment of the ruin is the Abbot's Kitchen, with its high, octagonal stone roof and lantern. Inside is a small museum of antiquities associated with the abbey. A picnic area allows visitors to eat their own food in the grounds, with the pinnacle of Glastonbury Tor and the tower of St Michael's Chapel soaring into the sky above them as sentinels of a long-lost age.

GREAT BEDWYN, Wiltshire
See Crofton Beam Engines

HAILES ABBEY (NT), Gloucestershire

Open daily; NE of Winchcombe off A46. Map Ref: SP0529

Cleared of its swags of ivy, and with its crumbling walls cleaned of the centuries' all, Hailes Abbey stands as a broken and jagged shell of its one-time magnificence. Only three cloister arcades and the occasional arch still rise to any height, but as you pause and catch the torn-off silhouette against a break of trees, the senses stir. It is not so hard to imagine the soft sound of sandalled feet on stone, and the brushing whisper of a monk's robe. Putting fact to such fancy is an excellent collection of relics in the adjacent museum.

Hailes Abbey was founded in 1246 with much pomp by the

On Glastonbury Tor is the tower of St Michael's Chapel, ruined by a landslip in 1271

Earl of Cornwall, younger brother of Henry III, as a thanksgiving for having survived a shipwreck. He became a rich and powerful landowner under the Cistercian order, and the presentation to the abbey of a phial of the Holy Blood furthered its career by bringing national fame and even more prosperity. Chaucer had his pardoner 'swear by it', and even Henry VIII made a pilgrimage to this idyllic wooded vale beneath the Cotswold escarpment. But the abbey suffered drastically at the Dissolution, and its buildings were subsequently ravaged by time and the stone stealers who were building homesteads in the valley.

Before leaving this quiet spot, make a visit to the tiny church opposite. It was 100 years old before the abbey was built, and preserves both a wealth of medieval wall paintings and an array of heraldic floor tiles. Its ancient walls hold the aura of antiquity.

A pleasant, well-marked route over the gentle rolling hillside takes the walker from Hailes Abbey along the ancient pilgrims' path for some 3m to the interesting old town of Winchcombe. Its abbey has long since gone, but it is well blessed with tea shops and inns, plus a local museum with a set of seven-holed stocks and the finest collection of police memorabilia in the country. Sudeley Castle, about half a mile distant, is clearly sign-posted from Winchcombe.

HARDY'S COTTAGE, Higher Bockhampton, Dorset

Open by written appointment to tenant; 3m NE of Dorchester, ½m S of A35. Map Ref: SY7292

Literary pilgrims eagerly find their way to this thatched brick cottage (NT) in a primrose wood at the top of the hill off Cuckoo Lane, for it was here in the home built by his great-grandfather that Thomas Hardy was born in 1840. He wove Dorset rural life into all his well-loved novels, and the cottage of his birth features in detail in *Under the Greenwood Tree*. It now houses the personal and literary memorabilia of his life.

This is a visit best undertaken by handfuls of visitors rather than coachloads, for it is only without haste that you can appreciate the intimate character of the writer, his family and their home. Neither must you miss the delightful details – such as the peep-hole in the porch where Hardy's grandfather kept a watchful eye on visiting excise men searching for his smuggled brandy!

Hardy's 'Egdon Heath', which stretches out behind the cottage, is managed by the Forestry Commission.

HELSTON, Cornwall
See Flambard's Triple Theme Park & Poldark Mine

HIGHER BOCKHAMPTON, Dorset
See Hardy's Cottage

KILLERTON HOUSE (NT), Devon

Open spring to autumn, gardens open all year; 5m NE of Exeter off B3185, off B3181. Map Ref: SX9701

Extensive Killerton Estate spreads out over a Devon hilltop as an impressive setting for the fine Georgian house at its heart. Its pride is the Paulise de Bush collection of period costumes, which is displayed in room settings furnished in styles covering the last two centuries. Large gardens with many rare trees and shrubs are contained within some 300 acres of glorious grounds. There is a restaurant and shop available.

KINGSTON LACY HOUSE, Dorset

Open spring to autumn; 1½m W of Wimborne Minster on B3082. Map Ref: ST9701

Art lovers will find one of the country's finest private

This hard Land's End granite rises above the sea 28 miles west as the Isles of Scilly

collections in this 17th-century house, which was remodelled by Sir Charles Barry in 1835. Works include such old masters as Van Dyck, Lely, Titian, Reynolds, Rubens and Velasquez. Kingston Lacy House and garden are now in the hands of the National Trust, so visitors are catered for by the standard shop and refreshments.

KNIGHTSHAYES COURT (NT), Devon

Open spring to autumn; 2m NE of Tiverton off A396. Map Ref: SS9515

A combined visit to Tiverton and Knightshayes Court – some 2m – makes an interesting outing. The old wool mill town of Tiverton was where author R D Blackmore went to school, and the triangular green – by the Loman Bridge – is where he set the fight between Ridd and Snell in *Lorna Doone*. A more factual history of the town is displayed in what is generally considered one of the best local museums in the county, and can be visited all year. Preservation and restoration of the Grand Western Canal near by has allowed the establishment of a horse-drawn passenger service through the delightful Devon countryside.

Woodlands are the predominant feature of

Knightshayes, a Victorian house set deep in glorious wooded and shrub-filled gardens which are particularly memorable when the rhododendrons and azaleas are ablaze with blossom. Refreshments, a shop and a garden centre are available on site.

LACOCK (NT), Wiltshire

Open spring to autumn; 3m S of Chippenham off A350. Map Ref: ST9268

Lacock village is locked tight into our national heritage – a lovely jumble of cheerfully unrelated styles, including grey stone and red brick, overhanging gables and lichen-encrusted tiles, whitewashed façades and half-timbered walls. Nothing is more recent than the 18th century, and many of the buildings are a great deal older.

Lacock Abbey is on the edge of the village. An Augustinian nunnery in the Middle Ages, it was one of the last monastic houses to suffer from the Dissolution, and was restored after the Reformation by Sir William Sharington as a family home. The Tudor mansion retains the cloisters, sacristy and nuns' chapter house, now joined by a later Gothic hall and an octagonal tower which forms a romantic cornerstone to the old grey stone house, with its tall and twisted chimneys. It was in this corner tower that Sharington locked his heiress after she had fallen in love with John Talbot, of whom Sir William disapproved. In a dramatic lover's leap, she jumped from the tower into Talbot's waiting arms. The story had a happy ending, as the couple were later wed with Sharington's blessings.

A later Talbot, William Henry Fox, inherited the abbey in the early 19th century and pioneered the art of photography. His first successful photograph – one of the oriel windows – is to be seen in the house, and a gallery of his work and early equipment is staged in a beautiful 16th-century barn at the abbey gates.

LAND'S END, Cornwall

Open all year; off A30. Map Ref: SW3425

Who has not heard of Land's End, the starting point to the measure we give to express the length of the kingdom 'from Land's End to John O'Groats'? Some 200 acres of the most westerly tip of mainland England, it dips its toe into the Atlantic off a windswept peninsula, punctuated and jagged with the passage of time. A leisure and exhibition complex illustrates the relationship between this rugged landscape and its peoples, from the early Celtic cultures to Cornishmen. It also has natural history displays. On a clear day it is possible to see the Isles of Scilly, some 28m west, from the headland.

LANHYDROCK (NT), Cornwall

House open spring to autumn, gardens winter; 2m SE of Bodmin off B3268. Map Ref: SX0863

A long beech and sycamore avenue leads to this restored 17th-century house, much of which was destroyed in a disastrous fire 100 years ago. Rebuilding the mansion was in accordance with the original plan, and surviving from the old house is a 116ft long gallery, featuring a ceiling richly carved with biblical scenes. The north wing and the two-storeyed gatehouse are also original. Less grand but just as interesting is the social history encapsulated in the Victorian servants' quarters. Tea is still served – but National Trust style. The bronze vases in the rose-filled gardens are the work of Ballin, goldsmith to Louis XIV of France.

LONGLEAT, Wiltshire

Open all year, Safari Park closed winter; 5m SW of Warminster off A362. Map Ref: ST8043

There is more to Longleat than its lions – though to be fair, it is they who have made the name of this great Wiltshire estate world-famous, by becoming the uncrowned monarchs of an animal world settled in Europe's first safari park. In the beautiful parkland, judiciously planned to include natural boundaries formed by woods, lakes and ditches, visitors can picnic among the zebras, camels and giraffes – but are warned to keep to the safety of their cars when travelling through the lions' domain.

Longleat has a long reputation of leading the field in revolutionary ideas. When Sir John Thynne rebuilt an Augustinian priory to his own designs here, he took the bold step of having rooms facing over the park rather than turned in to the courtyards. The golden-stone Italian Baroque house was the first stately home to be opened to the public, and the Marquess of Bath has extended the original attractions to visitors on an impressive scale.

In the house are the treasures of some 400 years, held in every corner from the grand state rooms to the Victorian kitchens – plus many interesting exhibitions. Of particular note are an original first-folio Shakespeare, letters by Queen Elizabeth I and Glastonbury Abbey's Saxon charter of AD681. Visitors are fully catered for by the usual facilities, and besides the gardens and safari park there are numerous other attractions, including a narrow-gauge railway, an adventure playground and a pets' corner.

LULLINGSTONE SILK FARM,

See Worldwide Butterflies

MINACK THEATRE, Cornwall

S of Porthcurno off B3315. Map Ref: SW3822

Just south of the village of Porthcurno – fortunate in having a white sand beach – is the fascinating Minack Theatre, which is built on the edge of cliffs from the bed-rock stone. There can be few settings as dramatic as here, where the stage is cleft to the cliff edge, affording a spectacular backdrop of natural seascape.

MONTACUTE HOUSE (NT), Somerset

Open spring to autumn; off A3088. Map Ref: ST4916

Montacute House has been held in trust for the nation for half a century, and in that time has been furnished in a manner befitting this gabled and turreted Elizabethan mansion of golden Ham Hill stone. The National Trust has also arranged for a fine collection of Tudor and Jacobean portraits from the National Portrait Gallery to be on permanent view in the 189ft long gallery. There is some splendid heraldic glass and panelling elsewhere, and formal gardens and refreshments invite the visitor to stay that bit longer.

NATIONAL SHIRE HORSE CENTRE, Dunstone, Devon

Open all year; E of Yealmpton off A379. Map Ref: SX5751

There is more to this centre than its name implies, although it is the noble horses which are the major attraction. Here on a farm worked by the traditional and true horsepower the great Shires regularly parade, with their foals in season, each day at 11.30, 2.30 and 4.15. At other times they can be seen in their stables.

A blacksmith at his forge, a wheelwright and a saddler, a potter and a glass engraver work in the crafts centre, and agricultural tools and equipment are to be seen in the farm museum. There is also a butterfly centre and a bird sanctuary, and displays of falconry are held twice daily. Children can amuse themselves with the pets – or in an adventure playground featuring a free-fall slide and assault course – while their elders take a quiet walk by the River Yealm, passing a lime kiln and

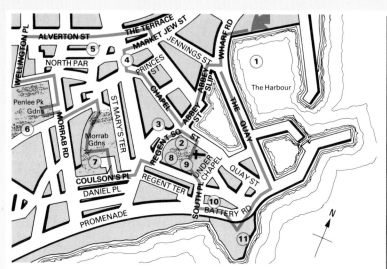

A kindly climate

Balmy Penzance takes its name and existence from the one time chapel-crowned headland which thrusts into Mount's Bay. In its lee, Pen sans (Cornish for holy headland) has grown from a humble fishing cove to the capital of Penwith, despite being burnt to ashes by the Spaniards in 1595. No buildings survive from before that date, but to compensate the town has a rich legacy from the Georgian era.

1 THE HARBOUR
Stacked high on the wharves in the heyday of sail were tin blocks and fish barrels. Today, although those ancient trades and a 300-strong fishing fleet have gone, the harbour is still full of life and colour. Colossal red buoys identify the Trinity House building; the Barbican Craft Centre and Aquarium was formerly an old warehouse; and from the South Pier the MV *Scillonian* makes a daily 40m voyage to the Scilly Isles.

2 CHAPEL STREET
Memories of an older Penzance – of smuggling and dark lanterns – seem to linger in this ancient way that leads from the harbour. Its 17th- and 18th-century buildings now find a variety of pleasing uses. The 400-year-old Admiral Benbow Inn (with its rooftop pirate), and Roland Morris's Maritime Museum opposite, are run by Roland Morris – diver and finder of the wreck of the *Association*. The Turk's Head Inn, with its fine signboard, is the oldest in town, dating back to the 13th century. No. 18 boasts a ghost – a board outside tells the story.

3 THE EGYPTIAN HOUSE (NT)
The most remarkable building in Penzance is at Nos 6 & 7 Chapel Street, the Egyptian House.

house, now the Camelot Restaurant. Farther along, in the old Municipal Buildings, is the Geological Museum – where local specimens can be seen.

6 PENLEE GARDENS
Once the lush 15-acre surround of Penlee House (1866), the gardens are now a public park. By the house stands an 8ft, 10th-century cross (formerly the town's market cross), one of only

Balmy Penzance tolerates outdoor palms and band concerts

Built in 1835/6 and reflecting the then popular interest in Egyptology, it housed the collection of John Lanvin, a local mineralogist.

4 MARKET PLACE
The shopping centre of the town is Market Place, Market Jew Street (derived from the Cornish words *Marghas Yow*, or Thursday Market) and Alverton Street. These are dominated by the high-domed Market House, which was completed on the day of Queen Victoria's coronation. In front of the massive portico is a statue of Sir Humphry Davy – Penzance's most famous son, a brilliant chemist, inventor of the miner's safety lamp and President of the Royal Society.

5 ALVERTON STREET
Alverton Street has a fine example of a mid 18th-century Cornish granite

two to bear the name of a Cornish king.

7 MORRAB GARDENS
Morrab Place is probably the finest example of the early 19th-century granite or stucco terraces which elegantly line the way to Morrab Gardens. With their bamboo and tree ferns, the gardens offer a few acres of sub-tropical greenery in the heart of Penzance. Embellishing them are a large fountain and a traditional ironwork bandstand.

8 REGENT SQUARE
The square is a delightful little enclave of relaxed Regency style houses built in the 1830s. The road twists through the centre and offers a close view.

9 ST MARY'S CHURCH
The church stands on the site of an earlier St Mary's Chapel, which was destroyed by the Spaniards.

10 ST ANTHONY'S GARDENS
The site of 12th-century St Anthony's Chapel (patron saint of fishermen) – the earliest place of worship in Penzance – is marked by these gardens. Although containing an archway believed to have come from the chapel, a more certain relic is a 4ft piece of granite depicting Christ in a loincloth. This stands in St Mary's Churchyard.

11 BATTERY ROCKS
This, the wave-washed tip of the 'Holy Headland', is almost covered by a war memorial and swimming pool. Its name comes from a small fort built in 1740.

EARLY CLOSING: *Wed*

MARKET DAY: *Tue & Thu*

PARKING: *Green Market, Guildhall, Harbour, Wellington Place*

OPENING TIMES:
Roland Morris's Maritime Museum: open *Apr–Oct*
Barbican Craft Workshop: open all year
Geological Museum: open *May–Sept. Mon–Fri, pm only*
Penlee House Museum & Art Gallery: open all year *Mon–Fri, Sat am only*

ROUTE DIRECTIONS
From the harbour (1) turn l. out of the car park along Wharf Rd. Turn r. up Abbey Slip and keep forward into Abbey St then go r. into Chapel St (2), passing the Egyptian House (3). Turn r. into Market Pl (4) and Market Jew St; cross over and turn l. along The Terrace, and then cross Causeway Hd to reach Alverton St (5). Cross by mini-roundabout and turn l. into Wellington Pl. Turn l. at the foot of the car park (signposted 'Pedestrian exit to Morrab Rd') and then turn r. at Morrab Rd. At this point a detour can be made by turning r. into Penlee Gardens (6). Return, cross the road and go ahead down an unsigned alley. At the end turn r. to enter Morrab Gardens (7). Bear r. to pass Morrab Library, turn downhill and bear l. to exit from the gardens into Coulson's Pl. Immediately turn l. and then go forward into Coulson's Bldngs. Turn l. to go uphill, and then turn r. into Regent Sq (8). Turn r. into Chapel St. Turn r. into St Mary's Churchyard (9) and cross seawards into South Pl. Go left and continue through St Anthony's Gardens (10). Cross the Promenade to Battery Rocks (11) and return to the Harbour along the Quay.

salmon leap. There are ample facilities.

NEWQUAY, Cornwall
See Trerice Manor

NORTHLEACH,
Gloucestershire
See Cotswold Countryside Collection

PARNHAM HOUSE, Dorset

Open spring to autumn; 1m S of Beaminster on A3066. Map Ref: ST4700

Parnham House is the home of John Makepeace, and it is to see the outstanding furniture designed by him and the work of his students that visitors are attracted to this lovely old Tudor mansion. It is here that cabinet- and furniture-making skills are to be seen at their traditional and contemporary best and most modernly exciting. Intensive and comprehensive courses are based here, and completed work is exhibited in the house.

POLDARK MINE, Cornwall

Open spring to autumn; 4m NE of Helston on B3297. Map Ref: SW6831

The history of Cornish tin mining is well illustrated at this show mine, which has three different levels so that visitors can view it according to their own capabilities. At ground level are lawns and gardens with working antiques and a 40ft high beam engine. Children can find amusement in their own quarter, and there is a restaurant with a shop, garden centre and picnic area too. A cinema programme and no fewer than nine museums take the visitor into greater depth and – literally – by a guided tour into the actual mine itself. Family tickets are available.

POOLE, Dorset

Map Ref: SZ0190

Compton Acres Gardens,
Canford Cliffs Road

Open spring to autumn; off B3065

Overlooking Poole Harbour are the famous private gardens of Compton Acres, where concentrated in some 15 acres is a fine collection of water, rock, heather, English, Japanese, Italian and Roman gardens, beautified by bronze and marble statues. Stepping stones and bridges span streams, linking the seven gardens by

pretty paths. There is a shop and garden centre, refreshments are available and lovely views extend over Brownsea Island to the Purbeck Hills beyond.

Maritime Museum, Paradise Street, The Quay

Open all year

Ever since Canute picked Poole as his harbour base in 1015, this town on Dorset's heath and pinewood shore has thrived on the sea-faring trades. Today its harbour and fine beach are alive in summer with holiday-makers, and the town's old and new buildings mix happily in its bustling centre.

On the quay beside the boat-filled harbour – next to the Customs House and Harbour Office – Poole's maritime heritage is housed in the cellars of an old Woolhouse dating from 1422. Exhibits trace the history of local commerce and families, particulary those involved in the 18th-century trade with Newfoundland. A collection of local boats and the tools of craftsmen, merchants, seamen and fishermen are complemented by contemporary accounts, ship models and paintings – many by the artist Gribble.

Among the maritime buildings on Poole's old waterfront is the 18th-century Customs House

Poole Pottery, The Quay

Open weekdays all year

The potters of Poole have carried the name of this popular holiday resort far and wide since they started producing 'Poole Pottery' in 1921. The pottery itself was founded some 50 years earlier. The range of buildings in which it is situated testify to a long maritime history. There is a shop and a tearoom attached.

PORTHCURNO, Cornwall
See Minack Theatre

PUDDLETOWN, Dorset
See Athelhampton House

ROYAL SIGNALS MUSEUM,
Dorset

Open weekdays; 3m NE of Blandford Camp off A354. Map Ref: ST9208

The history of army communications is illustrated here through radio and line systems, complemented by exhibitions of uniforms, badges, medals and paintings.

ST MAWES CASTLE,
Cornwall

Open. Map Ref: SW8433

St Mawes, steeply clustered down to the quay where medieval shipping once brought trade, has not succumbed to the intense pressures of tourism which have spoilt so many other similarly-sited resorts. St Mawes Castle, built by Henry VIII on a strategic tip south of the town, is also a survivor of the centuries. It succeeded in its purpose as a defensive stronghold and has withstood 400 years to stand today in excellent repair. From it a superb view extends across Carrick Roads to Pendennis Castle.

ST MICHAEL'S MOUNT
(NT), Cornwall

Open all year; 3m E of Penzance. Map Ref: SW5129

Old St Michael's is a pocket-sized packet of history. The small granite island in Mount's Bay can be reached by way of a causeway at low tide, or by boat during the summer months from Marazion. Entirely owned by the National Trust, it has a castle and priory built in the 11th century by Edward the Confessor above the small harbour and hamlet. A 14th-century chapel houses a fine collection of furniture, pictures and armoury. Refreshments are available.

SEA LIFE CENTRE, Lodmoor
Country Park, Weymouth, Dorset

Open daily. Map Ref: SY6880

When the weather is too bad to enjoy Weymouth's wonderful sandy bay, Georgian esplanade or the landscaped gardens of its headland, why not take a short trip to the east of the town to see creatures who love to live in wet conditions?

Here at Britain's largest marine-life display is an exciting water underworld that can be explored from such intriguing vantage points as the Ocean Tunnel, the Cliffwalk, the Island Walkway and in Rockpool 'touch tanks'. Man's relationship with the oceans of the world and a Blue Whale splash pool are also well worth finding time for. A butterfly farm, playground, shop and refreshments are offered too.

SHAFTESBURY, Dorset

On A30. Map Ref: ST8622

Gold Hill, one of the few remaining cobbled streets in southern England, has 18th-century cottages clinging tenaciously to one side of a steep street and heavy buttresses holding up a medieval wall on the other – thought to have been part of the long demolished abbey, burial place of Edward the Martyr. Relics from the ruins are preserved in the Abbey Museum. Thomas Hardy featured Shaftesbury in his novels, under its original name of Shaston. Shaftesbury has moved with the times, but something of its thousand-year development can still be traced in the quiet corners and busy streets. Its hilltop position makes it a good vantage point from which to scan the Blackmoor Vale, with superb views extending all the way to Glastonbury Tor.

SHEPPY'S CIDER FARM,
Three Bridges, Bradford-on-Tone, Taunton, Somerset

Open all year; 3½m SW of Taunton on A38. Map Ref: ST1722

'Zummerzet Zider' is more than a folk expression at Sheppy's Farm, for here – deep in the Vale of Taunton Deane – the Sheppy family has made cider since the early 1800s. Now, as one of the last true farm cider makers, they invite the public to see where and how their gold-medal draught is created.

Sheppy's cider orchards cover some 42 acres, fruited with such old names as Kingston Black, Dabinett, Stoke Red, Tremlett's Bitter and Yarlington Mill. An excellent farm and cider museum illustrates tools and equipment of old, and in the cellar a modern press room brings the old skills into the present day. The apple crop is processed in autumn, so a visit then includes the potent smell of cider in the making. A wide range of goods is sold in the shop, including superb farm produce such as cheese, cream, and of course, the golden cider.

SHERBORNE CASTLE,
Dorset

Open; on A30. Map Ref: ST6416

Golden stone enriches the beauty of Sherborne's many old buildings, some of which date from its medieval monastic past. The great abbey church has a glorious, fan-vaulted nave and choir, and is one of the town's outstanding features, but many of the dissolved monastery's buildings were converted to more secular purposes. For instance, 16th-century Sherborne School took over the abbot's hall, library and kitchen, while a conduit in Cheap Street was originally the washroom from the abbey cloisters.

Sherborne's pair of castles is found about half a mile east of the town. The Elizabethan New Castle, built for Sir Walter Raleigh, is open to the public and features fine period furniture, paintings and porcelain. It is set in some 20 acres, landscaped by Capability Brown, and in its park are the picturesque ruins of Sherborne's 12th-century castle, which was demolished by Cromwell's troops. It is in the gardens, where now there are lakeside lawns, a cascade and an orangery, that local lore says Sir Walter sat smoking the 'new-fangled tobacco' and a servant threw a flagon of ale over him thinking his adventurous master was on fire!

See also Worldwide Butterflies & Lullingstone Silk Farm.

SLIMBRIDGE WILDFOWL
TRUST, Gloucestershire

Open daily; 2m NW of Slimbridge off A38. Map Ref: SO7204

The world's largest collection of wildfowl has made its home

among the River Severn's tidal mud flats on the Berkeley estate, some five miles from its old castle (see page 66). Established in 1946 by Sir Peter Scott around his Slimbridge home, this famous trust has some 100 acres of lake-laced wetlands which are alive with speckled and striped blobs of birds, bobbing and weaving their various ways among the waterweeds. Here visitors can walk among geese from places as distant as the Soviet Arctic and Hawaii.

Specially-built hides have been made so that visitors can watch the wildfowl without disturbing them. Every need of the guests is considered – including sensitively-constructed facilities for disabled people. Even the visually handicapped can enjoy studying the role of wildfowl in our natural heritage through commentaries, and tactile exhibits which allow them unusual participation.

STONEHENGE, Wiltshire

Open all year; 3m W of Amesbury off A303. Map Ref: SU1242

In the great rolling chalklands of Salisbury Plain is the heartland of prehistoric Britain – and at the very centre of its ancient administrative, social and cultural territory is Stonehenge. An excellent introduction to this mystical and enigmatic spot is a tour along the A360 ridge road, which appears close to cloud and sky, to meet the A303 at Long Barrow Cross roads, 2m west of Stonehenge. Hereabouts are long and round barrows, the burial mounds of Neolithic and Bronze Age peoples, and the rectangular markings of old Celtic farms and fields.

At the base of five of these prehistoric parishes is the strange symbolic stone circle that is Stonehenge. Academics have argued its purpose for centuries. That it was the centre of some religious practice is generally accepted, and the alignment of the axes of the stones to the rising sun on midsummer's day gives credence to the theory that from it an ancient calendar was devised.

Stonehenge is an awe-inspiring monument to a lost and forgotten people. For whatever purpose it was designed, its complex construction of great Blue Stones – many weighing over two tons and all hauled from the Preseli Hills of South Wales – and 50-ton sandstone blocks from the Marlborough Downs will remain the greatest mystery in the history of man. It is still a centre for revived Druid ceremonies, and attracts many thousands of people to witness the summer solstice.

STOURHEAD HOUSE & GARDENS (NT), Wiltshire

Open spring to autumn, gardens all year; off B3092. Map Ref: ST7635

It is fitting that the National Trust – custodians of so much priceless heritage – should have their Wessex headquarters at Stourhead, for here are the most stately of all stately-home gardens. Landscaped in classical style, the 18th-century lake-watered grounds form a living portrait painted in brilliant blossom, touched with the softening shade of trees, the sparkle of water, and viewed from the stone temples of Flora, Apollo and the Pantheon before a background of ancient beech woods. The mansion is contemporary and has some fine Chippendale furniture.

Whether used originally as temple or ancient solar calculator, Stonehenge holds a spell that few can resist

SUDELEY CASTLE, Gloucestershire

Open spring to autumn; S of Winchcombe off A46. Map Ref: SP0228

Sudeley, according to some researchers, was the inspiration for P G Wodehouse's 'Blandings'. It is a honey-stone castle standing in the wooded Winchcombe Valley under the bluff of the Cotswold scarpline, and it has been both prize and pawn in England's vigorous political past. A thousand years of history focuses on the site, where castles have been built since the time of Ethelred the Unready, and the hands of all its masters have shaped it. But it is the castle's mistresses who have had the most influence. A favoured royal residence, it was the home of Queen Katherine Parr (Henry Tudor's sixth wife), who is buried in the castle chapel. Sudeley suffered badly in the Civil War, and the ruins of its once-great banqueting hall are stark reminders of that violent period. After years of neglect, its Victorian mistress, Emma Dent, devoted all her energy to restoring the castle and amassing a fine art collection with which to beautify it. Its present mistress has continued the legacy by opening the stately old doors of her home to the public.

As well as the treasures and collections of antique art, a suite of studios has been created where craftsmen of traditional skills can be seen at work in a 'gallery of arts in action'.

Falconry displays, changing exhibitions and a full programme of special events attract visitors to this lively centre, where you can keep busy all day – wandering in the lovely gardens, or lingering over a cup of tea and home made cakes from the castle kitchen.

TAUNTON, Devon
See Sheppy's Cider Farm

TEWKESBURY ABBEY, Gloucestershire

On A38. Map Ref: SO8933

Tewkesbury Abbey is the focal point of this ancient riverside town. Sited on the navigable Avon where it joins the Severn, it enjoyed the advantage of river transport long before roads were improved. War-worn armies of the red and white roses fled here after the momentous Battle of Tewkesbury, and it was here too where noble families who owned the 'Honor of Gloster' and *Domesday's* royal borough were carried to their final

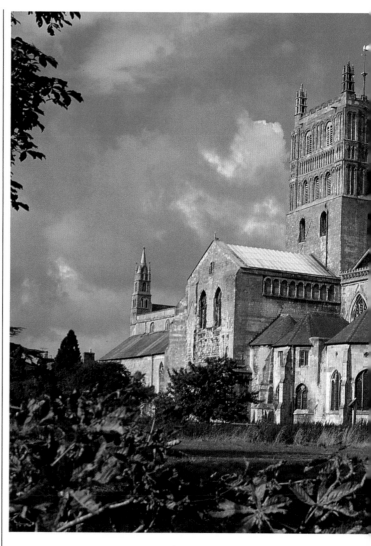

Norman masons shipped stone from northern France to build Severn-side Tewkesbury Abbey

resting place. Their ornate memorials furnish the abbey's inner chapels.

Edging the abbey lawns is a lovely terrace of cottages, built about 1500. A splendid half-timbered house overhanging the street contains a museum to John Moore, the notable author who captured his home town in his 'Brensham' trilogy.

TINTAGEL CASTLE, Cornwall

Open daily; W of Tintagel off B3263. Map Ref: SX0588

Tintagel sets the romantic senses tingling, for here in a land of legend is a web of mystery and magic that has so tangled the Arthurian saga in fact and fiction that one is indivisible from the other.

The village itself has a post office which was originally a 14th-century manor house, and a church which preserves Norman work. Down the lane are ruins that remain from a great castle of 1145. Below is a small beach close to Merlin's Cave, under the castle, where King Arthur was said to have been held in secret before the glorious age of Camelot. It was to this secluded spot also that he is claimed to have returned to fight the last fatal battle, at Slaughter Bridge.

Tintagel Castle is spread over two sites. The main part is on the mainland, while the other – dating back some 18 centuries – includes an inner monastery site connected by a causeway. Extensive surveys have revealed numerous old sites, including signs that the area was probably a Roman village.

TIVERTON, Devon
See Knightshayes Court

TORBAY & DARTMOUTH RAILWAY, Devon

Open early spring to autumn; Paignton Station. Map Ref: SX8860

One of south Devon's two steam train services, this is not a restored line but a continuation of its former British Rail run; only the ownership has changed.

Under the Dart Valley Light Railway Company it continues to perpetuate the days of steam for the benefit of visitors to the Devon coast, running about 7m from Paignton to Kingswear (and stopping at Goodrington Sands and Churston) for a ferry crossing to Dartmouth.

In the harbour town of Paignton the train runs from the BR station at the town centre end of Torbay Road, where the entrance is plainly marked by a pair of old GWR iron gates. Both Kingswear and Dartmouth are set on the steep hillsides of the Dart Estuary. Kingswear, the railway terminus, is on the east bank and the ferry point is close by. Dartmouth stands on the opposite bank and is cobbled together around the church and quay, incorporating various flights of steep and often narrow steps. An impressive chain of castles along the estuary, a bold cove, a small enclosed harbour, a shopping centre beneath a beautiful carved-timber arcade and a view of the Royal Naval Training College make this old port a memorable destination on a real train ride.

TORRINGTON, Devon

Map Ref: SS4919

Dartington Glass Centre, School Lane

Open all year; off A386

The new Glass Centre at Dartington's Torrington factory in School Lane has been designed specifically for visitors, and is already established as one of North Devon's major attractions.

A gallery of exhibits tracing the development of English glassware since 1650, together with a dazzling display of Dartington's own crystal glass produced over the last 20 years, leads to the centre. Inside is a working replica of an 18th-century glass cone, where skilled craftsmen perform the magical ritual of manufacturing glass, using tools and techniques which have hardly changed in 400 years.

Factory tours allow visitors to watch the whole glass-making process from overhead viewing galleries, and in the tempting factory shop is Dartington lead crystal glassware at very advantageous prices. A restaurant offers a selection of snacks and hot meals.

TOTNES MOTOR MUSEUM, Devon

Open spring to autumn; on A385. Map Ref: SX8060

Totnes claims, by legendary right, to be where Brutus stood to survey the area before founding the British race – and the spot is marked by a stone near East Gate, off the main Fore Street. The old, walled town itself is on a hill and still busy with boats.

Transport takes on a varied guise at Totnes, where there is a river cruise to Dartmouth and a steam-train run to Buckfastleigh. Opposite the quay is an excellent motor museum.

From Totnes Motor Museum the vintage, the veteran and the pick of the world's motors purr out of Devon to race across Europe and as far afield as New Zealand, competing most week-ends of the year. They leave behind an incredibly-varied range from the oldest members of the collection, including a 1922 Voisin and the prestigious Rolls and Bentley, the Alpha Romeo and Ferrari, together with a whole gallery of motor-cycles and models. Memorabilia on display forms a montage of motoring history comprising everything from elegant veiled hats to pit signals. Each motor's pedigree is displayed alongside.

TRERICE MANOR (NT), Cornwall

Open spring to autumn; 3m SE of Newquay on unclass road off A3058. Map Ref: SW8458

When Sir John Arundell settled in his native Cornwall after serving in Elizabeth I's army in the Low Countries, he incorporated various aspects of European style in his newly-built manor. The plasterwork on the ceiling and fireplaces is the finest feature of this picturesque Elizabethan house (NT), with its curvy gables, and old Sir John would surely have been gratified to know that his home would be preserved for the nation. So little has it changed that today's Elizabethans can fully appreciate the way their earlier counterparts lived – except, of course, they would have not been able to avail themselves of National Trust refreshments. They would doubtless have also been amazed at the collection of lawn mowers in the barn.

VERWOOD, Dorset
See Dorset Heavy Horse Centre

WELLS, Somerset

Map Ref: ST5445

Bishop's Palace, Wells Cathedral

Open spring to autumn

Wells is the smallest city in England, and it is to the majestic cathedral – richly ornate, with the finest collection of sculptures in Europe – that one is inevitably drawn. Parking in the Market Square affords the opportunity of seeing its medieval buildings, narrow streets and bustle on the way in. The Tourist Information Office is centrally sited in the old Town Hall, so details of local current events can be found easily. Water flowing beside the pavements of the High Street springs from the bottom of the bishop's garden, and gave Wells its name.

Bishop's Palace, alongside the cathedral green, is a beautiful building in an idyllic setting completed by a moat graced with swans. A pause here may be rewarded by the sight of those elegant creatures ringing a bell by the drawbridge – asking for food! The gatehouse dates back to the 14th century and the Bishop's Chapel is a century older – as is the banqueting hall, now a preserved ruin. Of similar age is the undercroft. Changing fashions and faces are seen in the portraits in the Long

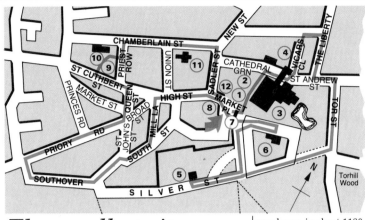

The smallest city

The City of Wells, known as the capital of
the Mendips, has a population of under
9,000, making it one of England's smallest.
It is home to small local industries, chiefly
paper-making and dairy farming, and much
of its rich architectural heritage has been
retained.

1 THE PENNILESS PORCH
This gate into the close was
so called because it once
attracted beggars and
paupers who sought alms
from people visiting the
cathedral. It was built in
1450.

2 CATHEDRAL CLOSE
Many of the buildings that
stand around the close
have histories that stretch

*Tradition has it that Wells
Cathedral is near the
springs from which its
name derives*

back to at least the 15th
century, but these ancient
origins are often disguised
by later façades. Of
particular interest is the
series on the north side of
the green. The Deanery
dates from the 15th
century, but has windows
installed at the close of the
17th century. Next to it is
the Chancellor's House;
Tudor with an 18th-
century facing. It houses
Wells Museum.

3 WELLS CATHEDRAL
One of the loveliest of
Britain's cathedrals, Wells
was begun in about 1180
and completed during a
second, astonishingly-
creative building period
which ended in 1340. On
the west front is the
greatest array of British
13th-century sculpture to
be found anywhere. To the
south of the building are
the cloisters, and above the
East Cloister is one of the
largest medieval libraries
in England. The Chapter
House, added in the early
14th century, is a
delightful octagonal
structure – as is also the
Lady Chapel at the eastern
end. Perhaps the most eye-
catching feature is the
astronomical clock.

4 THE COLLEGE OF VICARS
Known more recently as
Vicars Close, this is
believed to be the oldest
intact 14th-century street
in Europe. The college
itself was founded in 1348
and finally disbanded in
1934. It consists of terraced
houses, of which No. 22 has
been restored to its original
appearance.

5 THE BISHOP'S BARN
Built in the 15th century,
this cross-shaped barn is
110ft long and is used for
social events.

6 BISHOP'S PALACE
This is one of the oldest
inhabited houses in
England. Its outer walls
date back to 1206 and give
the building the
appearance of a castle. The
moat which surrounds the
palace receives water from
the wells in the Bishop's
Garden, from which the
city derives its name.

7 BISHOP'S EYE
One of Bishop Bekynton's
many improvements to the
close, this gateway, built in
1450, leads into the Market
Place.

8 THE CROWN INN
A 17th-century tavern with
a black-and-white frontage.
From one of its windows
William Penn, the pioneer
Quaker, is said to have
preached in 1685 before
being arrested.

9 ST CUTHBERT'S CHURCH
This fine example of
Perpendicular architecture
is the largest church in
Somerset, and was at one
time the focal point of
Wells.

10 ALMSHOUSES
An interesting 15th-
century building donated
to the city by Bishop
Bubwith. It was probably
unique in that it doubled
as a guildhall.

EARLY CLOSING: *Wed*

MARKET DAYS: *Wed &
Sat*

PARKING: *Market Pl*

OPENING TIMES:
Wells Museum: *open all
year. Apr–Sept, daily pm
only. Oct–Mar, Wed, Sat, &
Sun pm only*
Bishop's Palace: *open
Easter–Oct. Thu and Sun,
May–Sept most Weds. Open
daily Aug*

ROUTE DIRECTIONS
*Start at the north-east
corner of the Market Pl, at
the Penniless Porch (1).
Turn r. into Cathedral
Close (2). Pass by the porch
of Wells Cathedral (3) and
turn l. into The College of
Vicars (Vicars Close) (4). At
the end, bear r. From here
turn r. into The Liberty
then l. into St Andrew's St
and immediately r. into Tor
St. By the entrance to
Torhill Wood cross over
and turn r. then follow the
footpath until the moat of
the Bishop's Palace is
reached. Continue forward
into Silver St, where the
Bishop's Barn (5) is on the
r. From here, return to the
moat, then go l. and walk
along the footpath to its
north end. Turn r. for the
Bishop's Palace (6). Return
alongside the moat and
pass through the Bishop's
Eye (7) into the Market Pl
once more. From this
standpoint, the Crown Inn
(8) is to the r. of the Town
Hall. Turn l. here into the
High St, then l. again into
Mill La. Next, bear r. into
South St and follow the
pavement round into
Southover. At the end turn
r. into Priory Rd. Take the
second l. into Queen St,
pass the end of Priest Row
and walk into St Cuthbert
St. Cross over to St
Cuthbert's Church (9) and,
on leaving, turn r. and pass
through the churchyard to
the Almshouses (10).
Return to Priest Row and
turn l. At the junction turn
r. into Chamberlain St to
pass the Church of SS
Joseph and Teresa (11) on
the r. At the end turn r. into
Sadler St then l., past a
Commemorative Plaque
(12), into the Market Pl to
complete the walk.*

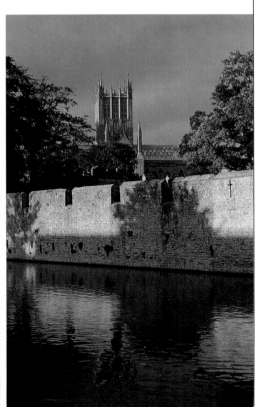

Gallery and State Rooms. Here are serenity, peace and beauty at their best, so linger awhile and drink them all in slowly – as you would a mellowed wine.

WEST SOMERSET RAILWAY, Minehead, Somerset

Open spring to autumn; 5m NW of Taunton on A358. Map Ref: SS1629

Re-opened in 1976, Britain's longest private railway line carries steam trains from the coast at Minehead to Watchet and Bishops Lydeard throughout the summer, and on special days off season. Souvenirs and refreshments are sold at the Minehead terminus.

WESTONBIRT ARBORETUM, Gloucestershire

Open all year; 3m SW of Tetbury on A433. Map Ref: ST8489

Britain's largest arboretum, at Westonbirt, is one of the West Country's greatest natural attractions. Every season has something to delight the eye amongst magnificent trees and shrubs in over 600 acres landscaped. Beautiful throughout the year, spring tempts especially with tender greens laced with sunlit silver leaves. It is matched only by the great drifts of brilliant azaleas and rhododendrons that bloom later on, or by autumn's fiery blaze of maples and other acers.

The visitors' centre runs a continuous audio-visual presentation relating to the arboretum, its management by the Forestry Commission and its objectives. There is also a brief history of the Holford family, who rebuilt the village of Westonbirt to fit in with the designs for their mansion.

WEYMOUTH, Dorset
See Sealife Centre

WILTON, Wiltshire

Map Ref: SU0931

Carpet Factory, King Street

Open weekdays; on A30

The oldest carpet factory in the world is at Wilton, and its fine, world-famous products take their name from the little Wiltshire town to where the 8th Earl of Pembroke once smuggled a couple of French Huguenot weavers. The craft of carpet weaving became so successful, bringing trade and industry to the town, that it

acquired royal status from William III in 1699. The Royal Wilton Carpet Factory exhibits old carpet-making crafts and offers tours of the modern works.

Wilton House

Open spring & summer; off A30

The River Wylye gave its name to both an old Saxon county and this little market town, which in turn gave it to the carpets for which it is now famed (see entry). Its early monastic beginnings brought prosperity until the Abbess refused the Bishop of Salisbury land for his new cathedral. Henry VIII's zealous force finally sacked the Benedictine convent, robbing Wilton of its abbey but providing the 1st Earl of Pembroke with site and stone for a magnificent house.

Wilton House suffered badly through fire in 1647 and was subsequently rebuilt by Inigo Jones. Holbein and James Wyatt added their talents during successive alterations, and the Earls of Pembroke gradually filled it with art treasures over the years. Exhibitions of some 7,000 miniature model soldiers, a palatial dolls' house, a working model railway and a tableau of toys through the ages are displayed in superb settings. A lovely Palladian-style bridge is a feature of the beautiful grounds. There are refreshments available, and a garden centre.

WIMBORNE MINSTER, Dorset
See Kingston Lacy House

WINCHCOMBE, Gloucestershire
See Hailes Abbey

Wilton's impressive Palladian bridge was built by the 9th Earl in the 18th century

WORLDWIDE BUTTERFLIES & LULLINGSTONE SILK FARM, Compton House, Sherborne, Dorset

Open spring to autumn; 2½m W – entrance on A30. Map Ref: ST5916

Stately homes have been put to varied uses over recent years, but Compton House must be unique inasmuch as it has two farms inside it. But farming also has different connotations these days, and in this case refers to butterflies and silkworms.

Worldwide Butterflies is an apt title, for the beautiful creatures here come from many different countries. A tropicana in the garden allows visitors to walk among free-flying specimens.

Lullingstone Silk Farm produces the only silk reared in England – exclusively for royalty. Thread for the last two coronations, and the wedding dresses worn by the Queen and the Princess of Wales, came from here. The long and intricate process, from minute eggs hatching to the silkworms spinning their cocoons, is shown by accelerated video film and eventually a live demonstration of reeling. After all that you can appreciate more fully why pure silk is the sovereign yarn. A good gift shop on the premises specialises in silk and butterfly items, and a picnic area gives visitors some freedom in the grounds.

YEOVILTON, Somerset
See Fleet Air Arm Museum

TOUR 1 53 MILES

Around the New Forest

From Christchurch the tour enters the New Forest, crossing Hinchelsea Moor before entering mixed woodland and the Rhinefield and Bolderwood Ornamental Drives. Later it passes through wood and heathland to Fordingbridge, then from Ringwood follows the River Avon basin back to Christchurch.

The drive starts from Christchurch, a pleasant priory town retaining some of its ancient character. The quay beside the River Stour is busy with small craft, and an old mill stands near by.

From Christchurch follow signs Lyndhurst, Southampton to leave by the A35. In 2 miles at a roundabout take the 1st exit and continue to Hinton (Cat and Fiddle PH). In 3 miles turn on to the B3058 signed Wootton, New Milton and pass the Brown Hills Car Park and Picnic site (on the left). At the Rising Sun PH in Wootton turn left, then left again on to the unclassified road, signed Brockenhurst. After ½ mile pass the Broadley Picnic Site and in a further ½ mile pass Wootton Bridge Car Park and Picnic Site. In ¼ mile at a T-junction turn right, signed Brockenhurst, and after a further 1½ miles reach Hinchelsea Viewpoint. Continue for another 2 miles to the edge of Brockenhurst. This picturesque village retains a timeless peace, and ponies crop the village green.

Keep forward, signposted Rhinefield, and after 1¾ miles pass Whitefield Picnic Site and Car Park. After 1½ miles enter Rhinefield Ornamental Drive. The drive is bordered by fine specimens of conifers and rhododendrons, most of which were planted in 1859. It is possible to park at either end of the Drive, and explore further on foot. There are three Forest walks, the short ½-mile Brook Hill Walk in the north; Blackwater Walk to the south and the aptly named Tall Trees Walk along the Ornamental Drive.

After 1¼ miles cross the main road (A35) and enter Bolderwood Ornamental Drive. After ½ mile pass on the right the 600-year-old Knightwood Oak. In 2 miles pass Bolderwood Picnic Site and Car Park. On the left here, a small former farm has been transformed into a sanctuary for wild deer.

In ¼ mile at the T-junction turn left, signed Linwood, Stoney Cross. After 2 miles turn right, signed Stoney Cross, Fritham. In 2¾ miles at the T-junction turn right, signed Stoney Cross, Cadnam, passing the Stoney Cross Plain Car Park. In 1 mile turn left on to the A31, signed Southampton. After 1 mile turn left on to the unclassified road, signed Rufus Stone and shortly pass the Rufus Stone Car Park and Picnic Site. The Rufus Stone is said to mark the spot where William II, son of the Conqueror and commonly known as King Rufus, met an untimely death while hunting in the forest.

In 1¾ miles at the village of Brook turn sharp left on to the B3078 and continue to Fordingbridge. Turn left into the High Street, signed Damerham, then bear right. In 1¾ miles at Sandleheath turn left on to the unclassified road, signed Alderholt. After ¼ mile pass Alderholt Mill. In 1 mile at a T-junction at the edge of Alderholt turn right then immediately left, signed Ringwood, Ibsley. After 5¼ miles join the B3081, signed Ringwood. In ¾ mile turn left and join the A31. After ½ mile branch left, signed Ringwood, then at the roundabout take the 3rd exit on to the B3347 to enter Ringwood. Situated on the River Avon and noted for its trout fishing, the town has several Georgian and Queen Anne period buildings in the centre.

At the roundabout take the 2nd exit, signed Sopley. At the next roundabout turn left to leave by Christchurch Road. After 5¾ miles at Sopley join the one-way system and follow signs Christchurch. In 2¾ miles at a roundabout take the 3rd exit on to the A35 and return to Christchurch.

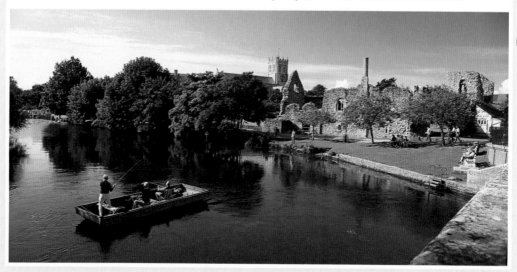

Salmon fishing on the Avon near the superb priory and ruined castle at Christchurch

TOUR 2 48 MILES

Views from the Downs

This drive takes in several attractive villages, the seaside resort of Seaford and the county town of East Sussex, Lewes. There are fine views of the Downs, the sea and the valleys of the Ouse and Cuckmere.

The drive starts from Brighton, a town which in Regency times became the most fashionable resort in England.

From Brighton follow signs to Lewes to leave by the A27. After 3 miles the drive leaves the built-up districts and passes Stanmer Park – the home of the University of Sussex. Here branch left on to the B2123, signed Falmer/Rottingdean, then at the roundabout turn right to cross the main road, still signed Rottingdean. An ascent is then made, crossing pleasant downland to reach a height of 536ft before descending past the residential area of Woodingdean into the attractive village of Rottingdean.

At the far end turn left at the traffic-lights on to the A259 (no sign) and proceed with views of the chalk cliffs and the sea through Saltdean, Telscombe Cliffs and Peacehaven. After a short climb, later descend to the busy cross-channel port of Newhaven in the Ouse Valley. At the one-way system turn left then bear right, following the Seaford and Eastbourne signs. Of interest in the town is Fort Newhaven – a coastal artillery fort converted into a museum.

Cross the River Ouse and skirt Denton then Bishopstone before entering the residential town and resort of Seaford. Follow the main A259 Eastbourne road through the town and in just over ¾ mile turn left on to an unclassified road, signed Alfriston. Alfriston is one of the most attractive villages in Sussex.

At the market cross bear right and in 1¼ miles past Drusillas Zoo Park (on the right). At the next roundabout take the first exit to join the A27, signed Lewes, and follow the northern slopes of the Downs.

Underneath the chestnut tree in Alfriston High Street is a pleasant place to pause

Four miles farther a short detour can be made by turning left on to an unclassified road to visit the beautiful Georgian house of Firle Place.

The main tour continues along the A27 and in a mile it turns right, unclassified, signed Glynde and Ringmere. Shortly enter the village of Glynde and keep forward, passing the Elizabethan manor of Glynde Place on the right. In ¾ mile bear left, signed Ringmere. Pass the partly Tudor mansion of Glyndebourne – famous for its opera house.

On reaching the junction with the B2192 turn left, signed Lewes. There are fine downland views on the left and across the Ouse Valley to the right before turning left after 1½ miles on to the A26 in order to visit Lewes – the county town of East Sussex. Interesting features in the town include the Norman castle with its Barbican House Museum of Sussex Archaeology, and the Museum of Local History in Anne of Cleves' House.

On entering the town keep forward at the mini-roundabouts (signed town centre) and cross the River Ouse. Turn left then right with the one-way system and ascend the main street. At the far end branch right, signed London, East Grinstead, then at the T-junction turn right again to leave by the A275. Later descend beneath the slopes of Offham Hill into Offham, then in ½ mile turn left on to the B2116, signed Hassocks. Continue along the B2116 to Westmeston and here go forward with Underhill Road, unclassified (signed Narrow Lane). In ¾ mile turn left, signed The Beacon, and ascend a narrow winding road (1 in 10 gradient) to the summit of Ditchling Beacon. At 813ft it is one of the highest points on the South Downs and makes an excellent viewpoint.

Descend across undulating downland and in 2¼ miles pass a picnic site on the left. At the next T-junction turn left then turn right (no sign) and continue the descent to enter the suburbs of Brighton. After 3 miles turn left at the roundabout (signed town centre), then at traffic-lights turn right, A27, for the return.

ALFRISTON, East Sussex

Map Ref: TQ5103

Behind the High Street lined with lovely old timbered buildings, and on the edge of the green, lies Alfriston Clergy House. This was the first property purchased by the newly formed National Trust in 1896, for the princely sum of £10.

Thatched and half-timbered, the house was built in the 14th century to house the Roman Catholic parish priests of the area. The hall – open to the timbered roof – forms the central part of the building, with two-storey sections at either end. It was on the upper floor of these sections that the priests once lived.

Be sure not to leave this tiny market town without visiting its lovely cruciform parish church, which has some of the best flint work in the country. It is known as the Cathedral of the Downs because of its great size, and also overlooks the green.

Three ancient and picturesque pubs in the village are the Smugglers Inn (whose name betrays a one-time landlord's alternative trade), the 500-year-old Star and the George Inn – which claims to have been licensed for six centuries, since 1397.

Drusillas Zoo Park, East Sussex

Open daily; off B2108

You probably would not expect the opportunity to buy fresh-baked bread at a zoo, but a cottage bakery is just one of many attractions offered by this amusement park. Others include a leathercraft shop, a garden centre and an English wine centre, which sometimes hosts a wine festival during September.

Not least in popularity are the animals, which make up one of the best small zoos in the country and include a varied collection of small mammals. Rare farm breeds are also on show, plus penguins, flamingoes and a delightful butterfly house.

A recent addition to the zoo park is a lovely Japanese garden, and if you feel like giving your legs a rest you can view all these and more attractions from the comfort of a miniature railway that runs round the grounds.

ALRESFORD, Hampshire
See Mid Hants Railway

AMBERLEY, West Sussex
See Chalk Pits Museum

ARUNDEL CASTLE & WILDFOWL TRUST, West Sussex

Castle open spring to autumn; Wildfowl Trust daily. Map Ref: TQ0107

Visitors to Arundel will have no problem finding the castle, since its massive grey outline can be seen from miles away, commandingly sited on the top of a hill overlooking the town. Arundel High Street, lined enticingly with shops, public houses and restaurants, meanders from the River Arun bridge to the castle entrance. Home of the Dukes of Norfolk for more than seven centuries, the stronghold owes much of its present-day appearance to romantic 19th-century restoration. Behind the burly walls are sumptuously furnished rooms and priceless art treasures, attractively displayed for public viewing and enjoyment.

Alongside the River Arun is the Wildfowl Trust, one of seven reserves set up by Sir Peter Scott. Here in 60 acres of wetlands, ponds and reed beds, overlooked by hides and crossed by a network of public paths, can be seen over 1,000 wildfowl from home and abroad. It is a lovely place to take children – especially in the school holidays, when there are activity sessions during which youngsters can make brass rubbings, badges and masks of endangered species. Giant jigsaws in the reception area are great favourites too, and the Trust's restaurant – which has superb views over a pond full of Eider duck – should not be missed.

ASHFORD, Kent
See Intelligence Corps Museum

ASHURST, Hampshire
See New Forest Butterfly Farm

AUDLEY END HOUSE (EH), Essex

Open spring to autumn; off B1383. Map Ref: TL5238

In its day, Audley End was said to equal Hampton Court for splendour and magnificence, and today this distinguished Jacobean mansion overlooking one of Capability Brown's exquisite landscaped parks is still among the finest houses that the public might hope to visit.

Built on a grand scale in the early 1600s for the first Earl of Suffolk (who was Lord Chamberlain and then Lord Treasurer to James 1), the house was remodelled by subsequent owners Sir John Griffin Griffin and Lord Braybrook.

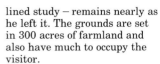

The interior is displayed as it was in the 18th and 19th centuries, and is richly decorated and furnished – particularly the state rooms, great hall and chapel – whilst retaining a romantic and comfortable feel. Outside in the extensive grounds are elegant garden buildings designed by Robert Adam, who was also responsible for one of the bridges that span the River Cam here.

Other features include the rose garden, the Concorde Temple, a miniature railway, and the Stable Exhibition of farming in Victorian times. Part of the exhibition is an interesting collection of old wagons and the estate fire engine.

AYOT ST LAWRENCE (NT), Hertfordshire

Open spring to autumn; off B653. Map Ref: TL1916

Here at Ayot St Lawrence is the house in which author George Bernard Shaw lived from 1906 until his death in 1950. Shaw's Corner, as the house is called, has been kept very much as it was in the author's lifetime, and many of his literary and personal possessions can be seen in the downstairs rooms. His work room was the study, and in it

has been preserved a large chest scattered with all the tools of his trade – pens, paper, dictionaries and so on. The dining room was where he liked to read with his meals, and the drawing room was the undisputed domain of his wife. One feels as if the Shaws have just slipped out for a moment and will soon be back.

In the garden where Shaw liked to walk every evening, whatever the weather, is the revolving summer house where he was best able to escape interruption and write. The wicker chair and table where he worked, and all his writing materials, are still to be seen there.

BATEMAN'S (NT), Burwash, East Sussex

Open spring to summer; on A265. Map Ref: TQ6724

Anyone who has read and loved Rudyard Kipling's *Puck of Pook's Hill* will recognise much of the area surrounding Bateman's, for this lovely 17th-century house of local sandstone was the writer's home from 1902 until his death in 1936. Much of the house – and in particular, the book-

Bateman's, a 17th-century ironmaster's house that was home to Rudyard Kipling

lined study – remains nearly as he left it. The grounds are set in 300 acres of farmland and also have much to occupy the visitor.

As well as the great author's 1928 Rolls Royce in the garage, there are oasthouses, a rose garden, a great pond that was built so that the Kipling children and their friends could boat and bathe, the River Dudwell and – perhaps most important of all – the Water Mill that featured so often in the author's books.

Kipling purchased the mill in 1905, and had a turbine installed to provide Bateman's with electricity, which it did for 25 years. The water mill gradually fell into disrepair, but, fortunately, has recently been restored to working order. Visitors can watch the mill grinding corn every Saturday afternoon in season. South, at Brightling, is the odd pyramid tomb of Mad Jack Fuller, MP and eccentric, who died in 1834.

BATTLE ABBEY & BATTLE & DISTRICT HISTORICAL MUSEUM, East Sussex

Abbey open all year, museum open spring to autumn; on A2100. Map Ref: TQ7415

William the Conqueror made a vow before the Battle of Hastings that if he was victor he would give thanks to God by building an extensive abbey on the site. He won the fight, and St Martin's Abbey, consecrated in 1094, was built with the high altar of the church placed on the spot where King Harold fell.

Thanks to King Henry VIII the church was destroyed some five centuries later, and a stone memorial marks the spot where Harold was killed. Still, plenty remains for visitors to see, including the great gatehouse towers rising over the town, the monks' dormitory – roofless but well preserved – excavated foundations of part of the abbey church and the chapter house. Visitors can also walk round the site of the battlefield and imagine the events of 1066.

Near by is the Battle and District Historical Museum in Langton House, where the story of the famous battle is explained. Exhibits on display here include a replica of the Bayeux Tapestry, a vivid diorama of Battle's history from Neolithic to present times, and a variety of local archaeological finds.

BEACONSFIELD, Buckinghamshire
See Bekonscot Model Village

BEAULIEU, Hampshire

Open daily; on B3054. Map Ref: SU3802

Beaulieu is one of the top tourist attractions in the country, with a vast range of things to see and do. The National Motor Museum is the biggest draw and houses hundreds of exhibits, from a magnificent 1909 *Silver Ghost* to the humble *Mini*; from the first petrol-engined car of 1895 to the most recent Formula 1 racing models. Donald Campbell's *Bluebird* is there, plus comprehensive collections of motor cycles, commercial vehicles and all the components and accessories that go with motor transport.

A viewing gallery gives visitors the chance to watch restoration work in the adjoining workshops.

'Wheels', the latest major development, is an exciting automated trip which carries visitors in moving seats through a century of motoring. Other rides include the high-level monorail – which actually goes through the motor-museum building – and veteran bus rides. These are both fun and good ways to travel between attractions.

Also of interest is the Palace House, which was built in the 14th century as the gatehouse to the abbey and is now the family home of Lord Montagu. Near by are ruins of the Cistercian abbey, which was founded in 1204 by King John and destroyed by Henry VIII.

BEKONSCOT MODEL VILLAGE, Beaconsfield, Buckinghamshire

Open spring to late autumn; off A40. Map Ref: SU9490

Beaconsfield's Bekonscot Model Village makes an outing guaranteed to delight grandparents and grandchildren alike, for visitors can immerse themselves in a miniature world of the 1930s as they walk through 1½ acres of houses, churches, castles, hotels and shops – all to the scale of one inch to the foot. Everything is in a pretty rock-garden setting, and there are many working models – including one of the finest model railways running in the UK. With this are a model airport, docklands and a funfair.

The entire complex grew out of a London accountant's hobby and is the oldest of its kind in the world, dating from 1929. Not only is it a must for model-making enthusiasts, but the tiny perfect lawns, miniature shrubs, dwarf conifers and

multitude of bedding and herbaceous plants make it popular with gardeners too.

BLENHEIM PALACE, Woodstock, Oxfordshire

Open spring to autumn, park open all year; off A34. Map Ref: SP4416

On the edge of Woodstock – a lovely riverside town full of inviting teashops, restaurants, pubs, hotels and charming old stone houses – is the huge and magnificent Italianate palace of Blenheim, set in immense and very English parkland. Designed by Sir John Vanbrugh

for the 1st Duke of Marlborough in recognition of the Duke's victory over the French, it was started in 1704 and completed after the death of the Duke in 1722.

Much of the cost of the building was defrayed by Parliament as a reward for the Duke's victory. The house is rich in furnishings and treasures, but has achieved even greater fame as the birthplace of Sir Winston Churchill in 1874. His remains lie near by in Bladon churchyard, within sight of the palace. In the vast grounds, exquisitely landscaped by Capability Brown, visitors can

Blenheim Palace carries the name of the battle which caused it to be built

walk through a deer park, enjoy boat trips on the beautiful lake or ride on a narrow-gauge railway between the house and a popular garden centre.

BLUEBELL RAILWAY,
Horsted Keynes & Sheffield Park, West Sussex & East Sussex

Trains run in summer and various single days; off A275. Map Ref: TQ4124

It is a relief sometimes to escape from this 'new' age of high-speed travel, and the many preserved steam railways operating around the country give travellers the opportunity to do just that. Among them is the Bluebell, which offers pure nostalgia and five miles of glorious Sussex countryside – carpeted with bluebells in spring – between Horsted Keynes and Sheffield Park, near Uckfield.

When a team of steam enthusiasts got together in 1960 and began to operate regular steam services on the old standard-gauge East Grinstead to Lewes line, they were the first voluntary body in this country to do so. Since 1960 about five million people have travelled in the Bluebell Railway's 50 carriages, pulled by 30 or so locomotives spanning more than a century of railway history.

Sheffield Park Gardens form a magnificent, lake-watered setting for a house built by James Wyatt and are known for their magnificent shows of rhododendrons and azaleas in Spring.

BODIAM CASTLE (NT), East Sussex

Open spring to autumn; off A229. Map Ref: TQ7825

When the sun shines on Bodiam Castle, the sight of that mighty structure mirrored in its water-lilied moat is breathtaking, dramatic and not easily forgotten. One of the best-preserved examples of medieval military architecture in the country, it was built in the 14th century to discourage French raiders from sailing up the River Rother. Outside it is a perfect example of a moated and curtain-walled fortress. Inside, however, it was dismantled in the mid 1600s, and only the hollow shell remains. Floors have been replaced in some of the towers to enable visitors to see the interior, and the exterior was restored in the 1920s. Objects discovered during the excavations can be seen in a small museum adjoining the National Trust shop and ticket office.

BOSHAM, West Sussex

Map Ref: SU8004

This pretty waterfront village, with its many picturesque old houses, is situated on a creek off Chichester Harbour. It is a place loved by yachtsmen and artists alike, and the people of Bosham (pronounced Bozzum) are quite adamant that it was here – not Southampton – that King Canute ordered the waves to retreat. They back up their claim by pointing to a tomb, discovered in Bosham's lovely old church some 100 years ago, which is said to be that of Canute's daughter.

Although this particular claim to historical fame remains a matter for debate, another can be substantiated by the Bayeux Tapestry, for it was from here that Harold set sail for Normandy to meet with William before the events which led to the Battle of Hastings. The tapestry shows King Harold outside Bosham Church.

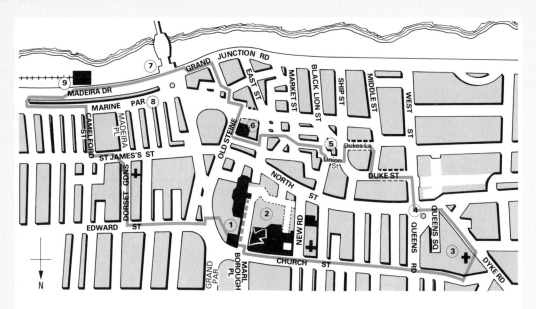

Regency by the sea

In 1754 Dr Richard Russell moved to Brighton, and his belief in curing most ills by bathing in and drinking sea water transformed the rather poor fishing village of Brighthelmstone into one of the most fashionable resorts along the south coast.

1 ROYAL PAVILION
When in 1783 the Prince Regent, soon to become George IV, made his first visit to the town, he rented a small farmhouse in The Steine. He later commissioned Henry Holland to rebuild it as an elegant, classical villa, which was later transformed by John Nash into the exotic and bizarre extravaganza that can be seen today.

2 THE DOME
The Dome, built in the same style as the Pavilion between 1803 and 1805 as stables and a riding school for use by the Prince Regent, has since been divided into an art gallery and museum, a concert hall and an exhibition hall. Of particular interest is the seaside exhibition on the upper floor.

3 ST NICHOLAS CHURCH
This largely 14th-century church contains an elaborately-carved Norman font depicting the last supper and scenes from the life of St Nicholas. Among those buried in the churchyard is Martha Gunn, 'queen' of the 'Dippers' – the attendants who looked after the women bathers in the 18th century.

4 THE CLOCK TOWER
Like many ornate clock towers, this one was erected in 1888 to commemorate Queen Victoria's Jubilee the previous year.

5 THE LANES
This attractive corner of the town is all that is left of the 17th-century fishing village of Brighthelmstone. Today the narrow passageways connect the many antique shops, jewellers, picture galleries, pubs and cafés.

6 THE OLD STEINE
Next to Steine House, once the home of Mrs

Essence of a seaside holiday

Fitzherbert (the Prince Regent's lover) stands Marlborough House, now the tourist information centre. Originally built for the 4th Duke of Marlborough, it was sold in 1786 and subsequently transformed by Robert Adam.

7 PALACE PIER
Built in 1899 and opened to the public in 1901, Palace Pier stands just west of the site of the old Chain Pier, which was the first pleasure pier ever built in England.

8 AQUARIUM AND DOLPHINARIUM
Established by a private company in 1869, the aquarium has over 10,000 fish from all over the world, kept in a series of dramatic under-ground caverns.

9 VOLKS RAILWAY
Opened in 1883, this was the first public electric railway in Britain. The engineer responsible for it was Magnus Volk, a leading pioneer in the use of electricity at the time.

PARKING: *Cannon Pl, Church St, Clarence St, North Rd, Regency St*

OPENING TIMES:
Royal Pavilion: open all year, except Christmas
Art Gallery & Museum: open all year, except Good Fri & Christmas. Tue–Sat all day, Sun pm only
Aquarium & Dolphinarium: open all year
Volks Railway: open daily, summer only

ROUTE DIRECTIONS
The walk starts by the George IV statue, near the junction of Marlborough Pl and Church St. Turn l. along Church St past the entrances to the Royal Pavilion (1) and the Dome (2). Continue along Church St over Queens Rd and turn l. into the churchyard of St Nicholas Church (3). Leave by a footpath to the l. of the church which joins Dyke Rd. Continue to the traffic lights and negotiate the junction around the clock tower (4) by crossing Queens Rd and North St into West St. Turn l. into Duke St, r. into Middle St and shortly turn l. again into Dukes La, which enters The Lanes (5). Continue through an arcade into Ship St and turn l. Immediately turn r. into Union St (a footpath through The Lanes) and at the end turn r. into Meeting House La and follow it round to the l. Continue through the narrow passageway into a paved square. Cross the square, descend the steps, and turn r, passing the Druid's Head. Continue until the lane opens out and cross into Market St. On reaching the Sussex public house, take the footpath alongside it which emerges into East St. Turn l. and then r. into Steine La and continue to Old Steine (6). Turn r. here and continue to Pool Valley and turn r. At the Bus Station bear l. and cross over to the sea-front. Turn l. and continue along Grand Junction Rd to Palace Pier (7). Continue into Madeira Dr, passing the Aquarium and Dolphinarium (8) on the l, to reach the Volks Railway (9) terminus. From here ascend the staircase at the end of the shopping arcade up to Marine Par. Turn sharp l. here and then turn r. into Camelford St. At the end turn l. into St James's St then r. into Dorset Gdns. Turn l. at the end into Edward St and on reaching Grand Par, cross and turn r. along by the Royal Pavilion then turn l. back to the George IV statue.

BOX HILL, Surrey

Exhibition, information rooms & shop open spring to autumn, site open all year; off A24. Map Ref: TQ1751

Hundreds of acres of downs, woodland and country park form a lovely setting for Box Hill, the whole comprising an area of outstanding beauty which offers walks to suit all energy levels. Rising some 400ft above the River Mole, the hill is a noted viewpoint and was named from the box trees that once grew all around its flanks – some of which remain today. Box wood is very dense, and was once in great demand for wood engraving and chess pieces.

At the summit of the hill are an exhibition room and a 19th-century fort, which is being restored. Much of the area is owned by the National Trust, including the aptly named Little Switzerland beauty spot, which lies to the north.

BROADLANDS, Romsey, Hampshire

Open spring to late summer; main entrance on A31, Romsey by-pass. Map Ref: SU3521

In 1978 Lord and Lady Mountbatten made the decision to open their beautiful riverside home to the public. It was a project into which Lord Mountbatten threw himself wholeheartedly, and one year later Broadlands was officially opened to the public by the Prince of Wales. Tragically, only six months later Lord and Lady Mountbatten were the victims of an IRA attack in which they lost their lives. Their grandson, Lord Romsey, felt the most fitting memorial he could offer was to continue his grandparents' plans and, in addition, to convert the stable building for a Mountbatten exhibition.

Today, many thousands of people must be thankful that Lord Romsey allowed the 'show to go on' in a house with such an interesting history and distinguished connections. Not only has Broadlands been home to the Mountbattens, but it also once belonged to the Victorian Prime Minister Lord Palmerston. In more recent years the Queen and Prince Philip, and Prince Charles and Princess Diana, have stayed there for parts of their respective honeymoons. Beautiful grounds landscaped by Capability Brown overlook the River Test, and behind an exterior which is one of the finest examples of Georgian architecture in the country are

rooms which encapsulate the rare combination of exquisite elegance and homeliness.

BUCKLERS HARD, Hampshire

Open all year; off B3054. Map Ref: SU4000

On the edge of the New Forest is the small riverside village of Bucklers Hard, a place where time seems to have stood still for the last century or so. No cars are allowed there, so visitors must leave their vehicles in the place provided and walk a short distance. Although today this Beaulieu River village – much-loved by yachtsmen – is a scene of tranquillity, that was not always the case.

At one time it was a bustling ship-building yard in which wooden war vessels, including some for Admiral Nelson's fleet, were made from New Forest oak.

A small but fascinating

Chalky Box Hill, in places barely covered by vegetation, is an important habitat for wild plants and creatures

maritime museum here relates the history, and the pretty 18th-century houses that form the short village street survive as the only part of the 2nd Duke of Montague's town- and dock-planning aspirations to reach fruition. His idea was to provide a complex which could handle the arrival of merchandise from his considerable foreign estates. Today, some of the houses have been used to recreate scenes from those times. As well as exploring this tiny village, visitors can enjoy river cruises, which leave from the pier at half-hourly intervals during the summer. Also, there is a beautiful riverside walk between Bucklers Hard and Beaulieu.

BURWASH, East Sussex
See Bateman's

The pilgrim's goal

Despite the ravages of World War II, Canterbury still retains its medieval character, with narrow streets and ancient buildings. Dominating them all is the incomparable cathedral, the setting for many dramatic events in past centuries.

1 ST AUGUSTINE'S ABBEY
The impressive gateway of St Augustine's Abbey, the Fyndon Gate, stands at the top of Lady Wootton's Green. The abbey entrance is to the left of the gate and leads through to the abbey ruins.

2 ROMAN PAVEMENT
Beneath one of the new shops in the Longmarket precinct is a well-preserved Roman tessellated pavement which came from one of the rooms in a large courtyard building dating from AD100.

3 CHRISTCHURCH GATE
An elaborate example of Perpendicular architecture, this impressive gateway was built between 1502 and 1519.

4 CHRISTCHURCH CATHEDRAL
The oldest part of the present cathedral, the crypt, dates from 1100 – although there are traces of earlier work. In 1170 the famous and dramatic murder of Archbishop Thomas Becket took place here, and from that time the cathedral became the setting for the shrine of the martyr, attracting thousands of pilgrims. The nave, one of the glories of western architecture, was rebuilt in 1400.

5 CATHEDRAL CLOISTERS
Originally the Great Cloister was the centre of the monastery that used to stand next to the cathedral. The cloisters were built in the 14th century, and one of their outstanding features is the collection of over 800 roof bosses.

6 THE KING'S SCHOOL
A large courtyard, Green Court, is the centre of this famous public school. The lovely external staircase in the north-west corner is one of the best-known pieces of Norman architecture in Britain.

7 ST ALPHEGE'S CHURCH
Even in 1166 this church was described as 'old', but its actual age is uncertain. It contains several excellent brasses.

8 WESTGATE
Said to be the finest city gate in England, this massive fortification was built by Archbishop Simon of Sudbury in 1380.

9 WEAVER'S HOUSE
Attractively set beside the River Stour, this was built for a rich merchant in 1561.

10 ST THOMAS'S (EASTBRIDGE) HOSPITAL
Within this building is a superb Norman undercroft, a 12th-century refectory and a beautiful 14th-

In the 17th-century, Huguenot weavers came to Canterbury and occupied these Tudor cottages

century chapel.

11 ROYAL MUSEUM (BEANEY INSTITUTE)
An imposing Victorian building housing a good collection of Roman, Saxon and medieval finds.

12 CANTERBURY HERITAGE CENTRE (POOR PRIESTS' HOSPITAL)
This medieval building has had many uses and is now a museum of Canterbury's heritage. Preserved here is one of the oldest railway engines in the world, the *Invicta*.

13 CANTERBURY CASTLE
All that now remains of Canterbury's Norman castle is the keep.

14 CITY WALLS
About half of Canterbury's original Roman and medieval wall survives.

EARLY CLOSING: *Thu*

MARKET DAY: *Wed*

PARKING: *Castle St, Lower Chantry La, Quenin Gate off Broad St, St George's La*

OPENING TIMES:
St Augustine's Abbey: open all year. Mon – Sat all day. Sun pm only

Roman Pavement: open all year. Summer all day. Winter pm only

Westgate Museum: open as above

St Thomas's Hospital: open all year

Royal Museum: open all year. Mon – Sat

Canterbury Heritage Centre: open Apr – Sep, Mon – Sat all day. Reduced opening hours Oct – Mar

ROUTE DIRECTIONS
Start from the city wall by the Quenin Gate car park in Broad St. Cross Broad St and go down Lady Wootton's Grn to St Augustine's Abbey (1). Return to Broad St, turn l. (SW) to Burgate and turn r. Shortly turn l. along Butchery La for Roman Pavement (2). Return to Burgate, turn l. then turn r. through Christchurch Gate (3) and keep to the l. side of cathedral precincts past the west end of the cathedral (4). Follow the path through the Cathedral Cloisters (5), turning r. after Chapter House and l. through Dark Entry into Green Court of the King's School (6). Go l. round Green Court and l. through Green Court Gate into Mint Yd. Mint Yd Gate leads into Palace St, and there turn l. Take first r. down St Alphege La to St Alphege's Church (7), then l. along King St and r. down The Friars. Turn r. along St Peter's St to Westgate (8) then return down St Peter's St to the Weavers House (9) and St Thomas's Hospital (10), opposite. Turn r. down Stour St, with the Royal Museum (11) on l. Pass Canterbury Heritage Centre (12) on r. Turn l. into Hospital La and r. down Castle St. Opposite the Castle (13), a footpath (SP East Station and Wincheap) leads to Castle Row. Cross into Dane John Gdns and go up the path to the city walls (14). Follow the walls round to St George's St and return to Broad St.

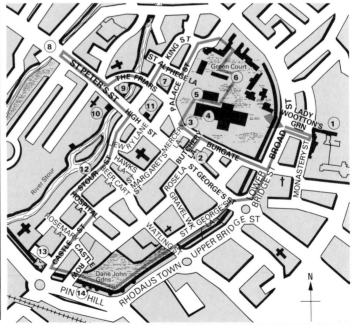

CANTERBURY, Kent

Map Ref: TR1457

Canterbury, which has a history that can be traced back to prehistoric times, has been famed as a religious centre and place of pilgrimage since before the medieval period. Inevitably, the city has changed over the centuries, but there are still numerous remains from Roman, Norman and medieval times to link the past with the present – and modern tourists flock there to enjoy the unique blend of ancient history and modern amenities. Towering over the city is the cathedral where Archbishop Thomas Becket was murdered in 1170, an event which began the city's history as a pilgrimage centre.

Dating back to 1070, after a fire destroyed the original building, it is a magnificent piece of architecture containing some of the finest stained glass in England, as well as delicate carvings, old paintings and the historic tombs of the Black Prince, Henry IV and his queen. Also, of course, there is the shrine of Thomas Becket himself.

The cathedral is only the beginning of this city's historical wealth. A huge keep testifies to the Norman castle which stood there; the ruins of St Augustine's abbey continue the ecclesiastical story; the church of St Martin is the oldest parish church to have been in continuous use in the country; the gorgeous Tudor weavers' cottages overhang the River Stour; and in Canterbury's underground museum are preserved the remains of a Roman town house, with magnificent mosaics.

The recently opened Museum of Canterbury's Heritage, which is housed in the restored Poor Priests' Hospital, traces the city's history from Roman to present times. Against this historic backcloth is a modern city that offers all the visitor could wish for in the way of amenities – an excellent pedestrianised centre, side streets full of inviting antique shops, galleries, tea rooms, pubs, snack bars and restaurants offering every type of cuisine. The city also offers a wide range of tours – on foot, by bus and on the river. Details of these are available from the Tourist Information Centre, and it must be said that one of the most pleasant ways of seeing Canterbury is from a hired rowing boat on the Stour.

CHALK PITS MUSEUM, Amberley, West Sussex

Open spring to autumn; off B2139. Map Ref: TQ0313

A disused lime quarry at Amberley has been given a new lease of life as home to the Chalk Pits Museum of industrial history in the south of England. For well over a century chalk was extracted from the quarry to make lime. Surviving from then are buildings and a narrow-gauge railway that have been preserved to form the basis of outdoor displays and exhibits covering some 36 acres. A particular section explains the lime-making process, but other local trades and industries are featured too, including brick making, timber and concrete.

Some of the buildings contain fascinating static displays, while others house fully operational workshops for a blacksmith, cobbler, potter, and a printer – who produces much of the museum's literature. Visitors also have a chance to ride on the narrow-gauge railway and experience for themselves the travelling conditions that quarry workers had to endure. Another feature is a comprehensive road exhibition, including signs, street furniture and an interesting collection of old vehicles. Do save a little time for the nearby village of Amberley itself, which is a pretty combination of stone, flint and half-timbered houses in colourful gardens on the River Arun.

Greyfriars straddles the River Stour in Canterbury, and was founded in 1267 as England's first Franciscan friary

CHARTWELL (NT), Kent

Open spring to late autumn, Tue–Thu, Sat & Sun; off B2026. Map Ref: TQ4551

This unpretentious Victorian house was bought in 1922 by Winston Churchill, who carried out considerable alterations to both the building and its grounds before happily pursuing his many literary and artistic interests there until his death some 40 years later. Most of the rooms on view have been left just as they were in his lifetime, and they vividly evoke the great man's career. His own paintings adorn their walls, and hang in his garden studio. Part of the house is given over to the Churchill Museum, which displays uniforms, gifts from other world leaders, his Nobel prize, and a collection of photographs depicting much of his life.

Outside in the beautiful grounds are landscaped lawns which stretch away to a lake on which glide the famous black swans.

Due to the large number of visitors to Chartwell, admission to the house is by timed and numbered tickets. Waiting time, which can be spent in the garden, may be considerable in summer.

CHAWTON, Hampshire
See Jane Austen Museum

CHERTSEY, Surrey
See Thorpe Park

CHESSINGTON WORLD OF ADVENTURE, Surrey

Attractions open spring to autumn, zoo all year; off junction 9, M25 & on A243. Map Ref: TQ1863

Chessington has come a long way since 1931, when London businessman Reginald Goddard bought the house and grounds and opened a private zoo there. Two years later it was host to a circus with performing animals, and much later in the 1960s it had fairground rides and side shows. In July 1987 the completely revamped 'Chessington World of Adventure' was opened by Prince Edward – and it is certainly a place to visit with the grandchildren.

Fun-packed rides can be taken into mysterious and fascinating lands that delight and amuse rather than scare, and an 'optical' ride offers a strange trip into the 'Fifth Dimension'.

A circus extravaganza provides thrills by performing artists – and there is a chance for children to step into the limelight by putting on their own shows, helped by the professionals, at the 'Circus Academy'.

The zoo at Chessington remains a popular attraction, with its great variety of creatures from all over the world. Visitors can enjoy both a bird's-eye view of the animals and an entertaining commentary by Johnny Morris when they ride on the 'Safari Skyway' monorail.

CHICHESTER, West Sussex

Map Ref: SU8604

Standing between the sea and the South Downs, Chichester offers the combined advantages of being the South Coast's most popular yachting centre and a bustling market town. The city was founded by the Romans in AD43, and much of the wall which they built around the original site is intact. Four streets converge from the points of the compass to a 50ft-high market cross, where farmers and growers gather each week to attend the cattle market.

Although the foundations of the city are Roman, most of the best architecture is Georgian – as shown particularly in the Pallants and Little London, where the Old Corn Store houses the City Museum. Attractive and elegant houses in those areas once belonged to wool merchants.

Chichester's Norman cathedral contains much of interest and beauty, including two outstanding works of modern art – a painting by Graham Sutherland and a tapestry designed by John Piper. Its interesting 15th-century belfry is the only surviving English example of a detached bell tower.

Roman remains, including mosaic pavements recently discovered under the cathedral foundations, are kept in the Guildhall Museum, which is also well worth a visit.

The modern city has all the amenities a visitor could wish for, including the internationally renowned Festival Theatre, where excellent productions feature top actors.

CHILHAM CASTLE GARDENS, Kent

Open spring to autumn; off A252. Map Ref: TR0653

Before passing through the gates into Chilham Castle Gardens, take time to admire the village itself, with its fine central square lined with black-

and-white timbered houses and lovely 15th-century flintstone church.

The main gates to the castle lead off the village square – although the main vehicular entrance is on the Maidstone-to-Canterbury road – and from this entrance can be seen the splendid Jacobean mansion and massive flintstone Norman keep to which it is annexed. Although the public cannot actually go inside the mansion or keep, they can have a good look round the outside of the buildings.

Chilham's main attractions are its wonderful gardens and parkland, designed by Capability Brown on a hillside overlooking a river valley and lake.

The views here are breathtaking, and beautiful walks can be enjoyed among borders and beds, in woodland and along the lakeside. Petland has friendly farmyard animals much loved by children, and the birds-of-prey collection is seen in full flight during displays of

Fine art in Chichester's Norman cathedral spans the centuries, and includes powerful modern works like this tapestry by John Piper

falconry. Jousting and tournaments are enjoyable old-time features of the summer months.

Although Chilham's hillside site means that visitors are faced with a fair number of steps and slopes, there are seats thoughtfully and strategically placed along the way which provide a welcome respite. The parkland, where the medieval jousting takes place, is a gentle 10-minute walk from the castle.

CLIVEDEN (NT),
Buckinghamshire

Grounds open spring to year end; on B476. Map Ref: SU9185

Even the driveway to Cliveden is a treat – first passing through a valley of rhododendrons, then beside a huge marble fountain and along a stately avenue of lime trees. The building, a magnificent Italianate mansion which was once the home of the Astors, is now a luxury hotel – but the grounds remain open to the public.

From the terrace behind the house you can enjoy one of the finest views from any country estate, extending along a beautifully wooded stretch of the River Thames known as Cliveden Reach. The grounds slope gently down to a pleasant riverside walk and have vast lawns patterned with low box hedges, an Italian layout, water features, topiary and an unusual rose garden. Scattered all around them are fine statues, Roman carvings and pavilions.

COLCHESTER & ESSEX MUSEUM, Colchester Castle, Essex

Open daily. Map Ref: TL9925

In England's oldest recorded town, this museum reflects the long and varied history of the area in both the building itself and the exhibits it contains. Housing the displays is a massive castle keep – the largest ever built in Europe, and the only surviving part of a huge Norman fortress. It was built largely of Roman bricks from the temple of Claudius, and a staircase leads down to vaults which survive from the substructure of that ancient place.

Parts of the town walls also survive, plus seven medieval churches. Not surprisingly, the museum has one of the finest Roman collections in the country, together with outstanding finds from a 1st-century AD Iron Age burial mound.

Other superb displays to be seen relate to the Middle Ages, when the town's livelihood depended on its market, its fishery and a domestic cloth-making industry. The castle stands in a pleasant park near the centre of the town.

DEVIL'S DYKE, West Sussex

Map Ref: TQ2611

This popular beauty spot and viewpoint on the South Downs is also something of a curiosity – a deep V-shaped cleft in the crest of a hill which, according to local legend, was carved by the Devil in an attempt to let in the sea and flood the local churches. He failed, of course.

Sinister legends aside, the dyke is often busy with children running up and down its steep slopes, hang glider pilots launching themselves from its summit and walkers enjoying far-reaching views extending from the ridge across the downs to Brighton and Hove. One of the best vantage points is to be found in the large car park at the top.

DUXFORD AIRFIELD, Cambridgeshire
See Imperial War Museum

EPPING FOREST & MUSEUM, Essex

Map Ref: TL4602

It is quite astonishing that this lovely area of great hornbeam trees, sunlit glades and rough heaths should have survived so close to London, but since it was first thrown open by Queen Victoria as a public place it has been a treasured breathing space for the people of the capital. Like many of England's forests, it was created by the Normans for hunting and remained a royal preserve for many centuries. The deer are still here, notably the black fallow deer (actually dark brown), which are peculiar to Epping Forest and are protected in a special sanctuary. At one time the forest trees were managed and cropped for their timber.

Recreational facilities are many, including pleasant walks, lakes and ponds for both anglers and inland sailors, and bridleways for riders. Much of the forest is accessible by road. If you are planning a day there, why not first call at the Epping Forest Museum, which is appropriately housed in Queen Elizabeth's Hunting Lodge on the Rangers Road near Chingford.

Originally the space between the beams of this lovely timbered 15th-century building was left open so that queen and courtiers could watch the chase from the upper floors. Now it houses exhibits relating to the natural history of the area, and contributes to the work of the Epping Forest Conservation Centre.

EXBURY GARDENS, Hampshire

Open spring to mid summer, late summer to autumn; off B3054. Map Ref: SU4200

May and early June are undoubtedly the best months to visit Exbury, because that is when the magnificent collection of rhododendrons is in full bloom.

Lionel de Rothschild – the gardens' creator – was passionate about them, and in the 1920s and 30s he spent part of his great wealth on importing hundreds of species. He also employed a vast workforce to clear ground between the mature woodland, and lay out the beautiful gardens seen today. Not content with the natural species of this colourful Himalayan bush, he began to experiment with hybrids, eventually adding more than 400 new types both to his own collection and to gardening posterity.

The result is quite breathtaking. A network of paths leads through the woodland and around the ponds, showing off the garden to its best advantage and sometimes taking in views across the Beaulieu River. The 2-acre rock garden is also splendid, and most of the plants are labelled – perhaps to make it easier to match them up with those for sale in the plant shop. There is a café to provide refreshments, and picnic tables if you have brought your own.

FARNHAM BIRDWORLD & UNDERWATERWORLD, Surrey

Open daily; 3½ m SW Farnham on A325. Map Ref: SU8042

A very pleasant and leisurely half-day can be spent here in 17 acres of gardens and parkland which feature an interesting collection of birds ranging from the tiny tanager to the great ostrich.

In between are colourful macaws and peacocks, noble eagles and the flightless penguins. A recent addition to the aviaries is an imaginative 'Sea Shore Walk', in which a coastal environment has been created, complete with waves. It is so realistic that shoreline species of birds have successfully bred there. The complex also has an aquarium – 'Underwaterworld' – where hundreds of freshwater, marine and tropical fish are displayed. The gardens are attractive and well kept, and everything is on a level. There is a café for refreshments, and picnic tables are provided.

FISHBOURNE ROMAN PALACE, West Sussex

Open all year; off A27. Map Ref: SU8304

Discovery of this huge palace was one of the most exciting finds in Britain, for when the six-acre site was excavated, archaeologists unearthed remains of the country's largest Roman building yet identified. Sections of walls, baths and the heating system are visible, plus superb mosaic floors which include one very intricate panel measuring 17ft square and incorporating at its centre a winged boy sitting astride a dolphin. The palace was occupied during the 1st and 3rd centuries AD, and is thought to have originally been the home of Cogidubnus – a Briton whom the Romans made viceroy.

Archaeologists did not discover the site until 1960, although it is known that in medieval times a ploughman cut a furrow across one of its mosaic pavements. Since its excavation, the Sussex Archaeological Society has done an admirable job of making the

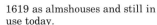

site interesting and accessible to visitors.

The comprehensive museum gives an excellent idea of what life was like in the palace, and a formal garden planted in the ancient courtyard contains the species that would have been there in Roman times.

FRENSHAM PONDS, Surrey

Map Ref: SU8440

There are two ponds at Frensham: the Great Pond, which is one of the largest lakes in southern England, and the Little Pond – which is by no means small. Together they make such a landmark that during World War II they were both drained to prevent them being used for navigation by enemy aircraft. Today the ponds are extremely popular for all kinds of recreation – sailing, windsurfing, angling and birdwatching. Grebes, coots, mallards and other wildfowl frequent the waters, and over 100 species of birds have been recorded in the surrounding heaths and woodland. There is

always plenty to look at here, and there is no need to get out of the car if you manage to park at a good vantage point. However, on a nice day there are some very pleasant walks around the ponds, and through the surrounding Frensham Common – part of a country park of which the National Trust owns nearly 1,000 acres.

GUILDFORD, Surrey

Map Ref: SU9949

Charles Dickens thought Guildford High Street 'the most beautiful in the kingdom', and present-day visitors continue to be charmed by its unspoilt Georgian character. A good blend of excellent shopping facilities and interesting old buildings makes the city a pleasant place to be, and in the High Street at the hub of things is the impressive Guildhall – its 17th-century façade concealing a Tudor ancestry. Its clock, bearing the date 1683, protrudes far out across the street. A little farther along is the Abbots Hospital, built in

1619 as almshouses and still in use today.

Guildford House dates from about 1660 and now contains the town's art gallery. At the top of the street is the Royal Grammar School, which was founded in 1507, and a ruined castle sits on top of its mound off Castle Street. The surrounding ditch defences have been transformed into colourful flower gardens, and a small museum adjoins the grounds. By far the most imposing building in Guildford is its cathedral – a red-brick, simplified-Gothic structure which looks down over the town from the top of Stag Hill. Started in 1936, it was delayed by World War II and was eventually consecrated in 1961.

Visitors wishing to be entertained have plenty of choice. The Yvonne Arnaud Theatre, by the river, is very highly regarded; there is open-air theatre at the castle during the summer; and the Civic Hall is the home of the Guildford Philharmonic Orchestra and can seat over 1,000 for concerts.

HATFIELD HOUSE, Hertfordshire

Open spring to autumn except Mon & BH; opposite Hatfield BR station. Map Ref: TZ2308

Built in 1611 for Robert Cecil – the 1st Earl of Salisbury – Hatfield House is still home to the Cecil family, but is a splendid place for visitors to spend the day too. The mansion itself is magnificent, measuring nearly 300ft long and 150ft wide, with rooms of equally impressive proportions. Treasures within are fine tapestries, furniture and paintings, including famous portraits and some possessions of Elizabeth I. It is for its Elizabethan connections that Hatfield is best known, for the queen spent much of her childhood in the Old Palace, of which a surviving wing can be seen in the west garden.

It was in the gardens at Hatfield that Elizabeth first heard of her accession to the throne, and they are still superb, encompassing styles ranging from formal parterre and knot to 'wilderness' and scented. Special exhibitions at the house include 'Fashion Through the Ages', a motor-vehicle collection and Model Soldiers.

Devil's Dyke: according to legend the devil's unsuccessful attempt to dig through the Weald and let in the sea to flood all the local churches

HAWK CONSERVANCY,
Weyhill, Hampshire

Open spring to autumn. Map Ref: SU3146

Birds of prey hold a special fascination, and this fine collection provides a marvellous opportunity to study them at close quarters. Hawks, falcons, owls, eagles, vultures and kites from Britain and many other parts of the world can be seen at Weyhill, where the aim is to encourage an appreciation of these elegant creatures.

When the weather permits, some of the birds are exercised at regular intervals throughout the day, giving visitors the opportunity of marvelling at their stunning flying skills. Keen photographers will also find plenty of scope. Refreshments are available, and there is a shop.

HAWKINGE, Kent
See Kent Battle of Britain Museum

HERSTMONCEUX CASTLE,
East Sussex

Open spring to late summer; off A271. Map Ref: TQ6312

This mellow brick castle within its moat is one of the most picturesque in Britain, and has a particularly fine gatehouse. In the past visitors have been drawn there by the Royal Greenwich Observatory, which was relocated from its previous London site in 1948. Among the attractions were exhibitions covering subjects such as astronomy and natural history, a video theatre and – of course – the telescopes. However, at the time this book was being published there were plans afoot to move the Observatory yet again, selling off the castle by the end of 1988 and completing the departure by 1990. Anyone thinking of visiting should check first to ensure that there is still something there to see.

HEVER CASTLE, Kent

Open spring to late autumn; off B2026. Map Ref: TQ4744

Although its origins are in the 13th century, this beautiful moated manor house had its heyday in Tudor times, when it was the girlhood home of Anne Boleyn. Henry VIII was a frequent visitor during their courtship. Although the castle later suffered from some neglect, it was totally and sympathetically restored at the beginning of this century by William Waldorf Astor.

It was he who built the group of Tudor-style houses across the moat – now used for group accommodation and banqueting – and who laid out the Italian garden as a setting for Roman statues that he had acquired during his years as American Minister to Italy. The gardens also contain fine topiary and a maze, and Hever's open-air theatre season is well known. Refreshments are available, and there is a shop and garden centre.

HOLLYCOMBE STEAM COLLECTION, Liphook, Hampshire

Open spring to autumn; 1½m SE Liphook on unclassified Midhurst road. Map Ref: SU8331

At Hollycombe steam fairground rides to the tunes of an old steam organ can be enjoyed, and a 2ft-gauge steam railway is ready to whisk visitors through lovely woodland banks of rhododendrons and azaleas to a lofty viewpoint offering a splendid panorama of the South Downs.

Also in this fine collection is a tram which runs between a saw mill and a steam farm, where demonstrations of steam ploughing, threshing and rolling are often held.

Traction-engine rides are available too, and still undergoing restoration at the time of publishing was the entire engine room of an old paddle steamer.

If you should tire of steam rides and nostalgia, you can take time to stroll through lovely woodland gardens, or watch genuine historic film in the bioscope show. Refreshments are available, and there is a picnic area.

HORSTED KEYNES, West Sussex
See Bluebell Railway

IMPERIAL WAR MUSEUM,
Duxford Airfield, Cambridgeshire

Open spring to autumn; on A505. Map Ref: TL4746

The Imperial War Museum has an outstanding collection of over 90 aircraft at Duxford, the Battle of Britain airfield where Douglas Bader was stationed, including a World War I *Bristol Fighter*, a *B17 Flying Fortress* and a *Vulcan* bomber from the 1970s. A *Sunderland* flying boat and *Lancaster* bomber are also in the collection, plus a number of civil aircraft,

including a *Concorde* which you can actually go inside.

Military exhibits include a *Conqueror* tank and an exhibition of 20th-century artillery. The caravan which Montgomery used during all his campaigns is worth a peep, and closer to home is a wartime prefab as it would have been in 1940.

There is certainly a lot of ground to cover, but transport around the site is provided, and there are plenty of benches if you feel like a rest.

Around five special events are organised each year, when aircraft exhibits are flown and vehicles demonstrated. Pleasure flights are sometimes available, or you can experience the same sensations without having to leave the ground in a flight simulator.

INTELLIGENCE CORPS MUSEUM, Ashford, Kent

Open by appointment only (0233) 25251 ext 208. Map Ref: TR0142

Background to the development of army intelligence services is given at this interesting museum in Ashford's Templar Barracks, starting from the Boer War.

Falconry demonstrations are given regularly by experts at the Hawk Conservancy, Weyhill

From then the story unfolds through World War II and touches the work of the SOE, the desert campaigns, combat intelligence and aircraft intelligence. Hostilities in Malaya, Borneo, Cyprus and the Falklands are all covered, and displays include diaries, photographs, uniforms, weapons and the Corps' Roll of Honour.

ISLE OF WIGHT, Hampshire

Blackgang Chine Theme Park

Open spring to autumn; off A3055. Map Ref: SZ4876

Opened as scenic gardens in 1843, and covering some 20 acres, Blackgang Chine has been described as the Isle of Wight's answer to Disneyland, and it certainly has amusements for every age and taste. Among them are the Wild West Town, Jungleland, Nurseryland and a Smugglers' Cave. A dinosaur park is dotted with huge models of those prehistoric giants, and the Crooked House, which is based on the nursery rhyme, is ever

popular. All these attractions are floodlit on summer evenings, which is also just the right time to enjoy a complete contrast by strolling through beautiful water gardens to the Look Out, where there are wonderful coastal views. There is an interesting maritime exhibition too, as well as a collection of wreck and smuggling pictures, and a display which tells the story of the Blackgang landslips.

Across the road from the Theme Park (you can buy a combined ticket) is a replica of a Victorian water-powered sawmill, complete with a forge and wheelwright's shop. An exhibition there tells the story of wood, woodland skills and traditional trades. Near by is a viewpoint car park and picnic area from where it is possible to see right across the bays of the south-west shoreline to The Needles, and the Dorset coast beyond.

Carisbrooke Castle (EH)

Open all year; on B3401. Map Ref: SZ4887

Carisbrooke Castle's long and varied history includes a visit by William the Conqueror in 1082, and its use until 1944 as the official residence of the

Island Governor. As you walk around its battlements today you might spare a thought for Charles I, who took the same stroll every day for almost a year during his imprisonment in 1647. His son Henry and daughter Elizabeth were incarcerated at Carisbrooke in 1650.

The castle was besieged on a number of occasions, but only surrendered once – in 1136, when the castle wells dried up. These water sources can still be seen, although one is reached by climbing 71 steps to the massive shell-keep. The other, more conveniently positioned in the castle courtyard, has an interesting 16th-century well house and winding wheel, which donkeys were trained to use. Prisoners were once used to work the wheel. The method is demonstrated today, but the bucket is only lowered a token distance, and several donkeys share the task.

Also in the castle is the Isle of Wight Museum, which includes amongst its range of exhibits an excellent archaeological collection, a 16th-century parish gun and a nightcap that belonged to Charles I. Also of interest is the oldest working chamber organ in the country (1602).

Old Park Tropical Bird Gardens & Glassmaking, St Lawrence

Open all year; off A3055. Map Ref: SZ5376

Most aviaries have some kind of mesh between the observer and the observed, but not this one. Here there is a series of walk-through sections in which visitors can move among the free-flying, colourful inhabitants, of which there are over 400. Among many species are exotic cockatoos, macaws and toucans, while away from the aviaries are pleasant walks along a lake thronging with flamingoes, spoonbills and ducks.

At the same location is Isle of Wight Glass, where you can watch the glassblower at his work and view some of the beautiful and unique pieces which have been made there. Both attractions are in the grounds of the Old Park Hotel. Refreshments are available.

Osborne House (EH)

Open spring to autumn; off A3021. Map Ref: SZ5194

'Dear modest, unpretentious Osborne' was Queen Victoria's favourite home, and the place where she died in 1901. Built as a retreat from the pomp and ceremony of Windsor, it was designed by Prince Albert in consultation with his builder. The Prince had likened the Solent to the Bay of Naples, and envisaged an Italian-style villa with terraced gardens overlooking the water – a plan which he carried out with great success. The State Apartments are now open to the public, still furnished as they were in Victorian times and containing many interesting works of art. Among them are life-size marble statues of Victoria's four oldest children.

A few years after the family moved into Osborne, the Swiss Cottage was built as a play house for the royal children. Here, under the direction of their father, they learned through play the arts of cooking, sewing, carpentry and gardening. He even paid them the market price for their crops! This too can be visited, and there is a small museum in the house.

Parkhurst Forest

Map Ref: SZ4790

Much of these 1,000-acre woodlands are made up of conifers managed by the Forestry Commission, which has done an admirable job of providing access to visitors, including a good car park

among the trees and an adjacent picnic area. Trails of varying lengths have been marked, but visitors are free to follow the many gravel roads or green paths at will for pleasant, unplanned walks. Bird watchers should stay till dusk in early June for a chance to sight a nightjar or long-eared owl – and even more exciting for the amateur naturalist are the red squirrels, of which the Isle of Wight boasts a thriving population.

Extremely shy and elusive, these enchanting creatures are best sought early – and quietly. Please remember, though, that they are very rare and are protected by the Wildlife and Countryside Act; they must not be disturbed.

JANE AUSTEN MUSEUM, Chawton, Hampshire

Open all year, but restricted in winter; off A31. Map Ref: SU7037

Jane Austen spent most of the last eight years of her life in this unassuming house in the Hampshire village of Chawton, during which time she wrote the novels *Persuasion, Emma* and *Mansfield Park*, amongst

others. It is known that she drew inspiration from local society for some of her characters.

Her former home is now a museum devoted to her life and work, and is furnished in much the same way as it was in her day. Many of her personal possessions are there, her portrait hangs on one wall and visitors can see both her writing desk and her bureau – as well as a beautiful patchwork quilt which she made with her mother. The garden has been restored, and visitors may picnic there. You may notice two great oak trees just outside the garden wall; Jane Austen planted them herself in 1809.

KENT & EAST SUSSEX RAILWAY, Tenterden, Kent

Map Refs: TQ8833 & TQ8927

It is a curious thing that few people can remain unmoved in the presence of a preserved steam train – even those who lived in the age of steam and complained that trains were noisy and dirty. This is, of course, marvellous news for the dedicated bands of enthusiasts who now operate steam routes

on a self-supporting commercial basis all over Britain – including those responsible for the Kent & East Sussex line.

From delightful Tenterden Town Station, this service operates through 5m of Kent countryside to Wittersham Road Station, using lovingly-restored locomotives and rolling stock.

For a special treat you could book yourself on to the special evening dining trains, which operate every Saturday from April to October, plus Fridays in June and July.

KENT BATTLE OF BRITAIN MUSEUM, Hawkinge, Kent

Open spring to autumn; off A260. Map Ref: TR2139

Here is an aircraft museum with a difference, for the exhibits are remains of actual planes which fought the Battle of Britain – both British and German. It is certainly the largest and most comprehensive collection of its kind, and is appropriately housed in the buildings of the former Battle of Britain RAF station at Hawkinge.

Additionally, in the Dowding

Memorial Hangar are full-size replicas of the *Hurricane, Spitfire* and *ME109* aeroplanes that have been featured in films.

LEWES, East Sussex
Map Ref: TQ4110

Lewes, the charming county town of East Sussex, is a picturesque collection of timbered cottages, Georgian houses, steep streets and tiny passageways full of alluring shops and eating houses. It stands on the River Ouse, with the South Downs rising all around it, and nearly every building within its boundaries is of interest. However, the attractive timber-framed Anne of Cleves' House – so named because it was part of her divorce settlement from Henry VIII – must be one of the most frequently visited, and contains a fascinating folk museum with a collection of Sussex ironwork and a history gallery.

The town's other claim to historical fame is the great keep of its Norman castle, from which there are good views. The fine-looking outer gatehouse, known as the Barbican House, was built in the 14th century and contains a museum of Sussex archaeology. A special date in the local calendar of events is 5 November, for this is when the martyrdom by burning of Protestants imprisoned in cellars at the old Star Inn – now Lewes Town Hall – is remembered with a colourful parade of costumed figures marching down the high street, and carrying flaming torches.

LIPHOOK, Hampshire.
See Hollycombe Steam Collection

LONDON
See page 108

LUTON HOO, Luton, Bedfordshire

Open spring to autumn; entrance at Park St Gates; off A1081. Map Ref: TL0821

An imposing mansion house built in 1768 by Robert Adam, Luton Hoo was badly damaged by fire in 1843 and was consequently considerably remodelled.

Its strange name comes from the Anglo Saxon *Hoo*, meaning 'the spur of a hill'. Today the

Hampshire's popular Watercress steam line is a long, restored section of the Alton to Winchester Mid Hants Railway

house is most famous for its incomparable Wernher Collection of fine art, including intricate Beauvais tapestries dating from the early 18th century and English porcelain and china featuring examples of Chelsea, Worcester, Staffordshire, Derby and Rockingham.

One of the nation's finest groups of Italian Renaissance bronzes in private hands can also be seen, plus paintings including works by Rembrandt and Titian; a Russian Room containing personal mementoes of the Russian Imperial family, together with some of the robes worn at the court of the Tsars; and a fabulous collection of Fabergé jewellery.

The grounds of the mansion were laid out by Capability Brown. One of the terraces is particularly lovely, with its fine display of roses, yew hedges and topiary.

LYMPNE, Kent
See Port Lympne Zoo Park, Mansion & Gardens

MIDDLE WALLOP, Hampshire
See Museum of Army Flying

MID HANTS RAILWAY, Alresford & Alton, Hampshire

Open spring to late autumn; off A31. Map Ref: SU5832 & SU7139

Ten miles of track between lovely Alresford and the old market town of Alton provide the route for the steam-hauled Mid Hants Railway, popularly known as the 'Watercress Line' from its past association with Hampshire's watercress industry. The trains also call at Ropley station, where there are old locomotives and stock to be seen in various stages of restoration.

Mid Hants is another revived railway which can offer a special dining train on alternate Saturday evenings throughout the season, but you will need to book well in advance for this popular trip – and expect to find watercress somewhere on the menu!

While visiting the railway, do take the time to stroll around Alresford. It is a particularly attractive place with a wide main street, lots of interesting antique shops, bookshops, art shops and – perhaps best of all – teashops. There is also a delightful river walk which runs between Alresford and Old Alresford past two old mills, which are now private homes, and, of course, several watercress beds.

LONDON
Events & outdoor attractions

Changing of the Guard, Buckingham Palace, SW1

There is nothing quite like the Changing of the Guard at Buckingham Palace. It takes place on the palace forecourt at 11.30, seven days a week, and is perhaps the best known of London's royal ceremonies. At the appointed time the old guard is relieved by the new, which is preceded by a band as it marches from one of the barracks. The regiments from which the guard is drawn are usually the Foot Guards – the Scots, Irish, Welsh, Coldstream or Grenadiers.

Greenwich
Map Ref: TQ3977

Perhaps the best and most enjoyable way of getting to Greenwich is on one of the many Thames-cruise boats that sail from the piers at Charing Cross and Westminster. Nearest the river can be seen a cluster of buildings that were mainly designed by Webb and Wren and now house the Royal Naval College, featuring the painted Hall – which took 20 years to paint, and was where Nelson 'lay in state' before his funeral. Both the hall and the chapel are open daily. Beyond the college – in the delightfully 17th-century Italianate Queen's House by Inigo Jones – is the National Maritime Museum, the largest and most extensive of its kind in the world.

Brilliantly illustrative of Britain's seafaring history, its many fascinating exhibits include Nelson's Trafalgar coat, complete with the hole made by the fatal shot. A particular delight are some of the best seascapes ever painted. Moored near the pier in front of the Maritime Museum are the famous tea and wool clipper, *Cutty Sark*, and *Gypsy Moth IV* – the yacht in which Sir Francis Chichester sailed single-handedly round the world in 1966/67. He was the first person to achieve this feat, and for his efforts was knighted at Greenwich by the Queen.

Providing a beautiful and fitting backcloth to the Naval College and Maritime Museum is Greenwich Park, royal grounds that are elegantly landscaped and formal in part, and the home of deer. In the centre of the park is the old Royal Observatory, which now houses an impressive collection of historic time-keeping, astrological and navigational instruments. A brass strip mounted on stone marks the

West wing of the Royal Naval College at Greenwich, an imposing group by John Webb, Christopher Wren and various other neo-classical architects

meridian – the accepted 0 line for the world since 1884.

Boats leave Greenwich regularly to visit the Thames Barrier, which was opened in 1984 and immediately dubbed by some 'the 8th wonder of the world'. The massive flood-prevention scheme spans the river and has a visitor centre which displays many exhibits. A dramatic audio visual show is worth seeing.

Kew Gardens
Open daily

A showcase of the plant kingdom, the superb Royal Botanic Gardens at Kew were started more than two centuries ago on a modest nine-acre site by George III's mother, Princess Augusta. They now extend over more than 300 acres and are among the most important in the world as a repository of plant lore and science.

Each season brings its own special delights, from tiny alpine flowers to orchids and delicate exotics that will thrive

only in the magnificent Palm House. The Princess of Wales Conservatory even has a Mangrove Swamp. In addition to many glasshouse exhibits, various outdoor garden areas and the museums, there is an exotic pagoda built entirely for decorative purposes by Sir William Chambers in 1761. The gardens suffered serious damage during the hurricane-force storms of October 1987.

Lord Mayor's Show

Each year on Michaelmas Day (29 September) a new Lord Mayor of London is elected with great pomp and tradition. The retiring incumbent and his aldermen first attend a service at St Lawrence Jewry, then make their way to the Guildhall to select one of the candidates put forward for the post by the Livery companies. When the choice has been made, the old and new Lord Mayors ride together in the state coach to the Mansion House, and all the city bells ring out to proclaim the fact.

On the second Saturday in November the new Lord Mayor of London publically takes office in a 600-year old ceremony in which he rides to

can be seen in summer.

Open-air concerts are also a regular feature, with military and brass bands giving frequent free performances at lunchtimes.

Public amenities offered by the park include games fields, archery, tennis and boating on Nash's great artificial lake. The park's other waterway is the Regent's Canal, which is sited on the northern boundary and is part of the Grand Union Canal – which cuts right through the precincts of the zoo, between the Snowdon Aviary and the deer and antelope terraces.

Visitors can actually reach the zoo by taking the boat from Little Venice, a quiet and leafy backwater of Paddington.

Galleries, exhibitions and displays

Age Exchange Reminiscence Centre, Blackheath SE3

Open Mon–Sat

A most unusual attraction in Blackheath opened its doors to the public for the first time on 29 May 1987, and proved an instant success.

Known as the Age Exchange Reminiscence Centre, it is designed as a shop-cum-museum furnished with a growing number of everyday objects dating from the turn of the century. Older folk are encouraged to drop in and talk about their memories with others of a like mind, and younger folk eager to learn about living history have only to step over the threshold to hear it from first-hand observers.

Memories of those willing to reminisce on tape or paper are stored in a memory bank and translated by the Age Exchange Trust into exhibitions, books and plays designed to reach the community as a whole. It is certainly a successful bridge across the so-called generation gap.

National Portrait Gallery, 2 St Martin's Place, WC2

Open all year

Just round the corner from the National Gallery in Trafalgar Square is the National Portrait Gallery, where visitors are asked to take a lift to the top of the building and there begin a fascinating tour among paintings, miniatures, engravings, cartoons, photographs and sculptures of personalities who have made a name for themselves in history. Portraits are displayed more or less chronologically in rooms attractively designed and

the Royal Courts of Justice in a superb 18th-century coach drawn by six horses and accompanied by an impressive bodyguard of pikemen and musketeers.

The coach is preceded by colourful floats illustrating different aspects of London's history, and on the following Monday the Lord Mayor gives a lavish banquet at the Guildhall. This is traditionally attended by the Prime Minister and the Archbishop of Canterbury.

Regent's Park, Marylebone Road, SW1

Open all year

Regent's Park has become synonymous with the zoo which occupies its north-eastern corner. Founded in the 19th century by Sir Stamford Raffles, the zoo was opened to the public in 1847 and now has one of the most comprehensive collections of animals in the world. Over 8,000 can be seen, from common British fauna to endangered species which are hard to find anywhere in the world. Among several international 'firsts' achieved here were the Reptile House of 1849, the Aquarium of 1853 and the Insect House of 1889.

Cages have given way to terraces offering less restricted accommodation and more natural environments for the animals, and the zoo's reputation for excellent care of its charges is second to none. An essential part of that care is a professionally complete veterinary and research support service.

Originally part of the great royal hunting ground of Marylebone Park, Regent's Park itself eventually came within the Prince Regent's grand plan for a vast neo-classical redevelopment under the talented hand of John Nash. At first the intention was to build on the park itself, but thankfully this did not happen and the 20th century can enjoy the legacy of this marvellous open space surrounded by the gleaming white stucco of elegant Regency terraces.

The layout remains as Nash designed it and is focused on the Inner Circle, which encloses Queen Mary's Garden – with its lovely little lake, shaded avenues, cascades of colourful rockery plants and some of the most beautiful rose beds in the capital. Here also is the popular Open-air Theatre, where Shakespearian and other plays furnished to reflect a fitting historical period. There are special exhibitions several times a year.

A delightful variety of famous and infamous people are on view, including royalty through the ages and celebrities from the arts, literature and sport. The portrait of the Queen by Annigoni, and Brian Organ's portraits of the Prince of Wales and Lady Diana (before her marriage), are of particular interest.

Opposite the gallery is a fine statue of Edith Cavell, the famous World War I nurse.

The Queen's Gallery,
Buckingham Palace Road, SW1

Open all year except Mon & BH

The building which contains the Queen's Gallery was originally designed as a conservatory by John Nash, and subsequently converted into a chapel.

After suffering some serious bomb damage in 1940, part of it was rebuilt as Buckingham Palace's private chapel and part as the art gallery that exists today. It houses a constantly changing exhibition of art treasures from the royal collection.

The Tate Gallery, Millbank, SW1

Open all year

Not only did the sugar magnate Sir Henry Tate finance the building of this gallery to house the nation's growing collection of British art, but he also donated 67 paintings and three pieces of sculpture to start things off. The Tate Gallery was officially opened in 1897, with further wings added to house the works of Turner, the modern foreign collection and the sculpture. In the British collection, which is arranged mainly in chronological order, are all the best-loved British painters – with Hogarth, Blake, Constable and Turner particularly well represented.

The foreign collection traces the development of art from impressionism up to the present day and features paintings by Cézanne, Matisse, Picasso and Chagall; in the Sculpture Gallery are works by Henry Moore, Barbara Hepworth and Alberto Giacometti. The Tate strives and succeeds in reflecting the constantly changing face of contemporary art, and some of its more avant-garde purchases have been known to raise a few eyebrows.

Its ever-changing galleries are always full of interesting surprises.

Museums

Museums in and around London range from the tiny and specific to the vast and general, featuring old, present-day and futuristic displays. The following small selection is particularly recommended, but there are plenty of others to excite interest and satisfy curiosity.

Imperial War Museum,
Southwark, SE1

Open all year

Housed in a building that was once the Bedlam lunatic asylum, this museum encompasses every aspect of the two world wars and includes much about other military operations that have involved Britain and the Commonwealth since 1914.

An outstanding display of tanks, aeroplanes, weapons, uniforms and other objects of war is of particular note, as is a collection of printings and drawings by war artists that is probably unequalled anywhere in Europe.

Madame Tussaud's & London Planetarium, Marylebone Road, NW1

Open daily

Founded in Paris and brought to London by Madame Tussaud in 1802, this much-loved waxworks museum was given a permanent home in the Marylebone Road in 1835. Its exhibits form a constantly changing parade of the famous and infamous from every walk of life, both present and past, often portrayed as parts of small, informal gatherings against suitable backcloths. The macabre and eerie Chamber of Horrors reconstructs spine-chilling crimes from the past.

In an adjacent building is the London Planetarium where a facsimile of the night sky is projected on to the inside of a huge copper dome and described in an accompanying commentary. An exhibition entitled 'The Astronomers' features wax figures of scientists such as Einstein and Galileo, together with working models of their inventions.

Very early seaplane in the RAF Museum at Hendon, north London

Natural History Museum, Cromwell Road, SW7

Open all year

One of the best loved of London's museums is the Natural History in South Kensington, where generations of schoolchildren have gawked at dinosaurs in the elegant halls of this most Victorian of buildings. As the museum covers a massive four-acre site it is advisable to arm yourself with a guidebook and decide beforehand on the exhibits you can comfortably get round in the time available. The choice of what to forgo is a tough one, but displays not to be missed include: the dinosaurs and their relatives – including the new discovery, 'Claws'; the life-size model of a blue whale; a Coelacanth, which is a type of fish known as a living fossil; the British bird pavilion, where there are recordings of many different birdsongs; and the Hall of Human Biology, where visitors can get a better understanding of their own bodies.

RAF Museum, Battle of Britain Museum & Bomber Command Museum, Hendon, NW9

Open all year

These three museums are on the site of the former Hendon airfield and cover most aspects of military aviation. In the RAF Museum are displays which comprehensively detail the history of the force, including among its exhibits some 40 aircraft housed in a World War I hangar. In the adjacent Battle of Britain Museum are British, German and Italian aircraft of 1940s vintage, with pride of place given to the *Spitfire* and *Hurricane*. On the first floor is an operations room as it would have appeared at the height of the Battle of Britain, and in the same complex is the huge Bomber Command Museum – an exciting collection including the *Lancaster, Wellington* and *Vulcan* bomber aircraft.

Science Museum, Exhibition Road, SW7

Open all year

A great place to mystify if not lose the grandchildren, the science museum has 60 galleries on six floors featuring collections covering more than 100 different subject areas and examining the history, development and understanding of science, industry, technology and medicine from antiquity to the present day.

There are exhibitions on road, sea, air, rail and space travel too, plus astronomy, telecommunications, printing, lighting, domestic appliances and much, much more. In the basement is 'Launch Pad', where children can absorb an introduction to science without realising it by watching video screens, pushing buttons and pulling levers to operate the many exciting 'hands-on' exhibits.

The British Museum, Great Russell Street, WC1

Open all year

Founded in 1753, this museum contains one of the world's richest collections of archaeological and historic treasures. There is so much to see under one roof that it is advisable to buy a guidebook and decide beforehand what you can comfortably look at in the time available – you can always go back!

Finds from all over the world span a time range from prehistory to comparatively modern periods and include the controversial Elgin Marbles from Greece; Egyptian Mummies; two of only four existing original copies of *Magna Carta*; Nelson's sketch plan for the Battle of Trafalgar – and the exquisite 7th-century Sutton Hoo treasure found in Suffolk.

Each year the British Museum stages special exhibitions that focus and expand on specific aspects of the collections.

Victoria & Albert Museum, Cromwell Road, SW7

Open all year except Fri

Almost always affectionately referred to as the 'V and A', this national museum of art and design follows its subject thoroughly through every century since the death of Christ and into nearly every country in the world.

Here it is possible to wander back into time by walking through rooms furnished according to historical periods, then explore galleries devoted to an infinite variety of special subjects like jewellery, dress, paintings – even the fakes of John Constable. Superb collections have been amassed of water-colour paintings, miniatures, Indian art and British sculpture, not to mention the greatest array of Italian Renaissance sculpture outside Italy.

Just one word of advice, however – the museum has an eight mile labyrinth of galleries, so it makes good sense to buy a guide and be selective each time you visit.

MUSEUM OF ARMY FLYING, Middle Wallop, Hampshire

Open daily; on A343. Map Ref: SU2937

A century of army flying is covered by this exciting aviation museum, from the early man-carrying kites and balloons to the missile-firing jet helicopters of today. Lots of aircraft are on display, including old bi-planes, the *Auster* and various helicopters which have taken over the majority of the army's modern flying operations.

There are lots of special displays and dioramas too, many relating to the pioneer days of flying during World War I. A particularly interesting section tells of the Glider Pilot Regiment during World War II, and of their involvement with the D-Day invasion and the crossing of the Rhine. Middle Wallop is the home of the Army Air Corps, and the place where its new pilots are trained. You are likely to see a certain amount of activity in the air there, as well as the 'grounded' exhibits.

NEW FOREST BUTTERFLY FARM, Ashurst, Hampshire

Open spring to autumn. Map Ref: SU3310

In the heart of the New Forest it is possible to see a huge variety of butterflies at very close quarters, all in a large heated glasshouse at the local butterfly farm. These delightful insects fly free, and even land on unsuspecting visitors walking round the tropical gardens that keep their colourful inhabitants comfortable. There are species from all over the world, some with wing-spans of several inches. British butterflies are housed in a separate section more suited to their own climate, and other displays relate to the life-cycles of butterflies and to conservation matters.

Creatures of less endearing natures include tarantulas, praying mantis, scorpions, ants and locusts – thankfully secured in their own glass enclosures. There is also a natural beehive, while outside the glasshouses is a dragonfly pond. You can complete your visit with a woodland ride on a traditional wagon, drawn by shire horses through a secluded part of the estate.

OLD WARDEN, Bedfordshire
See Shuttleworth Collection

OXFORD, Oxfordshire

Map Ref: SP5106

The mellow, honey-coloured stones and spires of Oxford's ancient university buildings give the city centre a timelessness which is easily appreciated, for most of the colleges are within a short walking distance of the High Street. Some actually open on to it, and it is easy to see the contrast between their quiet cloisters and the busy world outside. Some can be visited, but access may be restricted to certain times, so preliminary enquiries at Oxford's Information Centre in St Aldates are advisable. Christ Church, the largest and noblest of all, was founded by Cardinal Wolsey in 1525 and used by Charles I as his headquarters during the Civil War.

Magdalen (pronounced 'Maudlin') is renowned as the most beautiful, and it has changed little since it was built at the end of the 15th century. At sunrise on May Day the college choir climbs to the top of Magdalen's square tower and sings a latin hymn. Merton, Balliol, University College and St Edmund Hall are the oldest foundations, all having been in existence by the end of the 13th century.

Oxford also has the oldest museum in the country, the Ashmolean, which dates from the 17th century and contains collections of international importance. The Museum of the History of Science has the finest collection of early astronomical, mathematical and optical instruments in the world and the Museum of Oxford tells the story of the city from earliest times. A museum with a difference is the Rotunda Museum of Antique Dolls' Houses, two miles from the city centre at Iffley Turn. Some 50 dolls' houses are displayed – together with their furnishings, kitchen equipment and china – dating back as far as 1700.

In contrast to all this culture and antiquity are delightful

A beautiful swallowtail (top) and its companions overshadow their bright food plants at the New Forest Butterfly Farm

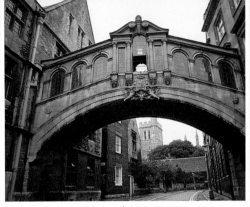

City of spires

For centuries Oxford has been famous as a seat of learning, and the scholarly atmosphere of the magnificent university buildings, the colleges, and the time-honoured traditions unique to Oxford student life are an intrinsic part of the city's charm.

1 UNIVERSITY BOTANIC GARDEN
During 1621 this garden, the oldest of its kind in Britain, was laid out as a Physic Garden. To one side, near the river, are greenhouses where more delicate and exotic plants are grown.

2 CHRIST CHURCH MEADOW
Keepers still watch the gates into the Meadow to prevent, according to the notice board, undesirables entering – and they lock the gates at dusk.

3 CHRIST CHURCH & CATHEDRAL
Christ Church was founded as Cardinal College by Cardinal Wolsey in 1525. However, by 1546 Wolsey had fallen from grace and Henry VIII refounded it as Christ Church. The present cathedral, the smallest in Britain, dates mainly from the 12th and 13th centuries. The huge quadrangle of the college is one of the most awe-inspiring in Oxford.

4 MUSEUM OF OXFORD
The museum, housed in the old city library, is a branch of the Oxfordshire County Museum at Woodstock. Its exhibits illustrate the history of Oxford from

Neolithic times to the present day.

5 CARFAX
Carfax, the name a derivation of the Old French word *carrefour* (meaning four forks), is the crossroads at the centre of the old city.

6 MARTYRS' MEMORIAL
Three bishops were burnt at the stake here in the 16th century for their Protestant beliefs during Queen Mary's reinstatement of the Catholic faith.

7 THE ASHMOLEAN MUSEUM
The rare and exotic treasures that fill the Ashmolean's galleries – based on a collection begun in the 17th century – come from all corners of the world. A very important part of the museum is its art collection.

8 MUSEUM OF THE HISTORY OF SCIENCE
Designed by Thomas Wood, this is one of the best examples in Oxford of 17th-century architecture.

9 SHELDONIAN THEATRE
With the sculpted heads of Roman emperors ranged on pillars around its

semicircular front, the 17th-century Sheldonian Theatre is one of the city's most distinctive buildings.

10 THE BODLEIAN LIBRARY
The Bodleian collection of today was really begun by Sir Thomas Bodley in 1598. Now it contains over 5 million books and 134,000 manuscripts and is one of the six libraries in Britain entitled to a copy of every book published in the UK.

11 NEW COLLEGE
New College Lane seems remote from the rest of the city as it leads between high walls to New College. This, despite its name, was founded in 1379.

12 ST EDMUND HALL
St Edmund, founded in 1220 and the only survivor of the medieval halls, is now a college.

13 RADCLIFFE CAMERA
This huge, 18th-century domed building at the very heart of the university dominates Radcliffe Square.

14 ST MARY THE VIRGIN
Oxford University's parish church, St Mary's, has been the scene of all university gatherings for nearly 400 years.

Oxford's 20th-century 'Bridge of Sighs', at Hertford College

15 BRASENOSE COLLEGE
The curious name of this college is thought to be a derivation of bronze nose – the nickname given to an old door knocker once adorning the door.

EARLY CLOSING: *Thu*

MARKET DAY: *Wed*

PARKING: *Westgate*

OPENING TIMES:
Botanic Gn: open all year
Museum of Oxford: open all year, Tue – Sat
Ashmolean Museum: open all year, Tue – Sat; Sun pm only
Museum of the History of Science: open all year, Mon – Fri

ROUTE DIRECTIONS
Start at Magdalen Bridge and pass the University Botanic Garden (1). Turn l. into Rose La. Follow the path through Christ Church Meadow (2) to Christ Church Cathedral (3). Walk through Christ Church College and leave by Tom Gate and turn r. along St Aldate's past Museum of Oxford (4) to Carfax (5). Continue along Cornmarket St into Magdalen St past Martyrs' Memorial (6) and turn l. into Beaumont St to the Ashmolean Museum (7). Return to Magdalen St, cross over and turn r. then shortly l. into Broad St to the Museum of the History of Science (8). From the Sheldonian Theatre (9), turn r. into Catte St for the Bodleian Library (10), then pass under arch into New College Lane, passing New College (11). Continue into Queen's La with St Edmund Hall (12) on l. On reaching the High St turn r. then r. again up Catte St to Radcliffe Sq and Camera (13). Opposite is St Mary's Church (14), with Brasenose College (15) adjacent. From Radcliffe Camera, proceed along Brasenose La, then turn l. into Turl St. Cross the High St into Alfred St and turn l. into Bear La to reach Oriel St. Continue l. into Merton St and turn r. at High St to return to Magdalen Bridge.

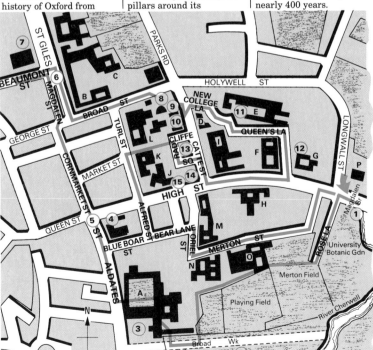

riverside walks by the Cherwell (pronounced Charwell), or by the Thames (called the Isis here). One along the riverbank and through the large Christ Church Meadow is particularly lovely, and might be followed by a visit to the University Botanic Garden, just beside Magdalen Bridge.

Boat trips are available too, and boats for hire – but remember that punting is something of an acquired skill! Events on the river include Eights Week, when rowing eights compete for the Head of the River title. This usually takes place towards the end of May each year.

Shopping facilities in the town are excellent, and there is a large new precinct as well as attractive streets of unusual shops and good book stores. An efficient park-and-ride system operates from the edge of the city.

PORT LYMPNE ZOO PARK, MANSION & GARDENS, Lympne, Kent

Open daily; off A20. Map Ref: TR1134

Port Lympne mansion was built by architect Sir Herbert Baker and has many unusual internal features, including the Rex Whistler Tent Room, a Moroccan patio and the hexagonal library where the Treaty of Paris was signed after World War I. In the long gallery is a curious, concentrically patterned marble mosaic-work floor.

The gardens cover 15 acres and are spectacular, with views that extend as far as the coast of France if conditions are right. Beyond the house and gardens is the famous zoo park, where Indian elephants, wolves, rhinos, African leopards, Siberian and Indian tigers, monkeys, chimpanzees and other animals live.

Usually it is possible to take a safari-trailer ride through the animal paddocks – but it is advisable to check this in advance of your visit, especially if you are relying on the service to get you round.

PORTSMOUTH, Hampshire

Map Ref: SU6400

Portsmouth is known to have been a harbour since Roman times, and has had important naval connections since the 14th century, so it is entirely fitting that two of the world's most famous wooden warships should be displayed there.

Nelson's flagship HMS *Victory*, one of the most

outstanding examples of ship restoration in the world, is still in commission staffed by men from the navy and Marines who show visitors round the ship. Opposite the dockland is the Royal Naval Museum, which exhibits many relics of Nelson and his men, a panorama of the Battle of Trafalgar with sound effects and a history of the navy in general.

The nation held its breath when Henry VIII's warship the *Mary Rose* was raised from the bed of the Solent in 1982, but after many years of work she is now on display and surrounded by special viewing galleries which allow visitors to watch her slow but sure restoration. In a Georgian timber boathouse near by is an exhibition of objects found on the vessel, and a re-creation of what life on board a Tudor warship must have been like.

ROMNEY, HYTHE AND DYMCHURCH RAILWAY, Kent

Trains run spring to late summer, & weekends in Mar & Oct; off A259. Map Ref: TR1634

The Romney, Hythe and Dymchurch runs for nearly 14 miles across Romney marsh, between Hythe and Dungeness, and is the world's smallest public railway; it is also the only one on 15in-gauge track. The superb steam and diesel locomotives that haul the trains are one third the size of their standard counterparts, and the steam models are based on the

high-speed locomotives of the 1920s. They have wonderfully nostalgic names – *Green Goddess, Black Prince, Hercules* and *Hurricane* – that evoke their golden age.

Visitors to this charming railway can make as long or short a journey as they wish, the full stretch taking three hours – or more if passengers decide to break their journeys at any of the six stations, and perhaps visit the exhibition at the railway's New Romney headquarters. There are cafés and shops at all the major stations, and a wealth of attractions within walking distance – not the least of which is the coast.

ROMSEY, Hampshire
See Broadlands

RYCOTE CHAPEL (EH), Oxfordshire

Open daily except two days a week in winter. Map Ref: SP6604

Originally built by the Quartermaine family from Thame, and consecrated in 1449, this lovely medieval chapel has superb contemporary benches and Jacobean pews.

Golden stars that decorate the barrel-vaulted roof were cut from rare European playing cards. The building has royal connections too, for both Princess Elizabeth (in the reign of her sister Mary) and Charles I visited it.

RYE, East Sussex

Map Ref: TQ9220

It is difficult to imagine that in medieval times this sleepy seaside town, with its lovely old buildings and cobbled streets, was heavily fortified against the French and attached to the Cinque Ports. Its importance waned as its harbour gradually silted up during the 16th century, but the town's one-time status has left it a rich legacy of historically interesting buildings. Not far from the Norman church – which has a 16th-century clock with an 18ft pendulum – is the three-storey Ypres Tower, built as a castle in the 13th century and used as a prison between the 1500s and 1800s. Today it houses an interesting Cinque Ports exhibition, and other local history material.

Some of Rye's oldest and loveliest houses are in Mermaid Street, Church Square, Watchbell Street and the High Street. The 15th-century Mermaid Inn is one of the oldest in the country, and in West Street is 18th-century Lamb House (NT) – home of the American author Henry James from 1898 until his death in 1916. Well worth a visit, this is where James wrote many of his later novels. The house and lovely walled gardens are owned by the National Trust.

HMS Warrior, moored at Portsmouth, was launched in 1860 as the world's first iron-hulled steam battleship

ST ALBANS, Hertfordshire

Map Ref: TL1407

This city grew out of the Roman town of *Verulamium,* and was named after Britain's first Christian martyr – a Roman soldier who was executed in about AD209 for shielding a Christian priest. A shrine is known to have existed here in the 5th century, when the Romans departed, and the Saxons built the first abbey on the site in the 8th century.

The present cathedral contains the restored remnants of the shrine and is based on the Norman abbey, of which the only other surviving remnant is the Waxhouse Gate – where candles were once made and sold to visiting pilgrims. The city is also renowned as the home of the only English Pope to date – Nicholas Breakspear, who was elected in 1154 and took the name Adrian IV.

Remains of the Roman town can be seen in Verulamium Park and comprise sections of the 3rd-century wall, remnants of a street of shops and – preserved in a special building – a hypocaust heating system. The associated museum of Roman finds is superb, and the nearby Roman Theatre of between AD140 and 150 is frequently used for plays and other functions.

Later history can be traced throughout the town. French Row is a medieval street off the High Street, named after French soldiers who were quartered there in 1216 by the barons who needed their help in the fight against King John. Nearby Romeland is where the townsfolk rioted in 1381 in support of the Peasant's Revolt, and St Peter's Street saw a major battle when Yorkists defeated the Lancastrians and captured Henry VI, in the Wars of the Roses.

St Albans City Museum is a fascinating place, with reconstructed workshops and the Salaman collection of craft tools. Other displays relate to the natural history and geology of south-west Hertfordshire. Of an entirely different nature is the Organ Museum, with its unique collection of automatically operated organs and other musical instruments.

This is a lovely city, its streets lined with historic buildings, and a town trail is available from the Tourist Information Office to enable the most to be made of a visit. Just outside the city is the Kingsbury Watermill Museum, a 16th-century corn mill with working waterwheel. Three floors of the mill are open to the public.

Gardens of the Rose, St Albans, Hertfordshire

Open early summer to autumn; 2m S of city off Watford Road

The Royal National Rose Society has its headquarters here, and in some 12 acres of gardens has one of the most important collections of roses in the world. Around 30,000 are grown in attractively laid-out beds and borders featuring several model gardens and a number of special garden ornaments.

As well as the popular hybrid teas and floribundas, there are climbers, miniatures, standards, shrubs and even wild roses. At the centre of the gardens is the Princess Mary Walk, a wide flagstone path which is flanked by masses of rose bushes and leads to a delightful circular pool with a fountain.

The pool is encircled by a pergola, upon which varieties of climbers are displayed. All around the garden are wooden seats where visitors can sit and survey the wonderful colours and enjoy the rich fragrances. One area is set aside as a trial ground, and it is there where the real work of the society is carried out. New varieties sent from all over the world by both professional and amateur rose breeders are planted, and judged over three years for their garden suitability. There is a licensed cafeteria and a gift shop within the main building; special events include pruning and planting demonstrations, and the National Summer Show and Festival which lasts for two days.

SHEFFIELD PARK, East Sussex
See Bluebell Railway

SHERBORNE ST JOHN, Hampshire
See Vyne, The

SHERE, Surrey

Map Ref: TQ0747

Situated on the edge of the North Downs by the River Tillingbourne, this lovely village has long been a favourite with artists and boasts many old and attractive cottages.

The local museum is interesting, and the church features in *Domesday.* Its Norman tower supports a fine medieval shingled spire. This is a good place to stop off and while away an hour or two strolling by the river, browsing in antique shops or having afternoon tea.

SHUTTLEWORTH COLLECTION OF HISTORIC AEROPLANES & CARS, Old Warden Airfield, Bedfordshire

Open daily; on A1. Map Ref: TL1343

This classic grass aerodrome, with its six hangars, is the home of around 30 historic aeroplanes, all of which are still capable of flight. Indeed, some are occasionally flown for displays. Stars of the show are the 1909 *Bleriot* and a 1941 *Spitfire*, the rest of the exhibits falling somewhere within that span of years. Also on show is a collection of roadworthy vehicles dating from an 1898 *Panhard Levassor*, while in the coachroom is a display of carriages from an earlier age.

Near by in the pretty village of Old Warden – where the first Warden pear was grown – is the Shuttleworth family home, now an agricultural college.

SINGLETON, West Sussex
See Weald & Downland Open Air Museum

SOUTHAMPTON, Hampshire

Map Ref: SU4112

Beneath the commercialised exterior of Southampton, with its modern port, excellent shopping centre, sports and leisure facilities and university, lies the true character of a city that has a maritime history stretching back hundreds of years. Evidence of ancient times is seen in the High Street, where the 13th-century drum tower of the Bargate marks the old northern entrance into the medieval town. It contains a museum. The city's Maritime Museum, housed in a 600-year-old building that was once a wool warehouse, does a great deal to unravel the mysteries of Southampton's seafaring past. Southampton's maritime present is the huge development, now in its second stage, taking place in the dockland area and known as Ocean World. Opened in 1986, this has plenty of good places to eat, inviting boutiques in which to shop, lots of street entertainment in season to amuse the grandchildren – and a bustling marina. From here harbour and river trips can be taken, including a Howard's Way (of TV fame) cruise up the Hamble River; Southampton is also on the Rivers Itchen and Test. It is even possible to take an evening meal on board a sailing barge in the harbour.

The Southampton Hall of

Aviation is a museum dedicated to historical aircraft that have associations with Southampton. There are usually about eight on display at any given time, as well as considerable collections of aviation memorabilia. Of particular interest are one of the last *Spitfires* to be made, the Snider Trophy model built for speed racing and the *Gnat* – later models of which are still used by the RAF's acrobatic team. All were built in the Southampton area.

SOUTHSEA, Hampshire

Map Ref: SZ6498

D-Day from the points of view of the people on both sides who were directly involved in the war is the theme of the D-Day Museum, which tells the story in pictures, re-creations of wartime scenes, plans and displays of vehicles, uniforms and weapons used at that time. The focal point is a superb embroidery in testimony to 'Operation Overlord' – the most important of history's seaborne invasions.

Children will enjoy the nearby Sealife Centre, and also the Cumberland House Natural Science Museum & Aquarium.

The Royal Marines Museum is housed in an original Royal Marine Artillery Officers' Mess, and provides a chronological history of the Royal Marines from 1664 to the present day. Uniforms, medals and badges are on display, as well as an exhibition opened in 1982 called 'The Royal Marines through the 70s and into the 80s'. This covers Northern Ireland and the Arctic Commandos – together with other corps activities that have taken place over the last 10 or so years. In 1983 a further dimension was given to the museum in the shape of the Falklands Display.

STOUR VALLEY, Essex & Suffolk

Map Ref: TM2633

Follow the winding River Stour along the boundaries of Essex and Suffolk, through villages such as Langham – with its

Timber-framed Bayleaf house, pride of the Weald and Downland's collection of re-erected domestic buildings

lavish church – or Belchamp, where the brook drops down into the river, and it is possible to see some of the finest of England's countryside. Much has remained virtually unchanged in the last 100 or so years, and certainly Flatford has altered little since John Constable captured the scene around Willy Lotts Cottage. Both this and Flatford Mill – featured in Constable's most famous painting, *The Haywain* – are owned by the National Trust and can be viewed from the outside only.

Just upstream from the mill is Bridge Cottage, a restored thatched cottage which houses an exhibition dedicated to the artist. Constable himself came from a milling family in East Bergholt, on the Suffolk side of the river, but he made many of the other charming villages and picturesque farms of this beautiful landscape the subject of his works.

STRATFIELD SAYE HOUSE & WELLINGTON COUNTRY PARK, Hampshire

House open weekends Easter & April, then daily in summer except Fri May–Sep, grounds open spring to autumn & winter weekends; off A33/B3349. Map Ref: SU6961

This famous home of the Dukes of Wellington, in its glorious park, was built in 1630 and presented by a grateful nation to the 1st Duke of Wellington in 1817, after his victory over Napoleon Bonaparte. Inside is a superb collection of paintings, prints and furniture belonging to the great soldier, and the Wellington Exhibition recreates many scenes from the life of the 'iron' Duke.

Many costumes and personal effects are featured, including the magnificent funeral carriage weighing 18 tons and standing 17ft high. Even the Duke's beloved horse – ridden at the Battle of Waterloo – is not forgotten, and Copenhagen's grave is to be seen within the grounds.

Just a five-minute drive from Stratfield Saye House is Wellington Country Park, which has 550 acres of unspoilt countryside with boating and fishing lakes, miles of lovely nature trails through woodland and meadows, a miniature steam railway and the many fascinating exhibits in the National Dairy Museum, all in a peaceful rural setting.

TENTERDEN, Kent
See Kent & East Sussex Railway

THORPE PARK, Chertsey, Surrey

Open daily spring to late summer; on A320. Map Ref: TQ0268

Entertainment of many varieties is offered by Thorpe Park, an excellent family venue set in 500 acres of amusements, lakes and refreshment facilities. Fully operational Thorpe Farm is set in the 1930s and farmed in the traditional way – and various rural skills such as bee-keeping, brewing, bread making and binding sheaves of corn are demonstrated there too.

Elsewhere are the Treasure Island train ride; Magic Mill fantasy boat trip; Space Station Zero adventure roller-coaster – and Thunder River, a rapid-water ride for all the family. Cinema 180 is a fascinating experience, and travel around the park by train or water-bus is free.

Additional charges are made for some sporting activities and coin-operated amusements, but more than 50 of the park's attractions are covered by the initial entrance fee. Certainly a day out for the grandchildren to remember.

VYNE, THE (NT), Sherborne St John, Hampshire

Open pm spring to autumn except Mon & Fri; on unclassified road to Bramley. Map Ref: SU6356

In the heart of rural Hampshire is The Vyne country house, which was built in the 16th century by William Sandys, Councillor to King Henry VI. The Sandys family lived there for more than 100 years, after which it became home to the Chutes – whose descendants lived there until 1956. The red-brick house has a 17th-century classical portico overlooking a fine lake to the rear, and contains many features to delight and interest the discerning visitor.

Of particular note are the superb hallway and staircase, the beautiful chapel and a long gallery with excellent linenfold panelling. One of two domed lodges is used as a teahouse.

WEALD & DOWNLAND OPEN-AIR MUSEUM, Singleton, West Sussex

Open daily spring to autumn, Wed & Sun in winter. Map Ref: SU8713

Historic buildings from all over South East England have been dismantled and re-erected in this 40-acre museum in the Lavant Valley, some dating as far back as the 14th century. They give an unusually clear insight into the rural England of yesteryear and include medieval houses, a Tudor market hall, a 19th-century schoolhouse and a blacksmith's forge.

Agricultural buildings are there too, and the Lurgashall Watermill still produces stone-ground flour. Rural industries and crafts are also displayed, including blacksmithing, carpentry, pottery and spinning. A charcoal burner's camp includes a traditional turf hut and demonstrates the old trade, which was essential to the local iron industry. Sometimes traditional farm skills such as heavy horse ploughing, sheep shearing and sheepdog trials are demonstrated.

There are picnic sites and light refreshments are available.

WEYHILL, Hampshire
See Hawk Conservancy

WHIPSNADE ZOO,
Bedfordshire

*Open daily; on B4540. Map Ref:
TL0117*

A real treat for all the family is
this superb 500-acre zoo, which
was opened in the 1930s and
has over 2,000 wild animals
living in parkland high in the
Chiltern countryside. The
emphasis is on space and
freedom – and the animals have
plenty of both, being able to
roam around in huge paddocks
and enjoy almost natural
habitats without apparently
being barred or fenced in.

All the favourites are there,
including lions, tigers and
bears, as well as rare birds and
other animals. Youngsters are
well catered for with the
children's zoo and farm, and
there is a superb dolphinarium.
For those who prefer to leave
their cars in the free car park
outside, a passenger steam
train – which passes through
the rhino enclosure – offers a
comfortable tour of the zoo.

WINDSOR, Berkshire.

Map Ref: SU9676

High above the winding
Thames and the Victorian and
Georgian architecture of
Windsor is the largest
inhabited castle in the world.
Royal families have made it
their home for the past 900

years, and though each has
added to the building's style,
much of the present-day
structure can be attributed to
George IV. He was responsible
for the massive Round Tower
which dominates Windsor's
skyline, and from which it is
possible to see 12 counties and
follow the meandering course of
the River Thames.

Much of the castle is open to
the public, including St
George's Chapel, the Round
Tower (with its pretty garden
below) and Queen Mary's Dolls'
House. Beautiful paintings and
exquisite porcelain are on show
in the state apartments.
Outside, a lovely tree-lined
avenue called the Long Walk
leads through Home Park (the
private gardens around the
castle), then out into Windsor
Great Park and up Snow Hill,
from where views of the castle
are breathtaking. Here the
Copper Horse, an equestrian
statue of George III, surveys the
scene. The Great Park itself
consists of some 4,800 acres of
beautiful woodland, open
parkland and formal gardens
laced with footpaths and roads.
At the southern end is Virginia
Water, a magnificent lake some
1½m long and formed on the
site of a large swamp by the
Duke of Cumberland in 1746.
Standing on the bank are
original Roman colonnades
brought from Leptis Magna in
1827, and a more modern

*Changing the guard at Windsor
Castle, royal stronghold and
home for nearly 1,000 years*

Totem Pole erected in 1958 to
commemorate the Centenary of
British Columbia.

Just a short drive from
Windsor is the famous Safari
Park, one of the first of its kind
in Britain. The open zoo
atmosphere there is made even
more exciting with drive-in
monkey and lion reserves.

WISLEY GARDENS, Surrey

*Open daily, RHS members only
Sun am; off A3. Map Ref:
TQ0659*

A day at Wisley is the best way
to enjoy every aspect of
gardening at its very finest, the
result of dedicated expert work
by the Royal Horticultural
Society.

Initial plantings began here
in 1878 on a 60-acre site, which
now covers some 250 acres with
formal, informal, ornamental
and wild layouts in
kaleidoscopic colour all the year
round. There are also
glasshouse displays, vegetable
gardens, orchards and a testing
ground for new and
experimental varieties of fruit
and vegetables – some of which
are available for visitors to buy.
There is always an expert on
hand to solve horticultural
problems, and a shop and plant
centre too.

**WOBURN ABBEY &
WILDLIFE KINGDOM,**
Bedfordshire

*Open daily in summer,
weekends in winter; on A50.
Map Ref: SP9433*

By looking carefully around the
parkland surrounding Woburn
Abbey it is possible to spot
herds of rare deer and other
exotic creatures which are the
inhabitants of the famous Wild
Animal Kingdom, which covers
some 3,000 acres and includes a
series of lakes.

The present abbey was
commissioned by John, the 4th
Duke of Woburn, in 1747 and is
built on the site of a 12th-
century monastery. It was
designed to retain as much as
possible of the ancient
ecclesiastical buildings, and the
elegant stately home that
resulted now houses works by
many famous artists, as well as
beautiful collections of
porcelain and silver. Splendid
rooms contain superb furniture
and other effects, while the
lavishly-decorated state
apartments, where monarchs
including Queen Victoria have
stayed, are on view.

WOODSTOCK, Oxfordshire
See Blenheim Palace

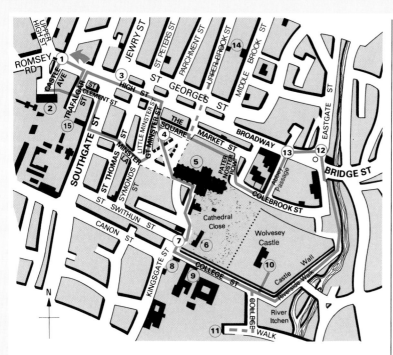

An ancient capital

For 200 years before the Norman Conquest the ancient cathedral city of Winchester was the true capital of England, a Saxon centre of government built on the site of the Roman town of *Venta Belgarum*.

1 WESTGATE
The Westgate, dating from the 12th to 14th centuries, is one of two surviving gates of the medieval city and stands on what is thought to be the site of the old Roman gate. It is now part of the City Museum.

2 GREAT HALL
The 13th-century Great Hall is all that survives of the Norman castle. It is a great aisled room with a timbered roof supported by eight columns of Purbeck marble. High on the west wall is the famous Round Table, a massive circle of oak measuring 18ft across and weighing 1¼ tons; it is known to be around 700 years old.

3 THE HIGH STREET
An attractive mixture of styles, from half-timbered Elizabethan to bow-fronted Regency, characterises the broad High Street.

4 CITY MUSEUM
Displayed on three floors of this fascinating museum are exhibits ranging from Roman mosaic pavements to medieval implements and objects relating to 19th-century life in the city.

5 CATHEDRAL
St Swithun, Bishop of Winchester in the 9th century and King Alfred's tutor, is the cathedral's patron saint. The site of his shrine, destroyed at the Reformation, can be seen in the retrochoir. The present cathedral, preceded by earlier minsters, dates from 1079, but the beautiful vaulted Gothic nave is 14th-century and is largely the work of Bishop William of Wykeham, who also founded Winchester College.

A particularly interesting memorial is that of deep-sea diver William Walker, which stands near the entrance to the Lady Chapel. When, early in this century, the east end of the cathedral was found to be sinking, he went down into the peat bog beneath the foundations and replaced the medieval timbers with concrete.

6 PILGRIMS' HALL
The Inner Close has many fine buildings, only one of which – the 14th-century Pilgrims' Hall, now part of the Pilgrims' School – is open to the public.

7 KINGSGATE
Above the 14th-century gate is the charming little church of St Swithun, reached by a stone staircase beside the archway.

8 JANE AUSTEN'S HOUSE
At the top of College St, on the right near Kingsgate, a plaque identifies the modest 18th-century house (not open) where Jane Austen died.

9 WINCHESTER COLLEGE
Founded in 1382 by William of Wykeham, the college is one of the country's leading public schools, and the earliest planned foundation. The chapel, hall and cloisters can usually be visited.

10 WOLVESEY CASTLE & BISHOP'S PALACE
Remains of the 12th-century castle of Bishop Henry de Bois survive from 'slighting' in the Civil War. Near by is the Bishop's Palace of 1684.

11 ST CROSS HOSPITAL *(detour)*
A one-mile detour from the main route leads along College Walk and across the watermeadows to the fine medieval almshouse of St Cross Hospital.

12 CITY MILL (NT)
A mill has stood on this site over the River Itchen since the 12th century. It is a delightful brick and tile building, built in the 18th century.

13 THE BROADWAY
The statue of King Alfred by Hamo Thornycroft, erected in 1901, dominates the eastern end of the High Street. Winchester was Alfred's capital and remained the first city in the kingdom until the Norman Conquest. The Guildhall, a large Victorian Gothic building, contains the city art gallery and Tourist Information Centre.

14 WINCHESTER HERITAGE CENTRE
Exhibition, including audio-visual displays, relating to the city's development.

15 SERLE'S HOUSE
This distinguished 18th-century mansion was the home of Colonel William Serle, who commanded the South Hampshire Militia. It is now a Regimental Museum.

EARLY CLOSING: *Thu*

MARKET DAYS: *Wed, Fri, Sat*

PARKING: *Chesil St, Friarsgate, Tower St, Upper Brook St*

OPENING TIMES:
Westgate: *open all year. Mon – Sat am and pm; Sun pm only; closed Mon, Oct – Mar*
Great Hall: *open as above*
City Museum: *open as above*
Winchester College: *open as above, but not closed winter Mons*
St Cross Hospital: *open all year except Sun*
Serle's House; *open all year, Mon – Fri*
Heritage Centre: *open all day Tue – Sun*
Wolvesey Castle: *open Apr – Sep, Mon – Sat all day, Sun pm only*

ROUTE DIRECTIONS
Start at Westgate (1) and go l. up Castle Ave to Great Hall (2). Walk down steps, l, to Trafalgar St, turn l. then shortly r. into High St (3). At City Cross go r. under archway to museum (4) and then bear l. to the cathedral (5). Walk through Inner Close (signed College and Water Meadow) past Pilgrims' Hall (6) to Kingsgate (7). Go through arch to College St past Jane Austen's House (8) and Winchester College (9). Shortly on the left is Wolvesey Castle (10). A detour to the right along College Walk leads through meadows to St Cross Hospital (11). Follow Riverside Walk and cross Bridge St for City Mill (12), emerge into Broadway (13) and turn l. past King Alfred statue to Abbey Passage l. by the Guildhall. Turn r. up Colebrook St and by Wessex Hotel take path through Cathedral Green to The Square. A detour can be made along Upper Brook St to the Heritage Centre (14). At end of Square, turn l. up Gt Minster St, then r. up Minster La to St Thomas St. Go up St Thomas Passage to Southgate St and Serle's House (15). Turn r. to St Clement St and l. for return to Trafalgar St.

Flamborough Head
Bridlington
Burton Agnes Hall
Great Driffield
Humanby
E
DS
Hornsea Pottery
Beverley
Burton Constable Hall
HULL
Withernsea
Barton-upon-Humber
Ulceby
Patrington
Immingham Dock
Spurn Head
Grimsby
Brigg
Cleethorpes
Caister
Market Rasen
LINCOLN WOLDS
Louth
Mablethorpe
Wragby
Alford
Horncastle
Spilsby
Skegness

Sleaford
Boston
The Wash
Swineshead
ntham
Holbeach
Holkham Hall
Hunstanton
Norfolk Lavender
Wells-next-the-Sea
Sheringham
Cromer
Great Bircham
Thursford Green
North Walsham
Blickling Hall
Sandringham
Fakenham
King's Lynn
Bourne
Spalding
Stamford
Burghley House
Wisbech
Norfolk Wildlife Park
Wroxham
Broadland Conservation Centre
Caister-on-Sea
Peterborough
March
Downham Market
Swaffam
East Dereham
NORWICH
Acle
Filby
Great Yarmouth
Wildfowl Trust
Watton
Wymondham
Pettifis Crafts & Falabella Gardens
Chatteris
Littleport
Brandon
Attleborough
Lowestoft
Oundle
Ely
Thetford
Diss
Bungay
Beccles
Thrapston
Huntingdon
Stretham
Soham
Halesworth
Southwold
Rushden
Godmanchester
Waterbeach
Eye
Saxmundham
St Neots
Anglesey Abbey
Newmarket
Stowmarket
Easton
Aldeburgh
Sandy
Cambridge
Bury St Edmunds
Woodbridge
Bedford
Shuttleworth Collection of Historic Aeroplanes & Cars
Imperial War Museum
Haverhill
Long Melford
Gainsborough Museum
IPSWICH
Orford Ness
Hollesley Bay
Ampthill
Royston
Saffron Walden
Sudbury
East Bergholt
Felixstowe
Letchworth
Audley End House
Stour Valley
Flatford Mill
Harwich
Hitchin
Baldock
Halstead
The Naze
Stevenage
Braintree
Colchester
Luton
Bishop's Stortford
Witham
Brightlingsea
Luton Hoo
St Lawrence
Ware
Harpenden
Hertford
West Mersea
Clacton-on-Sea
Berkhamsted
Hatfield House
Harlow
Colne Point
St Albans
Hoddesdon
Chelmsford
Maldon
Hemel Hempstead
Potters Bar
Gardens of the Rose
Epping Forest & Museum
Chigwell
Brentwood
Rettendon
Rayleigh
Foulness Island
Bekonscot Model Village
Romford
Basildon
Hadleigh
Watford
LONDON
Southend-on-Sea
Slough
Woolwich
Grays
Tilbury
Staines
Dartford
Gravesend
Sheerness
Isle of Sheppey
Margate
North Foreland
Thorpe Park
Orpington
Rochester
Gillingham
Herne Bay
Ramsgate
Chessington World of Adventure
Sittingbourne
Whitstable
Epsom
Croydon
Caterham
Faversham
Sandwich
Woking
Leatherhead
Godstone
Maidstone
Canterbury
Deal
Dorking
Box Hill
Reigate
Chartwell
Sevenoaks
Intelligence Corps Museum
Chilham Castle Gardens
Guildford
Shere
Gatwick
Hever Castle
Tonbridge
Ashford
Kent Battle of Britain Museum
Dover
Milford Ponds
East Grinstead
Biddenden
Crawley
Bluebell Railway
Tunbridge Wells
Lamberhurst
Port Lympne Zoo Park, Mansion & Gardens
Hythe
Folkestone
Horsham
Hayward Heath
Kent & East Sussex Railway
Tenterden
New Romney
Romney, Hythe and Dymchurch Railway
Billingshurst
Uckfield
Bodiam Castle
Rye
Chalk Pits Museum
Devil's Dyke
Hurstpierpoint
Bateman's
Battle
Winchelsea
Dungeness
Arundel
DOWNS
Hailsham
Herstmonceux Castle
Hastings
Lewes
Bexhill

121

TOUR 1 51 MILES

The White Peak of Derbyshire

As it winds through the south-eastern corner of the National Park this tour visits places of such diversity that it becomes an encapsulation of everything which is representative of the White Peak.

The drive starts in Matlock – the collective name for a loose gathering of individual settlements that were welded into a single spa resort in the 18th century.

From Matlock, follow signs Derby to leave the town by the A6, winding through a limestone gorge to the neighbouring spa village of Matlock Bath. The impressive Heights of Abraham can be ascended by cable car.

Continue along the A6 to Cromford, and in the village turn right on to the A5012, signed Newhaven. Cromford was where Arkwright built and operated the world's first water-powered cotton-spinning mill in 1771.

A short distance after leaving Cromford on the A5012 turn right for a long, winding climb through woodland on the Via Gellia valley road. After 4 miles reach crossroads and turn right on to the B5056, signed Bakewell. Continue across open countryside

Glorious greenery adorns the cliffsides on the long descent from Crich to the Derwent Valley in the White Peak District

for 1¾ miles, then turn right on to an unclassified road signed Winster. Descend steeply into Winster. Leave by the Bakewell Road, then ½ mile farther turn right and rejoin the B5056. Follow an undulating road for 2¾ miles, then cross a river bridge and turn right. Almost a mile farther on turn left on to the A6, signed Buxton, and shortly pass the car park for Haddon Hall. This magnificent medieval manor house of the Dukes of Rutland dates from the 12th to the 17th century.

Continue along the A6 to Bakewell. Bakewell is famous for the dessert sweet known as Bakewell Pudding, which can still be bought in the town.

Leave Bakewell by King Street, signed Monyash B5055. In almost ¾ mile turn left on to an unclassified road signed Youlgreave. At the next T-junction turn right and continue over higher ground for 1¾ miles before descending a 1-in-5 slope to cross the River Lathkill. Beyond the bridge take the next turning left to reach Youlgreave. At the church turn right (no sign), and in ¾ mile bear right signed Newhaven. After another ½ mile keep left, and in 2¾ miles pass on the left a turning into a picnic site. At the next T-junction turn right on to the A5012, then shortly turn left to join the A515, signed Ashbourne, and pass the Newhaven Hotel. After 6 miles at crossroads turn left on to an unclassified road signed Tissington. Drive through parkland to Tissington.

Return through the parkland, then turn left on to the A515 Ashbourne road and continue to Fenny Bentley. Continue past the village for ½ mile, then turn left on to the B5056, signed Bakewell. After 2¾ miles turn right on to an unclassified road signed Bradbourne. At the post office turn right signed Carsington, and follow a pleasant byroad – narrow in places – for about 1¾ miles, then turn left on to the B5035 Wirksworth road. After another 1¾ miles drive alongside the northern extremity of the new Carsington Reservoir. Stay on the B5035 for a further 1¼ miles, then turn right signed Wirksworth (unclassified; light traffic only) and descend to Wirksworth.

In the town centre turn left, then immediately right, with the B5035, signed Crich. Ascend on to higher ground, then follow a long descent into the Derwent Valley. At the foot of the descent turn right on to the A6, then cross the River Derwent and immediately go forward with the B3035 – still signed Crich. At the village cross turn left (unclassified) and follow signs to the Crich Tramway Museum. On 940ft Crich Stand is a tower with a light, raised as a memorial to the Sherwood Foresters. The tram museum is sited in an old limestone quarry.

Continue with the unclassified road to Holloway and turn right into Church Street, signed Riber. In ¾ mile go over crossroads into Riber Road. Follow this byroad for 1½ miles, meet a T-junction and turn left, then ¼ mile later keep left and pass on the right the turning to Riber Castle Wildlife Park. Descend steeply through hairpin bends, and at the foot of the slope turn right. Later turn left on to the A615 for Matlock.

TOUR 2 65 MILES

Evesham Vale & Shakespeare Country

The steep escarpment of the Cotswolds, with its stone-built houses, contrasts with the timber and thatch of the lush, fruit-growing Vale of Evesham on this tour. The route also gives a taste of Shakespeare's country along the Avon to Stratford, and allows for detours to Hidcote Gardens and Broadway Tower Country Park.

The drive starts from Stratford-upon-Avon, where Shakespeare was born and died.

Follow the Evesham road A439. After 7 miles reach Bideford-on-Avon. At the roundabout take the first exit on to the B4085, signed Broadway, and cross the 15th-century bridge. After ½ mile turn right for Cleeve Prior and South Littleton. One mile beyond South Littleton go over a level crossing, then take the first turning left on to an unclassified road (no sign) to reach Bretforton, where the B4035 is joined, and continue to Weston-sub-Edge.

At the Seagrave Arms turn right on to the B4632, signed Broadway. Pass through Willersley, and in 1¾ miles at the T-junction turn right on to the A44 into Broadway. Both Charles I and Cromwell used the 17th-century Lygon Arms.

By the Swan Hotel turn left on to an unclassified road, signed Snowshill. Ascend and later bear right into the secluded village of Snowshill. The Tudor manor has a lovely terraced garden.

Turn left at the church, then at the top go forward over the crossroads, signed Chipping Campden and Broadway Tower (care required). After 1¼ miles turn left, signposted Broadway, to Broadway Tower Country Park. At over 1,000ft the views from the 18th-century tower are magnificent.

After ½ mile cross the main road, signed Saintbury, passing Fish Hill Picnic Area,

In the heart of Shakespeare Country, in the secluded village of Snowshill, is the Tudor Snowshill Manor and its terraced garden

and after ¾ mile turn right, signed Chipping Campden. Continue for 1½ miles and at the crossroads turn right for Chipping Campden. A former centre of the wool industry, the town has an impressive 15th-century 'wool' church and a fine Jacobean Market Hall standing in the centre of the High Street.

Leave the town by Sheep Street B4081, signed Broad Campden, and after ¼ mile turn left on to an unclassified road for Broad Campden. In the village turn right then shortly right again and climb to Blockley. Turn left then shortly right on to the B4479, signed Moreton-in-Marsh. After 1½ miles at the T-junction turn left on to the A44 to pass through Bourton-on-the-Hill and later reach Moreton-in-Marsh. Follow the Oxford road A44 for 1¾ miles. After ¾ mile turn right on to an unclassified road for Chastleton. Half a mile on turn left and cross a cattle grid, then at the end turn right on to the A44. Beyond the Cross Hands public house turn left on to an unclassified road, signed Rollright. Two miles ahead on the right lie the Bronze Age Rollright Stones.

Turn left ½ mile past the Stones on to the A35, signed Stratford, and descend, via Long Compton, to Shipston-on-Stour. Turn left on to the Campden road B4035, and after 1¾ miles cross the main road. In 1½ miles keep forward on to an unclassified road via Charingworth to the pretty village of Ebrington. At the end of the main street bear right and then right again, signed The Hidcotes, keep forward for 2 miles then turn right for Hidcote Manor Gardens. Cultivated by an American and now owned by the National Trust, Hidcote is a series of small gardens, each given over to a theme or a kind of flower.

Return to the T-junction, turn left and then take the next turning on the right, signed Mickleton. At the main road turn right and immediately right again on to the B4636, signed Stratford, to enter Mickleton. At the end of the village bear left. After another 5½ miles reach the village of Clifton Chambers. Cross the River Stour and later turn left on to the A34 for the return to Stratford-upon-Avon.

AEROSPACE MUSEUM,
Cosford, Shropshire

*Open all year; off A41/A464.
Map Ref: SJ7905*

Memories of the last war are preserved in the RAF Aerospace Museum at Cosford, where over 50 aircraft exhibits include a Lincoln bomber, a Mosquito and a Beaufighter. In another hangar is a fine collection of rockets, including the notorious V1 'Doodlebug' and the V2 – Hitler's last vain effort to break the will of the British people. More up-to-date is a replica of the 'Moon buggy' used on the American space flights of the 1970s. Perhaps Cosford's most prized possession is one of the few remaining examples of Britain's great 'white elephant' aircraft – the TSR-2 – which was cancelled after millions of pounds had been spent and many man-hours expended in its development. Regular air shows are held at Cosford, and there is a picnic site and a good souvenir shop at this midland branch of the RAF Museum, Hendon.

ALTHORP HALL,
Northamptonshire

Open daily but may be closed without notice; on A428. Map Ref: SP6865

This charming Elizabethan mansion, extensively re-modelled by Henry Holland in the late 18th century, became a major visitor attraction when a daughter of the house – Lady Diana Spencer – became the Princess of Wales. It is still the home of the Spencer family, but liable to be closed to the public at short notice when the family is at home. It is also slightly difficult for access to the very young, old or disabled, and attracts large crowds. However, Althorp's collection of fine furniture, pictures and china is one of the best in England.

ALTON TOWERS,
Staffordshire

Open early spring to late autumn; off B5032. Map Ref: SK0742

Best known as Europe's premier leisure park, Alton Towers was originally the fairy-tale mock-Gothic home of the 15th Earl of Shrewsbury. If the dizzying rides of the 'Corkscrew', the 'Black Hole' and the 'Log Flume' are not for you, there's plenty more to see and enjoy in the 600-acre gardens. The hillsides above the beautiful Churnet Valley are resplendent with thousands of varieties of trees and flowering shrubs collected by the Shrewsburys – and in spring and early summer there are magnificent displays of rhododendrons and azaleas. The gentle hillside paths open up ever-changing views of fountains and other garden ornamentation, like the famous Pagoda, the Chinese Temple and the spectacular Rock Gardens.

ANGLESEY ABBEY (NT),
Cambridgeshire

Open spring to autumn; on B1102. Map Ref: TL5362

Anglesey Abbey, six miles from Cambridge on the B1102, was originally a 13th-century Augustinian monastery, but was extensively re-constructed around 1600 to create the present charming house, which incorporates the monastic undercroft. Some 100 acres of lovely gardens laid out earlier this century attract the most admiration, and a visitor centre explains how they were laid out and developed over the years by Lord Fairhaven. The tea room by the car park provides delicious home-made cakes and cream teas.

AVONCROFT MUSEUM OF BUILDINGS, Stoke Heath, Hereford & Worcester

Open spring to autumn; off A38. Map Ref: SO9468

Historic buildings that have been saved from destruction and lovingly restored are grouped together on this superb site. Long-forgotten standards of craftsmanship have been employed in the re-erection of the working windmill, the barns and granary, and the nail and chain-making workshop from the Black Country. Even older are the 15th- and 16th-century timber-framed houses – and the plodding shire horse and cart completes the picture of an older, slower pace of life.

BADDESLEY CLINTON (NT), Warwickshire
See Packwood House (NT)

BELVOIR CASTLE,
Leicestershire

Open early spring to autumn; between A52 & A607. Map Ref: SK8233

Palatial home of the Duke of Rutland, Belvoir (pronounced 'Beever') commands a ridge-top position overlooking the rich farmlands of the Vale of Belvoir, scene of new coal-mining operations. Apart from the fine-art collections and armour inside the house, a notable feature of Belvoir's many attractions are regular special events – including medieval jousting tournaments, mock battles and car rallies – which take place on Sundays throughout the season, at no extra charge.

BEWDLEY, Hereford & Worcester

Map Ref: SO7875

This attractive, Severn-side town, with its soaring bridge built by Thomas Telford in 1795, is a marvellous centre for a number of interesting attractions. Not least among them is the famous Severn Valley Railway, much seen on TV and in film clips, and one of Britain's finest restored steam lines. It follows the course of the winding Severn between Bridgnorth and Kidderminster, and the unique *frisson* of steam trains and station buildings as

they were in their hey-day adds magic to the sylvan riverside scenery. The Bewdley Museum at The Shambles, Load Street, often offers demonstrations of the traditional crafts of the area, including charcoal-burning from the nearby Wyre Forest, basket-making and coopering (barrel-making). The Lax Lane Craft Centre is a good place to learn the skills of brass-rubbing. Just outside the town on the Kidderminster road is the West Midland Safari and Leisure Park, a 200-acre wildlife refuge for giraffes, elephants, lions and other exotic beasts, which seem quite at home in the lush Worcestershire countryside. The park may be toured on the 'Rio Grande' railway.

BIRMINGHAM, West Midlands

Map Ref: SP0686

A birthplace of the Industrial Revolution, Birmingham's motorway links, modern airport and National Exhibition Centre assure the nation's second city of a bright future. The city has cherished its past, including a canal network which exceeds that of Venice, and in the Museum of Science and Industry is the oldest working steam engine in the world (1779). This regularly chugs away, and a full-size locomotive is moved a few yards back and forth with appropriate sound effects. Old-fashioned craftsmanship is celebrated in the engineering hall, while a World War II Hurricane and Spitfire are highlights in the aircraft section. More steam engines, rolling stock and carriages are to be seen in working order at the Birmingham Railway Museum, Warwick Road, Tyseley. The City Museum and Art Gallery is just the place for a rainy day in Brum, containing an outstanding collection of Pre-Raphaelite paintings and many others from just about every period of world history. Sarehole Mill, in Cole Bank Road at Hall Green, is an 18th-century water mill that has been beautifully restored to full working order.

BLICKLING HALL (NT), Norfolk

Open spring to autumn; off B1354. Map Ref: TG1728

Blickling is a lovely, orange-red brick mansion that dates from the 17th century and is set in beautiful gardens which are worth a visit in themselves. Inside, the superb Jacobean plasterwork ceiling in the gallery is a memorable highlight, but there are also fine collections of furniture, pictures and tapestries. It is probably the grounds, with their notable early 19th-century Orangery, which will remain in the memory.

Some pleasant surprises await those who think of Birmingham only as a brash, modern city — including the old canals, which exceed even the Venice network

BOLSOVER CASTLE (EH), Derbyshire

Open daily; on A632. Map Ref: SK4770

Standing high on a hilltop in the less fashionable part of Derbyshire, ringed by coal-mines, Bolsover Castle is a Norman stronghold that was extensively re-modelled and enlarged in the early 17th century. It houses fine fireplaces and ornate panelling, and an associated range of buildings includes a 170ft-long Riding School and Gallery.

BOSCOBEL HOUSE (EH), Shropshire

Open daily; off A5. Map Ref: SJ8308

Priest's holes are a common feature of many older country houses, but Boscobel positively bristles with them. Their most famous occupant was not a priest, but a king, for it was here that King Charles II came after his defeat in 1651 at the Battle of Worcester. When the chase got too hot, he is supposed to have fled into an oak tree to escape his pursuers. The original oak was gradually destroyed by souvenir hunters, but another still there is supposed to have been grown from one of its acorns. There is also a lovely box-hedged herb garden to be enjoyed.

BOSWORTH BATTLEFIELD VISITOR CENTRE & COUNTRY PARK, Sutton Cheney, Leicestershire

Open daily; off A441 on unclassified road 2m S Market Bosworth. Map Ref: SK4000

Here the course of English history was changed, when Plantagenet gave way to Tudor in the final battle of the Wars of the Roses. The Battle of Bosworth Field, which was fought on 22 August 1485, is brilliantly interpreted in the Visitor Centre housed in a former farm-house. There are dioramas, an exhibition hall, a film theatre and a good souvenir and bookshop – all of which tell the fascinating story of how Richard III lost his crown, and England gained a new dynasty. Outside, the course of the battle can be followed by carefully signed walks through the lush Leicestershire countryside. Regular battle re-enactments and other spectacular events are held in summer.

A colourful corner of a historic town – the Nutshell Pub in Bury St Edmunds

BROADLAND CONSERVATION CENTRE, Ranworth, Norfolk

Open spring to autumn; 3m N off A47. Map Ref: TG3514

Approached by a gentle nature trail through native woodland bursting with wildlife, this centre is an ideal introduction to the fascinating natural history of the Broads. It is a unique, floating building, thatched with traditional Norfolk reeds (the best thatching material and much sought-after today). Moored on Ranworth's Inner Broad, the centre is run by the Broads Authority and makes an ideal viewpoint for bird-watchers who do not relish the thought of hours spent in a draughty hide. It also tells the fascinating history of the Broads, which are now recognised as flooded medieval peat-diggings, not natural waterways.

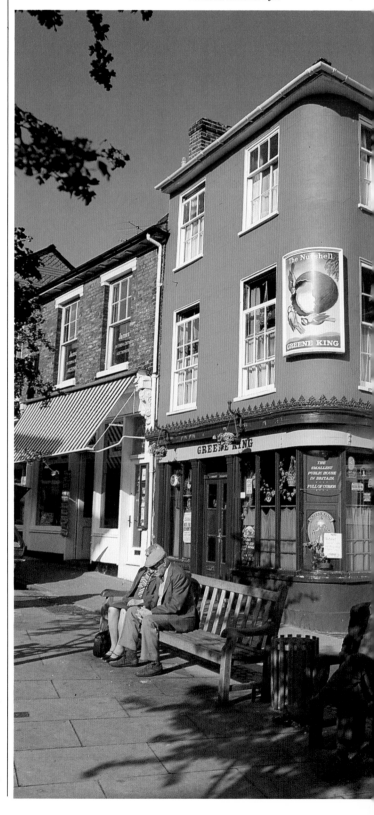

BROADWAY, Hereford & Worcester

Map Ref: SP0937

Broadway, once known as 'the Painted Lady of the Cotswolds', is almost entirely composed of fine houses and cottages in golden Cotswold limestone, which seems to reflect the rays of the sun. The Lygon Arms is a 16th-century coaching inn, and one of the most famous Cotswold hostelries. The more

energetic might wish to make the gentle climb to the commanding viewpoint of Broadway Tower for an outstanding view across the Vale of Evesham towards Worcester.

BUNGAY, Suffolk

Map Ref: TM3389

The Otter Trust – founded by naturalist Philip Wayre at Earsham, near Bungay – is an outstanding example of conservation in action. This 23-acre reserve on the banks of the River Waveney not only houses the world's largest collection of otters, but runs an active programme of breeding them safely in captivity and releasing them back into the wild to restore the dwindling native population. Other attractions include beautiful riverside walks and picnic areas, and three large lakes with a fascinating collection of wildfowl.

BURGHLEY HOUSE, Cambridgeshire

Open spring to autumn; off A1 1m SE Stamford (Lincolnshire). Map Ref: TF0406

Famous for the horse trials which take place each September, Burghley House also lays claim to be England's greatest Elizabethan mansion. The house was begun by Sir William Cecil – later Lord Burghley, Lord High Treasurer and chief advisor to Queen Elizabeth I – in 1552, and preserves the most spectacular double-hammer-beamed Great Hall of that earliest building. Also, Burghley houses the largest private collection of Italian Old Masters in the country, and the painted ceiling of Verrio's Heaven Room is a masterpiece of perspective.

BURTON UPON TRENT, Staffordshire

Map Ref: SK2423

The history of beer making in Britain is traced in the Bass Museum of Brewing History, which is housed in the company's joiner's shop of 1866, and describes the evolution of the industry from its small beginnings to today's multi-million pound concerns. Brewers were largely responsible for keeping the nation's native stock of shire horses going, when they became unpopular with farmers due to the advent of the tractor, and here at Burton, these great animals can still be seen.

BURY ST EDMUNDS, Suffolk

Map Ref: TL8564

Named after Edmund – last king of the East Angles, who was killed by the Danes in 869 and later martyred – this town retains its 11th-century street plan and has some fine Georgian houses. Pride of place must go to the ruined remains of the abbey, which now form the focal point of a country park. It was here that the barons swore on the high altar that they would force King John to accept the conditions of *Magna Carta.* Angel Corner (NT), a lovingly restored Queen Anne house on Angel Hill, contains one of the largest collections of clocks and watches in Britain, some dating from the 16th century. Moyse's Hall, in the Butter Market, is one of the oldest houses in East Anglia. Dating from about 1180, it now houses an interesting museum of Suffolk local history, archaeology and natural history. Military memorabilia can be seen in the Suffolk Regiment Museum, The Keep, Gibraltar Barracks, Out Risbygate.

BUTTERLEY, Derbyshire
See Midland Railway Centre

CAISTER-ON-SEA, Norfolk

Map Ref: TG5212

Thoughts of the earliest days of motoring are prompted by the Caister Castle Motor Museum, which has one of the finest automobilia collections in the country. The 15th-century castle also includes a 98ft tower and a substantial moat, reflecting the military importance of the coastal town – now a popular resort – since Roman times. Remains of the Roman town walls and a gateway can also be seen.

CAMBRIDGE, Cambridgeshire

Map Ref: TL4458

There are few more relaxing ways of spending a quiet summer's afternoon than sitting by the waters of the Cam in Cambridge's famous 'Backs' – lovely waterside lawns and meadows, literally at the backs of the city's great colleges, which somehow seem to have escaped the traffic scourge which bedevils Oxford. A peaceful stroll along waterways, and in and out of the venerable quadrangles of the colleges, is the best way to appreciate the town's unique tranquillity. Don't miss the

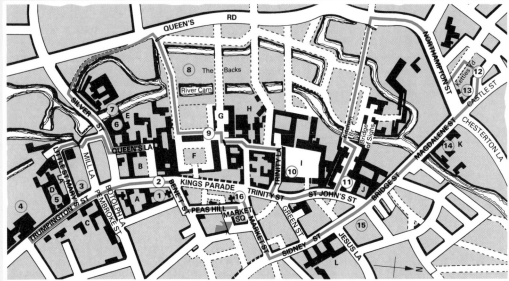

Cambridge cloisters & courts

An unforgettable sight of Cambridge is the view of The Backs, the river, and the magnificent Gothic chapel of King's College. The University was established in the 13th century and became one of the most celebrated centres of learning in Europe.

1 ST BENE'T'S CHURCH
The oldest building in Cambridgeshire, St Bene't's is believed to have been built about 1025.

2 KING'S PARADE
Once the main street of Cambridge, the Parade retains on the east side a number of interesting 18th- and 19th-century buildings, mostly converted into shops.

3 TRUMPINGTON STREET
Beyond St Botolph's, King's Parade becomes Trumpington Street. At the junction with Pembroke Street, notice the wide gutter – part of a 17th-century scheme designed to clean the city ditch. The chapel of Pembroke College, near by, was designed by Wren.

4 FITZWILLIAM MUSEUM
Egyptian, Greek, and Roman antiquities are among the many exhibits gathered together in this magnificent 19th-century building.

5 LITTLE ST MARY'S CHURCH
The original church on this site was dedicated to St Peter, and gave its name to Peterhouse College, which it served as a chapel.

6 QUEENS' COLLEGE
Queens' College was founded by two queens, Margaret of Anjou, wife of

Henry VI, and Elizabeth, wife of Edward IV.

7 THE MATHEMATICAL BRIDGE
This bridge was built for Queens' in 1749 on geometric principles, without the use of nails. When dismantled in 1867, it proved impossible to reassemble without bolts.

8 THE BACKS
The land was once a common, on which the townspeople pastured their animals.

9 KING'S COLLEGE CHAPEL
One of the finest Gothic churches in England, the chapel was built in three stages, from 1446 to 1515. To this last phase belongs the magnificent fan-vaulted ceiling.

10 TRINITY COLLEGE
The largest of all Cambridge's colleges, Trinity was created by Henry VIII from three medieval establishments.

11 ST JOHN'S COLLEGE
St John's has a magnificent three-storey gatehouse. The famous 'Bridge of Sighs', modelled on its more famous namesake in Venice, was built in 1831.

12 KETTLE'S YARD ART GALLERY
This collection was given to the university in 1960.

13 THE FOLK MUSEUM
Exhibits of local craft and industry.

14 MAGDALENE COLLEGE
The showpiece of Magdalene is the Samuel Pepys Library.

15 CHURCH OF THE HOLY SEPULCHRE
Only four round churches remain in England, and nearly all, like this one, had connections with the Crusades.

16 GREAT ST MARY'S
A fine example of the Perpendicular style, with slender, soaring columns supporting a vaulted roof with massive, carved bosses.

MARKET DAYS: *Mon-Sat*

PARKING: *Park St (off Bridge St), Pembroke St, Lyon Yard*

OPENING TIMES:
Fitzwilliam Museum:
open all year except Good Fri, Christmas & New Year. Tue-Sat all day, Sun pm only
Kettle's Yard Art Gallery: open all year except Christmas & New Year, pm only
Folk Museum: open all year except Bank Hols. Mon-Sat all day, Sun pm only
The Colleges: Most of the colleges admit visitors during the daylight hours, though not all their buildings are open to the public. In term-time, especially during examinations, opening hours may be restricted

ROUTE DIRECTIONS
Start in the market square and walk to r. of the Guildhall into Peas Hill, then turn r. into Bene't St, passing St Bene't's Church (1), and l. into King's Parade (2). Walk past Corpus Christi College, and

St Catharine's, opposite, and continue past St Botolph's Church into Trumpington St (3) for the Fitzwilliam Museum (4), next door to which is Peterhouse. Walk back to Little St Mary's La and turn l. to pass Little St Mary's Church (5). Continue up the lane to Granta Pl, and turn r. to reach Laundress La. At the end cross Silver St and turn r. then l. into Queens' La which leads to Queens' College (6). Return to Silver St and turn r. to cross the River Cam with the Mathematical Bridge (7) on the r. Take the path r, keeping r. at the fork, to cross The Backs (8) to Queens' Rd. Turn r. and r. again through the back gate of King's College, recrossing the river and turning l. to reach the chapel (9). On leaving, turn r. around the west end of the chapel and go through the gate, passing Clare College on l. Keep on, past the Old Schools, Senate House Passage and Trinity Hall down Trinity La and turn l. at the end down Trinity St. Pass Trinity College (10) and keep on into St John's St, turning l. through the gate of St John's College (11). Walk through to Third Court and go through the arch on the l. to cross the river by the Kitchen Bridge. Keep forward, passing New Court of St John's College to the gateway leading on to Queens' Rd. Turn r, then keep r. into Northampton St and cross into Kettle's Yd for the Art Gallery (12). Walk down the steps and turn r. for the Folk Museum (13). Cross to Magdalene St for Magdalene College (14) and the round church (15) and keep on into Sidney St, past Sidney Sussex College. Cross over, turn r. into Market St for Gt St Mary's Church (16) and the return to the Market Sq.

soaring fan vaulting of King's College Chapel, or the superb 'mathematical' bridge of Queen's College, or St John's with its copy of the Bridge of Sighs in Venice. Just outside the city on the A45 at Madingley is a restored post mill, and a little farther, the American Cemetery. Gardeners should not miss Unwins Seeds trial grounds at Histon.

CANNOCK CHASE, Staffordshire

Main access from A34/A513. Map Ref: SJ9917

Cannock Chase is 26 square miles of heathland, forest and delightful woodland glades just a stone's throw from the teeming cities of the West Midlands and Black Country. Although dark, regimented Forestry Commission conifers overshadow much of the land today, examples of the original oak and birch woodland can still be found in places like Brocton Coppice – an ideal place for a picnic. A short walk to Seven Springs – near the summit of this area of outstanding natural beauty – is well worth the effort. The Forestry Commission Information Centre is an excellent introduction to the fascinating wildlife of the area – notably the deer – and the German Military Cemetery commemorates the dead of two World Wars.

Outstanding views of the Peak District's countryside from the Black Rocks picnic site in Cromford – the town where Richard Arkwright set up the first water-powered cotton mill

CHATSWORTH HOUSE, Derbyshire
See under The North

COSFORD, Shropshire
See Aerospace Museum

COVENTRY, West Midlands

Map Ref: SP3379

Older visitors will for ever associate the ancient cathedral city of Coventry with the fearsome blitz of 1940, but it has risen from the ashes like the phoenix which it adopted as its symbol to become a leader in world-wide reconciliation and peace. The shell of the medieval cathedral of St Michael, with its soaring spire, has been retained as a quiet enclave in which to rest and contemplate the famous charred cross made from timbers of the burned-down roof. The modern cathedral, designed by Sir Basil Spence, still has its local critics but is gradually attaining the atmosphere of its predecessor through a fine collection of modern art. Of particular note are Sutherland's altar tapestry and Piper's Baptistry window. St Mary's Hall and the Golden Cross Inn are reminders of what was lost in that *blitzkrieg*, and Lady Godiva – Coventry's most famous daughter – still rides proudly on her plinth in Broadgate.

The city is inextricably linked with the motor industry, and the Museum of British Road Transport in St Agnes Lane and Hales Street illustrates the contribution that both Coventry and the Midlands in general have made to the development of transport since the 19th century.

CROMFORD, Derbyshire

Map Ref: SK2956

But for its isolation on the edge of the Peak District, Cromford might well have become a cradle of the Industrial Revolution to rival Birmingham or Manchester, for it was here in 1771 that Richard Arkwright first successfully harnessed the furious waters of the River Derwent to power his cotton mill – now being carefully restored by the Arkwright Society. Arkwright was also a model employer, providing his workforce with solid, gritstone cottages and a planned township round a spacious market square. Near by is Cromford Wharf, the restored terminus of the Cromford Canal, where visitors can step back in time for a leisurely horse-drawn boat trip through beautiful surroundings.

DOVEDALE, Derbyshire & Staffordshire

Map Ref: SK15

If you are feeling fit, you should cross the famous Stepping Stones and take the glorious, three-mile walk up the Derbyshire side to truly appreciate the dale's glories. Recently restored to give a sound, dry footing for its entire length, the path is easily managed by the average pedestrian. A succession of spectacular limestone buttresses with such evocative names as Dovedale Castle, Tissington Spires, the Lion Rock and Pickering Tor, spring from the lush woodland which clothes the sides of the dale.

DRAYTON MANOR PARK & ZOO, Tamworth, Staffordshire

Open spring to autumn; on A4091. Map Ref: SK1901

A good place to visit mid-week when the weekend crowds are absent, this family leisure park near Tamworth covers 160 acres and has a comprehensive zoo offering the chance to see exotic wildlife at close quarters. Dinosaurland reminds visitors of the monsters of the past, and the more adventurous (especially children) can enjoy the thrills of over 25 rides, including a Looping Roller Coaster, Log Flume, Paratower and Cable Cars.

DUDLEY, West Midlands

Map Ref: SO9490

The Black Country is black no more, but a new-found pride in its tremendous industrial heritage is evident at the open-air Black Country Museum, in Tipton Road, Dudley. Here, visitors can ride a tram back in time through displays reflecting the famous crafts and skills of the area. Among them are a chain-maker's house and an old-fashioned pub beside a canal boat wharf where narrowboat trips leave to chug through man-made tunnels in the limestone beneath Dudley Castle Hill. Regular demonstrations show how the chains were made, and how Brierley Hill crystal is produced.

DUXFORD AIRFIELD, Duxford, Cambridgeshire
See Imperial War Museum, under The South

EAST BERGHOLT, Suffolk
See Flatford Mill

EASTON, Suffolk

Map Ref: TM2858

Older visitors who recall days when chestnut-coated Suffolk Punches drew wagons and carts through the hayfields of East Anglia can relive those times at the Easton Farm Park, near Wickham Market, where there is a fascinating collection of rare farm-animal breeds. Visitors can also watch cows being milked, and see how that milk was treated in a Victorian dairy.

A priceless collection of stained glass dating back to the 14th century is one of the attractions to be found at Ely Cathedral – itself adorned with beautiful medieval panels

ELVASTON CASTLE COUNTRY PARK, Derbyshire

Open daily; off B5010. Map Ref: SK4032

Elvaston Castle is picturesquely situated in 200 acres of landscaped parkland, on the outskirts of Derby, comprising formal gardens, a walled Old English garden – where the scents of long-forgotten 'unfashionable' cottage flowers can be enjoyed – and exquisite topiary. Events are held in the grounds throughout the year, and informative exhibitions include displays by the Derbyshire Wildlife Trust, which has its headquarters here. The working estate museum recreates the lifestyle and craft skills associated with a country-house estate at the turn of the century.

ELY, Cambridgeshire

Map Ref: TL5380

Among the many glories of the Early English Ely Cathedral are its panels of stained glass, and a special museum shows how medieval craftsmen achieved such breathtaking results. Examples of glass from the 14th century to the present day are displayed in specially back-lit panels, and models depict how the windows were – and still are – designed and made. The museum was founded to rescue and preserve these priceless examples from redundant buildings.

FILBY, Norfolk

Map Ref: TG4613

Thrigby Hall Wildlife Gardens are just the place to unwind, either by viewing the collection of spectacular Asian animals or just enjoying the beautiful grounds. Mammals, reptiles and birds are displayed in the tropical houses, an ornamental lake is stocked with a wide range of waterfowl, and a yew tree walk provides welcome shade on hot, summer days. There is also an audio-visual theatre.

FLATFORD MILL (NT), East Bergholt, Suffolk

Off A12. Map Ref: TM0634

Constable's famous paintings come to life in this sleepy little

backwater off the A12, where the National Trust has preserved some of the best-known scenes in British fine art. The mill itself, on the River Stour, is now a field-studies centre where young people from all over Britain come to learn about the abundant local wildlife. Near by is the equally well-known Willy Lott's Cottage, hardly changed from the day that John Constable – a mill-owner's son from nearby East Bergholt – painted it and brought world-wide attention to the villages of Dedham Vale. The 14th-century parish church of East Bergholt has a unique, timber-framed belfry that stands away from the church itself, and is surrounded by mellow cottages of Elizabethan date.

GAINSBOROUGH MUSEUM, Sudbury, Suffolk

Open daily. Map Ref: TL8741

Thomas Gainsborough is one of Britain's best-loved artists, renowned both for his landscapes and for portraits. It is little wonder, then, that the ancient market town of Sudbury is so proud of the man who was born there in 1727 and remained until the age of 14, when he went to London to study.

Gainsborough's home in Sepulchre Street – since renamed Gainsborough Street – now houses a museum furnished in 18th-century style and containing a number of works by him and his contemporaries.

GREAT BIRCHAM, Norfolk

Map Ref: TF7632

Bircham Mill sits in broad acres of Norfolk countryside like a picture from a children's nursery rhyme. It is a tower windmill, built in 1846 and in continuous use for milling flour until the 1930s, when machine-powered mills took over. It is five floors high and commands fine views across the flat countryside. A small bakehouse museum shows what happened to the milled flour after it left the mill.

GREAT WITCHINGHAM, Norfolk
See Norfolk Wildlife Park

GREAT YARMOUTH, Norfolk

Map Ref: TG5207

An opportunity for a quiet breather away from the bright lights and 'Kiss me Quick' hats of bustling Great Yarmouth – premier visitor attraction on the Norfolk coast – is offered by the Tropical Butterfly Farm, on Marine Parade. Here, free-flying butterflies from every corner of the world flutter past and settle on your shoulders as you wander through glass-covered tropical gardens.

GUILSBOROUGH GRANGE WILDLIFE PARK, Northamptonshire

Open daily; 6m from junction 18 on M1. Map Ref: SP6773

Guilsborough Grange Wildlife Park is a marvellous stopping-off place when the roar of motorway traffic gets too much. More than 400 animals and 70 species of birds are kept there, in beautiful grounds surrounding a 19th-century country house. Special birds of prey displays are a feature, and the adventure play area and pets' corner are favourites with children.

HADDON HALL, Bakewell, Derbyshire
See under The North

HEREFORD, Hereford & Worcester

Map Ref: SO5139

This ancient city in the heart of cider country has a squat, pink-sandstone cathedral with a central tower that dates from the 14th century and overlooks lush farmland by the lovely River Wye. Of Norman foundation, the great church is dedicated to St Mary and St Ethelbert – a martyred King of East Anglia – and contains probably the best library of chained books in the country. Also of interest is the 14th-century Mappa Mundi, one of the earliest maps of the world.

The Museum of Cider, in Pomona Place, is an award-winning centre which shows cider-making through the ages. The ancient skills and machinery are shown in a reconstructed farm cider house and working 'French' cider-brandy distillery. There is also a cooper demonstrating barrel making.

HOCKLEY HEATH, Warwickshire
See Packwood House (NT)

HOLKHAM HALL, Norfolk

Open late spring to late summer;
1½m W of Wells-next-the-Sea, off
A149. Map Ref: TF8943

Holkham Hall could be said to
be the birthplace of the
Agrarian Revolution, for it was
the home of reformer Thomas
Coke (1752–1842), who – with
'Turnip' Townshend of
Raynham – campaigned for
agricultural improvement and
showed the rest of the world
just how to do it during the
18th century. Holkham itself is
a fine, Palladian-style country
house that is the home of the
Earls of Leicester and a
treasure house of art. The
Holkham Bygones collection
gives a flavour of life 'below
stairs' at the Big House.
Included are many Victorian
domestic items, a laundry,
harness room, shoe shop and
brewery. Craft displays take
place regularly, and steam
traction engines can be seen in
the grounds on summer
weekends.

IPSWICH, Suffolk

Map Ref: TM1644

Ipswich is the largest town in
Suffolk and has many
reminders of its eventful past,
including the Ancient or
'Sparrowe's' House of 1567, in
the Buttermarket. This is a fine
example of the ancient East
Anglian craft of pargeting, or
patterned plasterwork, and the
interior – now a bookshop –
shows original oak panelling
and heavy carved beams. Just
outside the town off the A45 at
Claydon is the Rosarium, a
unique garden devoted almost
entirely to roses. Most are of
the old-fashioned, heavily
scented varieties. More than
400 varieties, many very rare,
are on show.

IRONBRIDGE GORGE
MUSEUM, Shropshire

Open all year; off A442. Map
Ref: SJ6703

Named after the incredibly
delicate and graceful structure
of the world's finest iron bridge,
this fascinating township clings
to the sides of the Severn Gorge
and was where the Industrial
Revolution burst into fiery life
when Abraham Darby perfected
the technique of smelting iron
by burning coke instead of
charcoal. There is so much to
see in the extensive Ironbridge
Gorge Museum – which has set
new standards in industrial
archaeological interpretation –
that a day is not really enough.
There are some steep hills to
climb too, but the effort is well

worthwhile. Among the
highlights are the Blists Hill
Open Air Museum – a 42-acre
woodland site above the town,
where a carefully re-constructed
Victorian village shows how
people lived and worked in the
1890s. Gas-lit streets, a print
shop, offices and a
reconstructed toll house give a
real feel of the past, and there
are regular open days when
demonstrations and displays
take place.

The Coalbrookdale Museum
and Blast Furnace in
Ironbridge shows how Darby
made his breakthrough and has
an exciting audio-visual
display. Just as interesting are
the Coalport China Museum,
partly housed inside a Potteries
bottle kiln, and the Jackfield
Tile Museum – with a fine
display of these famous
products, which still adorn
many a fireplace. The best idea,
however, is to start at the
Severn Warehouse Museum
and Visitor Centre, just
upstream from the bridge,

The structure which gave its
name to Ironbridge, Shropshire:
the world's finest iron bridge
was built over the Severn in
1779

where you can plan the rest of
your visit to suit yourself.

KENILWORTH, Warwickshire

Map Ref: SP2872

Sandstone Kenilworth Castle
(EH) is one of the most
romantic ruins in Britain,
standing proudly above its
ancient town and flat
watermeadows which were once
flooded to create the Great
Mere to protect it from attack
from the west. The keep,
standing four-square at the
centre, was built between
1155-70, and the Great Hall –
now open to the Warwickshire
sky – was added by John of
Gaunt in the 14th century.
Here, Good Queen Bess was
lavishly entertained by the Earl
of Leicester, and his name is
perpetuated in the restored
Lord Leicester's Buildings.
There is easy access to all parts
of the castle.

Not far away down the
winding Warwickshire lanes is
Stoneleigh Abbey, originally a
Cistercian foundation and later
the family home of the Leighs –
among the first of the landed
gentry to open up their home to
the public.

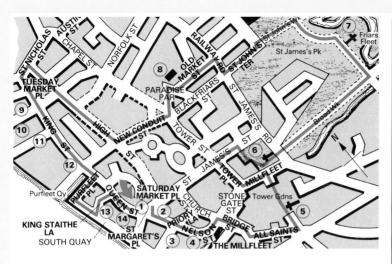

The Great Ouse port

Known locally simply as Lynn, the town of King's Lynn is historically a market produce centre which, over the years, has developed into an important port and industrial hub on the banks of the Great Ouse.

1 GUILDHALL
Although one complex, the Guildhall comprises four different parts built at differing times and in differing styles. The oldest is the original Guildhall of the Holy Trinity, which dates from 1421. It houses the Lynn Heritage Centre and a magnificent collection of civic regalia.

2 ST MARGARET'S CHURCH
The 12th-century towers of this lovely church form a prominent landmark. The interior was drastically remodelled in 1746, and further alterations were made in 1875. However, numerous internal features remain, including two superb 14th-century brasses.

3 ST MARGARET'S LANE
A glance to the right at the junction of this street with Priory Lane will reveal the Georgian façade of St Margaret's House. Next door is the Hanseatic Warehouse, built in the great days of Baltic trading during the 15th century. Ahead and to the right is the red-painted Hampton Court, a timber-framed merchant's house with origins dating from the 12th century.

4 NELSON STREET
Many 17th- and 18th-century buildings can be seen in this street. The traceried doorway of No. 9 is particularly interesting, and No. 15 is a fine two-and-a-half-storey Georgian house with a pedimented doorway and Tuscan columns.

8 LYNN MUSEUM
Formerly a chapel, this building now houses a wide range of local exhibits. Of special interest is a collection of pilgrims' badges from medieval times.

The stone which built the old King's Lynn custom house was shipped along the River Great Ouse in the late 17th century

5 ALL SAINTS' CHURCH
Mostly of 14th-century date, this church retains traces of a little Norman chapel that stood on the south side, and near by are well-preserved remains of an anchorite's cell.

6 THE GARDENS OF GREYFRIARS TOWER
Here is found the town's war memorial, under the shadow of a 14th-century octagonal tower which survives from a monastery which once covered a considerable area here.

7 RED MOUNT CHAPEL
A relic of the Virgin Mary was said to have been kept here, and the chapel was certainly a stopping place for early pilgrims on their way to Walsingham. The building was begun in 1485, and is an octagon of red brick, each side having an angled buttress.

9 THE CORN HALL
Ionic columns, a statue of Ceres – goddess of corn sheaves – and the town's coat of arms all decorate this exuberant structure.

10 GUILDHALL OF ST GEORGE
Constructed in the 15th century, this is the oldest and largest medieval guildhall in England.

11 MUSEUM OF SOCIAL HISTORY
The collections here give an insight into many local crafts and customs, and include an excellent toy collection.

12 THE CUSTOM HOUSE
Standing proudly alone by the quay, this was built in 1683 from stone shipped direct to the site along the navigations which contributed so much to Lynn's prosperity.

13 CLIFTON HOUSE
The earliest parts of this merchant's house date from the 12th century.

14 THORESBY COLLEGE
Originally this college was founded in 1500 for Trinity Guild priests. Its fine hammerbeam roof was restored in the 1960s.

EARLY CLOSING: *Wed*

MARKET DAY: *Tue, Fri & Sat*

PARKING: *Albert St, Baker La, King St, Queen St, Tuesday Market Pl*

OPENING TIMES:
Guildhall of St George: open all year Mon-Sat
Lynn Museum: *open all year Mon-Sat*
Museum of Social History: *open all year Tue-Sat*

ROUTE DIRECTIONS
Start at Saturday Market Pl and at the Guildhall of the Holy Trinity (1). Cross over into St Margaret's Place where St Margaret's Church (2) is on the l. Pass St Margaret's La (3), cross over Priory La and into Nelson St (4). Turn r. into Bridge St, along to All Saints' St, then turn l. along a path with All Saints' Church (5) on the r. At the end of the path under the arch turn l, then go across Millfleet and turn r. into Tower Pl. From here, turn r. into St James's St then turn r. again into the gardens of Greyfriars Tower (6). Leave by the steps, to reach Broad Walk. At an old archway turn l. into The Walks for Red Mount Chapel (7). Beyond the tennis-courts turn l. into St John's Ter. Turn r. at the traffic-lights into Railway Rd. Turn l. into Old Market St, to Lynn Museum (8). From here, walk along Paradise and turn r. into New Conduit St. Beyond the shopping precinct, turn r. into the High St and on to Tuesday Market Pl, in which is the Corn Hall (9). Enter King St with, on the r, the Fermoy Art Gallery contained in the Guildhall of St George (10). Farther along, at No 27, is the Museum of Social History (11). Pass the Custom House (12). Turn r. into Purfleet Pl, then l. beside the River Great Ouse, and then l. again into King Staithe La. Turn r. into Queen St. Here along on the r. is Clifton House (13). Continue until reaching Burkitt Court and Thoresby College (14). Return to Saturday Market Pl.

LEOMINSTER, Hereford & Worcester

Map Ref: SO4959

A leisurely stroll around this tightly packed jumble of delightful black-and-white half-timbered buildings is a step back into the Middle Ages – but without the stink and squalor. There is a surprise round every corner, and a sudden transition into another age when you find Georgian-style Broad Street. Just off Broad Street is the grey-stone priory church, said to be founded by Earl Leofric, husband of Coventry's Godiva. A ducking stool, used to punish nagging wives in the early 19th century, is preserved inside the three-naved church.

LICHFIELD, Staffordshire

Map Ref: SK1109

Lichfield Cathedral's triple spires are such a landmark locally that they are known as 'the Ladies of the Vale'. The cathedral itself is much restored, but contains some wonderful treasures – including the illuminated 7th-century manuscript of the St Chad Gospels, and a fine memorial sculpture by Chantrey. Try counting the statues on the magnificent west front, from Cathedral close; there are said to be no fewer than 113! In the Market Square (Breadmarket Street) of this busy little market town is the birthplace of the great lexicographer Dr Samuel Johnson, now a museum of his life and times. The Lichfield Heritage Exhibition and Treasury is a short step across the square, in the ancient Guild Chapel of St Mary's, where displays show the history of the city with clever use of audio-visual material.

LINCOLN, Lincolnshire

Map Ref: SK9771

Known as *Lindum Colonia* to the Romans, Lincoln bristles with history from its magnificent hill-top, triple-towered cathedral to what is thought to be the oldest inhabited dwelling in England – the 800-year-old Aaron the Jew's House, in The Strait. Astonishingly, modern traffic passes through Newport Arch, the only surviving Roman gateway still spanning an English street. But it is the majestic cathedral, standing on its 200ft limestone ridge, which overshadows the city. It was largely built in the Early English style in the 12th and 14th centuries, and now houses in its library the best surviving copy of *Magna Carta* and several very rare first editions.

The Close, near by, is also known as Minster Yard and contains a wonderful collection of old buildings, including a 13th-century tithe barn and the ancient Bishop's Palace. The

'The Ladies of the Vale' – as locals call the triple spires of Lichfield Cathedral – dominate the horizon in this view from West Gate

Norman castle, founded by William the Conqueror in 1068, provides a fine aerial view of the superb west front of the cathedral. One word of warning: despite the fact that Lincoln overlooks much low-lying country, be prepared to climb some quite steep hills as you explore this fascinating city.

LODE, Cambridgeshire
See Anglesey Abbey

LONG MELFORD, Suffolk

Map Ref: TL8646

Suffolk is full of lovely villages – such as Cavendish, Kersey and Lavenham – but perhaps the most stately is Long Melford. Its impressive main street is lined with splendid old buildings, and dominated by both a magnificent church – founded on medieval wealth won from wool – and a superb Elizabethan manor house. Melford Hall (NT) includes an original panelled banqueting hall little changed since it was built in 1578, a Regency library and a Victorian bedroom. A special Beatrix Potter display brings back memories of childhood bedtime stories.

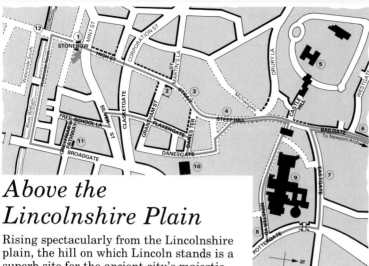

Above the Lincolnshire Plain

Rising spectacularly from the Lincolnshire plain, the hill on which Lincoln stands is a superb site for the ancient city's majestic, triple-towered cathedral – the third largest in the country. Around it wind narrow medieval streets with some of England's oldest houses.

1 THE STONEBOW AND GUILDHALL
This historic city gate stands on the site of the Roman and medieval south gates. The present gateway, with the Guildhall above, dates from the late 15th or early 16th century.

2 THE CARDINAL'S HAT
This fine 15th-century timbered house, once an inn, is thought to have been named after Cardinal Wolsey, who was Bishop of Lincoln in 1514-15.

3 THE STRAIT
The 'feel' of the medieval city begins in this narrow, cobbled street of quaint little shops as the walk approaches the part of Lincoln known as 'above hill'. No. 14 has a rounded gable decorated with a figure of the Lincoln Imp, while next to it is one of Lincoln's two Norman houses, the Jew's House.

4 STEEP HILL
This precipitous cobbled street was once the scene of a foolhardy exploit by a local MP, who drove a four-in-hand down it to win a bet.

5 LINCOLN CASTLE
Begun in 1068, Lincoln Castle has been repaired and added to in subsequent centuries, but the basic plan remains unchanged. The low tower in the north-east corner of the bailey, called Cobb Hall, was the castle dungeon. From its roof it is possible to walk along the battlements overlooking the medieval city to the 19th-century Observatory Tower. The top can be reached by a steep spiral staircase, and offers a most spectacular view of the city, the cathedral and the Lincolnshire plain beyond. On the south side of the bailey, steep steps lead to the Lucy Tower, or keep. Like the Observatory Tower, it stands on a motte or mound, making Lincoln one of only two Norman castles in England with two mounds.

6 BAILGATE AND THE NEWPORT ARCH
This unspoilt, village-like street of appealing old shop-fronts, inns and cottages leads to the Newport Arch – the only Roman gateway in the country that is still open to traffic.

7 EASTGATE
In the forecourt of the modern Eastgate Hotel are displayed the excavated remains of part of the east gateway of *Lindum Colonia*.

8 MINSTER YARD
In medieval times the cathedral and clergy houses stood in a walled, fortified precinct. Pottergate and the Exchequer Gate are among the 14th-century gates that still stand, whereas Priory Gate, where the walk enters the precinct, is a 19th-century replacement. The Old Bishops' Palace, the Precentory and the Chancery are among many interesting buildings in Minster Yard.

9 CATHEDRAL
No visitor to Lincoln can fail to be aware of the magnificent cathedral. Soaring majestically above the city on its hilltop site, its three towers dominate distant views of Lincoln from every direction. The beautiful Norman west front, where visitors enter the cathedral, dates in part from the 11th century. The Norman carvings of figures and animals on the west front are matched, at the opposite end of the cathedral, by the later craftsmanship of the Angel Choir. To the north-east of the cathedral lie the cloisters and the chapter house. Part of the medieval library survives, and here can be seen one of only four surviving original copies of *Magna Carta*.

10 USHER GALLERY
Opened in 1927, Lincoln's art gallery was financed by James Ward Usher, a local jeweller and keen collector who died in 1925. Paintings of many periods are displayed, and one room is devoted to memorabilia of Lincolnshire poet Alfred, Lord Tennyson.

11 CITY AND COUNTY MUSEUM
Situated behind the domed, early 20th-century library building, the museum is housed in part of a former Franciscan friary. Visitors may see both the fine vaulted undercroft and the upper storey, which has a magnificent barrel roof, not to mention a good collection of local archaeological and natural history finds.

12 HIGH BRIDGE
This stone bridge has spanned the River Witham here since Norman times, and the original vaulting can still be seen underneath.

EARLY CLOSING: *Wed*

MARKET DAY: *Fri & Sat*

PARKING: *St Rumbold's St, Saltergate, Flaxengate*

OPENING TIMES:
Lincoln Castle: open Mon-Sat all day, Sun pm only
Usher Gallery: open as above
City and County Museum: opens as above

ROUTE DIRECTIONS
Start at the Stonebow (1) and walk up the High St. At the top, pass the Cardinal's Hat (2) and bear r. into the Strait (3). Continue up Steep Hill (4). At the top, the castle (5) lies to the l. whilst straight on is Bailgate (6), with the Newport Arch at its far end. Return from the arch and turn left into Eastgate (7). At the end, turn r. through the Priory Gate and then follow Minster Yard (8) round to the r. Follow the path round the cloisters and the chapter house. Go through the Exchequer Gate, then turn l. to retrace your steps down Steep Hill. Bear l. into Danesgate, then, opposite the Usher Gallery (10), turn r. into Danes Terrace and l. into Flaxengate. Follow it down to the end, crossing Grantham St and Clasketgate, then turn l. and r. to cross Silver St into Free School La. Turn l. beyond the library into Greyfriars Pathway, passing the City and County Museum (11) on the l. Then turn r. into Broadgate and r. again by the Green Dragon Inn along Waterside North with the High Bridge (12) spanning the river in front. At the end turn r. into High St to return to the Stonebow.

Lincoln's aptly named Steep Hill leads up from the city's modern shopping centre to the 11th-century castle and three-towered majestic cathedral, which is seen for miles around

A Marcher stronghold

Set in the beautiful and unspoilt countryside of the Welsh Marches, Ludlow is a delightful blend of ancient border stronghold, medieval planned town and present-day country market centre. It amply justifies its reputation as one of the best county towns in England.

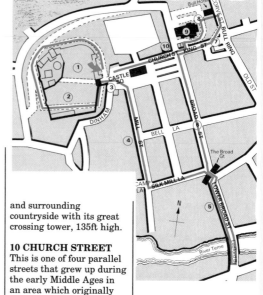

1 LUDLOW CASTLE
On two sides of the 900-year-old castle – now a dramatic ruin – the land falls steeply away to the rivers Teme and Corve. Breathtaking views may be enjoyed from the top of the keep. Perhaps the chief architectural treasure is the ruined Norman round chapel in the inner bailey – one of only five remaining in the country. The internationally famous Ludlow Festival always includes a Shakespeare play staged in the grounds of the castle.

2 CASTLE GARDENS AND DINHAM
Bright flower beds and a tree-lined promenade stand between the castle and Dinham, a winding medieval street named after a 7th-century settlement on the site. Dinham House, an elegant early 18th-century building, was briefly the home of Lucien Bonaparte, captured brother of Napoleon. It is now a craft centre.

3 CASTLE SQUARE
This was once the western end of the medieval high street. On the south side of the square is its oldest building, Castle Lodge, a 14th-century stone house with an overhanging first storey that was added later.

4 MILL STREET
Mill Street is a typical example of the straight streets that formed part of Ludlow's original 'grid-iron' arrangement, and much later lent itself perfectly to the elegant architecture of the Georgian era. At its foot is the site of Mill Gate, one of seven gates in the medieval town walls.

5 LOWER BROAD STREET
Perhaps Ludlow's first 'suburb', this street below the Broad Gate is lined with modest cottages that once housed workers in the cloth and glove-making industries.

6 BROAD STREET
Claimed by some to be Britain's most attractive street, Broad Street, like Mill Street, owes its beauty largely to medieval street planners and Georgian builders. An added delight, at the top of the street, is a range of timber-framed houses with projecting upper storeys supported by slender columns on the pavement.

7 BULL RING
This area is so called because bulls used to be stockaded here before sales. Its namesake, the Bull Ring Tavern, is an impressive black-and-white building, whilst at the northern end is the 15th-century Feathers Hotel, one of the most famous timber-framed buildings in the country.

8 CHURCHYARD AND COLLEGE STREET
The pleasant grassy area that surrounds the church is now a peaceful backwater and 'garden of rest'. An inscription on the north wall of the church records the burial nearby of the ashes of A E Housman (1859–1936), the *Shropshire Lad* poet.

9 CHURCH OF ST LAURENCE
Largest and stateliest of Shropshire parish churches, the mainly 15th-century St Laurence's is tucked away from Ludlow's main streets, yet still dominates the whole town and surrounding countryside with its great crossing tower, 135ft high.

10 CHURCH STREET
This is one of four parallel streets that grew up during the early Middle Ages in an area which originally formed one wide high street, or market place. At one end stands the classical stone Butter Cross, built in 1746. The first floor was once a school and is now Ludlow Museum.

EARLY CLOSING: *Thu*

MARKET DAY: *Mon*

PARKING: *Castle Sq, Castle St, Corve St, Station Dr*

OPENING TIMES:
Castle: *open daily Feb-Nov.*
Craft Centre, Dinham House: *open daily except Christmas*
Museum: *open Easter-end Sep, Mon-Sat. Also open Sun in June, July and Aug*

ROUTE DIRECTIONS
From Castle Sq walk west towards the castle (1), then turn r. down the path that leads round the castle's perimeter. Bear l. where the path forks to return through a walled-off section of the castle bailey, and then go through Castle Gardens (2), bordering Dinham, to Castle Sq (3). Turn r. beyond Castle Lodge and go down Mill St (4). Turn l. at the bottom into Silk Mill La and r. at the end, through the Broad Gate, along Lower Broad St (5) to Ludford Bridge. Retrace your steps through the gate and go up Broad St (6). At the top turn r. into King St, then l. into Bull Ring (7). Turn l. through the coaching yard of the Bull Hotel, go up the steps and through the passage into the churchyard (8). Turn l. to follow the path round the south side of the church (9), then turn l. and r. into Church St (10) and return to Castle Sq.

Ludlow's imposing castle, once the seat of the Lords President of the Marches, sits between the Rivers Teme and Corve

LUDLOW, Shropshire

Map Ref: SO5174

Ludlow is one of England's most perfect medieval towns, planned round the massive presence of Montgomery's red sandstone castle, which dominates the town. It was one of the nation's most important fortifications in its hey-day, and king-pin in the line of 'Marcher' strongholds which guarded the troubled Welsh border. The rest of Ludlow is an architectural feast, with particularly good examples of Shropshire 'magpie' black-and-white half-timbering – especially the 17th-century Feathers Hotel. Other periods are well represented by the gorgeous Georgian Butter Cross, and Broad Street. There's a good local museum too, also in Butter Cross.

MALVERN HILLS, Hereford & Worcester

Off A449. Map Ref: SO7641

This shapely mini-mountain range rises abruptly from the Vale of the Severn and provides an invigorating tramp of six or seven miles. From the summit of the 1,395ft Worcestershire Beacon are views which extend over much of Central England, taking in parts of 14 counties on a clear day. At the southern end of the ridge is the 1,114ft Herefordshire Beacon, crowned by a spectacular Iron Age hill

fort known locally as the British Camp. This can be easily climbed from the pub of the same name, in a col which slices through the range.

MARKET BOSWORTH, Leicester
See Bosworth Battlefield Visitor Centre and Country Park

MATLOCK BATH, Derbyshire

Map Ref: SK2958

Superb views for those with a head for heights can be enjoyed from the Heights of Abraham Cable Car, which spans the River Derwent gorge at Matlock Bath. The cars are safely enclosed, and don't be afraid when they stop mid-trip – it's just to allow other travellers to get in and out at either end! There's a splendid Alpine-style restaurant at the summit terminus, and a short step away is the Great Masson Cavern – where the history of lead mining in these limestone hills is interpreted in a lively way.

Down below in the Pavilion on the main street is more lead-mining history, in the Peak District Mining Museum. Opposite and up a steep road is Gulliver's Kingdom Theme Park, where more than 60 rides and attractions include a Wild West Street, complete with Fort Buffalo at one end.

High on the hillside beyond the awesome, 300ft wall of rock known as High Tor, is the 19th-century shell of Riber Castle, a landmark for miles around.

Built by the same John Smedley who founded Matlock's fame as a Victorian spa, it now houses a Fauna Reserve and Rare Breeds Farm, specialising in rarer European species such as the lynx.

MIDLAND RAILWAY CENTRE, Butterley, Derbyshire

Trains run early spring to early winter; off A610. Map Ref: SK4051

Midland Railway Centre – at Butterley, near Ripley – operates a regular steam train service the three miles to Ironville and provides an industrial history of the Golden Days of the former Midland Railway. Exhibits range from 1866 steam locomotives to 1960s diesels, and rolling stock spanning a period of 100 years.

MUCH WENLOCK, Shropshire

Map Ref: SO6199

Much Wenlock is a charming market town with many lovely half-timbered buildings, and a good centre for exploring A E Housman's Shropshire. Wenlock Edge (NT), subject of one of the poet's best-loved works, provides fine viewpoints of the Shropshire Hills from convenient lay-bys. Back in the town, Wenlock Priory (EH) is the ruined but still impressive remains of a 13th-century Cluniac house, with beautiful interlocking sculptured stonework.

Half-timbered buildings lining the streets of Much Wenlock add to the charm of this Shropshire market town

NAPTON-ON-THE-HILL,
Napton, Warwickshire

Map Ref: SP4661

The unique little museum known as the Napton Nickelodeon of Mechanical Music brings back the nostalgia and atmosphere associated with these machines. Tucked away in a corner of the High Street, it includes a Hurdy Gurdy Man, a Wurlitzer Photo-Player, and a Compton Cinema Organ – which is still used to accompany silent movies in an authentic replica of a 1930s picture house.

NATIONAL TRAMWAY
MUSEUM, Crich, Derbyshire
See under The North

NEWARK-ON-TRENT,
Nottinghamshire

Map Ref: SK7953

Reflected in the still waters of the River Trent, the ruins of Newark Castle have overseen the story of this delightful, mainly Georgian town for over 700 years. It was here that King John died in 1216 from a surfeit of food and drink after losing his treasure in the waters of the Wash. Five miles north of Newark on the busy A1 is the Vina Cooke Museum of Dolls and Bygone Childhood at The Old Rectory, in a charming 17th-century house at Cromwell.

NORFOLK LAVENDER,
North Lavenden, Norfolk

Open daily except Easter weekends; on A149. Map Ref: TF6737

Lavender is said to be an old-fashioned scent these days, but for many it remains the essence of traditional English cottage gardens. A visit to Norfolk Lavender at Caley Mill fills the senses with that subtle, tangy aroma, for it is the home of the largest growers and distillers of this aromatic oil in Britain. Between mid-July and mid-August, the floral harvest is in full swing – a never-to-be-forgotten experience – and the distillery can also be visited. At other times of the year visitors can enjoy an informative slide show, and delightful herb and rose gardens. Lavender products and other herbs are on sale in the shop, and there's a cottage tea room.

NORFOLK WILDLIFE
PARK, Great Witchingham, Norfolk

Open daily; 12m NW of Norwich on A1067. Map Ref: TG1020

This 40-acre wildlife park, founded in 1961 by the well-known naturalist Philip Wayre, is one of the best kinds of zoos. It breeds many more threatened animals than it takes from the

The art of an ancient tradition, seen in one of the White Peak area's famous well-dressings at Bakewell

wild, and wherever possible returns them to build up native populations. It is also the home of the Pheasant Trust, started in 1959 to encourage the captive breeding of rare species of wild pheasants.

NORTH LAVENDEN, Norfolk
See Norfolk Lavender

NORWICH, Norfolk

Map Ref: TG2208

Norwich, with its elegant Norman cathedral overlooking the River Wensum, has good claims to the title 'Capital of East Anglia'. Famous for its mustard, printing and insurance today, in medieval times its wealth was wool and this part of England was among the most populous and prosperous.

There are many fascinating glimpses of Norwich's ancient past in the busy streets, and many quiet corners – like the

tastefully restored, colour-washed buildings and cobbled streets around Elm Hill. Norwich Castle, originally a Norman foundation, was extensively remodelled in the 19th century. Today the Keep contains collections of art, archaeology, and natural history. There are more than 30 medieval churches to admire in the city, and museums ranging from the medieval merchant's house of Strangers' Hall in St Andrew's Street, to the Bridewell Museum off Bedford Street, which features local crafts.

NOTTINGHAM,
Nottinghamshire

Map Ref: SK5740

One of the great English cities, Nottingham will forever be associated with the legend of Robin Hood, whose statue still draws its bow beneath the castle walls. Founded by William the Conqueror shortly after his invasion, the castle was extensively reconstructed by the Duke of Newcastle in 1651, and converted into a mansion house. Today, it houses the city's museum and art gallery.

Also beneath the castle walls is the Trip to Jerusalem, said to be the oldest public house in the country. The Lace Centre, in Castle Road, houses a superb collection of the famous Nottingham lace in a 15th-century half-timbered building. Lace making is demonstrated on certain days. The Canal Museum, appropriately in Canal Street, tells the story of navigation on the Trent and local canals through the years.

**PACKWOOD HOUSE (NT), &
BADDESLEY CLINTON
(NT),** Hockley Heath,
Warwickshire

Both open spring to autumn; on unclassified road off A34. Map Ref: SP1772

Packwood is famous for its 'Sermon on the Mount' topiary garden, and the neatly clipped yews are certainly a sight to see. Note also the 30 'boles' or niches in the red-brick wall which encloses the garden; they were constructed to accommodate bee hives in the 17th century. The house itself is a timber-framed building of about 1560, but the structure is disappointingly concealed behind cement rendering and creepers. All is not as it seems inside either, for the 'Great Hall' was created earlier this century out of a cruck-framed barn.

A visit to Packwood can easily be combined with one to the nearby Baddesley Clinton, another National Trust property, and one of the best-preserved moated manor houses in the Midlands, dating back to 1300.

**PEAKIRK WILDFOWL
TRUST,** Peterborough,
Cambridgeshire
See Wildfowl Trusts

PEAK NATIONAL PARK,
Derbyshire, Staffordshire,
Cheshire

Around A57. Map Ref: SK0887

With about 17 million visits annually, the Peak is the country's most popular National Park, and most of the visitors come from the cities which encircle it. There are many recreational opportunities, and plenty of easy walks in the limestone dales or along the converted routes of the defunct Tissington, High Peak or Manifold Railways.

Perhaps the best-known attraction during the summer months is the ancient tradition of well-dressing. Intricate floral icons are constructed over village wells or springs, particularly in the White Peak area, to give thanks for the gift of water. They only stand in position for a week, but attract thousands of tourists who admire this age-old craft which is thought to have pagan origins.

PETERBOROUGH,
Cambridgeshire
See Wildfowl Trusts

**PETTITTS CRAFTS &
FALABELLA GARDENS,**
Reedham, Norfolk

Open spring to autumn; off B1140. Map Ref: TG4201

Pettitts Crafts and Falabella Gardens at Reedham, near Great Yarmouth, is particularly suited for elderly or disabled visitors, as there are no difficult steps to negotiate. Peacocks and ornamental pheasants strut around the lovely grounds, and displays of birds of prey and parrots can be seen in special areas.

RANWORTH, Norfolk
See Broadland Conservation Centre

REEDHAM, Norfolk
See Pettitts Crafts & Falabella Gardens

SANDRINGHAM, Norfolk

Open spring-late summer; off A149. Map Ref: TF6928

Open to the public when the distinguished residents are not at home, this house contains a fabulous collection of paintings of the Royal Family from 1845. It was bought by Queen Victoria for the Prince of Wales in 1862, and stands in a 7,000-acre estate, including a 300-acre country park.

SHALLOWFORD, Staffordshire

Map Ref: SJ8729

Anglers from all over the world make the pilgrimage to this cottage home of the 'Father' of their sport, in the tiny Staffordshire village of Shallowford. He was, of course, Izaac Walton – co-author with Charles Cotton of *The Compleat Angler* in the 17th century. Within easy distance of his beloved Dove, Walton's cottage has been restored and houses a small museum in his memory. The period garden is an ideal place to 'stand and stare'.

SHERWOOD FOREST VISITOR CENTRE AND COUNTRY PARK, Nottinghamshire

On B6005 & other roads. Map Ref: SK6267

Childhood memories of Robin Hood and his Merrie Men are brought to life in this superb visitor centre, at the heart of the best-preserved part of the medieval hunting forest which was traditionally his home and refuge. The centre – and the woodland trails which go out from it – are particularly well-suited for handicapped and disabled people, and there is even a nature trail for the visually handicapped.

Truth is, there were probably many Robin Hoods in various parts of the country, but Hollywood and the film-makers have ensured that Sherwood – which once extended to over 100,000 acres around Nottingham – is the favourite location.

SHIFNAL, Shropshire
See Boscobel House

SHREWSBURY, Shropshire

Map Ref: SJ4912

Shrewsbury, magnificently situated on a sweeping loop of the Severn, is an under-rated town which suffers from being by-passed by cars or trains en route to North Wales. This is a pity, because it has superb black-and-white half-timbered houses and narrow, winding streets which invite exploration.

Ruins of a Norman castle, much altered by Thomas Telford, were incorporated into a private house 200 years ago. It now contains the Shropshire Regimental Museum. Rowley's Mansion houses a museum of local history and art, and don't miss the lovely 14th-century complex of cottages, shops and a fine old hall in the area known as Bear Steps.

SPALDING, Lincolnshire

Map Ref: TF2422

A spectacular Flower Festival held here every May attracts visitors from all over Britain, but is best avoided by those who do not like crowds. Better to visit the 25 acres of lawns and gardens containing over a million bulbs at Springfield Gardens, on the eastern side of this River Welland town. Here, the show is continued into summer with the beautiful Summer Rose Garden, where more than 80 species of rose can be seen to their best advantage. Local history museums can be visited at Ayscoughfee Hall, and in Broad Street (by appointment).

STOKE BRUERNE, Northamptonshire
See Waterways Museum

STOKE HEATH, Hereford & Worcester
See Avoncroft Museum of Buildings

STOKESAY CASTLE, Shropshire

Open early spring to autumn; off A49. Map Ref: SO4381

Dating back to the 13th century, Stokesay is the country's oldest surviving fortified manor house, a little gem of medieval England which has miraculously escaped the march of time. It is, however, quite difficult of access – not being designed to cope with large numbers of visitors – so care must be taken on the tour of the house.

STOWMARKET MUSEUM OF EAST ANGLIAN LIFE, Suffolk

Open spring to autumn; off A45. Map Ref: TM0458

A typical 'Sleepy Suffolk' town with many good Georgian and Victorian houses grouped attractively round the market square, Stowmarket has the excellent Museum of East Anglian Life – an open-air site by the River Gipping where lively and interesting displays of Victorian, gypsy, farming and rural industrial life recreate local history. Craftsmen demonstrate the old-time skills of wood-working and wheelwrighting, and regular video shows cover other crafts. A working Suffolk Punch horse is resident, and its successor – a steam-powered traction engine – can also be seen.

STRATFORD-UPON-AVON, Warwickshire

Map Ref: SP2054

Shakespeare's home town is best avoided during the summer months, when it is thronged with tourists from all over the world on their pilgrimage to the birthplace of the bard. However, off-season visits reward visitors with glimpses of the old Warwickshire market town that Shakespeare himself might still recognise. Peace can be found, even in high summer, in the delightful Avon-side gardens around the Royal Shakespeare Memorial Theatre, an ugly red-brick building where some of the finest actors in the world have graced the stage.

The birthplace in Henley Street is a must for first-time visitors, but there is also the site of New Place – where the playwright returned to live on his retirement; Hall's Croft, home of his daughter and son-in-law; and Anne Hathaway's Cottage, home of his wife, in the nearby suburb of Shottery. The poet's grave can be seen in the lovely Holy Trinity Church, where he was also baptised.

The World of Shakespeare, near the Theatre, is a unique multi-media production which harks back to the days of Good Queen Bess. Those with interests in the more recent past will certainly enjoy the Stratford Motor Museum.

SUDBURY HALL (NT), Derbyshire

Open spring to autumn; off A50. Map Ref: SK1632

Sudbury Hall (NT) is a fine, red-brick 17th-century country mansion with exquisite plasterwork ceilings, excellent carving by Grinling Gibbons and murals by Laguerre. A special feature of interest to the children (or grandchildren) is the Museum of Childhood, a wonderful evocation of the world of a Victorian child, complete with toys, a schoolroom and dress of the period.

Many older visitors will recall with affection (or dread!) the hard wooden forms and cast-iron-legged desks of the schoolroom – with their slates and inkwells – in front of the blackboard and the teacher's high desk.

Traction engines at Stowmarket: one of the displays at the Museum of East Anglian Life

SULGRAVE MANOR,
Northamptonshire

Open all year except Jan; off B4525. Map Ref: SP5545

Sulgrave Manor is the Queen Anne ancestral home of the forebears of the first President of the United States of America, George Washington, and therefore attracts many transatlantic visitors. The first house on the site was built between 1539 and 1610 by Laurence Washington, whose tomb can be seen in the adjacent 14th-century village church.

There are many reminders and relics of the first Washingtons in the house, including George's black velvet coat, his saddle-bags and a fragment of his wife's wedding dress. Carved above the porch entrance is a representation of the original American flag, with only three stars and two stripes.

SUTTON CHENEY,
Leicestershire
See Bosworth Battlefield Visitor Centre & Country Park

SYMONDS YAT, Hereford & Worcester

Map Ref: SO5516

One of the country's most spectacular beauty spots, Symonds Yat is easily accessible and gives a bird's-eye view of the sweeping, tree-lined River Wye from a vantage point of nearly 500ft above its glittering surface at Yat Rock. If you come at the right time, you will also be able to see some of Britain's most exciting birds of prey – peregrine falcons, which regularly nest on the limestone cliffs. The Royal Society for the Protection of Birds sets up telescopes so that visitors can watch them swooping and diving above the river.

The Jubilee Maze and Museum of Mazes is not the place to go if you easily get lost! It is a fascinating place though, and traces the history of this strange desire to go round in ever-decreasing circles! Near by is the Herefordshire Rural Heritage Museum, where one of the country's largest collections of historic farm machinery is set in a delightful woodland location. The Symonds Yat Bird Park and World of Butterflies are just off the A40 at Whitchurch.

TAMWORTH, Staffordshire
See Drayton Manor Park & Zoo

THURSFORD GREEN, Norfolk

Map Ref: TF9734

If the strains of the mighty Wurlitzer cinema organ, barrel organs and the hiss of the showman's engine excite memories of the happy days of childhood, then a visit to the Thursford Collection – near Fakenham – is for you. This wonderful repository of fairground bygones stages live musical presentations every day, and midsummer musical evenings on that Wurlitzer organ are given every Tuesday by some of the country's leading organists. In addition to all the fun of the fair, there are ploughing engines, a miniature steam railway, and a children's playground.

UPTON HOUSE (NT), Warwickshire

Open spring to autumn; on A422. Map Ref: SP3645

Superb views across to the Cotswolds and the Vale of the Red Horse can be obtained from the grounds of this impressive, 17th-century country house. Inside are fine collections of porcelain, paintings, tapestries and furniture. Near by is the equally interesting Farnborough House, with its famous landscaped terrace and huge, spreading yew tree.

WARWICK, Warwickshire

Map Ref: SP2865

The towers, walls and turrets of Warwick Castle overlook Shakespeare's Avon in a composition that is the epitome of the English medieval fortress. Its undoubted attraction and popularity make it perhaps a place to be avoided at the height of the summer season, when it forms part of the 'Shakespeare Country' itinerary for many tourists, but at other times of the year it regains its peace. The medieval exterior hides a largely 17th-century interior, and among its fine collections are excellent examples of armour.

The rest of the town is just as interesting, but pride of place could be claimed by the delightful half-timbered building of Lord Leycester's Hospital, in the High Street. Built in 1383, this is still a home of rest for ex-servicemen and their wives.

Within the Church of St Mary, with its great tower, is the richly decorated, 15th-century Beauchamp Chapel. Elizabeth Oken's House contains a Doll Museum, and the 17th-century St John's House doubles as a craft and costume museum, alongside the Museum of the Royal Warwickshire Regiment. The County Museum is in the Old Market Hall.

WATERWAYS MUSEUM,
Stoke Bruerne,
Northamptonshire

Open daily; off A508. Map Ref: SP7449

Formerly a corn mill alongside the Grand Union Canal, this Waterways Museum gives a fascinating insight into what life was really like 'on the cut', as the canals were known. Visitors can step inside a real narrow boat to see how the canalfolk coped in their cramped little world, and admire the marvellous 'rose and castle' designs with which they adorned their floating homes.

Canal boat trips are made to the nearby Blisworth Tunnel – at 3,075yds, the longest still in use on British Waterways – and there are regular artists' weekends every year.

WELNEY, Cambridgeshire
See Wildfowl Trusts

WESTON PARK, Weston-under-Lizard, Staffordshire

Open spring to late summer; on M6 & 3m N of junction 3 on M54. Map Ref: SJ8010

Turn off the busy A5 Watling Street at Weston-under-Lizard to admire this lovely red-brick home of the Earl of Bradford, which stands in 1,000 acres of wooded parkland laid out by Capability Brown. The Earls of Bradford were great collectors of trees, and the extensive grounds are full of beautiful exotics screening a large adventure playground.

The house itself is full of magnificent works of art, from rose-red tapestries by Gobelin and Aubusson to paintings by Holbein, Van Dyck, Reynolds, Hoppner, Lely and Gainsborough.

WICKSTEED PARK,
Kettering, Northamptonshire

1½m SE of Kettering on A6. Map Ref: SP8778

One of the Midlands' premier amusement parks, Wicksteed boasts a large free playground with over 50 amusements, plus a further 36 'paid-for' entertainments. In addition, there are swimming and paddling pools, restaurants and picnic areas.

WILDFOWL TRUSTS,
Peakirk, Peterborough, Cambridgeshire; Welney, Wisbech, Cambridgeshire

Open daily; first off A15, second off A1101. Map Refs: TF1606 & TL5294

These two wildfowl refuges are outposts of Sir Peter Scott's famous original at Slimbridge, on the River Severn. The Peakirk centre, near Market Deeping, has 17 acres of water gardens which are home to nearly 700 ducks, geese and swans of 100 different species from all over the world.

The Welney Refuge, near Wisbech, is especially good in winter, when it is visited by over 3,000 Bewick's swans and thousands of other wildfowl, many of which migrate from Siberia and other Arctic regions. Pleasant summertime walks are laid to give visitors the chance to admire wild flowers, butterflies and other insects, as well as the abundant birdlife.

WYRE FOREST, Shropshire, Hereford & Worcester

On A456. Map Ref: SO7476

Straddling the border between Hereford & Worcester and Shropshire, this little bit of Old England has somehow escaped the changes wrought elsewhere in the countryside. In its ancient oak and birch woods is the timelessness of the primeval forest, an impression borne out by the fact that it is the home of several rare and shy species of wildlife. It is an ideal place to go for a quiet stroll, and to escape the pressures of the 20th century.

A sweeping view of Warwick, set on the Avon in Shakespeare Country, shows the towers of the popular medieval castle

The North

Scale: Approx 20 miles to 1 inch

N O R T H

S E A

Bamburgh Castle

Coquet Island
Amble

Newbiggin - by - the - Sea
Ashington
Bedlinggton
Blyth

Whitley Bay
Tynemouth
South Sheilds
NEWCASTLE UPON TYNE
Jarrow
Washington Waterfowl Park
SUNDERLAND
Washington

Houghton le Spring

Peterlee

Hartlepool

Redcar
Newton Aycliffe
Stockton on Tees   Saltburn-by-the-Sea
Middlesbrough
Darlington   *Guisborough*

Stokesley   Captain Cook Birthplace Museum & Heritage Trail   **Whitby**

Catterick   **N O R T H   Y O R K S**
Mount Grace Priory   **M O O R S**
Northallerton   North Yorkshire Moors Railway
Ryedale Folk Museum   *Scalby*
Kirkby Moorside   **Scarborough**
Masham   *Thirsk*   *Rievaulx Abbey*   Pickering
Seamer   *Filey*
Sherburn   *Humanby*   *Filey Bay*
Ripon   *Sherburn*   **T H E**   *Flamborough Head*
Boroughbridge   Castle Howard   **WOLDS**   *Bridlington Bay*
Easingwold   **Malton**   **Bridlington**
Sledmere Park   Burton Agnes Hall
Knaresborough   Great Driffield
YORK
Pocklington
arrogate   Wetherby
Tadcaster   Market Weighton   *Hornsea Pottery*
Yeadon   Beverley
LEEDS   Burton Constable Hall
Garforth   Selby
Castleford   *North Ferriby*   Withernsea
ouse   Knottingley   Goole   **HULL**
ewsbury   Wakefield   Thorne   Barton-upon-Humber   Patrington
Pontefract   *Ulceby*   *Immingham Dock*
Hemsworth   Spurn Head
Barnsley   **Scunthorpe**   **Grimsby**
Brigg   **Cleethorpes**
Doncaster
Caister
Rotherham   Bawtry   *Lincoln Wolds*
SHEFFIELD   Maltby   Gainsborough   Market Rasen   Louth
Dronfield   Retford   Mablethorpe
edwell & e John averns   **Worksop**   Wragby   Alford
Staveley   Bolsover Castle   Tuxford   Sherwood Forest Visitor Centre and Country Park
Chesterfield   Warsop   **Lincoln**   Horncastle   Spilsby
Skegness
Mansfield
atsworth ouse Hall   Kirkby-in-Ashfield   Sleaford
Alfreton   National Tramway Museum   Belper
Cromford   Midland Railway Centre   Hucknall   Newark-on-Trent
ashbourne   **NOTTINGHAM**   *Boston*
DERBY   Belvoir Castle   **Grantham**   Swineshead
The Wash
Elvaston Castle Country Park   Holkham Hall
Burton upon Trent   Hunstanton   Wells-next-the-Sea   Shering
Ashby de la Zouch   **Loughborough**   Melton Mowbray   Bourne   Norfolk Lavender   Great Bircham   Thursford Green   Blickling Hall
Coalville   Holbeach   Sandringham   Fakenham   Aylsham
Boswoth Battlefield Visitor Centre   **LEICESTER**   Oakham   Spalding   **King's Lynn**   Norfolk Wildlife Park   East Dereham
Stamford   Wisbech   Downham   Swaffam   **NORWICH**

145

TOUR 1 57 MILES

Pennine Waterfalls

The bustling market town of Hawes is the starting point for a tour which passes through Langstrothdale, and much of Wensleydale. It visits several waterfalls as well as the historic village of Castle Bolton – where Mary, Queen of Scots was imprisoned in the 16th century – Arkengarthdale, the most northerly Pennine Dale in Yorkshire and the famous Butter Tubs Pass.

Cataracts at the lower falls of Aysgarth Force, by the Yorkshire Dales park centre

The drive starts from Hawes, the friendly market town for upper Wensleydale. The Yorkshire Dales National Park Centre is housed in the former station yard, and visitors are welcome to call there for information.

Leave by the Sedbergh road, A684, and near the end of the main street turn left on to an unclassified road, signed Gayle and Kettlewell. Shortly cross the Duerley Beck (at Gayle) and follow a steep ascent through Sleddale. Fells rise to over 2,000ft on either side before reaching the summit, where there is a good viewpoint at 1,934ft – this being the highest road in North Yorkshire.

A long descent is then made into the valley of Oughtershaw Beck. Beyond the hamlet of Oughtershaw follow the Kettlewell road alongside the beck and enter Langstrothdale to reach the George Inn at Hubberholme. Here keep forward and continue to the Upper Wharfedale village of Buckden on the edge of a Norman hunting forest. Turn left on to the B6160, signed Aysgarth, and leave the valley to climb over 1,300ft along the Kidstones Pass. *A descent is then made into Bishopsdale to reach the edge of West Burton. Here turn left, then branch on to an unclassified road (still signed Aysgarth). In ¾ mile turn left on to the A684, and ¼ mile farther turn right on to an unclassified road, signed Aysgarth Force.*

On the steep descent the drive passes the Yorkshire Museum of Carriages and Horse-Drawn Vehicles before crossing the River Ure. After a short distance there is a Yorkshire Dales National Park Centre (on the left) which provides a convenient car park for drivers wishing to explore the nearby Aysgarth Force waterfall. Facilities for the disabled make it possible for visitors in wheelchairs to view the Lower Falls with ease.

Continue with the unclassified road and in ¾ mile turn right, signed Castle Bolton, and enter Carperby. Two miles farther, turn left for Castle Bolton. The impressive 14th-century stronghold here was once the prison of Mary, Queen of Scots. She and about 20 servants spent several months here in the troubled 16th century.

From this picturesque village follow the Reeth/Redmire road from ¾ mile, then at the T-junction turn left, signed Grinton and Reeth. A long climb is then made on to the lonely Redmire and Grinton Moors. After the summit, at over 1,500ft, there are fine views on the descent into Swaledale.

Near the foot of the hill turn left to reach Grinton. Here turn left on to the B6270 and cross the River Swale to Reeth. The small Swaledale village, formerly a lead-mining centre, stands at the confluence of Arkle Beck and the River Swale.

At the Buck Hotel turn right on to the unclassified Langthwaite road, which climbs above the valley slopes of Arkengarthdale. Half a mile beyond Langthwaite keep forward, signed Tan Hill. The drive then crosses the desolate Arkengarthdale Moor for 7½ miles to reach the Tan Hill Inn. At 1,732ft, this isolated hostelry on the route of the Pennine Way footpath is reputed to be the highest inn in England.

At the inn turn left (no sign) and follow a moorland road to enter West Stones Dale. Later there is a steep descent, with hairpin bends, before crossing the River Swale and turning left on to the B6270 to reach the edge of Keld.

To visit the waterfall of Kisdon Force, enter the village and follow the signs. Continue along the B6270 to Thwaite. Beyond this hamlet turn right on to an unclassified road, signed Hawes, and ascend the Butter Tubs Pass. After the summit of 1,726ft the drive descends into Wensleydale. Proceed through the hamlet of Simonstone and in ½ mile reach a T-junction. From here a short detour to the right may be made to visit the 100ft-high waterfall of Hardraw Force. Access is via the Green Dragon Inn at Hardraw. *The main drive turns left, then takes the next turning right for the return to Hawes.*

TOUR 2 60 MILES

Cumbrian Lakesides

From Keswick this tour quickly passes into enchanting countryside. First visiting Derwent Water and dark Borrowdale, it ascends Honister Pass to dramatic mountain scenery before dropping to Buttermere. Another high pass is taken to Bassenthwaite Lake and to quiet open moorland roads before the return to Keswick

Leave Keswick *by the Borrowdale road, B5289.* The drive soon follows the eastern shores of Derwent Water, with steep wooded slopes to the left. Farther on, the cliffs of Falcon Crag tower above the road to the left, and there are more excellent views over the lake. The road then enters the attractive valley of Borrowdale, keeping to the east bank of the River Derwent. Later the conical, tree-covered summit of Castle Crag is prominent to the right, and as Borrowdale widens out there are panoramic views of the numerous peaks ahead.

Continue through Rosthwaite and Seatoller, then begin the ascent of Honister Pass (1-in-4). The pass, which rises to 1,176ft, offers superb mountain scenery and on the descent there is a spectacular view down into Buttermere, with steep scree-covered slopes sweeping down to the road on either side.

After the descent, follow the waters of Buttermere and remain on the B5289 through the hamlet of Buttermere. The drive then follows the shore of Crummock Water, with more high peaks on either side of the road.

Almost 2 miles beyond the lake turn right (signed Lorton, Cockermouth), then in another 2 miles turn right on to an unclassified road and shortly go over the crossroads for High Lorton. At the end of the village turn right, signed Keswick, then at the T-junction turn right on to the B5292.* An ascent is then made over the Whinlatter Pass (1,043ft), and on the wooded descent there are views to the left overlooking Bassenthwaite Lake.

Continue the descent into Braithwaite village. Here turn left (signed Cockermouth A66), then turn left again to join the A66. Later the drive runs alongside Bassenthwaite Lake, with views of Skiddaw (3,054ft) across the water.

After 3½ miles, at the far end of the lake, turn right on to the B5291 (signed Castle Inn) then turn right again. In ¾ mile turn right and cross the river bridge. At the Castle Inn turn right then left over the main road to join the unclassified Uldale road. In 2¼ miles bear right and continue to Uldale. The rugged peaks of the Lakeland Fells now give way to gentler, undulating moorland scenery in the vicinity of Uldale.

At Uldale go over the crossroads with the Caldbeck road and ascend, then in 2¼ miles join the B5299. After another 1½ miles bear left and continue to Caldbeck. Here branch right on to an unclassified road, signed Hesket Newmarket. At Hesket Newmarket bear left, then ½ mile farther bear right, signed Mungrisdale. In 2½ miles pass the Horse and Farrier PH, then cross the river bridge and turn right. The drive now follows a moorland road to skirt the eastern flank of the 'Skiddaw massif', passing below the sheer rock face of Carrock Fell (2,174ft). Beyond the hamlet of Mungrisdale there are fine views ahead of Matterdale Common, with Souther Fell to the right.

Later, at the junction with the A66, turn right (signed Keswick). The peak of Saddleback (2,847ft) is now prominent to the right, and at the edge of Threlkeld the road passes directly below it.

Nearly 3 miles after the turning to Threlkeld branch left on to the A591 for the return to Keswick.

Bare Cumbrian hills behind the placid mirror of Derwent Water

ABBOT HALL ART GALLERY, Kendal, Cumbria

Open daily; off A684. Map Ref: SD5192

Artists have found Lakeland inspirational throughout the ages, and some who forged permanent links with the area are exhibited in this gallery on the banks of the River Kent, in old Westmorland. Period rooms of the impressive 18th-century Georgian house are adorned with elegant furniture by Gillow of Lancaster; watercolours by John Ruskin and portraits by Daniel Gardner and local artist George Romney hang on the walls. The gallery features a changing programme of exhibitions, and work by modern-day craftsmen and artists is on sale.

ALNWICK CASTLE, Northumberland

Open spring to autumn; off A1. Map Ref: NU1813

Even in a county renowned for its castles, the one at Alnwick reigns supreme. A great border fortress, it dominates its grey-stone town with a presence that justifies its unofficial title, the 'Windsor of the North', and although it is not so large as that Berkshire stronghold, it is equally imposing. A contributory factor is its spectacular setting above the River Aln.

The Percy family, one of the most famous in the history of Northumberland, founded a castle at Alnwick in the 12th century, and replaced it with the present building some 200 years later.

Take the opportunity before entering the impressive barbican to step back and look at the figures perched on the battlements. Some say that these stone soldiers were intended to frighten the approaching Scots, while the more cynical suggest that they are little more than upmarket garden gnomes!

Alnwick's sombre, weatherbeaten grey walls do little to prepare the visitor for its extravagant interior and wealth of *objets d'art*. Several Dukes of Northumberland – descendants of the Percys – refurbished the interior during the 18th and 19th centuries, and the present decor is the work of the 4th Duke. In the rich style of the Italian Renaissance, it provides the perfect setting for rare and precious works, including paintings by Van Dyck and Canaletto. The castle's collection of Meissen china is renowned.

This great building is more than just an historic house and fine-art museum; it is also the home of the present Duke of Northumberland, and family photographs – including ones of his daughters' weddings – provide warmth and save it from being simply a cold repository of the English heritage.

BAKEWELL, Derbyshire
See Haddon Hall and the Central Region

BAMBURGH CASTLE, Northumberland

Open spring to autumn. Map Ref: NU1834

A stroll along the dune-backed golden sands of Bamburgh is an essential precursor to visiting this huge citadel on its basalt crag, once the seat of the Kings of Northumbria, for it is seen at its spectacular best when viewed from the beach.

The great fortress dominates this stretch of beautiful Northumberland coast from an outcrop of a country-wide geological formation known as the Great Whin Sill. Weather permitting, views from its ramparts extend to the Farne islands and the Longstone Lighthouse – from where local girl Grace Darling set out to rescue the sailors of the wrecked ship *Forfarshire*.

After such a romantic and spectacular view, the interior of Bamburgh Castle may come as a disappointment, for little of the original Norman edifice remains. The Victorian industrialist Lord Armstrong rescued the fortress from ruin at the end of the last century, but his 'improvements' were heavy-handed and have been much criticised by historians.

The castle is still owned by an Armstrong, and in it is a museum of industrial archaeology dedicated to the First Lord Armstrong's achievements, including his famous armaments factory in Elswick, Newcastle.

BARDON MILL, Northumberland
See Vindolanda & Chesterholme

BASHALL EAVES, Lancashire
See Browsholme Hall

BEAMISH, Co Durham

Open all year; on A693. Map Ref: NZ2253

If the clang of a tram car bell, the smell of smoking chimneys and the warm aroma of newly-baked bread spark fond memories, take a trip to Beamish Museum, where the recent history of the North East is brought to life. This is pure nostalgia for many, and a real treat for youngsters used to the microchip technology of the 1980s.

Since it was started in 1970 the museum has saved vital historical detail relating to pit villages, engineering, railways and farming, along with the unique social history of the north east. Buildings have been dismantled brick by brick from all parts of the region, and rebuilt for posterity on 200 acres of rolling wooded countryside.

The museum is still developing, but complete at the time of publishing was an imposing visitor centre which undoubtedly contributed to the winning of the 1987 European Museum of the Year title.

Beamish is a real experience. There are steam trains at Rowley Station, and a fire in the grate of the waiting room. In the Co-op are the smells of a real grocers' shop and the chance to swap a 'divi' number with the museum staff – who

probably worked in the original Co-operative Store; the sound of a drill in the dentist's elegant town house is far too realisitic for comfort.

Before leaving the 1920s town, with its posh terrace, Co-op shops and printing works, call in at the Sun Inn pub and see dray horses belonging to Newcastle Breweries in the stables. If it's opening time you can actually enjoy a glass of real beer.

Then it's a tram ride to the pit village – but watch the steps, which seem so much higher than those of present-day buses. The colliery includes guided tours down a drift mine and a row of pit cottages from Francis Street in Hetton-le-Hole, near Sunderland. Each has been furnished and appointed in a different period; some have gardens with geese, while in another may be a woman baking the traditional North East bread – a 'stotty' cake. Galvanised tin baths hang in some back yards, and all have outside toilets, or 'netties'.

In complete contrast is Home Farm, a beautifully-restored farm house and buildings where the museum breeds livestock typical of the north.

Throughout the year this remarkable living museum is the venue for major events.

BERWICK-UPON-TWEED, Northumberland

Map Ref: NT9953

Perhaps the most impressive approach to Berwick-upon-Tweed is by rail over the Royal Border Bridge, which was designed by Robert Stephenson and is one of three spanning the River Tweed here.

As England's northernmost town, Berwick has traditionally been at the forefront of border disputes – and indeed, it changed hands 14 times between the Scots and the English. It has been the capital of the ancient Eastern Marches, and during Elizabethan times its town walls were fully restored. They are among the best-preserved in Europe.

Among the red-roofed, grey-stone houses are said to be more buildings scheduled for preservation than in any town of comparable size in the country.

Fine old buildings include the 18th-century Guildhall, in Marygate, where an eight o'clock curfew is still rung, and the oldest purpose-built barracks in the country, designed by Vanbrugh in 1717. They now house a superb museum complex, featuring the King's Own Scottish Borderers' Regimental Museum.

Despite its rich heritage and fine Elizabethan and Georgian buildings, this seaside town takes on a resort air during the summer season. Anyone visiting for the history and scenery would be well advised to avoid the high season. An early visit to miss the crowds could coincide with the annual 'Riding the Bounds' on 1 May.

BEVERLEY, Humberside

Map Ref: TA0339

Beverley Minster

In the Middle Ages the fine Gothic minster at Beverley was a place of pilgrimage for believers in the miracles of St

Memorabilia from all over the north east has been saved at Beamish, where trams still run

Gleaming brass craftsmanship on one of several Jowett cars in the Bradford Industrial Museum

John. This former Bishop of York, who is buried in the nave, founded Beverley Minster early in the 8th century.

St John is also remembered in his great church by the seven-ton Great John Bell.

The minster is quite rightly regarded as one of Europe's loveliest churches, and its twin towers present an impressive skyline above the flat Humberside landscape.

The work of brilliant craftsmen is revealed inside. Of particular note are the Percy tomb canopy, the elaborate 18th-century cover of the Norman font and 68 early-Tudor misericord seats, with their quaint carvings. Beside the high altar is the Saxon *fridstol* or sanctuary chair – for the minster once had the right of sanctuary. The great east window is the work of skilled 15th-century glassmakers.

Museum of Army Transport

Open all year

Testing an armoured vehicle for size proves to be an attraction that appeals to 'boys' of all ages at this museum, which is dedicated to every kind of transport used by the British Army. Popular exhibits include the Rolls Royce used by Field Marshal Montgomery, and the wagon used by Lord Roberts in the Boer War. Around 50 vehicles, from a three-wheels-in-a-row motor cycle to various prototypes are displayed.

A huge Blackburn Beverley Aircraft houses the History of Army Air Transport.

BLACKPOOL, Lancashire
See Sandcastle

BRADFORD INDUSTRIAL MUSEUM & NATIONAL MUSEUM OF PHOTOGRAPHY, FILM & TELEVISION, West Yorkshire

Both open all year. Map Ref: SE1733

Bradford's long association with the woollen industry is the subject of a fascinating industrial museum in Moorside Mills, where machinery and techniques developed locally are used to show how raw wool was turned into fine worsted cloth. The basic principles are still employed all over the world.

Originally the mill-owner and his family lived 'above the shop', and their home has been faithfully restored to its comfortable, turn-of-the-century style.

Bradford's other industrial achievements are also shown, and on display are Jowett cars, Scott motor cycles and the city's last tram – all made locally. Near by can be experienced the sounds and smells of steam engines which once powered the mill, and the aptly-named 'Bobbins' shop sells bargain-priced wool products.

Industry of a different sort and Britain's largest cinema screen can be seen at the National Museum of Photography, Film and Television, where a Canadian IMAX projection system shows international classic films and new releases on a huge curved screen measuring 52ft 4in high and 63ft 8in wide. It has been called the 'Cinema of the Future'.

Other galleries cover the history of photography and the part it plays in our lives, while a realistic national-newspaper editorial office is the backdrop for a photojournalism exhibition. Lord Lichfield helps to explain the history of portraiture.

There are television galleries too, and a Kodak museum on the evolution of the camera. Around 20,000 photographs and more than 15,000 pieces of historically-important equipment are on show.

BRITISH COMMERCIAL VEHICLE MUSEUM, Leyland, Lancashire

Open daily; off M6. Map Ref: SD5421

Telling the story of the British commercial-vehicle industry at this museum are more than 40 restored vehicles, ranging from horse and steam power to early petrol engines and models of today. Europe's largest museum of its type, it expertly illustrates how designs have changed to keep pace with expanding demand for passenger, heavy-goods and local-delivery transport. Check for special events throughout the year.

BROCKHOLE, Cumbria
See Lake District National Park Visitor Centre

BROWSHOLME HALL, Clitheroe, Lancashire

Limited opening spring & summer; 2½m NW Clitheroe at Bashall Eaves. Map Ref: SD6943

A warm, personal atmosphere is a major feature of Browsholme Hall, for this lovely Tudor mansion near Clitheroe at Bashall Eaves is still a family home and the

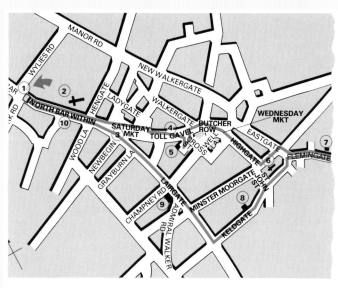

A Gothic skyline

Beverley has not just one, but two magnificent Gothic churches. Between them are narrow medieval streets and pleasant market squares graced by red-brick Georgian houses.

1 NORTH BAR AND BAR HOUSE
At one time a deep, wide ditch encircled the town, and the only way in was over one of five drawbridges which were each defended by a gateway, or bar. North Bar, the only survivor of these, was built in 1409.

2 ST MARY'S CHURCH
Were it not for the beautiful Minster, St Mary's Parish Church would easily be the most magnificent building in the town. The splendid West Front, with its pinnacled towers, was completed in 1420. In 1520, during morning service, the original Norman tower collapsed, killing many members of the congregation; it was replaced by a magnificent Tudor tower.

3 SATURDAY MARKET
This irregularly-shaped market place replaced the older market place – Wednesday Market – when the town spread north. It is dominated by the Market Cross, which was built in 1711 to replace an earlier one. Its stone pillars were supposed to be far enough apart to allow carriages to be driven through.

4 TOLL GAVEL
The curious name of this street dates from the days when tolls were collected. Number 44 used to be a chemist's shop, as the snakes entwined around the door posts show. Farther along at No. 65 is the former home of the 18th-century benefactress, Ann Routh.

5 THE GUILDHALL
A guildhall has stood on this site since about 1500, but it was largely rebuilt in 1762 by William Middleton. Later, the Mayor's Parlour and public gallery were added – the latter's pillars taken from the Minster in 1826.

6 THE MINSTER
Twin towers soar up above the rooftops of the town as a constant reminder that here is one of the most beautiful pieces of Gothic architecture in Europe. The church was actually begun during the 13th century, and although several phases of rebuilding followed, the whole harmonises completely. The wealth of beauty and detail throughout the Minster is immense, but carving both in stone and wood is one of its most outstanding features, and nowhere is this more apparent than in the choir.

7 MUSEUM OF ARMY TRANSPORT
Some 70 vehicles in a two-acre hall, ranging from a tiny *Gazelle* locomotive to a huge *Blackburn Beverley*, which houses the air-transport section.

8 KELDGATE
Ann Routh built an almshouse (now known as Ann Routh's Hospital) to the right of Keldgate in 1749. The plaque in the middle of the building is a memorial to philanthropy in Georgian Beverley.

9 THE HALL
Built in 1700, this fine house has reception rooms designed by Carr. Both the Chinese room and dining room have splendid stucco ceilings, and the design of the former incorporates musical instruments and has beautiful hand-painted Chinese wallpaper. Viewing is by arrangement with the Tourist Office.

10 NORTH BAR WITHIN
Standing on the left-hand side of the road is an 18th-century pub now called the Beverley Arms, but formerly known as the Blue Bell. The novelist Anthony Trollope stayed there in 1868.

EARLY CLOSING: *Thu*

MARKET DAY: *Sat*

PARKING: *Grayburn La, Morton La, Saturday Market, School La, Spencer St, Wilbert La*

OPENING TIMES:
Museum of Army Transport: Open all year
The Guildhall: Open Easter – Sep, Tue & BH. Other times by arrangement.

ROUTE DIRECTIONS
Start at North Bar (1) and walk along North Bar Within towards the town centre, passing St Mary's Church (2). Enter Saturday Mkt (3) and keep l, passing the Corn Exchange (now a cinema), and then continue into Toll Gavel (4). Cross Toll Gavel and enter Cross St to reach the Guildhall (5). Return to Toll Gavel and turn r. to enter Butcher Row. Leave by Wednesday Mkt to enter Highgate and reach the Minster (6). Leave the Minster by Eastgate and turn r. into Flemingate to reach the Army Transport Museum (7). Return to the Minster and leave by Keldgate (8), passing Ann Routh's Hospital and the Old School House, before turning r. into Lairgate, where The Hall (9) is, and return along North Bar Within (10) to North Bar.

It is difficult to believe that the magnificent Gothic nave of Beverley Minster was restored comparatively recently

owners – descendants of the original builders – are pleased to take on the task of guides and show people round.

Although official opening is limited to some weekends in spring and summer, the house can be viewed by appointment at other times by anyone keen to take in the fine oak panelling, tapestries, armour and family treasures.

The Prince Regent and Mrs Fitzherbert were the inspiration for the beautifully landscaped gardens surrounding the mansion.

BURTON AGNES HALL, Humberside

Open daily spring to autumn; on A166. Map Ref: TA1063

Four centuries of fabulous treasures fill Burton Agnes Hall, an outstanding Elizabethan mansion set in a sleepy village of the same name. In fact, there is so much to see there that visitors may find time slipping away.

No-one should miss either the house or the immaculate gardens. Work on the richly-mellowed red brick and stone-trimmed hall was started in 1598 and finished in 1610 by Sir Henry Griffith, and his descendants still live there. En route to the hall are clipped yew trees and manicured velvet lawns that will make keen gardeners green with envy.

Inside the house are richly-furnished rooms and impressive features such as the oak and plaster screen of the great hall, and a stone and alabaster chimney piece. The massive staircase and beautifully restored long gallery are justly famed.

BURTON CONSTABLE HALL, Sproatley, Humberside

Open spring to autumn. Map Ref: TA1836

Capability Brown's superb talent for landscaping can be enjoyed from a boat on the 22 acres of lakes that water the impressive 200-acre park in which this Elizabethan house stands. Rallies and fairs are held there throughout the summer, and young and old alike will appreciate the model railway and small zoo.

The house was built in 1570 and is the home of the 46th Lord Paramount of Seignory of Holderness. A highlight of any tour is the Long Room, which was created by Cuthbert Constable in 1736 and features a Flemish 15th-century stained-glass window. The interior was extensively remodelled in the 18th century and is furnished with one of the finest Chippendale collections in England. Visitors can follow a special 'Furniture Trail'.

CAPTAIN COOK BIRTHPLACE MUSEUM & HERITAGE TRAIL, Marton, Cleveland

Open all year; off A172. Map Ref: NZ5115

The Captain Cook Heritage Trail links places associated with the great explorer and starts at his birthplace at Stewart Park, in Middlesbrough. The actual site of the thatched cottage where he was born in 1728 is marked by a granite vase.

A visit to this fascinating museum will whet the appetite for the remainder of Cook's trail, which wends through the beautiful and deserted North York Moors to the fishing port of Whitby. Here the attentive beach comber might be lucky enough to pick up ammonite fossils, washed out of the local Blue Lias limestone.

The Cook Museum, set in parkland only a few miles from industrial Teeside, houses displays relating to James Cook's early life, as well as to his voyages of discovery to New Zealand, Australia and the South Pacific. A conservatory of exotic plants and an aviary of colourful parakeets remind the visitor of those faraway places.

CARK-IN-CARTMEL, Cumbria
See Holker Hall

CARLISLE, Cumbria

Map Ref: NY4056

'Carel' – as the locals call Carlisle – has 2,000 years of history and although industry has invaded the suburbs the heart of the city has retained its historic character.

It has always been important because of its strategic position on the Anglo-Scottish border, and it was first occupied by the Romans, who built Hadrian's Wall on the doorstep.

For centuries the city was a battlefield for the Scots and English, until 1745 when Bonnie Prince Charlie's troops were ousted. Today it fulfils a major role as the administrative and agricultural centre of Cumbria.

It is easy to explore the city's historic quarters without a great deal of footslogging. The Norman castle, built by William Rufus in 1092 and strengthened by David I, houses a museum dedicated to the former Border regiments. Sir Walter Scott, the writer synonymous with the Border region, was married in 1797 in the red sandstone cathedral – the second smallest in England. It too dates from the 12th century, and has one of the finest east windows in the country. The carved choir stalls and painted barrel-vault ceiling are superb.

As this is Roman country it comes as no surprise to find that Carlisle has its own excellent collection of Roman relics, and remains excavated from Hadrian's Wall can be seen in the city's museum and art gallery at the magnificent Jacobean Tullie House.

A recent addition to Carlisle's attractions is the Lane's Shopping Centre – a light and airy undercover complex, ideal for browsing on a rainy day.

CARNFORTH, Lancashire
See Steamtown Railway

CASTLEFIELD URBAN HERITAGE PARK, Manchester, Gt Manchester

Open daily. Map Ref: SJ8398

This unique urban heritage park takes its name from the Roman fort near by, and a reconstruction of the ancient north gate is an important feature among the several museums and historical sites that make up Castlefield.

In the world's earliest passenger railway station at Liverpool Street is the Greater Manchester Museum of Science and Industry, with displays of steam and textile machines that revolutionised the world – many in working order. Alongside is the Manchester Air and Space Museum, an impressive collection of historic aircraft and displays on aerospace technology.

As well as museums and a Roman fort, the park offers boat trips from Castlefield basin on the historic Bridgewater and Rochdale Canals. The Bridgewater was opened in 1761 as the world's first modern canal. Work continues at Castlefield, so repeat visits are likely to be rewarded by new attractions.

CASTLE HOWARD, Malton, North Yorkshire

Open spring to autumn; 3m off A64. Map Ref: SE7170

This incomparable 18th-century mansion is probably best-known as the backdrop for the acclaimed television adaptation of *Brideshead Revisited*. One of Vanbrugh's greatest works, it featured on the small screen as the home of the Flyte family.

Perhaps one of the most visually exciting stately homes in the country, it has grounds resplendent with lakes, fountains and follies – including a circular mausoleum designed by Hawksmoor to echo the central dome of the house itself. The lovely Temple of the Four Winds is also of note, and a pyramid crowns the huge gatehouse. No visitor should miss the outstanding collection of period costumes for which Castle Howard is also famed.

CASTLETON, Derbyshire
See Speedwell & Blue John Caverns

CHATSWORTH HOUSE, Derbyshire

Open spring to autumn; off B6012. Map Ref: SK2670

Ornamental waters, cascades and the highest fountain in Britain complement the beauty of this exceptional 17th-century mansion, unofficially known as the 'Palace of the Peak'. Before going into the house, drink in the beauty of its setting in acres of parkland on the banks of the River Derwent. Backed by wooded slopes in grounds crossed by chestnut avenues, Chatsworth was built by the 1st Duke of Devonshire and is still

At Castle Howard Vanbrugh and Hawksmoor created the ideal 18th-century Romantic landscape

the home of his family. It replaced an Elizabethan predecessor that was partly-designed by the 1st Duke's ancestress, the indomitable Bess of Hardwick.

Inside are magnificent state rooms and one of the finest collections of decorative art in the world, including paintings, sculpture, gold and silver plate. There is also a fine collection of books and furniture.

Chatsworth also has a farmyard where visitors can watch cows being milked and see various breeds of sheep, cattle, horses, pigs and poultry. There too is an exhibition about the management and working of farms and woods on the Chatsworth estate.

Particularly popular among various events held at Chatsworth throughout the year are the angling and game fairs.

CHESTER, Cheshire
Map Ref: SJ4066

The only sensible way to start a visit to this impressive city is with a tour of the walls – Britain's only Roman and medieval examples to have survived intact. Covering a total distance of two miles, the circuit affords panoramic views over the city and across the surrounding countryside. You can even see the racecourse, or Roodee, where the Chester Cup has been run every May since 1824.

Chester was founded by the Romans nearly 2,000 years ago and has been touched by almost

every era in history since then. It was an important county palatine under the Normans, whose earls were as powerful as kings, and it thrived as a port until the 15th century. During the 18th and 19th centuries it flourished as a commercial centre.

Around every corner in Chester is a clue to its rich heritage, but perhaps its best-known architectural landmark is the beautiful galleried tier of stylish shops known as The Rows. Black-and-white buildings are a hallmark of the city's age, including God's Providence House, Bishop Lloyd's House and Old Leche House. Not all are old, however, and some interesting Victorian 'romances' mix pleasingly with the real thing.

The beautiful sandstone cathedral dates mainly from the 14th century and is renowned for its ornate carved woodwork, the Lady Chapel, refectory and cloisters. Another church, partly-ruined St John's, has excellent Norman craftsmanship. Four separate regiments are featured in the Cheshire Military Museum in Chester Castle, which dates from the 13th century but was extensively restored by the Victorians, who left only the Agricola Tower untouched.

If you're looking for some relief from all this heritage, then a visit to Chester Zoo will make a refreshing change. It is second only to London Zoo and keeps more than 3,000 animals, including many rare and endangered species in pleasant and humane surroundings.

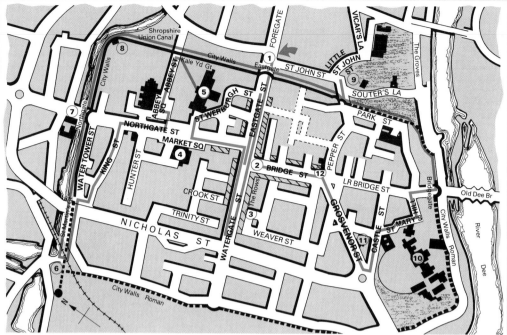

Heritage of Rome

Chester began life as a Roman military camp, the base for nearly 200 years of the famous 20th Legion, the *Valeria Victrix*. Within the walls, which have survived almost intact, the streets are lined with timbered buildings, including the famous Rows – raised walkways along the old Roman streets.

1 THE EASTGATE
Although the street which runs beneath it is now closed to traffic, the Eastgate was from Roman times right up to the present day the principal gate into the city.

2 THE ROWS
The Rows are unique raised galleries, with shops at first-floor level, dating back at least as far as the 13th century.

3 BISHOP LLOYD'S HOUSE
Several black-and-white houses in Watergate Street date back to the 16th and 17th centuries, and the most fascinating is Bishop Lloyd's house which was built in the early 17th century (open only by appointment).

4 TOWN HALL
The Victorian Gothic town hall dominates the market place and is best visited by arrangement with the Mayor's secretary.

5 ST WERBURGH'S CATHEDRAL
The origins of the cathedral, heavily restored in the 19th century, go back to the Anglo-Saxon foundation of the Abbey of St Werburgh. It is famous for its remarkably beautiful choir stalls.

CITY WALLS
Chester's city walls are the most complete anywhere in the country, and are remarkably well preserved. They date from Roman times, but throughout the medieval period they were strengthened and extended. The walk around the top of the walls is an ideal way to view the city.

6 WATER TOWER AND BONEWALDES-THORNE'S TOWER
These two medieval towers at the north-west corner of the walls were built to guard the river when Chester was a port. As early as the 14th century the Dee was silting up, and the Water Tower, which now contains a small museum of Chester's history, was built on an outlying spur of wall at that time.

7 BLUECOAT HOSPITAL
Below the Northgate can be seen the handsome Bluecoat Hospital, built in 1717 to house the 46 pupils of the school founded in 1700 by Ranulph Blundeville.

8 KING CHARLES' TOWER
From here Charles I watched the disastrous defeat of his army at the Battle of Rowton Moor, in 1645.

9 AMPHITHEATRE
By Newgate, steps lead to two relics of Roman *Deva*, the amphitheatre and the Roman Garden. The amphitheatre is one of the largest yet discovered in Britain – it could seat up to 7,000 spectators.

10 CHESTER CASTLE
Little remains of the original Norman Chester Castle except the mound, and one of the towers of the inner bailey.

11 GROSVENOR MUSEUM
The outstanding features of the museum are the models illustrating life in a Roman fort, and the remarkable remains of the Roman period which have been discovered in Chester.

12 CHESTER HERITAGE CENTRE
St Michael's Church in Bridge Street, declared redundant for religious purposes, was given a new lease of life in 1975 when it became the country's first Heritage Centre.

EARLY CLOSING: *Wed*

MARKET DAY: *Mon – Sat*

PARKING: *Castle Dr, Frodsham St, New Crane St, Newgate St, Pepper St*

OPENING TIMES:
Water Tower: open summer only Mon – Sat all day. Sun pm only
King Charles' Tower: open as above
Grosvenor Museum: open all year Mon – Sat all day, Sun pm only

Chester Heritage Centre: Open pm between Mar – Oct (exc Wed). Open all day Apr–Sep (exc Wed) and Sun pm

ROUTE DIRECTIONS
Start at the Eastgate (1) and walk down the l. side of the Rows (2) past Bishop Lloyd's House (3) to Weaver St. Cross and return down the opposite side of the Rows to Northgate St. Turn l. to reach the Market Sq and Town Hall (4), then cross to St Werburgh St and the cathedral (5). Leave the cathedral through the Slype and walk across to Abbey St, turning l. to reach Abbey Sq. Go through the arch, turn r. and cross over Northgate St. Continue to the Pied Bull Inn, turning l. into King St. At the end cross Water Tower St to ascend the city walls at St Martin's Gt. Detour l. along walls to the Bonewaldesthorne and Water Towers (6), then return and walk along walls past the Bluecoat Hospital (7) and King Charles' Tower (8). At Newgate descend for Amphitheatre (9). Return to the walls and ascend, then shortly descend the Wishing Steps and the Recorder's Steps to the street beside the River Dee. Turn r. by the Old Dee Bridge, cross over Lower Bridge St, then turn l. into Shipgate St and up St Mary's Hill. Walk l. down Castle St to castle (10). Return by Grosvenor St past the museum (11) to Bridge St and cross to the Chester Heritage Centre (12). Walk back up the Bridge St Rows to Eastgate St and back down the right-hand side of the Rows to complete the walk.

CHILLINGHAM PARK WILD WHITE CATTLE, Northumberland

Open spring to autumn; off B6348. Map Ref: NU0625

A stout pair of shoes, a strong pair of legs, binoculars and a little patience are vital for a visit to the unique Chillingham Park Wild White Cattle, thought to be descendants of wild oxen trapped in the park when it was created in 1220.

Today the animals can be viewed under the supervision of a knowledgeable and enthusiastic warden. However, be warned – there is no guarantee that the entire herd will be seen, for the animals are totally wild and often wander in remote areas of the 600-acre park. However, the reward for a long walk and a lengthy wait – the sight of the herd in their picturesque setting – is an exhilarating and unique experience.

An attractive alternative for anyone not feeling energetic is a tour of Chillingham Castle, which has recently been restored and opened to the public.

CLITHEROE, Lancashire
See Browsholme Hall

CONISTON, Cumbria

Map Ref: SD3097

Brantwood

Open all year; 2½m SE Coniston off B5285. Map Ref: SD3195

Some of the finest lake and mountain views in England can be seen from the gardens and windows of Brantwood, the Lake District home of John Ruskin – the influential English art critic and painter – between 1872 and 1900.

Views from a network of delightful nature trails around the estate confirm that this must be one of the most beautifully situated houses in England.

Those who can bear to tear themselves away from the scenery will find an extensive collection of Ruskin's watercolours and drawings inside the house.

Lake Coniston Steam Yacht *Gondola* (NT), Coniston Pier

Open spring to autumn

There can be few better ways to soak up the scenic delights of lovely Coniston Water than in the opulent splendour of the National Trust's vintage steam yacht *Gondola* – an excellent example of the way in which the Trust has diversified its interests in recent years.

The *Gondola* is pure Victoriana. Launched in 1859, the craft was restored to its former glory in 1980 and can accommodate up to 86 passengers in spacious, steam-heated saloons with sumptuously upholstered seats. Four or five sailings are made each day from Coniston Pier.

CRAGSIDE HOUSE & COUNTRY PARK (NT), Rothbury, Northumberland

House open spring to autumn, grounds all year; ½m E of Rothbury, car entrance 2m N on B6341. Map Ref: NU0501

Cragside's vast grounds are at their best in early summer, when great drifts of rhododendrons blaze with colour. Victorian industrialist Lord Armstrong planted a staggering seven million trees and shrubs in this 900-acre park, and his awe-inspiring creation can be equally well appreciated from signposted walks and a one-way system of drives.

In 1863 the house at Cragside was a simple shooting lodge, but it was extended throughout during the last century and is now a mansion surrounded by estate cottages. The whole park feels as if it was inspired by a Germanic influence.

Now owned by the National Trust, the house has been fully restored and furnished in contemporary Victorian style – even including original William Morris wallpaper.

The result is not to everyone's taste, for it is pure Victoriana, but as a shrine to that era and a monument to one man it is unfailingly impressive. Lord Armstrong's estate softened the harsh aspect of the area and became the setting for many 'firsts' in engineering skills and inventions – including hydro-electricity; it was the first house in the world to be lit by electricity generated by water power.

CRICH, Derbyshire
See National Tramway Museum

DACRE, Cumbria
See Dalemain

DALEMAIN, Dacre, Cumbria

Open spring to autumn; on A592. Map Ref: NY4726

Impressive features from several eras mingle at Dalemain, a medieval pele tower that was added to in Tudor times and given a Georgian façade in 1750. Inside, the visitor is faced with fine Tudor plasterwork, Queen Anne and 18th-century furniture, and a Victorian nursery. Other features include superb oak panelling and Chinese wallpaper.

Dalemain has two fascinating museums – one in the tower, dedicated to the Westmorland

Coniston Water can be explored in Victorian-style comfort on the steam-driven Gondola *(NT)*

Daffodils at Dove Cottage, once home to the great Lakeland poet, Wordsworth

and Cumberland Yeomanry, and one in the 16th-century cobbled courtyard, with a countryside theme. The historic gardens offer pleasant walking and clean Lakeland air.

DINTING RAILWAY CENTRE, Dinting Vale, Derbyshire

Open all year; off A57 in Dinting Lane. Map Ref: SK0194

Locomotives ranging from large express passenger types to smaller industrial models are on show at this operational museum, which should ideally be visited when at least one of the engines is 'steamed' – every Sunday from the end of March to the end of October, and on Bank Holidays; also on Wednesdays during July and August. Steam weekends are held through the year.

DOVE COTTAGE, Grasmere, Cumbria

Open daily. Map Ref: NY3306

William Wordsworth is remembered at tiny, 17th-century Dove Cottage, where the celebrated poet spent his most creative years in unabashed worship of the magnificent Lake District scenery around him. The delightful garden there is a re-creation of the original laid out by him and his sister Dorothy.

Original manuscripts – the results of some of those years – are among the treasures in the adjoining Wordsworth Museum, and personal belongings, photographs and paintings help to build up a picture of one of the country's best-loved poets.

After Wordsworth left the cottage in 1808 it became the home of Thomas de Quincy, famous for his book *Confessions of an English Opium Eater*.

DURHAM, Co Durham

Off A167. Map Ref: NZ2742

It is wise to park your car quickly and explore the heart of historic Durham City on foot, since that really is the best way to appreciate the narrow streets which climb from the River Wear to that masterpiece of Norman architecture, Durham Cathedral. Voted the best building in the world a few years ago, the great church dominates the city and quite literally puts every other building in its architectural shade.

Part of the cathedral's beauty is its simplicity, and one of the most moving moments for many visitors is to stand by the plain stone tomb of the gentle Ionian, St Cuthbert. The Galilee Chapel – at the opposite end of the cathedral – is the resting place for the great and scholarly Venerable Bede, while in the treasury are many valuable books, manuscripts and relics associated with St Cuthbert – as well as the original 12th-century knocker

from the north door!

Opposite the cathedral on Palace Green stands the imposing Durham Castle. Now part of the university, this was once the residence of the all-powerful Bishops of Durham and has a good Norman chapel. It is open to the public. There is also a public park and an unusual 18th-century deerhouse.

The cathedral and castle are almost surrounded by the River Wear, which loops the old town in a wooded gorge. Its banks offer delightful riverside walks, and rowing boats may be hired beside Old Elvet Bridge – the smart end of the city in the 18th century.

Durham boasts many other fine attractions, notably the Oriental Museum. Part of the university, this houses collections of artefacts from ancient Egypt, Japan, China and South East Asia. The Durham Light Infantry Museum and Arts Centre recalls the history of this famous regiment with displays of armaments, uniforms and medals.

ELLESMERE PORT BOAT MUSEUM, Cheshire

Open all year; near junction 9, M53. Map Ref: SJ4077

The leisurely pace of life on the waterways is featured by this award-winning museum, which is aptly situated in an historic dock complex at the junction of the Shropshire Union and Manchester Ship Canals.

It is a living, working boat museum where visitors may step back to 18th-century canal life and browse amongst the largest collection of historic canal craft in Europe.

More than 50 vessels are in the collection, ranging from a small weedcutter to a 300-ton coaster. The museum also features exhibitions on canals, horses and the town – as well as restored steam engines which are regularly 'steamed'.

Visitors are encouraged to board some of the boats, and there are trips for those who really want to capture the spirit of the waterways.

FILEY, North Yorkshire

Map Ref: TA1180

Filey Brigg, a mile-long natural breakwater of rocks, is a popular attraction of this North Yorkshire seaside town, and a fascinating nature trail makes exploring the local caves, coves, cliffs and rock pools an informative as well as an enjoyable experience.

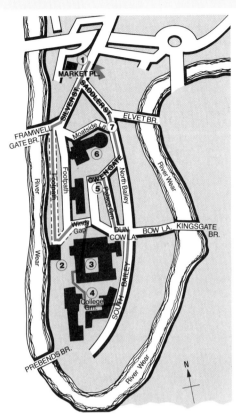

The fortress city

One of the most splendidly sited cities in Britain, Durham's rocky outcrop, washed on three sides by the River Wear, was from the earliest times a secure fortress against invading Scots and Danes. At its most powerful it was ruled by the Norman Prince Bishops as a city state, and it is to them that the town owes its great castle and cathedral.

1 TOWN HALL
Like so many town halls, this one is Victorian, but it is less flamboyant than some. It is worth visiting for its collection of mementoes of 'King Tom Thumb', a midget who lived in Durham for the last 17 years of his life.

2 ARCHAEOLOGY MUSEUM
This little museum is housed in an old fulling mill where woollen cloth was treated with fullers' earth to cleanse it of grease.

3 DURHAM CATHEDRAL
This great cathedral is considered by many to be the supreme example of Norman architecture in the world. The foundation stone was laid on August 11, 1093, and nearly all of the major work was completed by 1133 – a short span of time which gives the building a remarkable unity. Perhaps its greatest contribution to the history and progress of architecture was rib-vaulting. In the Galilee Chapel at the west end of the cathedral is the tomb of the Venerable Bede, the great early English historian whose remains were moved from Jarrow in 1020. The original Saxon church here was built in the 10th century to house the shrine of St Cuthbert, whose body was brought from Lindisfarne.

4 COLLEGE GREEN
This secluded open space is surrounded by pleasant houses of the 18th and early 19th centuries. One of the most interesting buildings is The Stables, close to the west end of the cathedral, which still has an original Norman north wall.

5 PALACE GREEN
Along the east side of the green are pretty, mock-Tudor almshouses, an elegant 18th-century hall, and the Bishop's Hospital, dating from 1666. On the other side, the old Tudor Grammar School adjoins the university buildings, and next to the University Library stands Bishop Cosin's Library, founded in 1669.

6 THE CASTLE
When the powers of the Prince Bishops, who ruled Durham as Counts Palatine for 800 years, were finally ended in 1836, the castle became the seat of the University of Durham – the first new university to be founded in England after Oxford and Cambridge. The castle itself was built soon after the Norman Conquest as a defence against the Scots, and in the succeeding centuries was enlarged and strengthened by the bishops.

7 NORTH BAILEY
Perhaps the finest street in Durham, North Bailey and its continuation, Saddler Street, are lined with well-preserved 18th-century houses.

EARLY CLOSING: *Wed*

MARKET DAY: *Sat*

PARKING: *Leazes Bowl, Milburngate*

OPENING TIMES:
Archaeology Museum: open Tue, Thu & Fri all day, Wed pm only
Castle: open all year. 1st 3 wks of Apr & Jul – Sep, Mon – Sat all day. Rest of year, Mon, Wed, Sat, pm only

ROUTE DIRECTIONS
Start at the Market Pl by the Town Hall (1) and walk down Silver St towards Framwellgate Br. A few yards before the bridge, turn l. down the steps and follow signs to the riverside footpath leading to the Archaeology Museum (2). From the museum, keep forward then turn sharp l. up a steep path to the cathedral walls, and follow signs for the cathedral. Enter Palace Gn and turn r. to reach the cathedral (3). Leave by the cloisters to emerge (turning l. and l. again) into College Gn (4) and walk round to the arched gateway into South Bailey. Turn l. here, then l. again into Palace Gn (5). Walk round the green past Bishop Cosin's Library and enter the castle (6) grounds. On leaving the castle, walk down to Owengate, turn l., then l. again into North Bailey (7) and continue along Saddler St to return to the Market Place.

Durham Cathedral's imposing twin towers symbolise the great power once wielded by its bishop as a ruling count palatine

Although Filey has the trappings of a family holiday resort, it remains a fishing port, a fact brought colourfully home by the brightly-painted boats bobbing around at Coble Landing. Well-known locally is the Filey Fishermen's Choir, which appears regularly at concerts.

In the last century Filey made a bid to become a spa resort, but luckily the resulting Victorian architecture – some of it particularly fine – did not swamp the quaint, 17th-century houses of the old village.

At the top of a lovely wooded road called the Ravine, which leads up from the beach, stands St Oswald's Church. This dates from the 12th century and is known for its great square medieval tower, topped by a 'weatherfish'! Local fishermen lost at sea are commemorated in one of the windows.

FOREST OF BOWLAND, Lancashire, West Yorkshire

Off M6. Map Ref: SD65 etc

This lonely, treeless expanse of hauntingly empty moorland and steep-sided fells has been designated an area of outstanding natural beauty and was once the hunting domain of the kings of England, who regarded the local deer as their own property. Hard punishments could be expected by locals caught poaching in those days, but now it is the preserve of fellwalkers and all lovers of unspoiled countryside. Excellent riverside scenery can be enjoyed, and near Preston at Beacon Fell is one of Britain's first country parks. Although popular throughout the year, the park is quite spectacular in winter – when conditions can be merciless and precautions should be taken against the cold.

GATESHEAD, Tyne & Wear
See Metrocentre

GRASMERE, Cumbria
See Dove Cottage

GROSMONT, North Yorkshire
See North Yorkshire Moors Railway

HADDON HALL, Bakewell, Derbyshire

Open spring to early autumn; 2m SE Bakewell, on A6. Map Ref: SK2366

According more to romantic tradition than historic fact, in the 16th century Dorothy Vernon eloped with her lover Sir John Manners from the terraced rose garden at Haddon Hall, a perfumed haven where belief in the tale burgeons.

The magnificent hall itself, owned by the Dukes of Rutland, survives as the most authentic and best-preserved medieval house in England. Although fiercely and comprehensively fortified, it never saw military action and so survived unscathed in its wooded parkland on the River Wye.

It also escaped the vagaries of architectural fashion which transformed many of its contemporaries into neo-classical palaces during the 18th century, because during that time it was uninhabited. Inside can be seen a great banqueting hall, old kitchens, a hand-carved and painted dining room and the beautiful Long Gallery – which overlooks the rose gardens. The setting is splendid and peaceful, the ideal spot in which to while away an English summer afternoon.

HARROGATE, North Yorkshire

Map Ref: SE3055

Until recently Harrogate was a fashionable spa resort where people came to 'take the waters' issuing from its 80 or so mineral springs, or endure a mud treatment at the Royal Baths. Today it is better known as a booming conference centre.

Although still one of Yorkshire's prettiest towns, Harrogate has changed to accommodate its new business and is no longer as refined and elegant as it once was. High Street chain stores have replaced some of the locally-owned shops, and there are times when even the genteel surroundings of Betty's famous tea rooms seem to become an extension of the conference facilities.

But the flowers are still there, and just a few minutes walk from the town centre are the lovely Valley Gardens, established in 1887 to celebrate Queen Victoria's Golden Jubilee. Here can be savoured acres of floral displays, pinewoods, a bowling green, a miniature golf course and tennis courts, all open throughout the year. Two of the country's best known flower shows are held here in spring and autumn respectively, and the earlier of the two celebrated its 60th anniversary in 1987. The Great Autumn Show is a national venue for chrysanthemum and dahlia competitions.

On summer Sunday afternoons the gardens are popular with music lovers, for band concerts are a regular feature. In August a free arts and craft market is held there too. A short distance from the town centre are the Harlow Car Gardens – 60 acres of beds, borders and woodland, including trial grounds for the Northern Horticultural Society.

To discover more about the town's growth as a spa, visit the recently-restored Royal Pump Room Museum – built as the country's first public baths in 1842.

HAVERTHWAITE, Cumbria
See Lakeside & Haverthwaite Railway

HIGH FORCE WATERFALL, Co Durham

Map Ref: NY4020

On its way through beautiful Teesdale the 270-mile Pennine Way – Britain's longest footpath – appropriately enough passes right alongside High Force, England's highest waterfall.

The walk on duckboards over marsh and through an indigenous juniper forest is not too strenuous, and the views of the falls and gorge below are spectacular.

However, be warned – in recent years there have been several tragic accidents as people have lost their footing on the slippery whinstone cliffs, which are sheer and unfenced. Great care should be taken, and it is advisable to wear boots or good shoes with plenty of grip.

Despite the danger High Force is a sight not to be missed, particularly after heavy rain, when huge quantities of foaming water plunge 70ft over the black rocks of the Great Whin Sill.

HOGHTON TOWER, Preston, Lancashire

Open spring to autumn; on A695. Map Ref: SD6125

The hilltop setting of 16th-century Hoghton Tower affords panoramic views of the Lake District Hills, the Welsh mountains, moorland slopes and the sea.

A highlight of the house is the magnificent banqueting hall, where James I is said to have knighted a joint of beef 'Sir Loin' in 1617. Visitors can also see the king's bedchamber, the audience room, a ballroom and other elegant state apartments. Another side of this impressive house is revealed in a tour of the underground passages, including the 'Lancashire Witches' dungeons.

Life in miniature can be seen in a collection of dolls' houses, and there is a permanent display of dolls as well. Don't leave the tower without discovering how a household coped without water on tap. This one used the Tudor Well House, with its horse-drawn pump and oak windlass.

HOLKER HALL, Cark-in-Cartmel, Cumbria

Open spring to autumn (except Sat). ½m N. on B5278. Map Ref: SD3677

There's something for everyone at this 16th-century hall, which is set in peaceful surroundings and is the home of the Lakeland Motor Museum. The collection comprises more than 80 vehicles and includes a full-size replica of Campbell's 'Bluebird'.

Several species of deer can be seen in the attractive grounds, where special events are held in summer, and exhibitions on the themes of Victorian and Edwardian kitchens, craft and the countryside are popular. The farm and adventure playground appeal to youngsters, and inside the hall

are fine carvings and furniture to be admired by their seniors.

HOLMES CHAPEL, Cheshire
See Jodrell Bank

HOLY ISLAND, Lindisfarne, Northumberland

Map Ref: NU1242

Ionian St Aidan established the tiny Holy Island, or Lindisfarne, as a cradle of Christianity when he and a group of monks founded a monastery there in the 7th century. This was destroyed by marauding Danes some 150 years later, and the ruins seen today are of a Benedictine priory established in 1082.

Also associated with the island is the gentle shepherd boy St Cuthbert, who spent much of his later life in retreat on the neighbouring Farne Islands.

Holy Island's fairy-tale castle (NT), perched on a rocky outcrop, was built in 1554 as a fort and refurbished at the turn of the century by Edwin Lutyens for the owner of *Country Life* magazine, Edward Hudson. Much of the dark oak

furniture in the castle, which was used as a holiday home, was designed by Lutyens.

Many old traditions survive among the dwindling island population, and brides still jump the Petting Stone in the yard of the 13th-century parish church. A clear jump over the stone supposedly ensures a happy marriage. Other customs are connected with the fishing industry – the most unusual concerning the word pig. No fishermen would ever mention the word, and even today the animals are called 'yon things' or 'grumfits'.

As the island can only be reached by causeway from the Northumberland mainland at low tide, thousands of visitors tend to flock there at once. However, it is not possible to fully appreciate the unique charm of Holy Island in the few hours afforded by the tide table, so why not check into a guest house and mingle with the locals instead of rushing to beat the North Sea?

Lutyens did not build the 16th-century castle on Holy Island, but he was responsible for its fairy-tale appearance

HORNSEA POTTERY,
Humberside

Open all year. Map Ref: TA2047

Visitors to this well-known pottery at Hornsea can learn about the skills and techniques of the potter's art, then buy the results of his craft at bargain prices in the popular seconds shop. But this is a visit offering more than industrial interest, for in the 28 acres of landscaped gardens around the centre are birds-of-prey and butterfly displays, plus a model village.

HORSESHOE PASS,
Cheshire into Clwyd (Wales)

Off A542. Map Ref: SJ1847

Pause on this high, winding pass through the Welsh border summits to admire breathtaking views of the Llantysilio Mountain to the west, and 1,844ft Cyrn-y-Brain — topped by Sir Watkin's Tower — to the north-east. Horseshoe Pass itself is 1,367ft above sea level.

A lovely feature of the River Dee is Horseshoe Falls, not as might be imagined a natural cascade, but a beautifully curving weir with an 18in fall, built to feed water into the Llangollen Canal. A feature of the canal, which winds through lovely countryside, cuts across the side of a mountain and vaults river valleys on graceful aqueducts, is narrow-boat trips starting from various points along its length.

HOUSESTEADS ROMAN FORT (NT), Northumberland

Open all year; ½m N of B6318. Map Ref: NY7968

A visit to Housesteads is worthwhile for the views alone, and the ancient Roman fort of *Vercovicium* occupies a commanding position there on an exposed whinstone ridge formed by the Great Whin Sill — and the scenery is breathtaking. Perhaps the most dramatically sited of any fort on Hadrian's Wall, Housesteads is also regarded as the most complete and is situated about half a mile from an excellent National Trust visitor centre. However, although the distance is short the walk is steep, and not suitable for anyone infirm. Those unable to tackle the climb should ask at the centre about special arrangements to gain vehicular access.

Excavations of the five-acre site have uncovered remains of a massive granary with an underground ventilation system, plus the only example of a Roman hospital in Britain. Youngsters are often found giggling over the 24-seater latrine, with flushing tank!

HULL, Humberside

Map Ref: TA0929

Town Docks Museum

Open all year

Hull's long association with the sea is told with eloquence in a splendid Victorian building that overlooks the old dock system. Exhibitions include: Whales and Whaling (with the country's best collection of carved and engraved whale bones); the local fishing industry; shipping; and inland waterways. Also, the building's magnificent marble-columned Court Room has been preserved. The museum is an important stop on the Hull's Maritime Heritage Trail.

William Wilberforce Historical Museum

Open all year

In a city that suffered greatly from bombing raids during World War II, the birthplace of the humanitarian William Wilberforce survives in the High Street as the oldest example of a prosperous merchant house. An MP and furious campaigner for the abolition of slavery, Wilberforce was born in the early 17th-century mansion in 1759, and the house now contains a museum in his memory. Inside are elegant Jacobean and Georgian rooms, together with displays relating to the great man's life and campaigns, including a section devoted to the evils of the slave trade.

The house itself shows a distinct Dutch influence and is unique in the street in having a front garden.

Housesteads Fort is dramatically sited beside Hadrian's Wall

HUTTON-IN-THE-FOREST, Skelton, Cumbria

*House open (limited) spring &
summer, gardens all year; on
B5305. Map Ref: NY4635*

Situated in the ancient Forest
of Inglewood, this unusual
house started life as a fortified
14th-century pele tower. It has
been added to over the
centuries, and features an
outstanding garden with
terraces, specimen trees, an
ornamental lake, forest walks
and a nature trail. Hutton is
the home of Lord Inglewood.

HUTTON-LE-HOLE, North
Yorkshire
See Ryedale Folk Museum

JODRELL BANK, Cheshire

*Open daily spring to autumn, &
winter weekends; off A535, 3m
NE Holmes Chapel. Map Ref:
SJ7970*

A whistle stop tour of the
galaxy awaits visitors deep in
the heart of Cheshire at Jodrell
Bank, including a three-
dimensional journey through
space in the planetarium,
where regular demonstrations
of the movement of stars and
planets are given.

Jodrell Bank became famous
after Manchester University
built a giant steerable radio
telescope there in 1957. The
instrument, known as Mark I,
has a 250ft reflector and
remains one of the largest of its
kind in the world. In the 1960s
it was joined by a Mark II
version, with a 125ft reflector
and an advanced digital control.

Cosmic scales and distances
are featured in the fascinating
exhibitions and displays, while
visitors more interested in life
on earth will appreciate the 35
acres of woodland, park and
gardens.

KENDAL, Cumbria
See Abbot Hall Art Gallery

KESWICK, Cumbria
See Lingholm Gardens

KIELDER RESERVOIR,
Northumberland

*Off B6320 at Bellingham, on
unclassified road to Falstone.
Map Ref: NY6788*

Kielder Reservoir might be
Europe's largest man-made
lake and a paradise for water-
sport enthusiasts, but it is
possible to enjoy a visit there
without even wetting your feet.
Opened in 1982 by the Queen,
it has 27 miles of shoreline
offering splendid walks on the
edge of the Northumberland
National Park and amidst a
huge man-made forest.

The best place to begin a visit
is the excellent Tower Knowe
Centre, where a video and
exhibition explain how the
massive Kielder project
involved flooding the entire
Upper North Tyne Valley.
Large picture windows allow
excellent views across the
water, and close to the centre is
a jetty from where a ferry runs
regular trips around the lake.

Water ski-ing, canoeing, wind
surfing, pony trekking, fishing
and bird watching are among
the many activities based on
the shore. However, one of the
best ways to enjoy Kielder is to
follow the Kielder Forest Drive,
a 12-mile route starting from
the 18th-century Kielder Castle
Visitors' Centre – once a
hunting lodge for the Dukes of
Northumberland. This toll road
winds through some wild and
desolate scenery before ending
at Redesdale, just a short
distance from the Scottish
border at Carter Bar.

KILLHOPE LEAD MINING
MUSEUM, nr St John's
Chapel, Co Durham

*Open spring to autumn (by
appointment for parties at other
times); off A689 N St John's
Chapel. Map Ref: NY8143*

Some of England's wildest and
most remote scenery can be
seen from this impressive lead-
mining centre, which has a
34ft-high water wheel fully
restored to its former glory. The
Park Level Lead Crushing Mill
provided employment for
Weardale men during the last
century, and this museum is a
monument to their powers of
endurance. Long journeys
across isolated moorland and
cramped living and working
conditions were the norm. The
exhibits are housed in the old
smithy, stables and bunk house,
and include working models.
There is also an audio-visual
presentation.

LAKE DISTRICT
NATIONAL PARK VISITOR
CENTRE, Brockhole, Cumbria

*Open spring to autumn and
other times by arrangement; on
A591. Map Ref: NY3901*

Comprehensive details about
the geology, wildlife and folk
culture of the Lake District are
available at this exciting
centre, which is accommodated
by a 19th-century house
picturesquely sited on the east
shore of Lake Windermere.
Amongst the displays is an
excellent 'Living Lakeland'
exhibition, and there are films
and audio-visual shows
throughout the day.

During the summer, launch
trips around the lake are
organised from here, and there
are special guided tours of the
centre's 32-acre garden. A
printed programme lists the
many seasonal events,
including Teddy Bears' Picnics,
the World of Beatrix Potter and
a Squirrel Nutkin Trail for
children.

LAKESIDE &
HAVERTHWAITE
RAILWAY, Haverthwaite,
Cumbria

*Site open daily, trains run
spring to autumn. Map Ref:
SD3483*

Here it is possible to recapture
the recently banished romance
of steam on comfortable trains
that run 3½ miles through the
lovely lake and river scenery of
the Leven Valley. Of standard
gauge, the railway conveniently
connects with Lake
Windermere's passenger ferries
at Lakeside, allowing a
continuance of the relaxing
journey by boat to Ambleside
and Bowness.

LANCASTER CASTLE,
Lancashire

*Open spring to late summer,
except when court is in session.
Map Ref: SD4761*

It is hardly surprising that
Lancaster Castle looks
formidable in its crowning
hilltop position above the River
Lune, for this great Norman
stronghold has for centuries
been the county gaol, and the
grim relics of a brutal past can
be seen there to this day.

Built after William the
Conqueror gave virtually the
whole of Lancashire to Roger de
Poitou, the castle has an
original keep with walls 78ft
high and 10ft thick. Other parts
of it were built by King John,
and the magnificent gateway
was added in the 14th century
by John of Gaunt, 1st Duke of
Lancaster.

The Crown Court, with its
barbaric branding iron, gained
infamy for handing out more
death sentences than any other
in the country. Visitors may
enter the aptly-named 'Drop
Room' adjoining Hanging
Corner, and the Gothic-style
Shire Hall houses coats of arms
which date back to the 12th
century.

Also interesting are St Mary's
Church, which contains 14th-
century carved stalls that came
from Cockersand Abbey, and a
Roman Catholic cathedral.

LEVENS HALL, Cumbria

Open spring to autumn; on A6.
Map Ref: SD4886

Works of art at Levens Hall are
not limited to the house, for the
gardens here include a famous
and delightful topiary that was
laid out in 1692 and has been
beautifully maintained in its
original design.

The Elizabethan mansion,
home of the Bagot family, was
extended from a fortified 13th-
century pele tower and contains
a fine collection of Jacobean
furniture. It is noted
particularly for its fine
plasterwork and panelling, plus
England's earliest recorded
patchwork – made in about
1708.

Steam engine enthusiasts will
be enthralled by a collection
featuring model table engines
which demonstrate the
development of steam power
from 1820 to 1920. Traction
engines are 'steamed' on some
Sundays and Bank Holidays.

LEYLAND, Lancashire
See British Commercial Vehicle
Museum

LINDISFARNE,
Northumberland
See Holy Island

LINGHOLM GARDENS,
Keswick, Cumbria

Open daily spring to autumn;
off A66 to Portinscale & 1m on
road to Grange. Map Ref:
NY2522

In spring a veritable 'Host of
golden daffodils' greets visitors
to this Lakeland home of Lord
Rochdale, forming a yellow
fringe to the wooded western
shore of Derwent Water and the
immaculate landscaped gardens
of Lingholm. Later in the year
Wordsworth's favourite bloom
is replaced by exotic and
luxurious displays of
rhododendrons and azaleas.

LITTLE MORETON HALL
(NT), Scholar Green, Cheshire

Open spring to autumn; E off
A34. Map Ref: SJ8358

A lovely water-filled moat
reflects the dazzling symmetry
of black and white timbering
for which this perfect
Elizabethan manor house is
possibly best known. Note in
particular the beautiful carved
gables, woodwork and plaster ·
before stepping inside to admire
the long wainscoted gallery,
chapel, great hall and fine oak
furniture. A knot garden is an
added attraction, and the main
approach is via a gatehouse.

LIVERPOOL, Merseyside
Map Ref: SJ3390

Albert Dock

Museum open daily, though
parts of the Maritime Park are
closed in winter.

Within living memory
Liverpool's historic waterfront
has degenerated from bustling
commerce to deserted
dereliction. However, a few
years ago commitments were
made to halt the march of decay,
and today the 7-mile chain of
wharves and warehouses has
been given a new lease of life
by the award-winning Albert
Dock complex – incorporating
the largest group of Grade I
listed buildings in Britain.

Preservation is only part of
the Albert Dock story, for the
project has created a living,
breathing maritime village
where spending time is easy
and enjoyable. Appetites honed
by the salt-sea air can be
satisfied in attractive
restaurants and wine bars, and
if the ozone is not enough to
prompt thoughts of food, a walk
round the huge Maritime
Museum will do the trick.

Here, in the 19th-century
dock buildings and scattered
widely across the cobbled
wharves amongst bollards,
capstans and other maritime
impedimentia are vessels of
every shape and pedigree, set
against the impressive backdrop
of the Royal Liver building and
its stern neighbours.

Exhibitions, displays, brass-
rubbing facilities and
demonstrations of marine
handicrafts complete the
ambitious and sympathetic
picture of Albert Dock, to which
it is rumoured that London's
Tate Gallery is coming in
search of a second home. But
it's big – so come well shod and
be prepared for some walking.

Croxteth Hall & Country Park

Open spring to autumn , with
some facilities in winter; 5m NE
of Liverpool city centre, signed
off A580 & A5088. Map Ref:
SJ4094

Set in 500 acres of beautiful
parkland, Croxteth Hall is the
former home of the Earls of
Sefton – but it is much more
than just another stately home.

The young and young-at-heart
will enjoy riding the miniature
railway before catching up with
milking time in the farmyard,
where several rare breeds of
animals can be seen. Elsewhere
in the lovely parkland of the
hall's extensive grounds is a
superb Victorian walled garden,
as well as a Victorian
home-farm.

Liverpool's restored Albert
Dock, with the twin-towered
Royal Liver building ahead

Inside the hall are
imaginatively laid-out displays
and furnished rooms on the
theme 'an Edwardian house
party'. Seasonal special events
and attractions are a feature of
the estate.

MALTON, North Yorkshire
See Castle Howard

MANCHESTER, Gt Manchester
See Castlefield Urban Heritage
Park

MARTON, Cleveland
See Captain Cook Birthplace
Museum & Heritage Trail

MARYPORT MUSEUM & PORT, Cumbria

Museum open all year. Map Ref:
NY0336

The history of this once
thriving port is told in
photographs at the town's
Maritime Museum, which
overlooks the harbour and
houses interesting displays of
curios handed down through
various seafaring families.
Among the more famous names

are Fletcher Christian and Thomas Ismay, whose company built the *Titanic*.

Tall sailing ships built at Maryport were launched broadside into the River Ellen, and during the Industrial Revolution the booming port was given its name by Lord of the Manor Colonel H Senhouse, after his wife. The sea is still Maryport's main attraction, fringed by miles of beach stretching to the north and south of the town.

An earlier era in Maryport's history is revealed on high ground to the north, where a Roman fort covered a 4½-acre site. Remains show that it was defended by a double ditch and became protector of a large civilian settlement with shops, workshops and taverns.

METROCENTRE, Gateshead, Tyne & Wear

On A69. Map Ref: NZ2563

The leafy, light and airy shopping malls of what claims to be Europe's largest out-of-town leisure complex make shopping relatively stress-free at the Metrocentre in Gateshead, where there are also glass lifts, fountains and special themed areas such as 'Antiques', and 'Children's Village'. A 10-screen cinema eliminates the traditional but irritating queue, parking is easy and the extra-wide malls are equally popular with wheelchair-bound shoppers and pushchair pushers.

MOUNT GRACE PRIORY (NT), Osmotherley, North Yorkshire

Open all year; 1m NW Osmotherley. Map Ref: SE4598

Carthusian monks who founded this ruined 14th-century priory included hermits who took vows of austerity, isolation and silence, and lived alone in self-contained cells. One of these in the inner cloisters has been restored, and visitors can see how the inhabitant would have lived entirely devoid of comfort and companionship. They only left their cells for a church service and a Saturday meal, and during the rest of the week took their food through a hatch so designed that they could neither touch nor see the server.

The remains are pleasant and peaceful to wander amongst, and include a small church in the Perpendicular style.

MUNCASTER CASTLE, GARDENS & BIRD GARDEN, Cumbria

Open spring to late summer; 1½m E Ravenglass on A595. Map Ref: SD1096

Exotic birds live in the beautiful grounds at Muncaster, a medieval castle and pele tower which was enlarged and refurbished by Anthony Salvin in the 19th century. At the lakesides are elegant flamingoes, ibis and storks, while the old courtyard is bright with the colour and chatter of smaller species.

Beautifully sited near Ravenglass, the castle's western aspect faces the sea and to the east rise the high Cumbrian Hills. Since the 19th century it has been the home of the Penningtons, and tradition holds that the family will have unbroken succession at Muncaster so long as an ancient enamelled and gilded bowl of green glass remains intact. Known as the 'Luck of Muncaster', it was given to the family by King Henry VI after they sheltered him following his defeat at the Battle of Towton in 1461.

A collection of 17th-century miniature furniture is just one of many other treasures in the castle.

NATIONAL TRAMWAY MUSEUM, Crich, Derbyshire

Open spring to autumn & weekends pre-Christmas; off B5035. Map Ref: SK3554

Not-so-old memories spring colourfully and vividly to life at this unique museum, which has a collection of more than 40 vintage British and European tramcars built between 1873 and 1953. The exhibits are contained in an old limestone quarry once worked by George Stephenson.

Many are in a working condition, and tram conductors issue certificates proving that passengers have ridden one of the oldtimers along the museum's mile of scenic track. A facsimile tramway period

Northdale Scar looms over the North Yorkshire Moors railway

street prompts more nostalgia, and there are various workshops, depots and a power station to explore.

Parents and grandparents will earn undying gratitude by remembering that a 'Santa Special' runs at weekends before Christmas.

NORTH YORKSHIRE MOORS RAILWAY, Pickering – Grosmont, North Yorkshire

Open spring to autumn & Xmas. Map Refs: SE7984 & NZ8205

Steam-train travel is making a real and profitable comeback in the capable hands of enthusiasts, and nowhere is this more true than on the North Yorkshire Moors, where an 18-mile stretch of spectacular countryside can be explored in this time-honoured fashion. Passengers can join the train at either Pickering, a delightful market town, or

Grosmont, where there is a loco shed. Along the route are various picturesque stations giving access for walkers to the interior of the North Yorks Moors National Park. Horse-drawn vehicles at Levisham offer an interesting means of exploring the local forest, while at Goatland are walks, waterfalls and a good pub lunch. Newtondale Halt affords splendid view points – but passengers who wish to alight there must tell the guard in advance.

The railway was founded in 1967 by a private company, but since 1972 it has been administered by a trust. Special events include summer evening dinner served aboard the North Yorkshire Pullman, and in December there are Santa Specials.

OSMOTHERLEY, North Yorkshire
See Mount Grace Priory (NT)

PILKINGTON GLASS MUSEUM, St Helens, Merseyside

Open all year; on A58. Map Ref: SJ5195

Some of the finest examples of glass in the world are on display at this museum, which is part of the famous Pilkington factory established here in the 18th century. Exhibits include Roman, French and English glassware, while displays trace the history of glassmaking back to the Egyptians. Various temporary exhibitions are staged at the museum through the year.

PORT SUNLIGHT HERITAGE CENTRE, Merseyside

Open all year; 3m SE Birkenhead. Map Ref: SJ3484

Now a conservation area, this unique village has a heritage centre which supplies 'history trail' leaflets and should be the first stop of any tour. The centre also details the founding and development of the world-famous 'model' community, which was created almost a century ago by William Hesketh Lever, the first Viscount Leverhulme. The heritage trail takes in the Lady Lever Art Gallery, with its outstanding collection of Wedgwood, 18th-century English furniture, Chinese porcelain and Victorian paintings.

Everyone of the 1,000 or so buildings in the village is listed as a place of architectural and historic interest, and it is explored by wide, tree-lined thoroughfares.

PRESTON, Lancashire
See Hoghton Tower

QUARRY BANK MILL (NT), Styal, Cheshire

Open all year; 1½m N Wilmslow. Map Ref: SJ8383

An award-winning museum which combines industrial and rural interest, Quarry Bank Mill is set in 252 acres of pleasant park and riverside woodland. Its main features are a working museum and cotton mill, where thundering looms can be heard, and intricate spinning watched as it produces cloth for sale in the museum shop.

The village and estate by the River Bollin were the creation of Samuel Greg, who founded them towards the end of the 18th century as an unusual self-contained community for a

workforce which stood at 450 by 1820. Visitors today can see detailed records of those times, revealing conditions of employment and working hours; an apprentice's day was from 5.30am to 8pm. Quarry Bank, which is run for the NT by an independent trust, is the most complete and least-altered factory colony surviving from the Industrial Revolution.

Visitors flock there on Bank Holidays and summer Sunday afternoons, so plan a weekday visit to really appreciate this Georgian cotton mill and estate.

RABY CASTLE, Staindrop, Co Durham

Open Easter and May to autumn; on A688, 1m N of Staindrop. Map Ref: NZ1221

A beautiful walled deer park surrounds Raby, probably the most intact medieval castle in the north of England. With its moat and nine impressive towers it might have come straight from a storybook, but in actual fact it dates from the 11th century and has additions contributed by almost every subsequent period. Its most visible ancestry is from the 14th century, and a major delight of this seat of Lord Barnard is the splendid medieval kitchen, with its rib vaulting and smoke-driven spit.

One of the north's greatest families – the Nevilles – owned the castle until 1569, when it was forfeited following their involvement in the ill-fated Rising of the North, which was intended to put Mary, Queen of Scots on the throne of England. In 1616 the great castle was acquired by James I's Secretary of State, Sir Henry Vane of Kent, and it has remained in his family ever since.

The castle is not only a fine example of elegant country-house living, with its octagonal drawing room, fine paintings and furniture, but also shows the below-stairs lives led by housemaids and estate workers.

RAVENGLASS & ESKDALE RAILWAY, Cumbria

Open spring to autumn (also reduced service all winter); off A595. Map Ref: SD0896

Seven miles of glorious Lakeland scenery awaits passengers boarding England's oldest narrow-gauge railway, which was established in 1875 to carry iron ore. Its little trains, mostly steam-hauled, run from the unspoiled coast to the foot of some of the highest hills in the Lake District. This is surely one of the prettiest

railways in the country, and on a sunny day travellers may even find themselves in an open-top carriage.

At Ravenglass there's a railway museum to explore, and stations operate at Eskdale Green and Beckfoot. The journey ends at Dalegarth, in Eskdale. *See also Muncaster Castle, Gardens & Bird Gardens, page 163.*

RIBCHESTER MUSEUM OF ROMAN ANTIQUITIES, Lancashire

Open daily, afternoons; off B6245. Map Ref: SD6535

For 300 years the wild country of this area was guarded by the Roman fort of *Bremetennacum*, the remains of which have been excavated. Finds including gold coins, pottery, brooches, lamps and a rare bronze parade helmet are housed in the site museum, while larger relics can be seen all over the village, incorporated in cottages and other buildings. The oak gallery in 13th-century St Wilfred's Church is supported by two Roman columns – and take a look at the pillars flanking the entrance to the White Bull pub; they are said to come from a Roman temple.

RICHMOND, North Yorkshire
Map Ref: NZ1700

Green Howards Regimental Museum

Open early spring to late autumn. Map Ref: NZ1701

Members of the famous Green Howards Regiment and their families helped to raise the cash needed to transform the medieval Holy Trinity Church in Richmond's market square into a regimental museum.

Now the history of one of the British Army's oldest and most romantic regiments is celebrated in an unusual and historic setting, incidently preserving a valuable old building. Formed in 1688 to fight for William of Orange against James II, for 300 years the Green Howards has drawn soldiers from the farming communities of Yorkshire, the steelworks, shipyards and foundries of Teeside and the mining villages of North Yorkshire and South Durham.

The story of the regiment unfolds from room to room, where outstanding collections of memorabilia include 80 uniforms dating back to 1780, various battle relics, medals, original paintings and even some of the earliest war photography.

Richmond Castle

Open all year; off A6108. Map Ref: NZ1700

One of England's earliest castles, this fine example is perched high above the River Swale in what is probably the most historic market town in Yorkshire. Built by the Normans, its 100ft-high keep commands superb views over the ancient community, and the shadows of its towers and massive 11th-century walls fall in the old market place. Picturesque Swaledale scenery straight from a James Herriot novel is the impressive backdrop against which this massive fortress is set.

RIEVAULX ABBEY (NT), North Yorkshire

Open all year; off B1257. Map Ref: SE5784

One of the best views of this beautiful, ruined abbey is from Rievaulx Terrace, a lovely landscaped garden area on high ground to the south, incorporating 18th-century garden temples. Founded in 1131, Rievaulx was the first church in the north of England to be built by Cistercian monks, who were given the land by Walter L'espec.

Although ruined, the abbey's setting in the richly-wooded valley of the River Rye makes it easy to imagine how Rievaulx

must have looked at the height of its glory, when it was the largest and most splendid Cistercian monastery in the country. The choir and refectory, both masterpieces of English architecture, are well preserved and of particular interest.

ROTHBURY, Northumberland
See Cragside House & Country Park

RYEDALE FOLK MUSEUM, Hutton-le-Hole, North Yorkshire

Open spring to autumn; 3m N of A170. Map Ref: SE7090

Living and working conditions of ordinary Yorkshire country folk are the subjects of this museum, which is set in wide grounds in the chocolate-box village of Hutton-le-Hole. When the museum opened in 1964 it was just a group of 18th-century farm buildings fronting on to the village green. These now serve as the entrance to a larger and living reminder of North Yorkshire's rural industry, including buildings that have been rescued from demolition and re-erected to create an appropriate atmosphere. Among them is a rare cruck-framed long house, with a witch post! Traditional thatch has been used to roof an Elizabethan manor house, and

Majestic even in ruin, Rievaulx's lofty arches evoke strong images of the past

a humbler but fully-furnished 18th-century cottage.

Regular craft demonstrations are a popular attraction here, and a Midsummer celebration is held in June.

ST HELENS, Merseyside
See Pilkington Glass Museum

ST JOHN'S CHAPEL, Co Durham
See Killhope Lead Mining Museum

SALTAIRE, West Yorkshire

Off A657. Map Ref: SE1437

The famous 'model' village of Saltaire stands today as a remarkable monument to one man — the benevolent Bradford wool merchant Titus Salt, who built it between 1851 and 1871 to provide everything needed for the welfare of his workers, including housing, hospital, school, church and leisure facilities . . . but no pub!

Salt didn't live in the village, but most of the streets are named after members of his family. Caroline Street was named after his wife, and George Street after his second son. Saltaire was designed by architects Lockwood and Mawson, generally regarded as

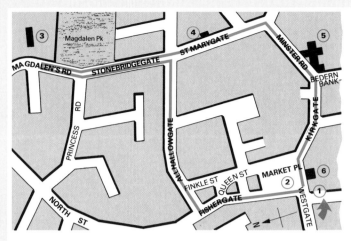

Where the Wakeman walked

The towers of one of England's oldest cathedrals watch over the ancient streets and buildings of Ripon. The basic street plan has remained substantially unchanged since the 13th century, and any visitor roaming the medieval thoroughfares will see Ripon's history written in the surrounding buildings.

1 WAKEMAN'S HOUSE

The Wakeman's House was originally built in the 14th century and stands at the corner of the Market Place. Nowadays there is no longer a wakeman in Ripon, but a mayor instead. Despite this, the age-old tradition of the Hornblower 'setting the watch' is still continued today. Each night at 9pm a figure wearing a tricorn hat sounds a horn at every corner of the market cross and in front of the mayor's house. Residents are proud to say: 'It's been going on for a thousand years without a break.'

2 THE OBELISK

Dominating the Market Square, the 90ft-high Obelisk was erected by William Aislabie at his own expense in 1781 to commemorate his Diamond Jubilee as the borough's Member of Parliament.

3 LEPER'S CHAPEL

This is the local name for the Chapel of the Hospital of St Mary Magdalene, a building which dates back to the 12th century, although it was considerably altered in medieval times.

4 RIPON PRISON & POLICE MUSEUM

Actually housed in the town's old prison, this museum contains various brutal reminders of 'rough justice', and is not for the squeamish. The displays tracing law and order in Ripon from 1604 to 1956 are, nevertheless, fascinating.

5 RIPON CATHEDRAL

Of the original 7th-century building founded here, only the remarkable crypt survives, the rest having been destroyed in 950. Much of the existing structure is 13th century, but there were many later alterations and extensive restoration was carried out in the 19th century. The choir screen has niches filled with brightly-painted statues of Ripon worthies spanning 1,200 years. They were donated by friends of the cathedral in 1947, to replace those lost at the time of the Reformation. The crypt remains little changed since St Wilfrid's day, when it was built as a relic chamber. Today it contains well-displayed church treasures.

6 THE TOWN HALL

Many of Ripon's treasures are housed here, but viewing is by arrangement only. The building itself dates from the early part of the 19th century and was designed by James Wyatt. On the front of the building, marked in glittering letters, are the words: 'Except ye Lord keep ye cittie, ye Wakeman waketh in vain.'

MARKET DAY: *Thu*

EARLY CLOSING: *Wed*

PARKING: *Fishergate, Market Place*

OPENING TIMES:
Ripon Prison & Police Museum: Open May – Sep Tue – Sat pm only

ROUTE DIRECTIONS
From the Market Pl, site of Wakeman's House (1) and the Obelisk (2), walk into Fishergate then r. into Allhallowgate. Next, turn l. at The Golden Fleece public house into Stonebridgegate. Keeping to the left-hand side, walk on into Magdalen Rd where, a little way up on the r, Leper's Chapel (3) is situated. From here, turn back and through Stonebridgegate once more and into Saint Marygate, passing Ripon Prison & Police Museum (4) on the l. At the eventual fork in the road, turn r. into Minster Rd, where Ripon Cathedral (5) is on the l. On from this point the road becomes Kirkgate, which leads back to the Market Pl where the imposing 19th-century Town Hall (6) is to be found on the l.

In present-day Ripon the medieval Wakeman's House stands as the enduring symbol of a centuries-old local tradition

the men who created Bradford in the middle of the last century.

A useful little visitors' guide details an interesting walk which takes in the Salt Mill Works by the Leeds and Liverpool Canal. In its prime the mill produced 30,000yds of cloth each day and employed 3,000 people. Saltaire's residential areas have changed little since they were built, and visitors will note that Sir Titus built executive housing as well as workers' terraces.

Finally, no-one should leave Saltaire without riding on the tram to the Glen, a wooded area above Roberts Park. It was built in 1895, and the original fare was 'a penny up and half a penny down'.

SANDCASTLE, Blackpool, Lancashire

Off M55. Map Ref: SD3035

Blackpool's proud boast is that the 'Sandcastle' is the world's greatest 'inside seaside', and it is certainly an excellent solution to those wet summer days. If a walk along the prom is rained off this is the place to be, splashing in huge leisure pools, daring the 300ft water slide, lying on terraced beaches among tropical trees close to restaurants, amusements and bars – a desert-island resort slap in the middle of town.

While youngsters will enjoy the fun pools, with their floating islands, obstacles and water cannons, more sporting members of the family might prefer a game of snooker or darts. Of course, you could just doze off under the palm trees and dream of faraway places!

SKIPTON CASTLE, North Yorkshire

Open all year. Map Ref: SD9851

Six massive towers joined by the intact curtain walls of this fully-roofed and -floored medieval fortress dominate the Skipton skyline from a wooded clifftop site. Founded 900 years ago, the castle was the home of the mighty Clifford family, and their motto *Desformais* is still proclaimed on the massive 14th-century gatehouse. In the charming 15th-century Conduit Court is a yew tree reputed to be more than 300 years old.

Skipton Castle was on the Lancastrian side in the War of the Roses, and an important Royalist stronghold during the Civil War. However, it was not strong enough to resist Cromwell's army, although it withstood three years of siege before it fell.

SLEDMERE PARK, Humberside

Open spring to autumn; junction of B1251 & B1253. Map Ref: SE9364

A Palladian mansion set in a beautifully-landscaped park designed by Capability Brown, Sledmere is the home of the Sykes, whose 18th-century ancestors were renowned agricultural innovators largely responsible for the transformation of the Wolds landscape from a bare waste into the fertile, wooded land of today. In the park is one of the loveliest parish churches in the country, and a feature of Sledmere itelf is a delightful Italian garden with columns, statues and an ornamental pond. The house itself was burnt down in 1911, but rebuilt in original 18th-century style. It contains some fine Chippendale, Sheraton and French furniture.

SPEEDWELL & BLUE JOHN CAVERNS, Castleton, Derbyshire

Open all year; off A625. Map Ref: SK1482

Castleton's 1-mile underground boat trip along an illuminated canal to Speedwell, the most spectacular of a group of limestone mines and caverns, is an event not to be missed. One of the tour's highlights is the 'Bottomless Pit', the only cave in Britain that is visited by boat, which was found by miners.

The Blue John Cavern is in the same group under the Derbyshire hillside, and is named from the blue, semi-precious stone that used to be mined there. Another feature of the cavern's extensive mineral formations are stalagmites and stalactites. Small items made from Blue John, which has almost been worked out in the area, can be bought locally.

SPROATLEY, Humberside
See Burton Constable Hall

STAINDROP, Co Durham
See Raby Castle

STEAMTOWN RAILWAY MUSEUM, Carnforth, Lancashire

Open all year; on A6. Map Ref: SD4970

Just 20 years ago British Rail closed its last operational steam shed, but now it enjoys a new lease of life as a working museum linked with two of the great romantic locos – *The*

Flying Scotsman and *Mallard.* Housed here are over 30 steam engines from Britain, France and Germany, some of which are steamed at weekends and throughout the summer.

STYAL, Cheshire
See Quarry Bank Mill (NT)

ULLSWATER STEAMERS

Off A592. Map Ref: NY4220

Cruise-and-lunch or cruise-and-walk alternatives are offered by this special service plying one of England's loveliest lakes, where regular scheduled trips and one-hour cruises are available on 19th-century steamers that have been converted to oil power. From their mountain-girded moorings at Glenridding the stately old ladies cruise the 9-mile length of Ullswater, stopping at pretty Pooley Bridge.

A combined cruise and lunch ticket allows time for a leisurely pub meal before returning on board to soak up the scenery, while the more energetic will appreciate the opportunity to take a lakeside walk.

VINDOLANDA & CHESTERHOLM, Bardon Mill, Northumberland

Open all year; off A69. Map Ref: NY7764

Vindolanda, a fort built by the Romans some 40 years before Hadrian's Wall was begun, is part of a frontier system that was masterminded by Agricola and called the Stanegate. It is an excellent site to visit, being considered one of the best-preserved Roman relics in Europe.

The museum is in the lovely country house of Chesterholm, which is set in picturesque ornamental gardens that are worth a visit in their own right. Exhibits show fascinating military and civilian finds, including sandals, shoes and even a child's money box. There are also some rather unsavoury Roman recipes!

WASHINGTON WATERFOWL PARK, Tyne & Wear

Open all year; follow signs to Washington District 15 from AIM. Map Ref: NZ3356

Feeding the birds is positively encouraged at this 103-acre Wildfowl Trust park, and bags of suitable morsels can be bought at the entrance. It might be noted that children are not the only ones spotted tossing dinner to some of the tamer birds in the attractively landscaped surroundings!

The waterfowl park, situated on the banks of the River Wear, is home to around 1,200 birds representing about 100 different species. These include Hawaiian geese – a rare breed saved from extinction by the efforts of the Trust – and a flock of Chilean flamingoes. Viewing hides allow visitors to observe visiting and migratory birds, and an inside viewing area with a tea room conveniently to hand is an excellent facility for when the weather is unkind.

YORK, North Yorkshire

Off A19/A66. Map Ref: SE6051

It is best to visit York outside the main summer season if you want to soak up the atmosphere of a great city steeped in many centuries of fascinating history. King George V said: 'The history of York is the history of England', and it really does seem that on every street corner another page of England's heritage is turned. The Romans and Vikings both left their marks, the medievals contributed folk architecture and Mystery Plays – and later centuries saw the rise of railways and invention of boxed chocolates.

This is a compact city that is easily explored on foot, although a visit to York must never be rushed. The city was the *Eboracum* of the Romans, but the present name derives from the Vikings' *Jorvick*. A good place to begin a visit is the 3m circuit of the city walls, which encompass a maze of narrow streets and – towering above the city's other ancient buildings – the glorious Minster.

The largest Gothic cathedral north of the Alps, it is famed for its beautiful medieval glass and has many other outstanding features that demand time and sympathy from the visitor. Not the least interesting is the continuous work of craftsmen in restoring and repairing, holding back the centuries. They are the living proof that modern skills easily match those of the medieval workers who built the minster between 1220 and 1470.

Following destruction by the Normans, York was rebuilt as a great medieval city, the best evidence of which is seen in the Shambles – where the old houses lean over and almost touch each other. Stonegate is another lovely street, and the location of some rather upmarket shops.

Ancient and modern come together at one of York's newest attractions, the fabulous Jorvick Viking Museum. Here visitors are transported in 'time cars' back to the 10th century to experience the sights, sounds and even the smells of the Scandinavian city. It is one of York's most popular attractions, so visitors should be prepared to queue. Out-of-season weekday visits are a good idea.

There are plenty of other interesting places including the National Railway Museum – a must for all steam enthusiasts and train spotters. The Castle Museum of Yorkshire Life, with its open-air period streets, is an ideal place to spend an afternoon. Its gardens are a pleasant and peaceful resort away from the crowds, and are the site of an astronomical observatory and ancient abbey ruins.

The city is particularly well blessed with ancient churches and other fine old buildings, many of which are open to the public and house museums.

As well as its remarkable heritage York can claim two infamous sons, Guy Fawkes – who was born in Petergate and executed for treason in 1605 – and legendary highwayman Dick Turpin, who was hanged in 1739 at York Tyburn, which stood near the area which is now York Racecourse. The spot is paved, and has seating – perhaps for visitors to sit and ponder the pros and cons of rough justice.

Near York Minster is Stonegate, where quality shops tempt both locals and tourists

Southern Scotland

Scale: Approx 16 miles to 1 inch

N O R T H

S E A

Firth of Forth

Girdle Ness

Aboyne
Peterculter
A93

Banchory

Ballater
Balmoral Castle & Crathie Church

Fasque
Laurencekirk
Inverbervie

Brechin
Montrose

JM Barrie's Birthplace Kirriemuir

Forfar
Glamis Castle
Lang Craig

Coupar Angus
Arbroath

Carnoustie
Monifieth

DUNDEE
Newport-on-Tay

Errol
Cupar
St Andrews Bay
St Andrews
Fife Ness

ermuchty
Falkland
Ladybank
Crail

nross
Glenrothes
Pittenweem
Anstruther
Isle of May

Buckhaven
Elie

Cowdenbeath
Ravenscraig Castle

Kirkcaldy

Kinghorn
North Berwick
Dunbar

Inverkeithing
Preston Mill

EDINBURGH
Musselburgh
Haddington
St Abb's Head

Dalkeith
Gifford
Grantshouse
Eyemouth

LAMMERMUIR HILLS
Duns
Berwick-upon-Tweed

Thirlestane Castle & and Border Country Life Museum
Lauder
Manderston

Holy Island

Peebles
Innerleithen
Mellerstain House
Coldstream
Bamburgh Castle

Scottish Museum of Woollen Textiles
Galashiels
Melrose
Scott's View
Kelso
Belford

Botanic Garden
Abbotsford
Selkirk

Bowhill
Wooler
Chillingham Park Wild White Cattle

Jedburgh

Hawick
CHEVIOT HILLS
Alnwick

fat
Cragside House & Country Park
Coquet Island
Amble

Kielder Water
Kielder Reservoir

Langholm
Otterburn
Newbiggin-by-the-Sea

Lockerbie
Morpeth
Ashington
Bedlinggton

Canonbie
Blyth

Longtown
Ponteland
Whitley Bay
Tynemouth

Gretna
Brampton
Housesteads Roman Fort
Haydon Bridge
Haltwhistle
Vindolanda & Chesterholm
Hexham
Corbridge
Gateshead
NEWCASTLE UPON TYNE
South Sheilds

Carlisle
Jarrow
Washington Waterfowl Park
SUNDERLAND

Wigton
Metrocentre
Washington

Hutton-in-the-Forest
Alston
Consett
Beamish
Houghton le Spring

ria
Durham
Peterlee

Cockermouth
Killhope Lead Mining Museum
Stanhope
Tow Law
Crook
Hartlepool

Keswick
Dalemain
Penrith
High Force Waterfall
Bishop Auckland

Lingholm Gardens
Ullswater Steamers
Appleby-in-Westmorland
West Auckland
Newton Aycliffe
Redcar

Dove Cottage
Brough
Barnard Castle
Raby Castle
Stockton on Tees
Salt

Kirkby Stephen
Darlington
Guisboroug

171

Captain C Birthpl
Stokesley

Dunnet Head
Stroma · Pentland Skerries
Duncansby Head
ster
Castletown
John
O'Groats
urso
Halkirk
Sinclair's
Bay
Noss Head
Wick
Latheron
elmsdale

Firth

Lossiemouth
Buckie
Cullen
Portsoy
Banff
Macduff
Rosehearty
Fraserburgh
Loch of
Strathbeg
Elgin
Forres
Rothes
Keith
Turriff
Peterhead
Charlestown
of Aberlour
Dufftown
Huntly
Glenlivet
Rhynie
Pitmedden
Garden
Ellon
Old Meldrum
Garten
Tomintoul
Grampian Transport
Museum
Inverurie
Alford
ce
ark
Craigievar
Castle
Aboyne
Peterculter
ABERDEEN
Girdle Ness
Braemar
Ballater
Banchory
Balmoral Castle
& Crathie Church
Loch Muick
Stonehaven
Fasque
Laurencekirk
Inverbervie
Brechin
Montrose
JM Barrie's
Birthplace
Kirriemuir
Blairgowrie
Forfar
Glamis Castle
Lang Craig
Coupar Angus
Arbroath
Carnoustie
Monifieth
DUNDEE
Newport-on-Tay
Perth
Errol
Bridge
of Earn
Cupar
St Andrews Bay
St Andrews
Fife Ness
Auchtermuchty
Crail
Falkland
Ladybank
Anstruther
Pittenweem
Isle
of May
Kinross
Glenrothes
Buckhaven
Elie
Cowdenbeath
Ravenscraig
Castle
line
Kirkcaldy
Kinghorn
North Berwick
Inverkeithing
uth
nsferry
Dunbar
Preston
Mill
EDINBURGH
Haddington
A1
Musselburgh
St Abb's Head
Livingston
Dalkeith
Gifford
Eyemouth
West
Linton
Grantshouse
LAMMERMUIR
HILLS
Thirlestane Castle &
and Border Country
Life Museum
Duns
Manderston
Berwick-upon-Tweed
Lauder
Peebles
Innerleithen
Mellerstain
House
Coldstream
Holy Island
Scottish
Museum of
Woollen Textiles
Galashiels
Melrose
Scott's View
Kelso
Belford
Bamburgh Castle
Biggar
Dawyck Botanic
Garden
Selkirk
Abbotsford
Wooler
Chillingham
Park Wild
White Cattle
Bowhill
Jedburgh
Hawick
Alnwick

NORTH

SEA

Firth of Forth

TOUR 1 108 MILES

Mountains and Lochsides

Starting with views of Gairloch's sandy bays and the island-studded expanse of Loch Maree, the drive follows the rivers and skirts the lochs of this gentle corner of Wester Ross, passing the beautiful Falls of Measach and the lush vegetation of Inverewe Gardens on its way.

The drive starts from Gairloch, a village with a fine, sandy beach occupying an attractive position on the shore of Loch Gairloch. A converted farmhouse contains the Gairloch Heritage Museum.

Leave by the A832 Kinlochewe road. After passing through Charlestown, the road proceeds inland along the River Kerry, and past Gairloch Dam before entering Slattadale Forest, with the Victoria falls on the right, and reaching the edge of Loch Maree. Across the water the mountain peaks of Letterewe Forest can be seen, with Slioch (3,215ft) rising prominently. The road widens as it runs alongside the loch, skirting the Beinn Eighe Nature Reserve on the approach to Kinlochewe. Several nature trails and a Visitor Centre have been provided in the Reserve.

At Kinlochewe keep on the A832 (single track) Achnasheen road. The drive climbs through Glen Docherty and later skirts Loch a' Chroisg before arriving at the hamlet of Achnasheen. *Continue forward, signed Inverness, along Strath Bran – with Loch Luichart on the right – as you approach Gorstan.*

At Gorstan turn left on to the A835, signed Ullapool. From here the drive follows the Black Water, then the Glascarnoch River, before passing the Loch Glascarnoch Reservoir on the right. Beyond the loch, bleak Dirrie More is crossed before reaching the Braemore road junction.

Turn left here on to the A832, where there is a car park for the Corrieshalloch Gorge (NTS). The Gorge and the spectacular Falls of Measach can be viewed from a suspension bridge which spans the deep and narrow chasm. The A832 climbs on to higher ground before descending to the Dundonnell River beneath the slopes of An Teallach (3,484ft). From Dundonnell the tour follows the shoreline of Little Loch Broom, passing Ardessie where there is a fish farm which is open to the public. Later the road crosses a headland and rejoins the coast at Gruinard Bay – noted for its sandy beaches. Gruinard Island, in the middle of the bay, was used as a germ warfare-testing ground in World War II; it is still infected with anthrax and landing is prohibited.

At the small hamlet of Laide the road swings southwards to the outskirts of Aultbea – a small crofting village situated on Loch Ewe.

Continue along the coast road. After 6 miles, on the right, is the entrance to Inverewe Gardens (NTS). These, begun in 1862, contain a remarkable collection of rare and sub-tropical plants. At Poolewe, the road turns southwards again and in one mile there is a viewpoint from where the length of Loch Maree can be seen. Higher ground, somewhat barren, is traversed before the return to Gairloch.

Gairloch village, on the shore of Loch Gairloch's tranquil expanse

TOUR 2 102 MILES

Peaks and Peat Hillsides

Leaving the bustling town of Oban, the tour climbs up to the forbidding Pass of Brander, crosses desolate Rannoch Moor, then goes through historic Glen Coe before returning to the less dramatic scenery – scattered with castle ruins – of Loch Linnhe.

The drive starts from Oban, a popular resort and the port serving the islands of Mull, Coll, Tiree, Lismore, Colonsay, Barra and South Uist. Of interest around the town are McCaig's Folly (the famous circular landmark above the harbour built to relieve unemployment in the late 19th century), the Caithness Glassworks and Macdonald's Mill, which demonstrates spinning and weaving.

Follow signs Crianlarich to leave by the A85. After 3 miles the road to the left leads to ruined 13th-century Dunstaffnage Castle (AM) which stands at the mouth of Loch Etive. Later, on the approach to Connel, the Falls of Lora can be seen below Connel Bridge. Continue beside the loch to Taynuilt. (A 1½-mile detour may be taken from here to the 18th-century Bonawe Iron Furnace (AM).)

At the crossroads turn left on to the B845, signed Village, and in 1½ mile turn right, (unclassified). Beyond Taynuilt, twin-peaked Ben Cruachan (3,695ft) rises to the left of the road. The main drive enters the wild Pass of Brander and later, on the left, are the Falls of Cruachan below the Cruachan Reservoir. The power station and Visitor Centre opposite are built underground. The road continues alongside Loch Awe and after 2¾ miles is the attractive church of St Conan, built between 1881 and 1930. Later, beyond Lochawe Post Office, there are views of the ruins of Kilchurn Castle (AM).

Pass Dalmally then 2 miles farther turn left on to the B8074, signed Glen Orchy. The single-track road passes through partly forested valley scenery, featuring several waterfalls. (An easier, alternative route to the Bridge of Orchy is via the A85 to Tyndrum, then left on to the A82; it is 5 miles longer.)

After 10¼ miles on the B8074 turn left on to the A82, signed Fort William, and continue to Bridge of Orchy. Beyond the village the road passes Loch Tulla, then climbs on to the bleak bog and lochan waste of Rannoch Moor. The Kings House Hotel, on a minor road to the right, faces Stob Dearg (3,345ft), left, one of Scotland's most famous rock peaks, which lies in a well-known winter sports district. From here the road descends into rugged Glen Coe, overshadowed by the peaks of Bidean nam Bian (left), at 3,766ft the highest mountain in Argyll, and its outliers, the

The circular McCaig's folly looks over the bustling harbour at Oban

Three Sisters. One mile beyond Loch Achtriochtan on the right is the Glen Coe Visitor Centre (NTS). This stands ½ mile from Signal Rock, from which the signal was given for the hideous massacre of the Macdonalds of Glencoe by the Campbells of Glen Lyon in 1692. Continue down the glen to Glencoe village. Two heather-thatched cottages in the main street house the Glencoe and North Lorn Folk Museum, with Macdonald and Jacobite relics.

From Glencoe follow signs Oban and Fort William and at the roundabout, 1¾ miles past the edge of Ballachulish, take the second exit A828, signed Oban. Shortly the road runs beneath the impressive Ballachulish Bridge, then past the Ballachulish Hotel. Near by is a monument to James of the Glen, wrongly hanged in 1752 after a notorious trial known as the Appin murder case. The drive then follows the Appin shore of Loch Linnhe, through Kentallen and Duror, with views of the Ardgour Hills across the loch. Early 16th-century Castle Stalker can be seen near Portnacroish, before the drive meets the edge of Loch Creran. It continues round the loch to the Sea Life Centre and Marine Aquarium at Barcaldine, with several picnic sites and forest walks along the way. Later there are views of Barcaldine Castle to the right. Continue through Benderloch, skirting Ardmucknish Bay; from here, the Moss of Achnacree can be seen to the left.

After 2¼ miles cross the cantilevered Connel bridge. At the T-junction turn left on to the A85 for the return to Oban.

ABBOTSFORD, Melrose, Borders

Open early spring to autumn; on B6360 1m SE Galashiels.
Map Ref: NT5034

Sir Walter Scott was at his happiest as laird of Abbotsford, and his study, extensive library, armoury, drawing room and dining room have been kept almost exactly as he knew them.

Among their treasures are historical relics ranging from Flora MacDonald's pocket book to a clasp (in the shape of golden bees) which fastened Napoleon's cloak at Waterloo. It is easy to imagine Sir Walter bent over the writing desk, letting his imagination flow into the latest chapter of another eagerly awaited Waverley novel, in the study so placed as to give him no distracting view of the lovely tree-lined course of the murmuring River Tweed that he loved so dearly.

ABERDEEN, Grampian

Map Ref: NJ9406

Hundreds of years before North Sea oil, Aberdeen was a flourishing mercantile city where many a medieval fortune was founded on trade with the Baltic and the Low Countries. The Shore Porters' Society of 1498 continues as the oldest company of its type in Britain.

Between the River Dee and the River Don, the city has nearly three miles of beaches and plenty of public open space. Hazelhead Park is on land granted to the citizens of Aberdeen by Robert the Bruce, and Duthie Park is famous for its winter gardens and hillsides ablaze with roses. Another 100,000 rose bushes bloom on the verges of the North Anderson Drive dual-carriageway.

Aberdeen Maritime Museum is in Provost Ross's House, which was built by a 16th-century merchant. Provost Skene's House – of similar date – is the museum of civic and domestic life and the Art Gallery displays a fine municipal collection.

ANSTRUTHER, Fife

Map Ref: NO5603

Although its substantial harbour no longer has its own fishing fleet, Anstruther has never lost the tang of the sea. The award-winning Scottish Fisheries Museum – transformed from a cluster of buildings which used to be a ships' chandlery, net loft and fishermen's store – features local fisherfolk and their activities. Exhibits deal with herring-fishing, whaling, boats and equipment, and there is a fine aquarium. Moored in the harbour is the red-painted North Carr light vessel, which was retired in 1975 from the vicious reefs off Fife Ness. It is also a museum of another and often forgotten aspect of seafaring life.

AVIEMORE, Highland

Map Ref: NH8912

Skiers think of it as a base for the Cairngorm snowfields, but Aviemore is a major all-year-round holiday resort. It has a station on the main Perth-Inverness line, but the adjacent Strathspey steam railway is the greater attraction and prompter of many nostalgic memories. From Easter to October enthusiasts operate steam-hauled services through the pinewoods to Boat of Garten. Timetables are available at the station. Just across the River Spey from Aviemore is Inverdruie, which has a whisky museum and a rainbow-trout fishery. Two miles south of Inverdruie there is a visitor centre at the start of a beautiful nature trail, with gentle gradients, which circles the woodland fringe round Loch an Eilein.

BALLATER, Grampian
See Balmoral Castle

**BALMORAL CASTLE &
CRATHIE CHURCH,**
Grampian

*Open spring & summer; on
B976 6m W Ballater.
Map Ref: NO2595*

Balmoral Castle – the Royal
Family's private Scottish home
since Victoria and Albert's time
– stands among lawns and
ornamental woodlands in a
curve of the River Dee. The
only part open to visitors is the
ballroom, with its exhibition of
Victorian paintings, furniture
and furnishings, but there are
plenty of enjoyable walks on
level drives and pathways
around the grounds and
gardens.

Just across the Dee is the
little church at Crathie, where
the Royal Family worship while
they are in residence at
Balmoral.

In 1894 the tiny parish found
it hard to raise funds for the
present building, so Queen
Victoria agreed to the grandest-
ever church bazaar in the castle
grounds, with princes and
princesses supervising several
of the stalls.

*The beautiful woodlands of
Balmoral, on the banks of the
River Dee, form the setting for
Balmoral Castle, the Royal
Family's home in Scotland*

**BANNOCKBURN
HERITAGE CENTRE (NTS),**
Stirling, Central

*Open spring to autumn; on
A872 ½m S Stirling.
Map Ref: NS7990*

With help from a dramatic,
action-packed mural and an
interesting audio-visual display,
this National Trust for Scotland
visitor centre tells the gripping
story of the most decisive battle
in Robert the Bruce's long and
determined campaign to regain
total control of Scotland from
the English.

At Bannockburn in June 1314
his heavily outnumbered army
was brilliantly directed to win a
crushing victory over Edward
II's forces.

BENMORE, Strathclyde
See Younger Botanic Garden

BLAIR ATHOLL, Tayside
See Blair Castle

BLAIR CASTLE, Blair Atholl,
Tayside

*Open spring to autumn; on
B8019. Map Ref: NN8666*

Every year, during the Atholl
Highland Gathering in the
grounds of Blair Castle, there is
a unique military occasion
when the Atholl Highlanders –
Europe's only remaining
private army – parade before
their commanding officer, the
Duke of Atholl. Dating in part
from the 12th century, the
white-walled castle has played
an important part in many
wars and risings.

These events are recalled in
several displays, but most of the
32 rooms open to visitors have
rather more peaceful themes.
Between them they house
splendid collections of furniture
and furnishings, family
portraits, tapestries and
porcelain.

**BLAIRDRUMMOND
SAFARI & LEISURE PARK,**
Central

*Open spring to autumn; off A84
5m NW Stirling.
Map Ref: NN7398*

Laid out on estate land
reclaimed in the early 19th
century from peat bogs which
were once on the bed of the
North Sea, Blairdrummond has
drive-through enclosures for
lions and tigers, a penguin pool,
a sea-lion show, a pets' farm
and cruises around a
chimpanzee island. There are
also lakeside picnic places,
where younger visitors can
swoop Tarzan-style across the
water on the 'Flying Fox' cable.

BOWHILL, Selkirk, Borders

House open summer, grounds spring to autumn; on B7039 3m W Selkirk. Map Ref: NT4227

This home of the Duke of Buccleuch and Queensberry is a 19th-century mansion containing Louis XV furniture, valuable porcelain, rooms with hand-painted 17th-century wallpaper from China, and an internationally renowned art collection including works by Leonardo, Canaletto, Gainsborough, Raeburn and Reynolds. Below stairs is the gleam of burnished copper in a restored Victorian kitchen. Nature trails in the beautifully wooded grounds circle a pair of lochs, run alongside the Yarrow Water and follow the Lime Avenue.

BRAEMAR, Grampian

Map Ref: NO1591

Perhaps the most famous sporting and social occasion on Deeside is the Braemar Gathering on the first Saturday in September, when members of the Royal Family join tens of thousands of spectators in enjoying athletics events, dancing and piping. Braemar's craft shops specialise in locally produced woodcarving and hornwork. Although it is a fine centre for serious hillwalking, there are lower-level paths here too – for instance, to the view indicator in the Morrone birchwood and juniper reserve, facing across the magnificent upper valley of the Dee to the Cairngorm Plateau. Braemar Castle was at different times in its turbulent history a Jacobite stronghold and a Hanoverian outpost garrisoned to keep the Jacobite clansmen in check.

CARRBRIDGE, Highland

Map Ref: NH9022

The place which pioneered ski-ing holidays in the Cairngorms, Carrbridge is a traditional stone-built village beside the elegantly arched Bridge of Carr, built in 1717 to allow burial parties to cross the River Dulnain – even when in spate. The Landmark Visitor Centre makes very full use of its 30-acre pinewood site, including a multi-screen historical show and a nature centre. One of the nature trails has a tree-top section with a walkway on stilts 20ft above the forest floor. There is also a modern sculpture park, plus an adventure playground with almost a mile of pathways in a woodland maze.

CHATELHERAULT, Hamilton, Strathclyde

Open all year; on A72 1m SE Hamilton. Map Ref: NS7353

Designed by William Adam, the Duke of Hamilton's remarkably ornate 18th-century hunting lodge occupies a hilltop site, with an invigorating view north, and has been completely restored as the centrepiece of a fine country park. Chatelherault's historic herd of unique white cattle graze in front of the lodge. Behind, the landscape makes a dramatic change as the woodland fringe drops down into the precipitous Avon Gorge. Miles of rebuilt footpaths run along both sides of the gorge, and cross it at three bridges. Many are fairly level; one follows the riverside track of a long-gone, horse-drawn mineral railway.

CLATTERINGSHAWS LOCH, Dumfries & Galloway

On A712, 6m W New Galloway. Map Ref: NX5476

Lochside Galloway Deer Museum, open from April to September, has fine displays on the wildlife of the district, forestry activities and the workings of the hydro-electric scheme for which Clatteringshaws is a reservoir. Red deer and wild goats have hillside enclosures farther west. A short walk leads to the site of Robert the Bruce's 1307 victory at the skirmish of Moss Raploch, and the 10-mile Raiders Road forest drive – open from June to September – follows an 18th-century cattle-rustlers' trail beside the rock pools of the Black Water of Dee.

COATBRIDGE, Strathclyde
See Summerlee

CRAIGIEVAR CASTLE (NTS), Grampian

Open spring to late summer, grounds open all year; on A980 6m S Alford. Map Ref: NJ5609

Of all the National Trust for Scotland's impressive properties in Grampian, Craigievar – with its pink-washed walls, tiny windows, corbelled turrets and balustraded roof-top tower – is the nearest to a 'fairytale' castle. It was completed in 1626 as the country home of a wealthy Baltic merchant of Aberdeen, William Forbes. He was known to his city neighbours – then, as now, difficult to impress – as 'Danzig Willie'. Craigievar has brilliant plasterwork, fine wood carvings and the neat but unflamboyant

furnishings of a comfortable home. The height of the building draws the eye to the ornamented roofline, but it also implies a fair number of steep stairways inside.

CULROSS, Fife

Map Ref: NS9885

Sir George Bruce of Culross (the 'l' is silent and the 'u' is long) was a brilliant engineer-businessman-laird at the turn of the 16th and 17th centuries. He exploited the coal seams and salt pans of his Fife-coast estate, and built up a very lucrative foreign trade. His own distinguished town house, Culross Palace (AM) (NTS), is open to the public. Completed in 1611 and unaltered since, it is under the guardianship of the Ancient Monuments scheme and owned by the National Trust for Scotland, which spearheaded a remarkable restoration project to keep the lower part of the town as nearly 17th-century as possible.

Unfortunately, the 20th-century skyline is very dull. The Culross Trail visits most of the carefully restored buildings, and in the Town House – another NTS property – the history of this fascinating little place is recalled in illustrations and an audio-visual display.

CULZEAN CASTLE & COUNTRY PARK (NTS), Maybole, Strathclyde

Castle open spring to autumn, country park all year; on A719 12m SW Ayr. Map Ref: NS2310

One of Robert Adam's finest buildings, 18th-century Culzean Castle stands on a striking clifftop site above the Firth of Clyde in more than 500 acres featuring woodlands, gardens, fields and shoreline. The whole property – castle and grounds – was presented in 1945 to the National Trust for Scotland. Among its many fine features are a supremely elegant oval staircase and a circular saloon whose windows look out over the sea to the mountain peaks of Arran and the 1,100ft rock of Ailsa Craig.

Adam's elegant home-farm complex houses a visitor centre which explains in a lively way the history, architecture, agriculture and personalities of Culzean, pronounced 'Cullane'. Miles of smoothly surfaced footpaths explore the wooded grounds and run along a clifftop which is well sheltered by oaks, sycamores and Corsican pines. Long stairways lead down past the sandstone cliffs to the shore.

DAWYCK BOTANIC GARDEN, Stobo, Borders

Open spring to late summer; on B712 8m SW Peebles. Map Ref: NT1635

Landlords from three different families cared for the arboretum at Dawyck before it was taken under the wing of the Royal Botanic Garden of Edinburgh. In one of the loveliest stretches of the upper Tweed Valley, its fine specimen trees, flowering shrubs and springtime bulb displays sweep up the glen of the Scrape Burn, which at one point tumbles under an attractive high-arched Dutch bridge. Well-graded walks climb through woodland and also lead to a little chapel housing memorials to many of the owners who made Dawyck such a delight.

DOUNE, Central

Map Ref: NN7201

Crossed pistols on coats of arms displayed at each entrance road to Doune recall the 17th-century craft for which it was once famous. Open all year, Doune Castle (AM), was a stronghold of the Earls of Moray, and has many striking apartments, including a Retainers' Hall hung with banners and a Lord's Hall with a colourful armorial screen. Doune Motor Museum is built beside Scotland's best-known speed hill-climb course. The Doune Nature Trail, running along the trackbed of an old railway, is suitable for wheelchair users and has information displayed in braille.

'Danzig Willie's' 17th-century home, Craigievar Castle (NT), adds a fairy-tale touch to the Grampian countryside

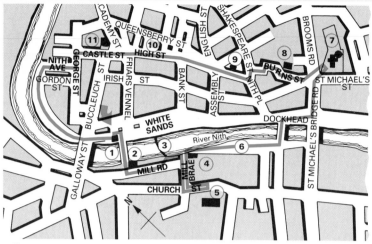

Queen of the South

Dumfries, the 'Queen of the South', was created a royal burgh in 1186. For three full centuries, it bore the brunt of the incessant wars and border raids between Scotland and England, but after the Union of 1707 was left in peace to develop trade and cultural connections.

1 THE OLD BRIDGE
Tradition says that the first wooden bridge across the Nith at this point was set up in the 13th century by the Lady Devorgilla in memory of her husband John Balliol.

2 OLD BRIDGE HOUSE
This is the oldest house in Dumfries, built by James Birkmyre in 1660. The last tenant of the house died in 1959, and it has now been restored as a museum. There are six furnished rooms of different periods.

3 THE CAUL
A weir set diagonally across the Nith, this once diverted water to 18th-century riverside mills. Small coasting vessels used to come to Dumfries, and at high tides even reached as far as the foot of the Caul.

4 ROBERT BURNS CENTRE
Situated in an 18th-century water mill, this award-winning centre outlines the connections between the town and Scotland's national poet.

5 DUMFRIES MUSEUM & CAMERA OBSCURA
This 18th-century windmill on the summit of Corberry Hill was, in 1834, taken over by the Dumfries and Maxwelltown Astronomical Society, who rebuilt it as an observatory, with a *camera obscura*. The museum includes fine displays of wildlife, archaeology and social history.

6 FALLOW DEER PARK
This riverside deer park by the Nith has its footpath well away from the water's edge, in case of floods.

7 ST MICHAEL'S CHURCH
The graveyard of this parish church is where Robert Burns was buried, with great ceremony, on 25 July 1796. In 1815 his coffin was moved to an ornate mausoleum, which stands in sharp contrast to the local red sandstone of the church itself. A brass tablet in the church indicates the pew at which Burns sat.

8 BURNS HOUSE
Robert Burns, and his wife Jean, moved to this house in 1793 where he died after having been taken seriously ill in 1796. The house is now a Burns museum, with many relics and original manuscripts.

9 GLOBE INN
In a passageway to the right of the High Street is the Globe Inn, Robert Burns' howff – or 'local' – during the time he lived in Dumfries. Several mementoes of the poet are kept here, including his favourite chair.

10 MIDSTEEPLE
Built in 1707, this 'island' in the High Street housed the courtroom, prison and town offices. Across the High Street is the County Hotel, in which Prince Charlie's Room recalls the stay of the Young Pretender for three days in 1745.

11 GREYFRIARS CHURCH
In the centre of the roundabout, in front of Greyfriars Church, is a statue of Robert Burns. The church dates from 1868, but the original Greyfriars monastery of Dumfries, now disappeared, was much older. It was at the altar of Greyfriars in 1306 that Robert the Bruce killed Sir John Comyn, representative in Scotland of the English King Edward I, and sparked off the War of Independence which put him on the Scottish throne.

EARLY CLOSING: *Thu*

MARKET DAY: *Wed*

PARKING: *Whitesands*

OPENING TIMES:
Old Bridge House: open Apr–Sep, Mon–Sat all day, except Tue. Sun pm only
Dumfries Museum & Camera Obscura: open Apr – Sep, Mon – Sat, Sun pm; Oct – Mar, daily except Sun & Mon
Robert Burns Centre: as above
Burns House: as above

ROUTE DIRECTIONS
Start at the Tourist Information centre in Whitesands. Go over The Old Bridge (1), noticing the Old Bridge House (2) and turn l. on to Mill Rd. Turn l. to the viewpoint overlooking the Caul (3); ahead is the Robert Burns Centre (4). Proceed up Mill Brae. Cross Church St and turn l. up the footpath into the museum grounds to the Dumfries Museum (5). Return to the foot of Mill Brae and turn r. into the park (6). Cross the suspension bridge and turn r. into Dockhead. Turn l. to reach St Michael's Church (7). From the church cross the main road and take the first r. into Burns St for Burns House (8). Continue forward and cross Shakespeare St. Turn l. then r. into High St, passing on r. a passageway to the Globe Inn (9). Keep the Midsteeple (10) on your r., and continue to Greyfriars Church (11). Go straight on along Castle St, l. into George St and r. down Nith Ave beside the old people's home. Turn l. and r. on to the riverside footpath to return to the Whitesands.

The Old Bridge at Dumfries

DRUMNADROCHIT,
Highland
See Loch Ness Monster Centre

DUMFRIES, Dumfries &
Galloway

Map Ref: NX9776

Built on both banks of the
River Nith, whose fast-flowing
waters rush over a weir in the
heart of the town, Dumfries
houses the major regional
museum for the whole Solway
area.

In the grounds is a fine 18th-
century hilltop windmill, which
acted for a time as an
astronomical observatory and
now has a camera obscura in
the tower. By the riverside is
the Old Bridge House, which
concentrates on old-style
furnishings and furniture –
including a fearsome turn-of-
the-century dentist's surgery.

Towards the end of his life,
Robert Burns lived and worked
in Dumfries, and the town is
proud of the connection. The
riverside Robert Burns Centre
has an audio-visual theatre and
a separate exhibition on the
history of Dumfries itself. Also
open is the Burns House, which
was his family home from 1793
onwards.

No Burns pilgrimage to
Dumfries is complete without a
visit to the Globe Inn, where

his memory is kept warmly
alive, and his chair is still in
his favourite place by the
fireside.

DUNS, Borders
See Manderston

DUNFERMLINE, Fife

Map Ref: NT0987

A maze-like one-way traffic
system here tends to exasperate
casual visitors, but
Dunfermline should not be
shrugged off on that account. It
was, after all, a royal residence
from the end of the 11th
century, and the preserved
ruins of its majestic
Romanesque abbey (AM) are
open all year. Robert the
Bruce's tomb lies below the
pulpit of the parish church.

Dunfermline, though, is best
known as the birthplace of
Andrew Carnegie, the weaver's
son who left for America when
he was 12, became an iron and
steel magnate in Pittsburgh,
and was by most reckonings the
richest man in the entire world
after he sold out in 1901.

The scale of Carnegie's
benefactions is staggering, and
estimated at today's values he
gave away a fortune of around
£1,750 million. Dunfermline
was given the first of the 2,811

*Dunfermline Abbey (AM), where
the preserved 12th-century nave
is an awesome example of early
Romanesque architecture*

Carnegie Free Libraries, which
were built all over the world,
and he also presented to the
town the beautiful Pittencrieff
estate. With its lawns and
gardens, woodlands and a deep
curving ravine, this remains
one of the finest town parks in
Britain. The whole incredible
story is told in the Carnegie
Birthplace Museum, in the
weaver's cottage which was his
humble family home.

DUNNET HEAD, Highland

*On B855 7m N Castleton. Map
Ref: ND2076*

This and not John o'Groats is
the actual most northerly place
in mainland Britain, a cliff-
ringed headland from whose
summit viewpoint expands a
stunning outlook north across
the Pentland Firth to Orkney
and west along the Caithness
and Sutherland coasts as far –
on a really clear day – as Cape
Wrath. The approach road
climbs easily over a peat
moorland dotted with brown
trout lochs. At the head
keeper's discretion, visitors
may be allowed afternoon
access to the lighthouse.

EAST LINTON, Lothian
See Preston Mill

EDINBURGH, Lothian

Map Ref: NT2573

Scotland's historic capital is a
striking city, with a Georgian
New Town which is one of the
highlights of European
architecture; a clifftop castle
(AM) dominating its busiest
streets; and a royal palace
whose parkland sweeps up to
the summit of an extinct
volcano.

Edinburgh can be an
exhilarating open-air city.
There are steepish walks to
panoramic viewpoints on
Arthur's Seat, the old volcano
in Holyrood Park; gentler
gradients on the pathways
round wooded Corstorphine
Hill; and a meandering
walkway for miles beside the
Water of Leith.

But Edinburgh is also a
festival city, crammed with
museums, galleries and
exhibitions of every kind. The
National Gallery of Scotland is
where the Old Masters are on
display, but there is also a
Scottish National Portrait
Gallery and a Scottish National
Gallery of Modern Art.

The castle is where one of the
most popular events at the time
of the Edinburgh Festival is
held – the always impressive
Military Tattoo, on the
Esplanade. From the castle, the
Royal Mile runs down to the
Queen's official residence in
Scotland – the Palace of
Holyrood House, which is open
to visitors outside the times of
any royal or state visits.

Add the high-level Outlook
Tower and Camera Obscura on
Castle Hill, the Royal Botanic
Garden's magnificent indoor
and outdoor displays at
Inverleith, the visitor centre at
the Royal Observatory on
Blackford Hill – and dozens
more places of genuine interest
and appeal – and you will see
that Edinburgh is
unmistakably a city of capital
status.

FALKLAND, Fife

Map Ref: NO2507

In 1970 this sensitively restored
royal burgh at the foot of the
Lomond Hills was declared the
first Conservation Area in
Scotland, but even it and its
fine private houses must take
second place to the superb 16th-
century architecture of
Falkland Palace, a much-loved
holiday and hunting retreat of
the Stuart kings and queens.
The palace also has the oldest
'real-tennis' court in Britain,

dating from 1539, and a bright,
carefully tended garden of
lawns, shrubs and herbaceous
borders. Although the National
Trust for Scotland opens the
palace and gardens to visitors,
it remains the property of Her
Majesty the Queen.

FASQUE, Fettercairn,
Grampian

*Open spring to late summer; on
B974 1m N Fettercairn. Map
Ref: NO6475*

Gladstones have owned the
mansion-house and estate of
Fasque since 1829, and it was
for some years the home of
William Ewart Gladstone – the
'Grand Old Man' of Victorian
politics and Prime Minister for
four terms between 1868 and
1894. As well as outlining the
family history, displays at
Fasque also tell the story of the
servants who were the
'downstairs' element in the
running of the household. It
remains very much a family
home rather than any kind of
impersonal museum.

FESHIEBRIDGE, Highland

Map Ref: NH8504

This hamlet is beside a bridge
where the River Feshie dashes
down its rocky course to the
Spey and has a picnic site on
the edge of the Inshriach Forest
plantations, which sweep up
into the foothills of the
Cairngorms. The road up the
east side of Glen Feshie passes
the Cairngorm Gliding Club's
riverside landing ground. On
the west side of the glen, the
Forestry Commission's Rock
Wood Ponds trail mixes a short
climb to a glorious ridgetop
viewpoint with level-ground
strolls to wildlife-observation
hides.

FETTERCAIRN, Grampian
See Fasque

FORT WILLIAM, Highland

Map Ref: NN1073

Under the great bulk of Ben
Nevis, Fort William is the scene
of some highly energetic
sporting events – like the
Scottish Six Days Motor Cycle
Trial in May, and the Ben
Nevis Hill Race every
September. But there is plenty
to see in the town without
breaking into a sweat. The
West Highland Museum and
the Cameron Centre have
comprehensive displays on local
history, including the stirring
days of the Jacobite Risings,
archaeology, geology and

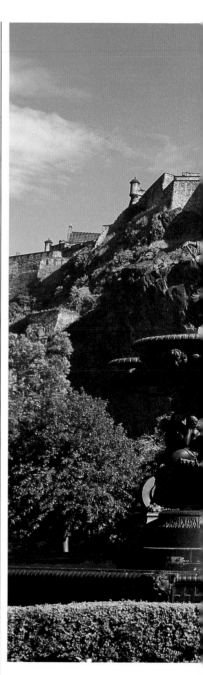

wildlife. The Ben Nevis
Exhibition tells the story of the
mountain, including the
exploits of the pioneer
meteorologists who kept a
weather observatory on its
wind-swept and often snow-
bound summit plateau in
operation from 1883 to 1904.

**GAIRLOCH HERITAGE
MUSEUM,** Highland

*Open spring to autumn; on
A832.*
Map Ref: NG8076

Backed by rugged hillsides and
looking west along a sea-loch to
what are often magnificent
sunsets, Gairloch has a fine
sandy beach, a golf course with
faraway mountain views, and
facilities for river, loch and sea-
angling. The Gairloch Heritage
Museum, open from May to

September, illustrates the history, fishing, crofting and wildlife of the district. On the south side of Loch Gairloch, the beautiful road through Badachro winds past wooded bays and rocky islands before heading over moorland to the sands of Opinan and a seaward viewpoint above the beaches at Red Point.

GIFFORD, Lothian

Map Ref: NT5368

Surrounded by farms and woodlands in the foothills of the Lammermuirs, Gifford is an attractive and well-preserved 'planned' village founded in the late 17th century. A memorial plaque beside the parish church recalls that the Reverend John Witherspoon, a son of the Gifford manse, was a signatory of the American Declaration of Independence.

There is a stately lime-tree avenue, and a pleasant parkland golf course is laid out near by. Railway historians come to trace the course of the modest Gifford and Garvald Light Railway, whose green tank engine and solitary coach puffed its way cross-country for the last time in 1948.

GLAMIS CASTLE, Tayside

Open spring to autumn; on A928, 4m S Kirriemuir. Map Ref: NO3848

Elizabeth Bowes Lyon, now the Queen Mother, spent much of her childhood here – which is why a rose named in her honour is called 'Elizabeth of Glamis'. Her family have owned Glamis (the 'i' is silent) since 1372. The

Home of the Military Tattoo, Edinburgh Castle looms majestically over busy city streets – a reminder of the more turbulent past

castle shows a mesmerising array of spires, turrets and battlemented towers to visitors approaching along its fine tree-lined avenue, and inside are valuable furnishings, paintings and collections of arms. The vaulted Duncan's Hall commemorates the murder in 1040 of King Duncan by Macbeth. Shakespeare's *Macbeth* places the actual killing here, when it really happened many miles away.

Outside, the woods and parkland of Glamis are much more cheerful, and include a nature trail, an Italian garden and an amazingly ornate sundial.

GLASGOW, Strathclyde

Map Ref: NS5965

The choice of Glasgow, first of all as the location for the National Garden Festival in 1988 and then as the European City of Culture in 1990, linked together two important strands in the city's life. It is remarkably well-endowed with public parks; and, as well as being the home of Scottish Opera, Scottish Ballet and the Scottish National Orchestra, it has one of the world's finest municipally owned art collections.

There are more than 60 public parks within the city limits, and a great number of public golf courses and bowling greens, on which retired people may play free of charge on most days of the week. Pollok Country Park's 361 acres include woodland and riverside nature trails, and the Palladian mansion of Pollok House is now a museum with valuable furnishings and a notable collection of Spanish paintings, while the estate also provided the site for the Burrell Gallery. This modern building houses the most magnificent presentation ever made to the city – the multi-million-pound, 8,000-piece art collection of the shipowner Sir William Burrell.

The older Art Gallery and Museum in Kelvingrove Park displays most of the city's British, French, Dutch and Italian paintings. The People's Palace in Glasgow Green is a museum of a different kind, concentrating on the city's own history, personalities, often fiery politics and industry. And the restored 16th-century Haggs Castle is a museum specifically for children.

Glasgow's Museum of Transport in the Kelvin Hall has a fine exhibition of Scottish cars – Albion, Argyll, Arrol-Johnston, Beardmore and Galloway; trams, buses, horse-drawn vehicles, locomotives and railway memorabilia; and the city's superb collection of ship models, many of them presentation pieces from the time when the Clyde was the world's most famous shipbuilding river.

GLEN AFFRIC, Highland

Off A831, 17m SW Beauly. Map Ref: NH2828

This has always been regarded as one of the most beautiful glens in the Highlands, and although it plays a part in major forestry and hydro-electric schemes, that judgement still holds good. In the lower part are forest walks

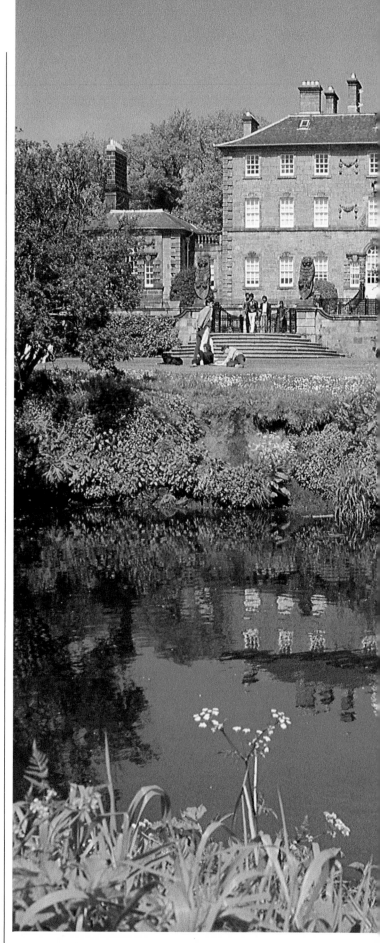

which show off the thundering gorge of the Dog Falls, edged with birch and pine. Farther up between Loch Benevean and Loch Affric is an easy river walk to another set of falls.

From the same starting point begins the Viewpoint Walk, which is steeper but offers a superb outlook over lochs, forests and deer-stalked mountains.

*A mansion turned museum:
Glasgow's Pollok House, set in
hundreds of acres of beautiful
park and woodland, now houses
a fascinating collection of
Spanish art*

GLENFINNAN, Highland
See Loch Shiel

GLENLIVET, Grampian

Map Ref: NJ1929

This is classic malt-whisky
country, where the River Livet
winds down between
alternating forests, tumbling
burns and open hillsides dotted
with the sites of old illicit stills.
In 1823 George Smith of
Glenlivet was the first
Highland distiller to take out a
government licence – something
his neighbours thought so
offensive that he had to ride
around armed with pistols for
his own defence.

'The Glenlivet' is still
produced in the original
location, and there is a visitor
centre which recalls the old
illegal days in displays which
supplement tours of the modern
distillery.

**GLENMORE FOREST
PARK,** Highland

*Off A951, 6m E Aviemore. Map
Ref: NH9709*

While the Cairngorm range
soars to a sub-arctic 4,000ft
plateau, this is the forested
area of the foothills around
chilly Loch Morlich – itself
1,048 feet above sea level. Scots
pine, spruce and larch combine
to give miles of not-too-
strenuous forest walks the
heady atmosphere of pinewood
resin. The higher-level treks
are much tougher. Birds of the
pinewoods – rarely seen
elsewhere – include redpoll,
siskin and the Scottish
crossbill. Altogether, in the
forest and on the loch, more
than 100 bird species have been
recorded. The Reindeer House,
near the Forestry Commission's
visitor centre, offers guided
tours to view Britain's only
reindeer herd feeding on the
high-level lichens. These were
established from Lapland stock
in 1952.

GLEN TROOL, Dumfries &
Galloway

*Off A714 at Bargrennan 1m E
of Glentrool village. Map Ref:
NX3778*

On entering this most
Highland-looking of the
Galloway glens, stop to admire
the rocky and beautiful Falls of
Minnoch, starting point of
forest walks. The public road
climbs towards a memorial
stone to Robert the Bruce's
victory at the Steps of Trool in
1307, a striking viewpoint over
the steeply banked Loch Trool
and its surrounding forests,

heathery crags and wild, open
hillsides streaked with whitewater burns. The private road
hairpinning down into the
oakwoods at the head of Loch
Trool is easy for walkers, but
the forest trail on the far side
does involve some very rough
going.

GORDON, Borders
See Mellerstain House

**GRAMPIAN TRANSPORT
MUSEUM,** Alford, Grampian

*Open spring to late summer; on
A944.
Map Ref: NJ5715.*

Most cherished exhibit at the
Grampian Transport Museum,
which displays cars, motor
cycles and commercial vehicles
from many different decades, is
the locally built Craigievar
Express, a steam-engined
tricycle of 1897. There is also a
splendid fairground organ.

Nearby Alford Station is now
a railway museum, from which
the narrow-gauge Alford Valley
Railway runs into Haughton
House Country Park and the
adjacent Murray Park. There
are picnic areas and easy
nature trails in the wooded
parkland, and walks beside the
River Don.

HADDINGTON, Lothian

*Off A1 13m W Edinburgh. Map
Ref: NT5173*

East Lothian is a district of
painstakingly restored villages,
and the old county town of
Haddington sets an even higher
standard, with more than 100
listed buildings in its Georgian
heart. Explorers are helped by a
signposted walk along streets,
pends and alleyways, and
should look out for the motif of
a goat eating grapes – the
Haddington coat of arms.

St Mary's parish church was
the subject of a long rebuilding
programme and is basically of
15th-century date. One notable
feature is the Lauderdale Aisle
– an Episcopal chapel in a
Presbyterian church, and the
focus of the strong local
ecumenical movement. St
Mary's Pleasance is a
reconstructed 17th-century
garden near by.

The Jane Welsh Carlyle
Museum was the childhood
home of the wife of the
Victorian philosopher and
historian Thomas Carlyle. Open
all year is a fascinating little
exhibition on the history and
architecture of the town in
Lady Kitty's Doocot, a restored
dovecot of 1771 in another
garden by the River Tyne.

HAMILTON, Strathclyde
See Chatelherault

**HIGHLAND FOLK
MUSEUM,** Kingussie, Lothian

*Open all year; off A86.
Map Ref: NH7500*

An amazing amount of material
about Highland life and work in
generations long gone by has
been assembled in the indoor
and outdoor displays here, set
in six acres of garden on the
edge of the village of 'King-*you*-
ssie', where wooded Glen
Gynack meets the plains of the
Spey.

Domestic and farming life,
transport, crafts and costumes
are all covered in detail.
Thatched buildings in the
museum grounds, like a
reconstructed turf house and a
primitive Hebridean 'black
house', show that Highland life
in past centuries was harder
than it sometimes seems
through a hopeful nostalgic
haze.

**HIGHLAND WILDLIFE
PARK,** Kincraig, Highland

*Open spring to autumn; on
B9152 8m SW Aviemore.
Map Ref: NH8681*

In these 250 acres of birchwood
and heather moorland above the
valley of the Spey, the ecological
clock has been turned back.

*A feline resident of the
Highland Wildlife Park, where
less familiar species – such as
wild boar – can also be seen*

Animals long since gone
from the Highland scene –
bison, wild boar, bears and
wolves – have been
reintroduced. Animals and
birds of the modern Highlands
have also been gathered
together: for instance, red and
roe deer, Highland cattle,
wildcats, pine martens, foxes,
eagles, grouse, capercaillie,
peregrine falcons. An extensive
drive-through area shows many
of the animals living in groups,
while others are in enclosures
in the walk-around section of
the park.

INVEREWE GARDEN,
Poolewe, Highland

*Open all year; on A832.
Map Ref: NG8681*

Mild Gulf Stream air and the
patient transformation, since
1862, of a rocky and barren
peninsula with shelter belts of
trees, have combined to make
this National Trust for Scotland
garden an unexpected blaze of
colour.

On the same latitude as
Leningrad and Labrador,
Inverewe has masses of
rhododendrons, azaleas,
camellias, magnolias,
herbaceous borders, heathers,
maples, cotoneasters – in total,
something like 2,500 different
species of trees, plants and
flowering shrubs. Curving
pathways, many suitable for
disabled people, wander
through the woodlands to
glorious viewpoints looking
across Loch Ewe to a sea or
mountain skyline.

ISLE OF ARRAN, Strathclyde

*Car ferries from Ardrossan to
Brodick (all year); Claonaig to
Lochranze (summer only). Map
Ref: NS0136*

It would be much easier to list
what Arran does *not* offer the
visitor than to call to mind all
its attractions. The northern
granite peaks are for the
serious climber and hill-walker,
but there are also walks in the
southern forests, as well as
strolls to places like the cliff-
tumbled Fallen Rocks at
Sannox and the old barytes
mine in a nearby glen.

Golfers are spoiled for choice,
with a different course for every
day of the week. Rivers, lochs
and the seas around the island
offer scope for anglers. There
are craft workshops, prehistoric
sites featuring standing stones
and stone circles, and
watersports of every
description. More than a dozen
villages ring the coast, some
with palm trees growing in the
mild maritime air.

Arran's stately home is
Brodick Castle, once a residence
of the Dukes of Hamilton and
the Dukes of Montrose, and now
one of the finest properties of
the National Trust for Scotland.

History and prehistory,
domestic and farming life over
the years, are illustrated in the
Isle of Arran Heritage Museum
at Rosaburn. Also, the wildlife
of an island with 3,000 red deer
in the northern hills, seals and
squirrels, seabirds and golden
eagles, is the main interest of
the Arran Nature Centre at
Cladach.

The Highland Capital

The traditional 'capital' of the Highlands, and its industrial and transport centre, Inverness has a history going well back into Pictish times. The town itself was created a royal burgh by David I in the 12th century, fortified by successive monarchs and eventually became a thriving commercial centre with strong links connecting it to Scandinavia, the Low Countries and the Mediterranean.

Abertarff House, Church Street, Inverness, now a centre for Highland language and culture

two main River Ness islands to be linked with each other and with both banks by a series of footbridges. These were swept away in the floods of 1849, but he had new suspension bridges set up – and they remain there still, connecting a series of wooded island walks.

8 EDEN COURT THEATRE
Opened in 1976, this very modern theatre is the main centre for plays, concerts and conferences in Inverness. The original Eden Court was a Bishop's Palace, and is now incorporated in the theatre complex.

9 ST ANDREW'S CATHEDRAL
The original cathedral plans by architect Dr Alexander Ross, who was later to be Provost of the town for a term of six years, included spires – which had to be omitted – on top of the square towers. With an interior as impressive as its Gothic exterior, St Andrew's was completed in 1869.

EARLY CLOSING: *Wed*

PARKING: *Castle St, Ardconnel St, Crown Rd, Rose St*

OPENING TIMES:
Town House: on enquiry at the Town House, Mon – Fri
Museum & Art Gallery: open all year, Mon – Sat

ROUTE DIRECTIONS
Start at the Town House (1) in High St (2). Turn l. up Castle Wynd, passing Inverness Museum (3) on r. Continue straight on up the steps and pathway to the castle (4). From the Flora Macdonald statue (5) bear l. downhill to exit and bear r. into View Place, then turn sharp r. on to Castle Rd and immediately l. round a church, then l. on to Ness Bank beside the River Ness (6). Follow the riverside pavement and go straight on along a riverside footpath. Just before this joins a public road, turn r. over a footbridge and l. on to another riverside path. Turn r. across a footbridge on to the first of the Ness Islands (7), and at the southern end cross a curving footbridge on to the next main island. From it, take another footbridge on to the far bank of the river and turn r. on to a footpath alongside the river bank. Follow the Ness Walk footway past the Eden Court Theatre (8) and St Andrew's Cathedral (9) to reach Ness Bridge. Turn r. to cross it and return to the Town House.

1 TOWN HOUSE
A Victorian-Gothic building of 1882, the Town House unexpectedly hosted a Cabinet meeting when Lloyd George visited the town in 1921. Beside the entrance is the restored mercat cross of Inverness, standing on the *Clach-na-Cuddain* – the stone of the tubs – on which women used to rest their baskets of washing.

2 HIGH STREET AND BRIDGE STREET
This route has been the main street of Inverness since the 1680s, when a toll-bridge was built across the River Ness. The latest Ness Bridge was opened in 1961. On the north-east corner of the Bridge Street-High Street junction is the old Tolbooth of 1791. Prisoners used to be held here while awaiting trial

by the circuit courts.

3 MUSEUM AND ART GALLERY
The present building was opened in 1966, on the site of an earlier museum. It houses collections and displays of Highland wildlife, history, weaponry, music and crofting, and there is a fine selection of Highland silverware.

4 INVERNESS CASTLE
An 18th-century stronghold called Fort George once stood here, but it was blown up by the Jacobites in the Rebellion of 1745. The site was cleared in 1834 and the first part of the present pink sandstone castle was built for the Sheriff Court. A second part, now council offices, was added in 1847.

5 FLORA MACDONALD STATUE
From the statue, set up in

1899 in memory of the famous Jacobite heroine, there is a fine view of the River Ness, and of two wooded crags on the western edge of the town. The one to the left is Tomnahurich, one of the most beautifully situated cemeteries in the country. To its right is Craig Phadrig, with the remains of a vitrified fort on the summit, said to be the site of the capital of the ancient Pictish kings.

6 RIVER NESS
In AD565, St Columba reported that one of his men was attacked by an *aquatilis bestia* – a water beast. Columba rebuked it, and it promptly swam away. This was the first written account of a monster, if not in Loch Ness itself, at least in its river.

7 NESS ISLANDS
In the 1830s, Joseph Mitchell, a civil engineer who lived in the town and worked with Thomas Telford, arranged for the

A peaceful scene on the island of mountains: one of the Isle of Skye's breathtaking views, at Tarskavaig

ISLE OF SKYE, Highland

Car ferries from Kyle of Lochalsh to Kyleakin (all year); Mallaig to Armadale, foot passengers (summer only). Map Ref: NG7526

Although Skye is an island of mountains – the Cuillin peaks are the most spectacular in Britain – it is also an island of long peninsulas and deeply indented sea-lochs. Coastline and mountains are handsomely matched; one of the most stunning views in the country is from Elgol, across Loch Scavaig, to the serrated Cuillin ridge.

Skye is the territory of several major clans. The MacLeod chiefs have been at Dunvegan for 30 generations, and the present clifftop castle there, open from Easter to October, is a treasure-house of clan history. There is also a display on the remote island group of St Kilda, once a MacLeod property, out on the Atlantic fringe.

The Clan Donald Centre in the part-ruined Armadale Castle has imaginative displays and an audio-visual programme on the 'Sea Kingdom'; the 'MacDonalds' lost Lordship of the Isles'; the rich culture of Gaelic Scotland; and the dispersal of MacDonalds overseas.

Skye also has smaller, thatched-cottage folk museums at Luib, Colbost and Kilmuir. Near the museum at Kilmuir, on a hillside with a majestic outlook across the Minch to the Western Isles, stands a memorial – a Celtic cross on the grave of Flora MacDonald – which people with a feeling for history come from all over the world to see.

JEDBURGH, Borders

Map Ref: NT6520

Located on one of the main roads from England into Scotland, this ancient royal burgh has always known how to look after itself. The traditional and very boisterous handball game played every February in the High Street started, according to a strong local

tradition, with the severed head of an English soldier. No wonder Jedburgh took so keenly to rugby, of which it is one of the Border strongholds.

The town centre is a model of restored buildings, many dating from the 17th and 18th centuries. Jedburgh Abbey's (AM) stately ruins are much older, and the high-set Jedburgh Castle belies its name by being a restored Georgian model prison.

Set in gardens back from a riverside walk, Queen Mary's House is believed to be where Mary, Queen of Scots lodged during a royal progress of the Borders in 1566. It is now a museum devoted to her, with an account of her turbulent life and many of her personal relics.

J M BARRIE'S BIRTHPLACE, Kirriemuir, Tayside

Open spring to late summer; in Brechin Rd. Map Ref: NO3854

If you have sat in a theatre, surrounded by excited children shouting their answer to the famous question, 'Do you believe in fairies?', you will appreciate the National Trust for Scotland's displays and audio presentation in the little cottage where J M Barrie was born in 1860. For 30 years, Barrie filled theatres in Britain and on Broadway – and he started young, putting on plays in the wash-house behind the cottage. There is a *Peter Pan* exhibition in that same little building, which was his inspiration for Wendy's house.

Barrie was capable of the grand gesture – making over the rights in *Peter Pan,* for instance, to the Great Ormond Street children's hospital. He is buried in Kirriemuir's beautiful hillside cemetery, where there is no imposing memorial, no mention of his membership of the Order of Merit – just a simple inscription on the family gravestone.

JOHN O'GROATS, Highland

On A39 14m N Wick. Map Ref: ND3773

Do not be misled by its association with Land's End into expecting some remote and rugged headland here. John o'Groats is a tidy village at the edge of the great sweep of well-worked farmland along the Caithness seaboard. There are souvenir and craft shops, holiday accommodation and a compact harbour. Summer cruises are run across the Pentland Firth to Orkney, and also round the mainland coast past thronging seabird cliffs and spiky offshore rock stacks near Duncansby Head. The lighthouse on Duncansby Head, a spectacular sea and island viewpoint, is easily reached by car.

John o'Groats is 874 miles by road from Land's End, and the first pedestrian to walk the whole distance did so in 1865. Dr Barbara Moore sparked off renewed interest in the 'end to end' walk during the 1960s, and there are now recognised record times for walkers, cyclists, tandem and tricycle riders – and even hitch-hikers.

KELSO, Borders

Map Ref: NT7233

Kelso's Georgian town centre is one of the most elegant in the Borders, and it also has a ruined 12th-century abbey (AM). Turret House, the town museum, has displays including a 19th-century market place and a reconstructed skinner's shop.

Kelso Racecourse has a programme of point-to-point and National Hunt racing from October to April, the Kelso Ram Sales in September are world-famous – and rugby and cricket are both played enthusiastically. The local beats on the River Tweed are among the finest salmon waters in the country.

The impressive Adam-designed Floors Castle is the home, in fact, of the Duke of Roxburghe and, in fiction, of young 'Tarzan' in the film *Greystoke.*

KINCRAIG, Highland
See Highland Wildlife Park

KINGUSSIE, Lothian
See Highland Folk Museum

KINROSS, Tayside

Map Ref: NO1102

Kinross, now bypassed by motorway traffic, is an old county town renowned for its Loch Leven trout fishing. A spring to late summer ferry runs to the wooded island where, in Loch Leven Castle (AM), Mary, Queen of Scots was kept prisoner for 11 months in 1567/68. During that time, disaffected courtiers forced her to abdicate from the throne, but were later outsmarted by her daring escape in which the hero was a 16-year-old boat-boy – Willie Douglas.

KIRRIEMUIR, Tayside
See J M Barrie's Birthplace

LANARK, Strathclyde
See New Lanark

LOCH GARTEN, Highland

Off B970 3m WSW Nethy Bridge. Map Ref: NH9718

In the mid-1950s – after a gap of half a century – ospreys returned to Scotland and nested in these Speyside pinewoods, where the RSPB now looks after a 1,500-acre reserve. Loch Garten's ospreys arrive from Africa in April, nest in clear view from the well-equipped visitor centre, and fly south again in August. They can also be seen from time to time, hunting over some nearby loch and swooping down to snatch fish straight from the water in their fearsome talons.

LOCH LOMOND, Central & Strathclyde

Map Ref: NS3598

One of Scotland's most beautiful inland lochs, Lomond begins in the north as a narrow waterway loomed over by 3,000ft peaks, then stretches south for 22 miles, gradually widening out to accommodate a cluster of lovely wooded islands. Lochside roads follow all of the west shore and some of the east, which is well supplied with car parks, picnic areas, and steep or gentle forest walks among oakwoods, spruce and larch.

Cruises or hire-boats operate at Balloch, Luss (the Victorian village which doubles as 'Glendarroch' in the television series *Take the High Road*), Inverbeg, Tarbet, Ardlui, Inversnaid, Rowardennan and Balmaha – which is also the starting point for the passenger-carrying mailboat service round the islands.

Just off Balmaha, a round-island nature trail on high and thickly wooded Inchcailloch is an unforgettable experience. More leisurely walking is available among the lawns and woodlands of Balloch Country Park, where the loch waters feed into the River Leven.

LOCH NESS MONSTER CENTRE, Drumnadrochit, Highland

Open spring to autumn; 15m SW Inverness. Map Ref: NH5030

Try to resist the temptation, when visiting this grand but mysterious waterway, to make jokes about the Loch Ness Monster. Many local people are firmly convinced that there is some unidentified creature in its chill and visually impenetrable depths, and heartily dislike the 'monster' tag. The centre has gathered together descriptions and observations from more than 50 years, including results of the massive 24-boat sonar sweep made in October 1987, which produced computer printouts from readings down as far as 720ft. There is also a fun element in several of the centre's displays!

LOCH SHIEL, Glenfinnan, Highland

On A830 17m W Fort William. Map Ref: NM9080

Loch Shiel slashes through the dramatic landscape of the Lochaber hills, 17 miles long but never more than a single mile wide. It starts at Glenfinnan, beyond the tall

memorial tower which recalls Bonnie Prince Charlie's raising of the standard to launch the final Jacobite Rising on 19 August 1745. From there, the outlook is down a narrow corridor of loch crammed between wild mountain sides. At its western end, Loch Shiel becomes milder and shallower to finish among the mosslands around the village of Acharacle, before being drained by the short River Shiel down to the sea.

MANDERSTON, Duns, Borders

Open spring to late summer; off A6105 1¼m E Duns. Map Ref: NT8154

In 1901, when Sir James Miller told his architect that 'it simply doesn't matter' how much the rebuilding of Manderston might cost, he really meant it. At today's values, the final bill was £15 million! The house is lavishly furnished, with a unique silver staircase and beautiful plaster ceilings; the marble dairy and sumptuous stables are simply amazing. A display in the old servants' hall features Sainfoin, Sir James's 1890 Derby winner, and Rock Sand, which won the 'Triple Crown' of Derby, St Leger and 2,000 Guineas in 1903.

MAYBOLE, Strathclyde
See Culzean Castle & Country Park

MELLERSTAIN HOUSE, Gordon, Borders

Open spring to late summer; off A6089 6m NW Kelso. Map Ref: NT6439

Home of the Earl of Haddington and one of Scotland's finest Georgian mansions, this house was built over several years under the direction of William Adam and his son Robert. It contains paintings by Van Dyck, Gainsborough, Constable, Raeburn, Ramsay and others, period furniture and the library – with its fine plasterwork ceiling and friezes – is one of Robert Adam's masterpieces.

Mellerstain has a lovely terraced garden, parkland and a lake, and is the venue for annual events like the Borders Vintage Automobile Club display.

MELROSE, Borders
See Abbotsford

NEW LANARK, Lanark, Strathclyde

Map Ref: NS8842

One of the most ambitious and best carried-out restoration projects in Britain is the revival of this late 18th- and early 19th-century cotton-mill village, built to take advantage of the water power of the Falls of Clyde. A heritage trail shows off the individual mill buildings, the model workers'

hedges have to be kept in trim. The National Trust for Scotland has also provided woodland walks and a picnic area here, plus a collection of rare breeds of Scottish livestock and a fascinating Museum of Farming Life.

PITTENWEEM, Fife

Map Ref: NO5402

This old royal burgh has a fine High Street lined with restored 16th- to 18th-century houses, and narrow wynds descending to the equally attractive Dutch-influenced buildings by the harbour. Pittenweem is 'the place of the cave', and takes its name from the restored cell of the 7th-century St Fillan, deeply recessed in a rock outcrop in Cove Wynd. A few miles inland is the basically 14th-century Kellie Castle, an impressive National Trust for Scotland property. The grounds include a Victorian walled garden.

POOLEWE, Highland
See Inverewe Garden

PRESTON MILL (NTS), East Linton, Lothian

Open spring to late autumn; on B1407 ¼m NE East Linton. Map Ref: NT5977

Every now and again travellers will find a cluster of buildings that have been put up for no aesthetic purpose but which instantly appeal to artists and photographers. This 16th-century water-driven grain mill, restored to full working order for the National Trust for Scotland, is one. Its arrangement of conical-roofed drying kiln, outside stairways, red tiling and casually placed outbuildings stand in perfect harmony.

RAVENSCRAIG CASTLE, Kirkcaldy, Fife

Open all year; off Dysart Road. Map Ref: NT2992

This royal stronghold of James II, poised above the Firth of Forth, illustrates an ominous turn in castle design (AM). Started in 1460, it was probably the first fortress in Scotland built to withstand artillery assaults. The footpath to it begins in Ravenscraig Park. The shoreline boundary wall was ordered by an Edwardian landowner who wanted to keep the *hoi polloi* out of his private estate. In the next generation, his son presented Ravenscraig to the town!

housing and the classically styled New Institution for the Formation of Character opened by the forward-thinking company chief, Robert Owen, in 1816 as the social and educational centre of the village.

The majestic gorge of the Falls of Clyde is a Scottish Wildlife Trust reserve where there is a good footpath system with only occasional steep stretches, and a visitor centre in the old New Lanark dyeworks.

PERTH, Tayside

Map Ref: NO1123

This historic town is attractively situated on both banks of the River Tay and features the 12th-century St John's Kirk – sensitively restored – where John Knox's incandescent sermon of 1559 sparked off the Scottish Reformation. Balhousie Castle is the regimental museum of the Black Watch, and Branklyn is the National Trust for Scotland's finest suburban garden.

There are pleasant low-ground strolls in the North and South Inch parks beside the Tay. Rising to the east of the town is wooded Kinnoull Hill, which has a network of footpaths starting from a comfortably high-level car park and leading to panoramic viewpoints like Kinnoull Tower – a folly overlooking the lower reaches of the Tay.

Preston Mill (NT), built 400 years ago and working again today

PITLOCHRY, Tayside

Map Ref: NN9458

Local landscapes here changed dramatically in the 1950s when the gorge of the River Tummel was dammed to form winding and wooded Loch Faskally. The hydro-electric power station beside the dam has a visitor centre (open spring to autumn), and windows looking into the specially-built salmon ladder.

Pitlochry's famous Festival Theatre presents plays from spring to autumn. There are many craft shops in the town, and facilities for walking, boating, angling, golf and curling. At Edradour, guided tours (with wheelchair access) are arranged, between Easter and October, of the smallest malt-whisky distillery in Scotland.

PITMEDDEN GARDEN, Grampian

Open all year, museum and visitor centre spring to late summer; on A920 6m WSW Ellon. Map Ref: NJ8828

Amateur gardeners go pale at the thought of the work involved in re-creating the colourful formal parterres of the 17th-century Great Garden of Pitmedden – 40,000 plants are put in place every May, and three miles of tiny boxwood

Mecca of Golf

Named after the patron saint of Scotland, this ancient town on the Fife coast has a cathedral that was founded in the 12th century, and was the centre of violent religious disputes at the time of the Reformation. The university was established in 1411. For many, of course, St Andrews is famous for one thing only – golf.

1 OLD COURSE
St Andrews is the home of golf, which was being played on the grassy links between the town and the River Eden earlier than 1552. Although not the first one in Scotland, the Society of St Andrews Golfers was founded in 1754, and ten years later reduced its course from 22 holes to 18. The public right of way across the first and eighteenth fairways of the Old Course is known as Granny Clark's Wynd. To the right can be seen one of the small bridges over the meandering Swilcan Burn. To the left is the Royal and Ancient clubhouse, opened in 1854.

2 LADE BRAES
This series of footpaths, in the wooded valley of the Kinness Burn, originally ran alongside a mill lade. On the far side of the burn are the new University Botanic Gardens.

3 WEST PORT
At the entrance to South Street, with its pends and closes and 18th-century houses, the medieval and Elizabethan West Port is one of the few surviving city gates in Scotland.

4 MADRAS COLLEGE
Set back from the street behind open lawns, the elegant Madras College – a school, and not part of the University – was founded in 1832. In front of it are ruins of the 16th-century Blackfriars Chapel.

5 TOWN HALL
This civic building in baronial style dates from 1860. Facing the Town Hall is Holy Trinity Church, transferred to this site early in the 15th century. Beyond the Town Hall, on the right-hand side of South Street, is the rear wall of St Mary's College, founded in the 16th century.

St Andrews' ruined 12th-century Cathedral – once the biggest church in Scotland

6 SOUTH COURT
In this was the town-house quarter of wealthy families, and their coats of arms can still be seen on the walls. South Court leads to the little Byre Theatre, originally founded in a cowshed on the site.

7 ST LEONARD'S SCHOOL
This girls' school was founded in 1877, and extended in 1961. Its library is in the 16th-century Queen Mary's House, believed to have been where Mary, Queen of Scots lodged during her visits to St Andrews.

8 CATHEDRAL
By far the biggest in Scotland, the Cathedral Church of St Andrew was established in 1160, completed in 1318 and ruined soon after the Reformation. Its styling moved from Romanesque to Gothic as the long work of building progressed.

9 CASTLE
Originally the Bishop's Palace, the Castle of St Andrews dates from the early 13th century. It was the focus of many attacks and sieges, especially in the religious troubles of the 1540s. The most notorious feature of the ruin is the Bottle Dungeon, which is still intact. Narrower at the top than at the middle or the bottom, it has no means of exit, apart from the roof. No prisoner ever escaped from it.

10 BOW BUTTS
Beyond the castle, the street known as The Scores leads past fine university buildings and the residence of the Principal. It finishes at a series of grassy mounds topped with the Martyrs' Monument. The hollow below the monument is still called the Bow Butts, as it was in medieval times, when the townsmen came for compulsory archery practice.

EARLY CLOSING: *Thu*

PARKING: *north end of Golf Place*

OPENING TIMES:
Cathedral: *open all year*
Castle: *open all year. Mon – Sat all day. Sun pm only*

ROUTE DIRECTIONS
Start at the car park in Golf Place. Follow road along north side of Old Course (1), and shortly turn l. on to path across fairways. Turn r. into The Links, then turn r. into Gibson Pl to cross bridge over burn and immediately l. on to path beside burn. Turn r. onto Links Crescent and cross it by footbridge. Then go straight on up footpath on far side, and r. before park wall. Follow path along wall, then go along Kennedy Gardens. At far end turn l. along Donaldson Gardens, r. at T-junction into Hepburn Gardens. Beyond junction with Buchan Gardens, after school sign, turn l. down wide path. Turn l. at foot of hill, through gate and along Lade Braes (2). At far end, go through gate, straight on at 'Lade Braes' sign, then l. and r. on to Argyle St. Go through West Port (3) into South St, past Madras College (4) and Town Hall (5). Turn r. into 'South Court' (6). Pass Byre Theatre, turn l. into Greenside Pl, l. into Abbey St, passing St Leonard's School (7), then r. back into South St. Turn l. at end of South St, then r. into cathedral (8) grounds. Return to gate, turn r. and go on along Gregory La. Turn l. on to East Scores, passing the castle (9). Go straight along The Scores, then bear r. on to footpath after junction with Murray Park. Turn r. to cross footbridge, then l. at far side and bear r., past Bow Butts (10), to car park.

ST ANDREWS, Fife

Map Ref: NO5016

'Where is the golf course?' has been the lugubrious question of more than one tournament player looking for the first time at the most famous golf course in the world. The Old Course at St Andrews – one of five in the town, all owned by a public trust – has no artificial landscaping, no trees, no elegant lakes; only the natural undulations of some of the world's finest linksland turf, and some wickedly placed sand bunkers.

St Andrews houses Scotland's oldest university, which was founded in 1411. Its ruined 12th-century cathedral, once the largest church in Scotland, is an ancient monument; so is the 13th-century castle, with its chilling bottle dungeon.

There is also an imaginative new Waterlife marine centre, the West Sands offer two straight miles of dune-backed beach, there is an attractive small harbour and even the putting greens – it goes without saying – are of the very highest quality.

SCOTTISH MUSEUM OF WOOLLEN TEXTILES, Walkerburn, Borders

Open all year. Map Ref: NT3537

How a woollen sweater once went from 'sheep's back to man's back' in 4 hours 40 minutes – through shearing, sorting, spinning, dyeing, knitting, stitching, washing and embroidering – is the theme of one display in this extensive exhibition on how the Borders textile trade developed from a cottage industry into the international business of today.

Information is given about natural dyeing with plants and tree barks, and traditional knitting patterns for fishermen's jerseys – with names like 'Herring Nets' and 'Heart in his Home' – are illustrated.

SCOTT'S VIEW, Borders

On B6356 3m SSE Earlston. Map Ref: NT5934

Connoisseur of Border landscape Sir Walter Scott greatly admired this glorious view, over a sweeping curve on the wooded course of the River Tweed to the three shapely peaks of the Eildon Hills. Tradition has it that the horses drawing his hearse to Dryburgh Abbey paused here for a moment, as they had always done at his command when he was alive.

SCOURIE, Highland

Map Ref: NC1544

On a rugged north-west coastline and facing a fine sandy beach, the little resort of Scourie has more than 30 hill lochs, some of which are reached only by cross-country hikes but all of interest to the visiting angler. North is an enterprising little road that wanders, with many sudden dips and climbs, on a circuit round the hamlets of Tarbet, Fanagmore and Foindle. A ferry runs from Tarbet to the spectacular bird sanctuary island of Handa. Cruises from Fanagmore explore the deep-set bays and mass of rocky islands in Loch Laxford.

SELKIRK, Borders
See Bowhill

STIRLING, Central

Map Ref: NS7993

Set on a cliff-ringed volcanic rock, Stirling Castle (AM) guarded the strategic crossing of the River Forth at a time when, west of the town, the peat mosses left by the receding North Sea were still treacherous marshland. Stuart kings favoured Stirling and built the present castle, which is open all year and features their Palace, the Chapel Royal, military buildings and the museum of the Argyll and Sutherland Highlanders.

The story of the castle, of the other historic buildings clustered near it at the 'top of the town', and of the battles fought within sight of it, are recounted in an audio-visual presentation in the National Trust for Scotland's visitor centre. This is sited on the castle esplanade.

STOBO, Borders
See Dawyck Botanic Garden

STRONE WOODLAND GARDEN, Cairndow, Strathclyde

Open spring to autumn; off A83 12m NW Arrochar. Map Ref: NN1710

Although it lies near the head of Loch Fyne, where hillsides rise almost directly from the water's edge, this estate woodland has soft pathways on mostly gentle gradients. Occasional steeper stretches are eased by flights of steps. Strone mixes conifers and deciduous woodland with a fine display of rhododendrons and areas of springtime wildflowers. All through the year, the River Kinglas tumbles cheerfully over rapids, a dam and a salmon leap. A Grand fir, planted in 1875, is an awesome sight as it soars straight-trunked to a height of over 200ft – the tallest tree in Britain.

A landscape of lochs: the Highland resort of Scourie

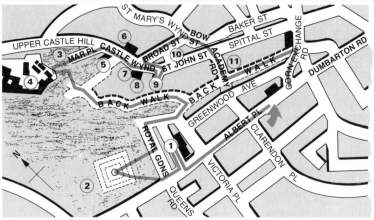

Bulwark of Independence

Dominated by its castle and royal palace on a crag-and-tail rock formation, Stirling is on a commanding site – once lapped by the North Sea – between Lowland Scotland and the Highlands. Near by, Robert the Bruce crushed Edward II's army in 1314, restoring Scotland's independence.

1 SMITH ART GALLERY & MUSEUM
In the heart of a Victorian suburb, laid out to a plan drawn up in 1848, the Smith Art Gallery was opened in 1874. Thomas Stuart Smith, who endowed it, left it to his own collection of 125 paintings. The museum section features a permanent local display entitled 'Stirling's Story'.

2 KING'S KNOT
Created in the 1620s, this geometrical garden in the then-popular 'knot' style is clearly visible from the castle above. The octagonal centrepiece may have featured in tournaments held here. Certainly, there was a jousting-ground on the far side of Dumbarton Road, in what is still called the King's Park, a royal property since at least the 12th century.

3 CASTLE ESPLANADE
Originally a parade-ground, the Esplanade is a splendid viewpoint towards the north and east. Over the lower-lying Gowan Hills, the outlook is down to the River Forth. Beside one of the windings is the ruin of Cambuskenneth Abbey, founded in 1147. Silhouetted against the skyline of the Ochil Hills, on Abbey Craig, is the 220ft tower of the Wallace Monument, completed in 1869 in memory of the hero of the Battle of Stirling Bridge in 1297.

4 STIRLING CASTLE
Known to have occupied its hilltop site earlier than 1124, this castle was a favourite residence of the Scottish monarchs up to the time of James VI, who became James I of the United Kingdom at the time of the Union of Crowns in 1603. Some of the most important buildings are the Palace, the Chapel Royal and the Great Hall, and the castle includes the regimental museum of the Argyll and Sutherland Highlanders.

5 PORTCULLIS HOTEL
For almost 100 years, from 1788, this building served as the Grammar School of Stirling. The road beside the hotel leads to an impressive stone pyramid which was erected in the 19th century in memory of the Covenanters – who fought for the Presbyterian cause in the 17th century.

6 ARGYLL LODGING
This splendid town mansion was built in 1630 for the 1st Earl of Stirling, but takes its name from a later owner, the 1st Marquis of Argyll.

7 MAR'S WARK
Only the frontage remains of this ambitious Renaissance-style palace, built in the 1570s for the Earl of Mar, Keeper of Stirling Castle and Regent of Scotland during the childhood of James VI.

8 CHURCH OF THE HOLY RUDE
This 15th-century church, one of the finest in Scotland, and fully restored in the 1930s, features a lofty nave with timbered ceiling. In 1656 a theological dispute led to the building of a wall to divide it in two, and thereafter there were separate congregations. The wall was removed only at the restoration.

9 GUILDHALL
Completed in 1639, this fine building was set up in accordance with the will of John Cowane, a wealthy member of the Merchant Guildry of Stirling. As Cowane's Hospital, it housed a number of Guild members 'decayed' by reason of ill health or ill fortune. The interior was rebuilt in 1852 and contains many Guild relics. Beside the Guildhall is a bowling green, opened in 1712 and still in use.

10 TOLBOOTH
This was built in 1704 as the town hall and town jail. From it, in 1820, John Baird and Andrew Hardie – two leaders of the Scottish Radical Rising – were led out to be executed beside the Mercat Cross. The present cross is a replacement set up in 1891, but it is topped by the stone unicorn which crowned the original.

11 HIGH SCHOOL
The old High School building stands in

Fit for kings: Stirling Castle, favourite home for Scottish monarchs

Academy Street. Behind it, the 18th-century Back Walk leads alongside the surviving town wall.

MARKET DAY: *Thu*

PARKING: *Allan Pk, Goosecroft Rd, Well Gn*

OPENING TIMES:
Smith Art Gallery & Museum: *open all year, Wed – Sun*
Stirling Castle: *open all year. Closed Sun am Oct – Mar*
Stirling Castle Visitor Centre: *open Feb – Dec*
Church of the Holy Rude: *open all year. Closes early pm Nov – Apr*
Guildhall: *as above*
Mar's Wark: *open all year*
Museum of the Argyll & Sutherland Highlanders: *open daily Etr – Sep; Oct, Mon – Fri*

ROUTE DIRECTIONS
Start this walk at Albert Halls. Go west along Albert Place to reach the Smith Art Gallery and Museum (1). Turn r. through gate into King's Knot garden (2). Return to gate, turn sharp l. into Royal Gardens and follow this road as it swings r. Bear l. uphill on broad path at grass islands. Turn sharp l. under the town wall on to Back Walk. Follow the pathway round the back of the cemetery and go forward between wall and railings, then on uphill and l. up steps on to Castle Esplanade (3). Enter castle (4). Return from castle, and follow the cobbled street downhill past the visitor centre. After Portcullis Hotel (5) go down Castle Wynd past Argyll Lodging (6) and Mar's Wark (7). Turn r. to Church of the Holy Rude (8) and Guildhall (9). Return from Guildhall, turn l. then r. into Broad St. Pass Tolbooth (10) and Mercat Cross. Turn r. into Bow St, go forward up footpath, passing Spittal's House. Cross into Academy Rd, and pass the Old High School (11). Turn l. on to Back Walk and return to Albert Halls via Corn Exchange Rd.

SUMMERLEE, Coatbridge, Strathclyde

Open all year; West Canal St.
Map Ref: NS7265

Dinosaurs at Summerlee are something else. Not prehistoric monsters, but the heavy industrial cranes which are just a few of the exhibits at this massive heritage park which traces the story of the old iron, steel and coal-mining industries which made Coatbridge the steel capital of Scotland.

A huge, purpose-built machine hall also features a reconstructed Victorian street, small modern workshops, and displays about very varied characters who are now, like their industry, figures from the past.

THIRLESTANE CASTLE & BORDER COUNTRY LIFE MUSEUM, Lauder, Borders

Open spring to late summer; off
A68 & A697.
Map Ref: NT5347

There was only ever one Duke of Lauderdale, and he was a close friend of Charles II who transformed an old Maitland family stronghold into this magnificent castle, which has state rooms that are among the finest apartments in Scotland. On a different scale, Thirlestane also has an extensive collection of historic toys.

The south wing is given over to the Border Country Life Museum, which recalls the way of life of farming families, fishermen, craftsmen and lairds in generations gone by. There is enough space here to devote each of the rooms to an individual theme.

THREAVE, Dumfries & Galloway

Map Ref: NX7560

There are three distinct locations to visit here. The showpiece grounds of Threave House, open all year, serve as the National Trust for Scotland's School of Gardening. The Trust also owns nearby Threave Castle, although this ruined river-island stronghold of the Douglases — open all year except on rare occasions when the short ferry-crossing is cancelled because of a spate on the River Dee — is administered as an ancient monument. Observation hides on the Threave Wildfowl Refuge, available from November to March, overlook the feeding and winter roosting grounds of great numbers and varieties of geese, ducks and swans.

A blaze of colour in the summer months, the Younger Botanic Garden, Benmore, has a wide range of flowering shrubs

TOMINTOUL, Grampian

Map Ref: NJ1619

Its position as the highest village in the Highlands, 1,150ft above sea level and not far from the ski-runs of the Lecht, gives a misleading impression of 'Tommin-towel' — a neat and regularly planned 18th-century village in an area of forests, angling rivers and sporting moorlands. There is a museum in the square, and the easy three-mile Tomintoul Country Walk circles the beautiful wooded valley of the River Avon.

TORRIDON ESTATE (NTS), Highland

Off A896 9m WSW Kinlochewe.
Map Ref: NG9055

The National Trust for Scotland's spectacular 16,000-acre Torridon estate includes the magnificent mountains of Beinn Alligin and Liathach, whose soaring crags and rock terraces rise to a pinnacled summit ridge reaching 3,456ft. At the roadside below Liathach is the Trust's Countryside Centre, which has a deer museum near by. The narrow and exhilarating road high above the north shore of Loch Torridon eventually plunges down one of the steepest road gradients in Scotland to reach the multi-level lochside village of Diabaig.

WALKERBURN, Borders
See Scottish Museum of Woollen Textiles

WICK, Highlands

Map Ref: ND3650

The winners of BBC Television's *Mastermind* are always presented with engraved Caithness glassware, and there are demonstrations of glassblowing at the factory at Wick. Most of the town was built around 1810, financed by the British Fisheries Society, and the harbour is still very active. Wick Heritage Centre has displays on fishing, kippering and coopering, and even includes a working lighthouse. There is recreational angling on the Wick River, which features in a torchlight sail during Gala Week. The walk round the South Head at the entrance to Wick Bay leads past curious rock formations and the natural archway of Brig o' Trams.

YOUNGER BOTANIC GARDEN, Benmore, Strathclyde

Open spring to autumn; on
A815 6m N Dunoon.
Map Ref: NS1484

Originally planted in the 19th century, this carefully run outstation of the Royal Botanic Garden in Edinburgh lies in the narrow valley of the short and winding River Eachaig, with forested hillsides to east and west. The grassy avenue of soaring Wellingtonias across the Eachaig bridge is a stately introduction to the garden, which has footpaths wandering through extensive low-ground woodlands and hillside viewpoints. Benmore is famous for its variety of flowering shrubs, especially the 250 species of rhododendron which provide a riot of early summer colour.

Wales

Scale: Approx 16 miles to 1 inch

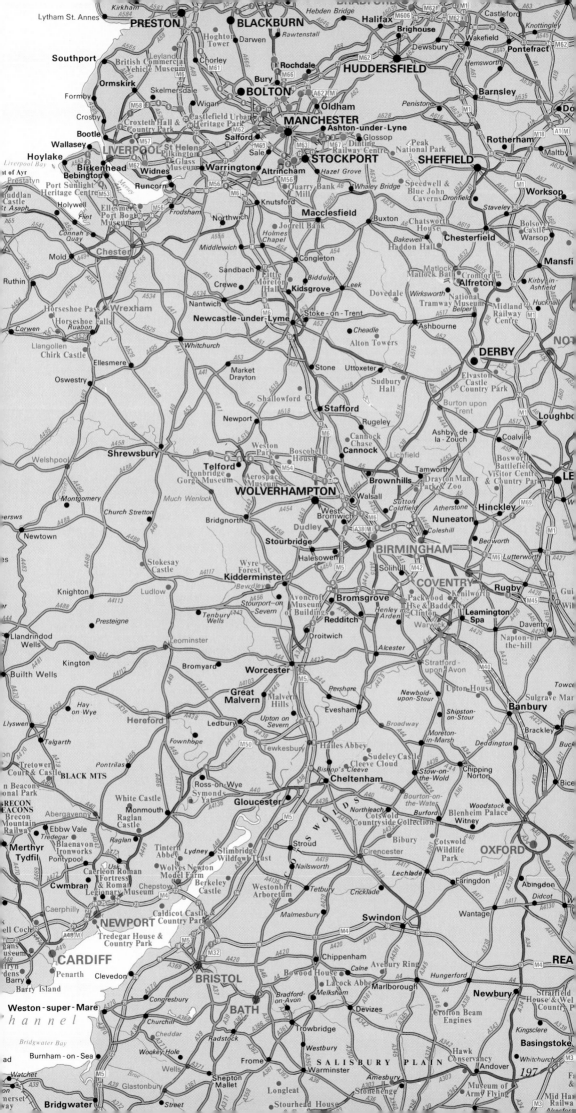

TOUR 1 90 MILES

Mountain Stronghold

Gwynedd the name lives again as a county, but Gwynedd the fortress – the strong land of mountains and lakes, dominated by Snowdon and moated by the Menai Strait – has never died.

The drive starts from the walled town of Caernarfon, a popular tourist centre overlooking the Menai Strait and dominated by a massive medieval castle. *Leave Caernarfon on the A487, signed Bangor, and drive alongside the Menai Strait to the popular yachting centre of Port Dinorwic. Continue, and in 1½ miles at a roundabout take the first exit, signed Holyhead. In ¾ mile at another roundabout take the first exit, signed Holyhead. In ¾ mile at another roundabout take the first exit to join the A5. Cross the Britannia Bridge into Anglesey, and immediately branch left then turn right on to the A4080 to reach Menai Bridge town. Here follow signs Bangor and cross Telford's suspension bridge, then at a roundabout take the first exit on to the A5122 to enter Bangor.* This delightful seaside town has a cathedral which claims the oldest bishopric in Britain, and buildings of the University College of Wales.

Leave Bangor on the A5122 Betws-y-coed road, and continue to the entrance of the Penrhyn Castle Estate (NT). This large, neo-Norman 'castle' actually dates from the 19th century and is superbly sited between Snowdon and the Menai Strait.

In ¾ mile at a roundabout take the second exit on to the A5 and almost immediately turn right on to the B4409 signed Caernarfon. In 3½ miles at a roundabout take the first exit on to the B4547 signed Llanberis. After 2 miles descend to a T-junction with the A4086. A detour can be taken from here by turning right on the A4086 to the edge of Llanrug, then left on to an unclassified road for Bryn Bras Castle. This early Victorian building is in Romanesque style and stands in fine wooded gardens.

A superb, sweeping view extending from Llyn Gwynant to Snowdon and along the Nant Gwynant Valley

The main drive turns left on to the A4086 to skirt the shore of Llyn Padarn and continue to Llanberis. On the far side of the lake runs the Llanberis narrow-gauge railway. The village is dominated by huge slate quarries, and is the start of the easiest route to the summit of Snowdon. Close by is the lower terminus of the rack-and-pinion Snowdon Mountain Railway – an alternative way to the top. Also here is the Oriel Eryri Welsh Environment Interpretation Centre, and across the valley at Gilfach Ddu is the Welsh Slate Museum – housed in buildings of the former Dinorwic quarry.

Continue along the A4086, passing 13th-century Dolbadarn Castle (AM Cadw), and skirt Llyn Peris. Beyond Nant Peris ascend to the summit of Llanberis Pass. Views extend north to 3,279ft Glyder Fawr, and south to the Snowdon massif, crowned by 3,560ft Yr Wyddfa. The Miner's Track can be taken from the top of the pass to the summit of Snowdon.

Descend to the Pen-y-Gwryd Hotel, at the head of the Gwryd Valley, and at the T-junction turn right on to the A498, signed Beddgelert. Continue to the viewpoint above Llyn Gwynant. From here a panorama extends to Snowdon and along the Nant Gwynant Valley.

Descend along the valley to Llyn Dinas. The ancient fort of Dinas Emrys stands at the west end of this attractive lake, and gives it its name. In the west is Yr Aran, at 2,451ft above sea level, a good viewpoint from which to appreciate the Snowdon range.

Skirt the shores of Llyn Dinas, passing the Sygun Copper Mine before reaching Beddgelert. Solid with old stone, this town is surrounded by mountains dominated in the south west by Moel Hebog – Mountain of the Hawk.

Keep forward on the A4085 Caernarfon road to reach Beddgelert Forest and picnic site. Continue to Rhyd Ddu, where a path leads to Snowdon, skirt Llyn Cwellyn, and follow the Afon Gwyrfai through Betws Garmon and Waunfawr to re-enter Caernarfon.

TOUR 2 60 MILES

Lakeland of Wales

A series of huge dams has turned the lovely mountain valleys of the Elan and its tributaries into a huge, forest-fringed lakeland with a beauty that is different but equally compelling.

The drive starts from Rhayader, a market town with 19th-century buildings among its modern shops. A large mound survives the castle which once stood here, high above a rocky reach of the River Wye. *Leave on the B4518 Elan Valley road and continue to the edge of Elan village, where there is a visitor centre. Keep forward on to an unclassified road for Caban Coch Dam and Reservoir.* Late in the 19th century, the Corporation of Birmingham built a reservoir system in the area now unofficially known as the Lakeland of Wales, creating a new landscape that is very beautiful and popular. However, it called for the drowning of a whole valley and its offshoots, complete with waterfalls, farms, meadows, houses and a church. Beneath the placid water is a house in which the poet Shelley lived for a while.

Continue to the Garreg-Ddu Viaduct and turn left to cross it. Proceed through pleasant woodland with the remains of Dol-y-Mynach Dam on the left, and enter the attractive Claerwen Valley. At an AA telephone box turn right to reach the Claerwen Dam and Reservoir. This vast, 600-acre lake is held back by a massive dam across the Afon Teifi.

Return across the Garreg-Ddu Viaduct and turn left, then follow the wooded shores of Garreg-Ddu Reservoir. A unique submerged dam separates this from the neighbouring Caban Coch Reservoir.

From the end of Garreg-Ddu Reservoir, ascend a short, winding stretch of road to Penygarreg Dam and Reservoir, then continue alongside Craig Goch Reservoir. A lake of 200 acres, this is the topmost part of the Elan Valley complex.

At the end of the reservoir cross a bridge and ascend, then turn left on to the Aberystwyth road. Continue along the wide moorland valley of the Afon Elan to a road summit of 1,320ft, then descend into the deep and wild Ystwyth Valley and in 4 miles reach Cwmystwyth. Ruins of mine workings hereabouts demonstrate the 19th century's insatiable appetite for minerals.

Beyond Cwmystwyth bear right to join the B4574 Devil's Bridge road. Ascend a wooded slope and reach the Arch Picnic Site. Descend with the Mynach Valley on the right, and enter Devil's Bridge. Here the Cwm Rheidol narrows to form a spectacular, 500ft-deep wooded gorge, and the Afon Mynach adds its own 300ft of impressive waterfalls to the grandeur.

Excellent views into the gorge can be enjoyed from the road, but the full splendour is best appreciated on a 100-step, spray-soaked descent into the valley bottom. At river level a small bridge and platform afford views of five separate waterfalls that make up the complete cascade. Devil's Bridge, named after the lower of three bridges across the gorge, is also a terminus for British Rail's last narrow-gauge railway – the Vale of Rheidol, which runs to Aberystwyth.

Leave Devil's Bridge village by crossing the Devil's Bridge on the A4120 Ponterwyd road. Continue high above the Rheidol Valley, and after a short distance reach Ysbyty Cynfyn. Several stones of the prehistoric circle in which this church was built have survived intact.

Continue, and in ½ mile turn right on to the B4343 Dyffryn Castell road. In 1¾ miles turn right signed Llangurig on to the A44 and reach Dyffryn Castell. A path leads from here to Plynlimon, a 2,470ft mountain which affords spectacular views.

Ascend to Eisteddfa Gurig and a 1,400ft road summit. Continue alongside the Afon Tarenig, and reach its confluence with the River Wye. In 5 miles enter Llangurig, then leave on the A470, signed Rhayader. Drive down the attractive Wye Valley and return to Rhayader.

The wild beauty of Cwmystwyth, where visitors can still see the ruins of 19th-century mine workings

ABERGAVENNY, Gwent

Map Ref: SO2914

Abergavenny is an excellent touring centre for the Black Mountains, Sugar Loaf, Skirrid Fawr and the Blorenge Mountains. Its carefully restored castle keep is an important landmark above peaceful meadows by the clear-flowing Usk, and an early 19th-century hunting lodge is the town's small but interesting museum. Exhibits include a Welsh farmhouse kitchen and saddlers' workshop. Nearby Llanthony Priory (AM Cadw) is a huge tranquil ruin, and at Llanfihangel Crucorney is the Skirrid Mountain Inn – Wales' oldest pub, where the notorious hanging judges held court in the 12th century. Abergavenny has a large park and a busy market day; in contrast, a tranquil afternoon can be spent boating on the Monmouthshire-Brecon Canal.

AFAN ARGOED COUNTRY PARK, West Glamorgan

Open early spring to autumn; on A4107. Map Ref: SS8195

Spectacular forested hills, steep valley sides, fast-flowing streams and extensive views have given this valley the local name 'Little Switzerland', and although some walks are on steepish slopes, others are quiet strolls through pretty glades. Forest and mountain tours by Land Rover are also offered. The award-winning Welsh Miners' Museum at Cynonville graphically portrays the miner's continual struggle. The miner's family is not forgotten either, and it is quite an experience to visit the reconstruction of a traditional miner's cottage. There is ample car parking, a cafeteria and excellent toilet facilities.

ANGLESEY, Gwynedd

Map Ref: SH47, etc

Much of Anglesey is officially designated an Area of Outstanding Natural Beauty, and its 125 miles of scenic coastline bring delight at every turn – sandy beaches and tiny fishing villages, quiet coves and rocky headlands alive with spindrift, sea holly and gorse. The walls of 13th-century Beaumaris Castle (AM Cadw) are dreamily reflected in its placid moat, and Telford's iron suspension bridge spans the Menai Strait. There, too, is the fascinating Museum of Childhood, with the Tegfryn Art Gallery and Penmon and Amlwch potteries near by. At Llanfairpwll, the old art of drying flowers has been revived, jewellery is produced from local stones at Beaumaris, and at Ty'n-y-gongl visitors can watch wrought-iron craftsmen at work.

Plas Newydd (NT) is an imposing 18th-century stately home at Llanfairpwll, full of wonderful treasures and richly furnished. There you can see the painter Rex Whistler's largest wall painting, and an impressive military museum. The car park is quarter of a mile away, but special arrangements may be made on request. A short way farther along the strait are Brynsiencyn and the Anglesey Sea Zoo, where many huge tanks house fascinating varied examples of the marine life of North Wales. Everything in the zoo is under cover, including trout ponds where visitors can feed the fish.

BALA LAKE, Gwynedd

On A494. Map Ref: SH9236

Bala Lake lies in wild mountain scenery of great beauty, bounded on the south and east by the 2,700ft Berwyn range and west by the 3,000ft twin peaks of Aran Benllyn and Aran Fawddwy. North rises the great bulk of Arenig Fawr. The narrow-gauge Bala Lake Railway affords wonderful views of the mountains as it makes its way along the southern shore between Bala and Llanuwchllyn.

BARRY ISLAND, South Glamorgan

Map Ref: ST1166

Really a peninsula reached by road across a low causeway, Barry Island is known for Whitmore Bay – an excellent beach sheltered by rocky Nell's Point and Friar's Point. Butlin's Pleasure Park overlooks the bay, and provides a wide range of amusements in a cheerful, gaudy atmosphere. Quiet, bracing walks can be enjoyed along Friar's Point and the promenade. On the far side of Nell's Point are Jackson's Bay and Barry Harbour, both filled with the colour and tranquillity of yachts and boats.

For a complete contrast, drive around the causeway to Cold Knap, a quiet pebble beach with ample car parking facing the sea and sheltered by cliffs. A short walk from Cold Knap is quiet Romilly Park, while a drive over a steep hill to the west leads to the wooded country park of Porthkerry, where there is also a pebble beach. There are barbecue and toilet facilities there too, and in the background, the spectacular Porthkerry railway viaduct strides across the valley. A mile away is the Welsh Hawking Centre.

The forested slopes at Afan Argoed account for this country park's local name of 'Little Switzerland'

Seaside gentility

An air of bygone gentility still clings to the hotels, guesthouses, churches and chapels which line the streets of Aberystwyth, a quiet and unassuming seaside resort that is also an important administrative centre.

1 VALE OF RHEIDOL LIGHT RAILWAY

The last narrow-gauge railway owned and operated by British Rail, the Vale of Rheidol runs for 12m through lovely scenery up to Devil's Bridge. The line was opened in 1902 to carry lead from several upland mines.

2 HARBOUR

When Daniel Defoe visited Aberystwyth in 1724 he reported that both town and harbour were very dirty and smoky from the huge quantities of coal and lead that were exported from here. Things are far different today, but reminders of the old industries survive.

3 ENOC HUWS SHOP

Set at the corner of Prospect Street, Enoc Huws' is a millinery and haberdashery 'shop' that is actually a cleverly mounted exhibition.

4 ABERYSTWYTH CASTLE

When Edward I decided to crush Welsh insurgency once and for all, he built powerful castles in the most strategically important places. Aberystwyth was completed in 1277, captured and destroyed by the Welsh five years later, and rebuilt by the king two years after that. Wales' last great guerilla leader, Owain Glyndwr, captured it in 1404 and held it for four years.

5 UNIVERSITY COLLEGE OF WALES

This was built by a Victorian railway magnate as a hotel for the thousands of tourists he hoped to entice to the town, but he became bankrupt and the building was subsequently bought by a group of Welsh businessmen as home for a new university. The building is in fact only the south wing of the original; the rest burned down in 1885. The main university buildings overlook the town from Penglais.

6 ST MICHAEL'S CHURCH

A massive stone tower, built in 1906, dominates this church, which itself dates from 20 years before that. Inside is a reredos which is a copy of Leonardo da Vinci's *Last Supper*.

7 LAURA PLACE

Most of Aberystwyth's Georgian buildings disappeared when the railway arrived in the 1860s, but some survived – notably those in Laura Place.

8 CEREDIGION MUSEUM

A converted theatre is the setting for this fascinating museum, in which can be seen folk memorabilia and domestic bric-à-brac of the past – including a cottage interior.

9 THE PIER

When it was opened to the public in 1865 the pier was 800ft long, but shortly afterwards 100ft of it was washed away by the sea. In 1938 it was severely damaged by a storm, but it still stands today as a popular place of entertainment.

10 MARINE TERRACE

Hotels and guesthouses line this thoroughfare, which leads to Constitution Hill – where a funicular railway built in 1895 carries passengers up and down the steep 1-in-2 slope.

11 TOWN HALL

Set at the end of Portland Street, the town hall was built in 1961 and opened a year later. It is a white building with a Palladian front to the centre block, and two plain Georgian-style wings.

EARLY CLOSING: *Wed*

MARKET DAY: *Mon*

PARKING: *Maesyrafon, railway station*

OPENING TIMES:
Vale of Rheidol Light Railway: open Easter – Oct
Ceredigion Museum: open all year. Weekdays

ROUTE DIRECTIONS
Start at the railway station, terminus of the branch line from Shrewsbury and of the Vale of Rheidol Light Railway (1). Walk west along Alexandra Rd, reach a roundabout and continue forward into Mill St. Just before reaching a bridge turn l. then r. to walk beneath its arches. From here there are views of the harbour (2). Ascend steps on r, then turn r. again and at the end turn l. into Bridge St. Turn l. into Princess St and keep forward into Vulcan St. Pass Enoc Huws Shop (3). Continue into Sea View Pl, join South Rd and reach New Promenade. Turn r. and enter the grounds of

A dramatic coastline, gentle seaside streets and a fine University campus make Aberystwyth a fascinating resort

the ruins of Aberystwyth Castle (4). Leave the castle by the main gate and take a path by a children's playground, with the University College of Wales (5) away to the l. Reach St Michael's Church (6). Walk through the churchyard into Laura Pl (7). Keep forward into New St, Eastgate and Portland St, then turn l. into Terrace Rd, passing the Ceredigion Museum (8). Turn l. into Corporation St, go past the library and turn r. down Crynfryn Row, a narrow passage which leads to the sea front. To the left is the pier (9). Turn r. along Marine Terr (10), then turn r. into Albert Pl and r. again into Queen's Rd, passing the Town Hall (11). Reach the end of Queen's Rd and continue into Thespian St. Turn r. into Alexandra Rd for the return to the railway station.

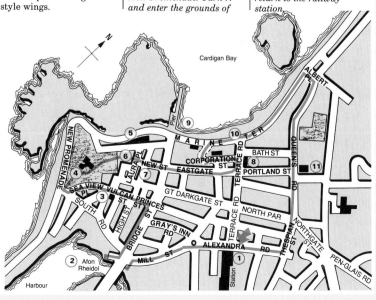

BEAUMARIS CASTLE (AM CADW), Anglesey

Open daily; on B5109. Map Ref: SH6076

Beaumaris Castle was begun in 1295, the last link in a chain built by King Edward 1 of England round the coast of North Wales. It is a symmetrical masterpiece of concentric defensive planning, but nowadays can be entered across a wooden bridge where once the drawbridge lay. Ahead is a glowering arched gateway, set between round and square towers guarding the entrance. In Beaumaris Gaol is a macabre treadmill where prisoners once laboured to raise water.

BETWS-Y-COED, Gwynedd

Map Ref: SH7956

At the junction of the Rivers Lledr, Llugwy and Conwy, this Snowdonian touring centre is at the start of an enchanting nature trail leading through deciduous woods to the Conwy Falls, one of the most spectacular waterfalls in Wales. A salmon leap allows the migrating fish to reach more easily their spawning grounds, upstream. Pont y Pair (Bridge of the Cauldron) crosses the River Llugwy on the Capel Curig side of the village, where there is also the summer Theatre, Nant y Nos. West are the famous Swallow Falls, where the River Llugwy cascades over a broken cliff between rocks and bright gorse. There is a car park, but a small charge is made to the falls.

Some 3½m from Betws-y-coed is the mountain-ringed village of Penmachno, from where easy walks lead to the Machno Falls or through Gwydyr Forest to Wybrant and Ty Mawr (NT), the 16th-century birthplace of Bishop William Morgan (who translated the bible into Welsh). Pentrefoelas Mill, driven by an overshot water wheel, dates from 1817 and still produces flour. Baskets and chairs in cane and willow are made in the village, and Penmachno Woollen Mill is a thriving concern perched on the edge of the Machno River. It now houses the 'Story of Wool'.

BLAENAU FFESTINIOG, Gwynedd

Map Ref: SH7045

At the head of the beautiful Vale of Ffestiniog is the mountain town of Blaenau Ffestiniog, surrounded by the majestic Moelwyn and Manod mountain ranges and a terminus of the narrow-gauge

With the soaring heights of Snowdonia in the background, the beautiful Bodnant Gardens in Gwynedd have a striking setting for their floral displays

Ffestiniog Railway from Porthmadog, on the coast. You can drive from the town up a winding mountain road to the Stwlam Dan, part of the Tanygrisiau hydro-electric scheme offering dramatic views from 1,000ft. While you're there visit Moelwyn Mill, a restored 18th-century water-powered fulling mill 200yds from Tanygrisiau Station.

At Llechwedd Slate Caverns the adventurous can choose between two underground rides – the Miners' Tramway, which trundles steadily into the open maw of the mountain, or Britain's steepest passenger underground railway to the Deep Mine. From the vast, 200ft Cathedral Cave leads a warren of narrow chambers that descends a further 61 steps before rejoining the carriages. Old works buildings on the surface have been converted into tourist attractions, and at the Slate Heritage Theatre a 25-minute programme illustrates the story of the industry since Roman times. Four rival railways that once competed for the Blaenau Ffestiniog slate trade have left Llechwedd a rich legacy of rolling stock and equipment.

North from Llechwedd along the Crimea Pass is the Gloddfa Ganol Tourist Centre, where you can try splitting slate – or watch a craftsman do it. The centre has used quarry buildings and tunnels to house a museum and gallery.

BLAENAVON IRONWORKS, Gwent

Open early spring to early winter; off B4248. Map Ref: SO2509

Located on the fringes of the Brecon Beacons National Park, Blaenavon has impressive, restored blast furnaces that were built in 1789 and reached their peak of production in the 1820s. Visitors can also see a water-balance lift, two typical cast houses of the early 19th century and the ruins of ironworkers' cottages. A viewing platform, interpretative facilities and fact sheets are also available. Not far away is the Big Pit, one of the oldest shaft mines in South Wales. It is now a fascinating mining museum offering underground tours and the chance to explore extensive surface remains dating from the Industrial Revolution.

BODNANT GARDEN (NT), Tal-y-cafn, Gwynedd

Open early spring to autumn; on A470, entrance ½m along Eglwysbach road. Map Ref: SH8072

These beautiful, 80-acre gardens, situated above the River Conwy, near Tal-y-cafn Bridge are especially famous for their magnificent collection of rhododendrons and camellias. The view along the length of the formal lily pond is reminiscent of the Taj Mahal, and magnificent displays of azalea, magnolia and many other species assure Bodnant's deserved reputation as certainly the finest garden in Wales – and one of the best in Britain.

BRECON, Powys

Map Ref: SO0428

This pleasant mid Wales town of Georgian and Jacobean houses is an ideal centre from which to explore the

surrounding Brecon Beacons
National Park. On its northern
outskirts is the imposing
cathedral, mostly of 13th- and
14th-century date, and once the
church of a Benedictine priory.
Among priory buildings that
have been restored is a fine
tithe barn. Beyond the
cathedral, a handsome 16th-
century stone bridge over the
Usk leads to Christ College
public school, originally built as
a Benedictine friary.

Brecon Castle is ruined, but
sections of the medieval town
walls can be seen at Captain's
Walk – an area named after
French prisoners who exercised
there during the Napoleonic
Wars. Also, it was from this
town that the 24th Foot (South
Wales Borderers) left for their
heroic stand at Rorke's Drift,
and they are remembered in an
admirable regimental museum.
Near by is the charming
Brecknock County Museum, in
the old Shire Hall. Here can be
seen archaeological and local
history exhibits and
reconstructions of a traditional

Welsh kitchen and a complete
smithy, as well as the town's
original assize court.

BRECON BEACONS
NATIONAL PARK (NT),
Powys

*Off A40/A470. Map Ref: SO02,
etc*

From the Beacons Mountain
Centre at Libanus, south of
Brecon, extends an impressive
panorama dominated by 2,906ft
Pen-y-Fan – often streaked with
snow well into spring. The park
embraces a wealth of similar
natural beauty, including
wooded gorges and waterfalls in
the limestone country around
Ystradfellte; the impressive
stalagmite and stalactite
formations at the Dan-yr-Ogof
showcaves, north of Craig-y-nos;
lakelands, forest and picnic
sites between Talybont and
Pontsticill – and canal cruising
in the borderlands around
Abergavenny.

It is great country for walkers,
but the weather changes

quickly and appropriate
clothing is essential.

Many of the local roads have
parking places from which
short strolls may be taken, and
those interested in history will
find many features to keep
them occupied. These include a
Roman fort and settlement at Y
Gaer, just west of Brecon, and
the evocative ruins of Carreg
Cennen Castle in the west.
Llanthony Priory is in the
Black Mountains.

BRECON MOUNTAIN
RAILWAY, Mid
Glamorgan/Powys

*Opening times on application;
off A465 2¾m NE Merthyr
Tydfil. Map Ref: SO0609 to
SO0512*

This – the first narrow-gauge
railway in Wales – starts at
Pant Station and runs for
2 miles through the
magnificent Brecon Beacons
National Park to Pontsticill, on
the forested shore of the Taf
Fechan Reservoir.

Port of princes

Caernarfon's grimly impressive castle and massive 13th-century town walls overshadow tiny, terraced houses, ancient inns and quaint shops, crowding together in narrow streets against their giant guardian.

1 SLATE QUAY
In the late 19th century cargo ships sailed to and from the harbour with loads of slate and coal, and recalling these days is the stone Harbour Master's Office of 1840.

2 CASTLE SQUARE
The Welsh call this Y Maes, which means The Field, and although the square is far from being a meadow, it is a pleasant open space that teems with life. Bronze statues of two of Wales' most famous figures – Lloyd George and Sir Hugh Owen – stand there.

3 HOLE IN THE WALL STREET
Terraces of colour-washed houses rise up on either side of this narrow street, which represents the heart of the ancient town of Caernarfon. On the right is the stone market building of 1832.

4 CAERNARFON CASTLE (AM CADW)
This massive fortress has dominated the town since Edward I built it as the chief stronghold in his chain of defensive castles around Wales. Today, although little more than an empty shell, its brown and cream stone walls and tall turreted towers present a façade which is as impressive as it ever was. It was here that the first Prince of Wales – Edward II – was born, and centuries later two other princes – Prince Edward (later Edward VIII) and Prince Charles were invested with the same title within the old walls.

5 ROYAL WELCH FUSILIERS REGIMENTAL MUSEUM
Housed in the Queen's Tower of the castle, the museum was set up in 1960 by trustees to represent almost 300 years of the regiment's history.

6 HIGH STREET
West Gate, at one end of the street, is known as the Golden Gate – possibly because lovely sunsets over the Menai Strait can be seen through it. East Gate at the other end had a large tower on it until 1963, when it was removed for safety reasons. At the base of the arch in Bank Quay is a very small cell which was used as the town lock-up until 1835.

7 NORTHGATE STREET
The Welsh call the street 'Stryd Pedwar a Chwech', meaning Four and Six Street – which apparently dates to the time when sailors could have a hammock for fourpence; an extra sixpence would secure female company as well.

Near the town wall is the famous Blackboy Inn, officially 17th-century, but possibly as much as 300 years older.

8 ST MARY'S CHURCH
Henry de Allerton, assistant master mason at the castle, founded St Mary's in 1307 for the garrison – but much of the present building was reconstructed in the 19th century.

9 VICTORIA DOCK
This was built during the 1870s as part of a much larger quayside development plan which never materialised. A small maritime museum, run by volunteers, is housed in a whitewashed stone building. Moored alongside is the SS *Seiont II*, which was purchased in 1980 for restoration.

10 THE PROMENADE
Dating from the 13th century, the promenade follows the seaward length of the walls and provides a very pleasant walk.

11 ANGLESEY HOTEL & HANGING TOWER
A customs house before 1822, when it was turned into a public house, the Anglesey Hotel is the last secular building in the town still attached to the castle walls. The squat, round tower next to the hotel is known as the hanging tower, because it used to be a place of execution.

EARLY CLOSING: *Thu*

MARKET DAY: *Sat*

PARKING: *Bank Quay, Slate Quarry*

OPENING TIMES:
Castle: open all year. Sun pm only Oct – Mar
Maritime Museum: open summer, hours vary

ROUTE DIRECTIONS
Start from the Slate Quay (1). Go up Castle Hill (to the r. of the castle) then turn r. into Castle Sq (2). Turn l. along Bridge St and turn l. into Turf Sq. Continue into Eastgate St to the arch in the town wall. Go through this and turn immediately l. into Hole in the Wall St (3). At the end turn r. into Castle Ditch to reach the Castle (4), where the Royal Welch Fusiliers Museum (5) is housed. Continue the walk along Castle Ditch and turn r. into Shire Hall St, then r. again into the High St (6). Turn l. into Northgate St (7), past the Blackboy Inn, and continue through the town-wall arch, then turn l. into Bank Quay. Turn l. into Market

St through another arch and turn immediately r. into Church La, which leads to St Mary's Church (8) in Church St. Leave the churchyard by turning l. through another wall arch to Victoria Dock (9). Continue towards the sea and turn l. along the Promenade (10), following the town walls to the Anglesey Hotel (11). (A short detour can be made from here across Aber Bridge. A walk to the l. affords some magnificent views of the castle.) Continue along from the hotel for the return to Slate Quay.

Sombre 13th-century castle towers loom over the ancient town of Caernarfon

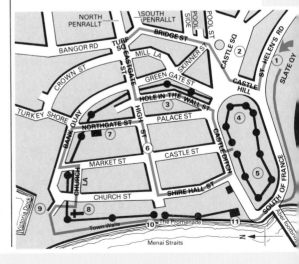

BRYNGARW COUNTRY PARK, Mid Glamorgan

Open all year; off A4065. Map Ref: SS9085

Nestling in the peaceful valley of the Afon Garw and secluded by acres of woodland is Bryngarw – former country home of the Traherne family – in 113 acres of park. Lawns and a Japanese garden contrast with wild, almost impenetrable wet coppices along the river, studded in season with the gold of marsh marigolds. Elsewhere are gently rolling meadows, woodlands, wet lands and pastures. There are easy walks around the park, and an information block with various facilities.

CADER IDRIS, Gwynedd

Off A487. Map Ref: SH7113

Cader Idris has been described as a crouching lion, and the mountain indeed dominates the road which winds through its foothills, overlooking the beautiful Mawddach Estuary, from Dolgellau to the Cregennen Lakes.

CAERLEON ROMAN FORTRESS (AM CADW) & ROMAN LEGIONARY MUSEUM, Gwent

Open daily; on A449. Map Ref: ST3390

Beneath modern Caerleon is *Isca Silurum*, chief fortress of the 2nd Augustan Legion of Rome. Established in AD75, it covered 50 acres and once held about 6,000 foot soldiers – plus horses. Parts remain of the barrack and administration blocks, shops and temples, and the excellent National Museum of Wales' Legionary Museum has a fascinating collection of Roman artefacts.

The most complete example of a Roman legionary bath building in Britain can also be seen, and a wooden walkway allows the site to be viewed from above. Tapes, videos and information panels provide details. The Amphitheatre (AM Cadw) was built about AD90 and held 6,000 spectators. A short walk from it are the Prysg Field barracks, the only remains of their type in Europe.

CAERNARFON, Gwynedd

Map Ref: SH4762

Caernarfon is the market and touring centre for Snowdonia National Park, the Lleyn Peninsula and the holiday island of Anglesey. Excellent shops are supplemented by a colourful Saturday market held in the square before the castle (AM Cadw) – a 13th-century stronghold that on 1 July 1969 was the setting for the investiture of the Prince of Wales. Open to visitors, it houses the Royal Welch Fusiliers Regimental Museum. Both the castle itself and the encircling town walls date from 1283 and were commissioned by Edward I.

At the Victoria Dock, the moored 87ft ex-dredger, *Seiont II* forms the basis of a small museum about the maritime history of Caernarfon and the Menai Strait. Also, the Roman fort of *Segontium* (AM Cadw) has been excavated, and has a fascinating museum.

CAERPHILLY CASTLE (AM CADW), South Glamorgan

Open daily; on A469. Map Ref: ST1587

Concentric Caerphilly Castle is the second-largest fortress in Europe and a monument to the warring Welsh and Normans. Its massive walls have been greatly restored in recent years, and the moat refilled. Extensive and easy walks explore the 30-acre site, and within the ruins is a vast, restored, 14th-century great hall. Among several unique features are a leaning tower and the ghost of the Green Lady – said to be a French princess who fell for a Welsh prince. Visitors can explore the castle's extensive water defences aboard a canopied boat, appropriately called *Green Lady*.

Over 1,900 years old, the remains of Isca Silurum, the main fortress of the 2nd Augustan Legion of Rome, lie beneath Caerleon in Gwent. This fortress once covered 50 acres and housed thousands of soldiers

CALDICOT CASTLE & COUNTRY PARK, Gwent

Open daily; on B4245. Map Ref: ST4888

Relic of a bloody past, Caldicot Castle is nowadays at the heart of a tree-scattered country park with green lawns and bright flower beds. Facilities are available for family barbecues, both in the park and in nearby Wentwood Forest. The round keep is the earliest part of the 12th-century castle buildings, although its mound and earthworks are older. Many of the towers house museum displays, including costume, furniture and fine art. Caldicot's 'medieval' banquets are of international repute.

CARDIFF, South Glamorgan

Map Ref: ST1876

Cardiff Castle, which dates back 1,900 years to the Romans, has been fully restored and stands in large grounds where peacocks display and visitors can picnic beneath huge shady trees. Just beyond the castle's eastern walls lies one of the finest civic centres in the world, a beautiful collection of buildings adorned with carved figures.

Literally across the road from the castle's south wall is a fine shopping centre with department stores, a colourful covered market that is reputed to have the finest wrought-iron structure since the Crystal Palace – and an unusual network of covered arcades.

Most of the centre is now pedestrianised, and in the heart is the magnificent St David's Hall – a 2,000-seat concert hall only recently completed, but already with a world reputation for music and drama.

Cardiff has over 2,700 acres of parks, one of the most beautiful of which is Bute, which offers a riverside walk from the city centre to Llandaff Cathedral. North of the centre is Roath Park, 100 acres of trees, shrubs, a vast rose garden and a 32-acre boating lake. There is also a sub-tropical greenhouse – another world of flowers, plants and butterflies.

Cardiff has several museums. In the civic centre is the marvellous National Museum of Wales, a vast, light and airy 'palace' entered through a great marbled hall under a 90ft dome. Its collections illustrate life in Wales and also include foreign exhibits and art treasures. A mile away at Cardiff Docks is the Maritime and Industrial Museum, with a collection of motive-power plants from the last two centuries. There is also an outside collection of railway engines and rolling stock, buses – even tug boats and cutters.

Beautiful Llandaff Cathedral nestles on low ground alongside the River Taff, near Llandaff Weir. In Cardiff – and yet within the ancient Llandaff City too – it is a building of great tranquillity and reverence, tracing its origins back to a religious community founded in the 6th century. *See also St Fagans Folk Museum.*

CARREG CENNEN CASTLE (AM CADW), Dyfed

Open daily; off A483. Map Ref: SN6619

There is a fairy-tale feeling about the way ancient Carreg Cennen Castle, approached through the delightful village of Trapp, perches dominantly on its high limestone crag. It is an excellent vantage point for views over the Vale of Cennen to the Black Mountain.

CASTELL COCH (AM CADW), Tongwynlais, South Glamorgan

Open daily; off A470. Map Ref: ST1382

This enchanting little castle stands among woods above Tongwynlais Gorge and the River Taff, its round towers and conical turrets soaring fantastically above the land.

The first castle in Britain made entirely of stone – Chepstow, in the beautiful border lands

Created by the fabulously wealthy Lord Bute and his architect – the 'eccentric genius' William Burges – the present building was begun in 1875 on the site of a ruined Norman castle.

A decorative extravaganza, its exotic interior design is surprising, enchanting and amusing. Fantastic murals depict Aesop's fables on the ceilings and walls of the drawing room, while figures from Greek mythology grace the mantel, and painted birds and carved butterflies adorn the vaulted ceiling. Castell Coch is a delight, but it contains steep stone stairways and has no facilities for those who would find them difficult.

CEFN COED COLLIERY MUSEUM, Crynant, West Glamorgan

Open spring to autumn; on A4109. Map Ref: SN7904

On the site of the former Cefn Coed Colliery – once the deepest anthracite mine in the world – this museum re-creates the atmosphere of a working pit in its heyday. Among many preserved features are the massive, brightly painted steam winding engine that once lowered and raised the cages, and six enormous boilers that powered it. In the dark and dank underground mining gallery, brilliantly brought to life by realistic sound effects, are exhibitions explaining the geology and mining history of the area. A variety of outdoor exhibits includes winding headgear and a colliery locomotive.

CHEPSTOW CASTLE (AM CADW), Gwent

Open daily; on A48. Map Ref: ST5393

A huge round tower protects the landward flank of Chepstow Castle, while on the other side are crenellated walls rising steeply to battlements atop unassailable cliffs above the River Wye. All around is the beautiful border landscape, and it is difficult to envisage the past strife that made the fortress so strategically important for hundreds of years. The first entirely stone castle to be built in Britain, it guarded the crossing from England into Wales. Visitors can trace the history of its fortification, from the 11th-century keep to 17th-century gun loops.

Chepstow's medieval town walls still enclose the steep, narrow streets, and before a by-pass was built the main road squeezed through a 14th-century town gatehouse – now tastefully restored as the Tourist Information Centre.

CHIRK CASTLE (NT), Clwyd

Open spring to late summer; off A5 ½m W Chirk. Map Ref: SJ2638

Commanding wide views and dominating the little border village of Chirk, this magnificent Marcher stronghold was built in 1310 by Roger Mortimer on land given to him in reward for suppressing the local Welsh princes. Its horrific dungeon is in complete contrast to elegant staterooms with elaborate decor and Adam-style furniture. Splendid gardens feature roses, yews, flowering shrubs and trees, and impressive ornamental gates – by the Davies brothers of Bersham – rival the castle itself as an attraction. Light lunches and teas are available at the shop.

CILGERRAN CASTLE (AM CADW), Dyfed

Open daily; off A484. Map Ref: SN1943

A romantic ruin in a commanding position above the River Teifi, this 13th-century castle is an excellent viewpoint and close to good walking country.

COLWYN BAY, Clwyd

Map Ref: SH8479

Entertainment for all ages is offered by this attractive seaside resort, where a long promenade, served by runabout buses, is fringed by sandy beaches offering safe bathing. Attractions include a paddling pool, miniature railway, donkey rides, amusements and boating.

At nearby Rhos-on-Sea is the tiny church of St Trillio, which is well worth a visit. Eiras Park – alongside the sea – covers 50 acres through which the pretty wooded Eiras Dingle runs. It offers 'endless' entertainments, including a boating lake and children's amusements, a cafeteria, various kiosks and much more. The modern Leisure Centre in Eiras Park extends the range still further, and has sports facilities.

From the pier at Rhos-on-Sea there is an easy drive to the Welsh Mountain Zoo – on a wooded hillside above Colwyn Bay – where birds of prey fly free each afternoon. The Tree Tops Safari Restaurant is an exciting and unique alternative to picnics on the lawns.

CONWY, Gwynedd

Map Ref: SH7877

A true fortified town, Conwy lies in the shadow of a huge castle (AM Cadw) with 21 crenellated towers and 1½ miles of massive curtain wall supported by complete town walls – all picturesquely sited on the river which gave it its name. Built by Edward I, the castle was his headquarters in the struggle against Prince Llywelyn of Wales, who besieged the king there in 1290. Richard II later sought shelter within Conwy's walls, but could not withstand the siege which led to his death. Cromwell's army took the castle in 1646, and when the Monarchy was restored it was given to the Earl of Conwy – who avariciously dismantled it for its timber, lead and iron.

This house, believed to be the smallest in Britain, nestles against its larger neighbours on Conwy's fish quay

The vessel carrying his spoils away was wrecked at sea.

Plas Mawr, a fine Elizabethan mansion, was built in 1577 and is now the home of the Royal Cambrian Academy of Art, which holds regular exhibitions. The Conwy Visitor Centre in Rosehill Street is a good starting point for a town tour, which should include its famous trio of river bridges: Telford's suspension bridge (NT), of 1826; Robert Stephenson's tubular bridge; and the modern, perfectly arched road bridge of 1958.

On the colourful fish quay is an intriguing house which is reputed to be the smallest in Britain and has been furnished as a mid-Victorian Welsh cottage. The quay itself is a popular attraction, where Conwy's river estuary bubbles with activity.

CRAIG-Y-NOS, Powys
See Dan-yr-Ogof Show Caves

CRICCIETH CASTLE (AM CADW), Gwynedd

Open daily; off A497. Map Ref: SH5038

Criccieth Castle, with its two great drum towers is strategically placed on a rocky headland thrusting into the sea at Tremadog Bay, on the Lleyn Peninsula.

The original castle was built in 1230, and in 1282 Edward I increased his hold on the land by strengthening the defences as a link in his chain of coastal fortresses. Criccieth never ranked with Conwy, Caernarfon or Beaumaris, but it was important enough for the king to visit on several occasions.

CRYNANT, West Glamorgan
See Cefn Coed Colliery Museum

CYNONVILLE, West Glamorgan
See Afan Argoed Country Park

DAN-YR-OGOF SHOW CAVES, Craig-y-nos, Powys

Open spring to autumn; on A4067. Map Ref: SN8316

Forested limestone landscapes swallow up the River Giedd at Sinc-y-Giedd, from where it flows 2½ miles underground to the Dan-yr-Ogof caves, which are partially open to the public. Their stalactites and stalagmites, chambers and underground lakes are floodlit, while above ground are a dinosaur park, ski slope, excellent restaurants, caravan site and the car park. The caves are not suitable for anyone who has difficulty with steps.

DENBIGH CASTLE (AM CADW), Clwyd

Open daily; off A543. Map Ref: SJ0566

Mellowed by mossy walls and ruination, Denbigh Castle has been described as Queen of the lower Vale of Clwyd and stands at 467ft above a strategic junction of valleys between the high ridge of the Clwydian Range and the Mynydd Hiraethog. It was built by the Earl of Lincoln in 1282 at the command of King Edward I, and is now the subject of a small but interesting museum. The famous African explorer H M Stanley – who found Dr Livingstone – was born in Denbigh.

DINAS MAWDDWY, Gwynedd
See Meirion Woollen Mill

The fortress town

Set against a backdrop of wooded hills above the wide river are the great towers of Conwy Castle – one of the best preserved medieval fortresses in Britain. The site was inaccessible until the 19th century, when Telford reached it with the first of the three bridges.

1 CONWY CASTLE (AM CADW)

Conwy Castle, the third of Edward I's great Welsh fortresses, consists of an inner and outer ward surrounded by eight great battlemented drum towers which are linked by a high curtain wall. Extra turrets were placed on the four eastern towers, as this was the residential half of the castle and required even greater protection. All the towers, apart from Chapel Tower, have lost their dividing floors.

2, 3 & 4 CONWY'S BRIDGES

Before Thomas Telford built his graceful suspension bridge (NT) here in 1826, the only way across the wide estuary was by ferry. In 1956 a new road bridge was built next to it and Telford's bridge is now for pedestrians only. The third is Stephenson's Tubular Railway Bridge, completed in 1848.

5 THE QUAY

Set beneath the castle walls, the quay is one of Conwy's most attractive features. Trawlers unload their catches there, and during the 19th century it was a loading area for slate export.

6 THE SMALLEST HOUSE IN GREAT BRITAIN

Wedged against the town wall between newer buildings is a red-painted mid-Victorian house which, measuring just 122ins high and 72ins wide, is claimed to be the smallest house in Britain.

7 TOWN WALL WALK

For most of the year it is possible to walk along the north-west section of the town walls, ascending from quay level to the highest point in the town. The views are tremendous.

8 CHAPEL STREET

To the left of the street lie the stone ruins of the medieval house, Parlwr Mawr, which was the family home of John Williams – who became Archbishop of York during the Civil War. As a supporter of the king he took refuge in Conwy, but later changed his allegiance and took part in the siege of the town.

9 PLAS MAWR

An Elizabethan adventurer built this stately mansion for himself in 1577, and today it is the town's finest building: the Royal Cambrian Academy of Art maintains the house, and uses it as its headquarters.

10 LANCASTER SQUARE

A statue of Llywelyn the Great, founder of Conwy Abbey, has occupied the centre of the square since 1898. Standing in one corner of the square is the former Boot Inn, now called the Alfredo Restaurant, which is believed to have been where Charlotte Brontë spent her honeymoon.

11 CONWY VISITOR CENTRE

Here, the past 800 years of Conwy's history are brought to life on film and through scenic displays.

12 ST MARY'S CHURCH

Eight hundred years ago a Cistercian abbey was founded in Conwy on the site now marked by St Mary's parish church, and parts of the walls and buttresses can be dated back to the original abbey church. There are many interesting monuments inside, plus an early Tudor font and a screen representing 15th-century craftsmanship at its best.

13 CASTLE HOTEL

The hotel stands on the site of an ancient spital – a medieval monastic hospital or guesthouse – remains of which survive in the stable yard. It is famous for its collection of old Welsh furniture, and pictures.

14 ABERCONWY HOUSE (NT)

Aberconwy House dates from the 14th century and is the oldest house in the town. Built by a prosperous merchant, it contains an exhibition depicting Conwy through the centuries.

EARLY CLOSING: *Wed*

MARKET DAYS: *Tue & Sat in summer, Sat in winter*

PARKING: *Morfa Bach (Llanrwst Rd), Vicarage Gardens (Rose Hill St)*

OPENING TIMES:
Castle: open all year except Christmas & New Year. Closed Sun pm Oct – Mar
***The Smallest House:** open summer only. Mon – Sun all day*
***Conwy Visitor Centre:** open all year.*
***Plas Mawr:** open all year except mid Dec – mid Jan*
***Aberconwy House:** open Apr – Sep. Closed Tue, and only open Sat & Sun in Oct*

Thanks to Thomas Telford's suspension bridge, visitors to Conwy no longer have to travel by ferry across the river estuary to the great fortress

ROUTE DIRECTIONS
Start in Castle Sq at the entrance to the castle (1). From the castle turn r. and before reaching the Conwy Road Br (2) bear r. down a path to Telford's Suspension Br (3), built alongside Stephenson's Tubular Railway Br (4). Return to the main road, cross and go down to The Quay (5). Continue into Lower Gate St, passing 'The Smallest House in Great Britain' (6) and go through the wall arch at the end. Continue up the steep slope to the l. to reach the A55. Here, either turn l. into Berry St, through the arch and turn immediately l. up the steps for the Wall Walk (7) – or for the less energetic, continue into Town Ditch Rd and Mount Pleasant, turn l. into Sychnant Pass Rd and keep l. for the arch at the top of Upper Gate St, which is the end of the Wall Walk. Continue down Upper Gate St into Chapel St (8) and turn r. into Crown La past Plas Mawr (9). Turn r. into the High St to Lancaster Sq (10) and turn l. into Rose Hill St past the Conwy Visitor Centre (11). Here turn l. along Church St and r. by the Baptist Church to reach St Mary's Church (12). Leave the churchyard by the path leading to the High St and turn r. past the Castle Hotel (13). Turn r. into Castle St, past Aberconwy House (14) on the corner, for the return to Castle Sq.

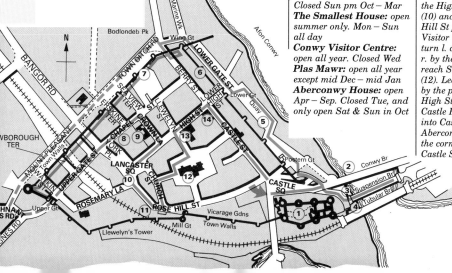

DOLAUCOTHI GOLD MINES (NT), Pumsaint, Dyfed

Open spring to autumn; on A482 between Lampeter & Llanwrda. Map Ref: SN6640

Dolaucothi was the only place in Britain where the Romans mined gold, and the workings that developed from their original excavations are surrounded by lush wooded hillsides overlooking the beautiful Cothi Valley. It is an exciting experience to put on a miner's helmet and lamp for a guided tour of the underground passages, or to follow the Miners' Way and share the secrets of nearly 2,000 years. Stout shoes are always recommended for exploring underground.

DOLGELLAU FOREST WALKS, Gwynedd

Off A470/A487. Map Ref: SH7217

The 7 mile Precipice Walk near Dolgellau has been adopted as a well-signposted nature trail which can be joined from the Llanfachreth Road. A forest walk starts at a picnic site opposite the Ty'n-y-groes Hotel – north of Dolgellau on the A470 – and runs 2 miles to Ganllwyd. From there a trail leads to Dolgefeilian Bridge picnic site, where the A470 crosses the river 8 miles north of Dolgellau. The Torrent Walk, approached off the A487 about 1 mile west from town, leads along the scenic Clywedog stream, with the rushing water often far below. These are all fairly easy walks, but good shoes are necessary.
See also Cader Idris.

DREFACH VELINDRE, Dyfed
See Museum of the Woollen Industry

DYFFRYN GARDENS, St Nicholas, South Glamorgan

Open spring to autumn; off A48, near Cardiff. Map Ref: ST0974

Tranquil, and a pleasurable venue for all the family, these gardens feature vast lawns and gentle walks amongst a great variety of mature trees, flowering shrubs, herbaceous borders and plant houses filled with colourful bloom. Water is a big attraction, including a pretty fountain pond, an eye-catching lily canal and a rock garden where the flowers burst over natural limestone rocks. You can buy souvenirs and refreshments are available.

Reminders of the industrial past at Kidwelly's Industrial Museum in Dyfed

DYLAN THOMAS BOATHOUSE MUSEUM, Laugharne, Dyfed

Open spring to late autumn; off A4066. Map Ref: SN3010

Dylan Thomas was Laugharne's most famous inhabitant – but, apart from his simple grave, the only evidence of him is the Boathouse, where he lived and wrote. A small white Georgian cottage under the hillside on a narrow cliff walk near Laugharne Castle is now a museum dedicated to the poet's life and work.

The town itself is fresh and charming, with modest Georgian houses and a white-towered town hall in the main street. Across the quiet estuary is Llanstephan Castle.

FAIRBOURNE, Gwynedd

Map Ref: SH6112

A growing resort south of the scenic Mawddach Estuary, Fairbourne is backed by dunelands which stretch north to Penrhyn Point. Across the water is Barmouth, with its sandy beaches, picturesque harbour, painted houses and bright sailing boats. Extending beyond the estuary are superb views to the Diffwys Mountains, with Cader Idris visible beyond the Cregennen Lakes at Arthog. The Butterfly Safari Centre is a collection of tropical houses where gorgeous butterflies flit freely.

Fairbourne Railway operates four 'Lilliputian' locomotives, brightly painted and polished brass replicas of their larger cousins. The line follows the coast across the dunes from Fairbourne to the mouth of the

mansion containing fine examples of period furniture. In the extensive grounds are peacocks and tropical birds.

HARLECH CASTLE (AM CADW), Gwynedd

Open daily; on A496. Map Ref: SH5831

Harlech is dominated by the brooding ramparts of its famous castle, built in 1283 on a rocky promontory which was on the shore before the sea retreated more than a mile. There is ample car parking at the beach.

HORSESHOE FALLS, Llangollen, Clwyd
See under Horseshoe Pass in The North

HORSESHOE PASS, Clwyd

Off A542. Map Ref: SJ1847

This is a spectacular pass through the border mountains with magnificent views of Eglwyseg Mountain and the Dee valley. *See also under The North.*

KIDWELLY, Dyfed

Map Ref: SN4006

This ancient town lies in lush green farming country at the confluence of the rivers Gwendraeth Fawr and Gwendraeth Fach. Other medieval survivals include the Church of St Mary the Virgin, and a great castle (AM Cadw) rising beyond the river. Maes Gwenllian – a memorial stone near the castle – commemorates the wife of Gruffydd ap Rhys, whose army attacked the castle in 1136.

LAUGHARNE, Dyfed
See Dylan Thomas Boathouse Museum

LLANBEDR, Gwynedd

Map Ref: SH5826

This is a good place from which to explore the Snowdonia National Park. The Cwm Nantcol Nature Trail riverside walk, which begins at the car park and camping site, is a delightful and fairly easy walk through beautiful country. Mochras Island, just 2 miles along the coast west of Llanbedr, is also known as Shell Island. A paradise for nature lovers, it is really a long peninsula that is accessible at low tide by causeway. Take care to avoid being cut off. Car parking and some facilities are available.

Mawddach Estuary. It was built in the 19th century as a horse-drawn tramway, converted to steam power in 1916 and rescued by enthusiasts in 1946.

FISHGUARD & GOODWICK, Dyfed

Map Ref: SM9537 & SM9438

Lower Fishguard, a picturesque cluster of old wharfs and cottages round a beautiful harbour, was used for the film of Dylan Thomas's *Under Milk Wood*. One headland is dominated by the ruins of an old fort and on the other is Fishguard town – a good shopping place where a well-established week-long music festival is held in July. The sturdy Royal Oak Inn on the Square has mementoes of a French landing in 1797, the last invasion of Britain.

GOWER PENINSULA, West Glamorgan

Map Ref: SS48 etc

From the Mumbles west of Swansea, the Gower stretches some 14 miles to Worm's Head – a sharp rocky headland with towering cliffs. On the other side is the small resort of Rhossili.

The southern coast of Gower – Britain's first designated area of outstanding natural beauty – has many beautiful bays and inland are pretty villages on narrow winding lanes.

GWYDIR CASTLE (AM CADW), Llanrwst, Gwynedd

Open all year; on A470. Map Ref: SH7961

Faithfully reconstructed after fire damage earlier this century, Gwydir is a Tudor

LLANBERIS, Gwynedd

Map Ref: SH5760

Beside the twin lakes of Padarn and Peris is Llanberis, a centre for the rugged and beautiful Llanberis Pass and the lower terminus of the Snowdon Mountain Railway. This unique rack-and-pinion line ferries passengers to the 3,566ft peak of Snowdon at 5mph, offering breathtaking views over rows of mountains. At the summit is a bar, restaurant and shop. The air at this height is noticeably cooler than at Llanberis, so a good coat or anorak should be taken to cover light summer clothes.

Above Lakes Padarn and Peris is the largest pumped water-storage scheme in Europe, and on the opposite side of Lake Padarn is the Welsh Slate Museum and Padarn Country Park. Oriel Eryri (The Snowdon Gallery) is an interpretative centre of the National Museum of Wales. Dolbadarn Castle (AM Cadw) is south of the village, and Bryn Bras Castle – 2 miles south on the scenic A4086 – has extensive grounds. For something different spend an hour at the oddly named Pretty Ugly Pottery, in Llandinorwig Old School.

The narrow-gauge Llanberis Lake Railway runs along the eastern shore of Lake Padarn from Gilfach Ddu to the lonely shore of Cei Llydan lake, where there are gorgeous sunny banks (in good weather) for picnics.

LLANGOLLEN, Clwyd

Map Ref: SJ2141

Though close to the low-lying English border, famous Llangollen is completely Welsh in its mountainous scenery and character. The town's 14th-century stone bridge, beneath which plunges the salmon-filled River Dee, has been called one of the Seven Wonders of Wales – though the International Music Festival in the beautiful Vale of Llangollen is perhaps better known. Early in June each year the festival's huge marquee seems to fill the valley floor, and the vale echoes to song, music and dance.

Car parks abound, and places to browse in the town include the local pottery and Llangollen Weavers. The town's station has a fine collection of locomotives, carriages, relics and photographs.

From the Grapes Hotel it is a gentle walk uphill to Plas Newydd, a black-and-white timbered mansion that for 50 years was home to the 'Ladies of Llangollen', Lady Eleanor Butler and Miss Sarah Ponsonby – whose home was a tourist attraction even then.

LLANGWM, Gwent
See Wolves Newton Model Farm

LLANRWST, Gwynedd

Map Ref: SH7961

This delightful market town is set amid rolling meadows beneath the pine-clad foothills of Snowdonia National Park. A three-arched bridge designed by Inigo Jones in 1636 spans the River Conwy, and the town is the main shopping centre of the upper Conwy valley. Near the station are remains of Plas Isaf, the home of William Salisbury, who first translated the Old Testament into Welsh.

Fron Canol, in School Bank Road, houses the North Wales Museum of Wild Life – a fine collection of local flora and fauna alongside big game trophies and stuffed birds from an era before cameras could do the catching. The old parish church has a magnificent carved rood loft from Maenan Abbey, while in the adjoining Gwydir Chapel (AM Cadw) there is the vast stone coffin (supposedly) of Llywelyn the Great, Prince of Wales.

LLYN BRIANNE, Dyfed & Powys

Off A483. Map Ref: SN7948

Opened in 1973, Brianne is formed from the headwaters of the River Tywi, and behind its dam an incredible 61 million cubic metres of water extend back into valley after valley between forested hills. A road that runs in spectacular roller-coaster fashion along the eastern shores affords magnificent views of the lake and its surrounding grandeur. Visitors can stop at an elevated viewing platform for more breathtaking views, and just south are the foaming Tywi Falls and Twm-Sion-Cati's cave – hideout of a Welsh Robin Hood-type outlaw.

MAESGWM FOREST VISITOR CENTRE, Gwynedd

Open spring to autumn; off A470 N of Dolgellau. Map Ref: SH7127

Among the first of its kind to be established in Wales, this visitor centre is in the midst of the Coed-y-Brenin forest – fourth largest in Wales – which blankets low-lying hills alongside the River Mawddach. Deep in the forest the Pistyll Cain Falls plunge in a series of whitewater runs between fern-covered rocks. The centre does not confine its exhibits to forest alone, but traces its development, topography, soils, natural vegetation, underlying geological formations and man's impact.

MARGAM PARK, West Glamorgan

Open early spring to late summer; access N of Pyle on A48. Map Ref: SS8184

Margam Park, near Port Talbot, offers wide variety within its 850 acres of countryside, including lakes, landscaped parkland and a wild mountainside with an Iron Age fort.

Margam Castle is an imposing Gothic-style mansion, partially restored and with exhibition rooms. Near by is a magnificent 18th-century orangery behind sparkling fountains, and the imposing ruins of a great 12th-century Cistercian abbey. Picturesque lakes offer fishing and boating, and guided walks with park rangers are conducted throughout the year. Other features include a putting course, one of the world's largest hedge mazes and a renowned outdoor display of sculpture.

There are plenty of seating, rest and picnic areas, and refreshments are available at the visitor centre. A road train offers an alternative means of exploration.

MEIRION WOOLLEN MILL,
Dinas Mawddwy, Gwynedd

Open spring to autumn; on A470. Map Ref: SH8514

This working woollen mill is situated in the Snowdonia National Park, beside Afon Dyfi, and produces high-quality woven fabrics that can be purchased as finished rugs, bedspreads and knitwear. Light meals and refreshments are served at the mill's delightful coffee shop throughout the day, and other places to visit include a medieval pack-horse bridge, The Railway Walk, and many reminders of the old Mawddwy Railway Station – now part of the extensive mill complex. Near by is an art and craft gallery which shows work by local people.

MUSEUM OF THE WOOLLEN INDUSTRY,
Drefach Velindre, Dyfed

Open spring to late summer; off A484. Map Ref: SN3538

In the most important woollen manufacturing centre of Wales, this museum contains an extensive collection of textile machinery and tools dating back to the 18th century. There is a car park and picnic area too, and visitors can follow a factory trail through evolutionary stages in the development of the woollen industry. Next door are the working Cambrian Mills, which are also open to visitors.

The canal at Llangollen on its scenic journey across the Pontcysyllte Aqueduct

NEATH ABBEY (AM CADW) & VALE OF NEATH, West Glamorgan

Open daily; off A465. Map Ref: SS7597

Just behind the industrial coast of South Wales, this beautiful vale stretches north from Neath to the Brecon Beacons National Park. Ruined Neath Abbey was founded in 1130 on a rocky terrace overlooking the river marshlands, and by the time of its dissolution it had become 'The fairest Abbey in all Wales'.

Flanked by high hills, the vale itself is wide and gentle, passing through the great Forest of Rheola and including the spectacular Aberdulais Falls (NT). In their wooded gorge survive the remains of 400 years of industrial activity. At Pelena is a recently built Mountain Centre, where visitors are welcome and which is a good base for walks in the Pelena Forest.

NEWPORT, Gwent
See Tredegar House & Country Park

PEMBREY COUNTRY PARK, Dyfed

Open daily; access ½m off A484. Map Ref: SN4000

This delightful 210-acre park of grass and woodland borders miles of sandy beach and can be explored by way-marked nature trails or guided walks with experienced leaders. Birdwatchers can use a permanent hide on the edge of extensive pine woods overlooking the beach. There are also sheltered picnic sites with tables and benches, an adventure playground for children, family barbecue areas (you can hire equipment from the centre) and a caravan and camp site near by. Ample car parking is available, and the Visitor Centre houses an information desk, first-aid facilities, displays and exhibitions, the Ranger Service and toilets.

PEMBROKE, Dyfed

Map Ref: SM9801

Pembroke Castle

Open all year; off B4320

Pembroke is an ancient borough built around a great castle perched on a rocky crag amid woods. Its massive fortifications centre on a great round tower, the hub of a 14 mile-wide medieval network of defences. Henry VII – the first

Tudor king – was born in the castle, beneath which is a vast cavern known as The Wogan.

Pembroke Dock

On A4139

The Royal Navy once built battleships here, and the harbour's placid waters still reflect fortified towers built as a defence against Napoleon. Splendid views extend to Milford Haven, a deep waterway used by the world's biggest oil tankers when berthing at Angle Bay. The MV *Tudor Princess* and other pleasure craft depart from Hobbs Point for cruises along the Haven, affording good views and opportunities to watch the varied bird life. Colourful regattas are organised by the local yachting and boating clubs, and there is excellent fishing. East of Pembroke are the picturesque ruins of Lamphey (AM Cadw), the old palace of the Bishops of St Davids.

PEMBROKESHIRE COAST NATIONAL PARK, Dyfed

Off A477 & B4546. Map Ref: SN10 to SN14

Here, in a 5 mile strip of beautiful countryside stretching 180 miles from Amroth on Carmarthen Bay to the Teifi Estuary near Cardigan is some of the finest walking country to be found in Britain. However, the land can be steep and difficult – but there are many places where the excellent views of sea, sand and rocky cliff may be enjoyed from a car.

There are field studies centres at Dale Fort and Orielton, near Pembroke, and just off the coast are the scenic islands of Caldey, Skokholm, Skomer, and Ramsey, where seals may be seen rolling and plunging in the surf. A little farther away on Grassholm is one of the world's largest gannetries. The park also embraces small towns, such as Haverfordwest, formerly the county town of

St David's Head, with its 100ft-high cliffs, forms a striking promontory on the Pembrokeshire coast

PORTHMADOG, Gwynedd

Map Ref: SH5638

On the Lleyn Peninsula between Tremadog Bay and towering hills is Porthmadog, at the mouth of the Glasyn River and close to sandy beaches. In Snowdon Street is a pottery where visitors can watch and try clay work, and the sailing ketch *Garlandstone* – at the town wharf – has been adapted as an interesting local Maritime Museum. Nearby Tremadog is the birthplace of T E Lawrence (Lawrence of Arabia).

The old Ffestiniog railway – which used to carry slates from the huge quarries of Blaenau Ffestiniog to Porthmadog Harbour – has been restored, and its quaint tank engines pull passenger trains through superb scenery to Llyn Ystradau and Tanygrisiau. Just below Ffestiniog are the Cynfal Waterfalls.

PORTMEIRION, Gwynedd

Map Ref: SH5837

A wooded peninsula, on the shores of Cardigan Bay, between Harlech and Porthmadog, is the setting for this tiny Italianate village, where trim lawns bordered by palms and cypresses evoke images of the Mediterranean. It was the dream of the late Sir Clough Williams-Ellis, and the pastel coloured buildings include a town hall, restaurant and a luxury hotel. There is ample parking.

POWIS CASTLE, Powys

See Welshpool

PRESTATYN, Clwyd

Map Ref: SJ0682

Within easy touring distance of Snowdonia and the beautiful Vale of Clwyd, this popular seaside resort has 4 miles of sand, an ultra-modern heated outdoor swimming pool, a promenade, a putting green and golf courses – plus an excellent sports centre in Princess Avenue and squash centre at Meliden. More outdoor amusements are at the Central Beach Royal Lido – a modern holiday complex in the centre of the sea front. Parking is available at Y Ffrith Beach and Central Beach.

PUMSAINT, Dyfed

See Dolaucothi Gold Mines

Pembrokeshire, which provide all the usual facilities and a wide diversity of shops.

PENARTH, South Glamorgan

Map Ref: ST1871

The seaside town of Penarth, near Cardiff, has an Edwardian promenade with flower gardens overlooking the Bristol Channel and the islands of Flatholm and Steepholm. There are also plenty of seats, and admission to the pier is free. A pleasant cliff walk leads south to St Mary's Well Bay, at Lavernock.

From the promenade a short, steep walk leads to Windsor gardens, which are beautifully laid-out with gently sloped paths and shallow steps. A pretty aviary is sheltered by yew hedges, and along the wooded Dingle is the Turner House Art Gallery – in a Georgian building well worth visiting for its fine collection of paintings and ceramics.

PORTHCAWL, Mid Glamorgan

Map Ref: SS8176

Several large bays forming the 'front' of this traditional seaside resort vary from miles of sand to rocky points and pools. There is a large and exciting funfair, and the long promenade offers easy walks and excellent shopping.

East of Porthcawl are the dunes of Merthyr Mawr Warren, beyond which is the quaint thatched-cottage village of Merthyr Mawr itself. Walks from the car park at ruined Candleston Castle cross the flower-covered duneland, and in the village is a miniature suspension bridge over the River Ogmore. Ancient 12th-century stepping stones are used to cross the River Ewenny to Ogmore Castle (AM Cadw), beside the river, and just west of Porthcawl is Kenfig Burrows – a nature reserve with excellent walking and bird hides.

RAGLAN CASTLE (AM CADW), Gwent

Open daily; off A40. Map Ref: SO4107

Although its size suggests an early foundation, Raglan belongs mainly to the 15th century and was the product of social grandeur rather than military necessity. Its great tower, strikingly positioned outside the castle wall, defied Cromwell's engineers until they undermined two of its six sides, leaving it in its present state. The yellow tower of Gwent remains the dominant feature, and the hall was the finest apartment. Hints of a previous splendour can be seen in the windows, the moulded roof, surviving corbels and a huge fireplace.

RHUDDLAN CASTLE (AM CADW), Clwyd

Open daily; on A547. Map Ref: SJ0278

Rhuddlan Castle's great round towers reflect enchantingly in the River Clwyd, much as they and their predecessors have done since William the Conqueror caused a motte-and-bailey stronghold to be built there in the 11th century. In Rhuddlan High Street is Old Parliament House, which is reputed to incorporate remains of a building where Edward I passed the Statute of Rhuddlan – his terms for Wales after the extinction of the Welsh princely line – in 1288.

Two miles south-west is Bodelwyddan and its curious 'marble' church, while east on the Dyserth Road is Bodrhyddan Hall, home of the Hereditary Constable of Rhuddlan Castle. This beautiful 17th-century house contains fascinating collections of pictures, armour and furniture.

RHYL, Clwyd

Map Ref: SJ0081

Rhyl offers 2 miles of promenade and just about everything that could be asked of a seaside resort. Attractions ranging from indoor surfing and a tropical lagoon to a roof-top monorail and pool-side sun-tan beds are available at the Sun Centre. On the East Parade are miniature golf, bowls, a playground and boating. Children's attractions are near Queen's Gardens. At the west end of the promenade is the Marine Lake Leisure Park, with rowing boats and cruises on a 'pirate ship'.

Rhyl also has one of the finest shopping centres in North Wales, and a superb night-life.

ST DAVID'S CATHEDRAL, Dyfed

Open all year; off A487. Map Ref: SM7525

Mellowed St David's Cathedral, devoted to Wales' patron saint, lies in a shallow valley that once hid it from seafaring marauders. It has the shrine of St David at its heart and fascinating carvings on its choir stalls. Irish oak has been used for the nave roof, and delicate fan vaulting can be seen above the Holy Trinity Chapel. Ruins of the Bishop's Palace (AM Cadw) enclose a fine lawn.

ST FAGANS FOLK MUSEUM, nr Cardiff, South Glamorgan

Open spring to autumn; off A48. Map Ref: ST1277

West of Cardiff at St Fagans is the Welsh Folk Museum, an excellent collection of re-erected buildings containing day-to-day items of domestic and working life from days gone by. A Tudor mansion set in beautiful formal gardens is completely furnished in period style, and everything from kitchen to bedrooms looks as though the inhabitants have just popped out for a minute. Every aspect of Welsh country life is represented in a vast collection: farmhouses from Denbighshire, a woollen mill from Breconshire, a barn from Flint, a chapel from Carmarthen, and many more examples of folk architecture. The trades and crafts of past times are also preserved, including woodturning and basket making. There is an excellent cafeteria.

ST NICHOLAS, South Glamorgan
See Dyffryn Gardens

SNOWDONIA NATIONAL PARK, Gwynedd

Map Ref: SH65, etc

With 840 square miles of glorious mountains, lakes and forests, this famous park also has three lovely estuaries and 25 miles of coastline. It can be entered in many ways – by car, special buses, narrow-gauge railway, or on foot along nature trails. Information centres have been established at Llanrwst, Llanberis, Blaenau Ffestiniog, Harlech, Aberdyfi, Bala, Conwy and Dolgellau.

Encircled by wooded hills, the stately ruins of Tintern Abbey are one of the most striking features of the Wye Valley. This beautiful abbey was founded in the mid-12th century

STRATA FLORIDA ABBEY, (AM CADW), Dyfed

Open daily; on unclassified road off B4343, 6m NE Tregaron. Map Ref: SN7465

Fed by the River Teifi, the great bog of Tregaron – home of the red kite – in turn nourishes a great flower-strewn plain that gave its name to Strata Florida, the 'plain of flowers'. Here stood the supreme Abbey of Wales, now an impressive ruin

with a unique, Norman-style arch and fine tiled pavements.

SWANSEA, West Glamorgan

Map Ref: SS6593

Swansea is the main shopping centre for south-west Wales, and has a colourful indoor market where you can buy a great variety of traditional Welsh foods – including lava bread – and superb fish.

Glyn Vivian Art Gallery in Alexandra Road has a fine collection of paintings and rare Swansea and Nantgarw porcelain, and the City Royal Institution Museum will keep children and adults absorbed for hours. In the Guildhall's magnificent Brangwyn Hall are the British Empire Panels, originally painted for the House of Lords, and in October the hall's concert programme culminates in the renowned Swansea Festival. Amongst traditional entertainment available in the town is the *Hwrnos*, a superb evening of traditional cuisine, folk music, singing and harp music. Swansea Leisure Centre, on Oystermouth Road, has an indoor beach and a wave-making machine.

No fewer than 48 parks exist along the bay, with the Botanical Gardens at Singleton among the most notable. The Mumbles is a small nearby resort with plenty of parking facing the sea. Visitors can wander the promenade among beached yachts, or choose from many cafés and restaurants. Around Mumbles Point, with its lighthouse, are beautiful sheltered bays which extend in a series of endless beaches along the Gower coastline.

TAL-Y-CAFN, Clwyd
See Bodnant Garden (NT)

TAL-Y-LLYN RAILWAY, Gwynedd

Open spring to autumn; off A493 & B4405. Map Ref: SH5800 to SH6806

Unique as the only narrow-gauge railway in the world with over a century of unbroken passenger service, the Tal-y-llyn runs from the sea at Tywyn to the slate quarries at Nant Gwynant, above Abergynolwyn. Wharf Station features a fascinating collection of railway relics, including a horse-hauled slate wagon and a peculiar 'host wagon' from Padarn. From Tywyn the route passes through gentle country, then at Dolgoch Viaduct enters the rugged hills to offer breathtaking views through overhanging trees to the Dolgoch Falls. The surroundings become more mountainous and wild as the valley narrows and the line follows the rocky slopes of Mynydd Pentre, to re-enter woodland before Abergynolwyn, in the foothills of Cader Idris. The terminus is along a short extension at Nant Gwernol. Refreshments are available in Tywyn and Abergynolwyn.

TENBY, Dyfed
Map Ref: SN1300

An ancient walled town on a rocky peninsula jutting into Carmarthen Bay, Tenby's stylish Georgian harbour, bright with painted houses and bobbing yachts, is reached along narrow medieval streets which are rich in character and charm.

The famous Tudor Merchant's House (NT) is a late 15th-century building characteristic of the architectural tradition in south-west Wales, preserving three storeys featuring the original floor beams, many of the joists and scarfed roof trusses. Each floor has its original fireplace and chimney, but the fascinating furnishings are of different periods. Many difficult steps have to be negotiated.

Some 500yds from the mainland is St Catherine's Island, and 2½ miles offshore is Caldey Island – both served by frequent boats in summer. Caldey has an ancient monastery where Cistercian monks make perfume from local flowers.

TINTERN ABBEY (AM CADW), Gwent

Open daily; on A466. Map Ref: SO5300

Wordsworth appreciated the serene beauty of this magnificent ruin, which dominates the village that grew around it between the wooded slopes of the Wye Valley. Near the river is the Anchor Inn, once the abbey's water gate, and in Tintern's former railway station is a small exhibition telling the story of the Wye Valley Railway.

TONGWYNLAIS, South Glamorgan
See Castell Coch

TREDEGAR HOUSE COUNTRY PARK, Newport, Gwent

Open spring to late summer; off A48 2mW Newport. Map Ref: ST2985

Now extensively restored, this stately Charles II mansion was acquired by Newport Borough Council in 1974 and stands in huge and lovely grounds in which many of the old estate buildings have been restored. There is a delightful children's farm too; also an aquarium and a large boating lake with facilities for fishing. Parking is free and there is a fine restaurant.

Around harbour walls

Two beaches of golden sand enclosed by rocky headlands and overlooked by ancient walls and a tumble of Georgian and Victorian houses help to make Tenby one of the most delightful of Welsh towns.

1 FIVE ARCHES
Originally this great bastion of stone was built as the west gate of the town wall. Three of the five were erected in recent times for traffic. The town walls were built in the 13th century and considerably strengthened in the 16th, when fears of a Spanish invasion were at their height.

2 WAR MEMORIAL GARDENS
In south-western Wales it is possible to grow plants which cannot withstand the colder weather elsewhere – and Tenby is especially sheltered, so palm trees can be seen in its pleasant and well laid-out gardens.

3 THE HARBOUR
The Harbour is given its particular charm by the higgledy-piggledy rows of brightly painted houses which surround it. Fishing boats still make use of the sheltered waters here, and the Sluice is a little loop of water used for the winter maintenance of boats. Around the Sluice are three-storeyed buildings which were built as fish markets and net stores. Overlooking the harbour is St Julian's Seaman's Church, and dotted along the walls are bollards made from cannons used by land batteries against Parliamentary ships in 1643.

4 CASTLE HILL
Stretches of broken walls and foundations are the surviving remnants of Tenby Castle, once a powerful fortress. The remains probably date from about 1153, but there was a castle here before that. To the south, and only 500yds offshore, is St Catherine's Island – on which stands a fort built in 1864 to protect the approaches to Milford Haven.

5 TENBY MUSEUM
Built partly into the remaining walls of the castle, the museum contains the Smith collection of animal remains and the Lyons collection of shells amongst various interesting displays.

6 TUDOR MERCHANT'S HOUSE (NT)
This special survivor of Tenby's mercantile past was probably built in the 15th century and considerably altered and extended in the 16th. In the late 1960s removal of old lime wash revealed the house's original painted wall decorations. The house contains furniture and fittings from many periods.

7 ST MARY'S CHURCH
One of the largest and most handsome parish churches in Wales, St Mary's was enlarged by the addition of chapels and a north aisle during the 15th century. At the same time it gained the beautiful wagon roof in the chancel – a feature especially noteworthy for its carved and painted bosses. There are many interesting tombs in the church, including one depicting a 15th-century cleric as a shrouded skeleton. A tablet commemorates Robert Recorde – inventor of the equals sign – who was born in the town in 1510.

8 ESPLANADE
Overlooking the South Beach, the Esplanade is lined with handsome Victorian and Edwardian buildings, nearly all of which are hotels. From here are marvellous views across to Caldey Island, the site of a monastery on and off for more than a thousand years.

EARLY CLOSING: *Wed*

PARKING: *Marsh Rd, North Beach, Upper Park Rd*

OPENING TIMES:
Tenby Museum: open all year
Tudor Merchant's House: open Easter – Sep. Mon – Fri and Sun pm

ROUTE DIRECTIONS
Start at Five Arches (1) and walk along South Parade, with the town wall on the r. On the l. at the junction with Upper Park Rd are the War Memorial Gardens (2). Continue for a short way along South Parade, then turn r. into Town Wall Arcade to reach Upper Frog St. Turn l, reach white Lion St, turn r. and then l. into the Norton. By the tourist information centre descend a zigzag path to the r. to reach North Beach. Turn r. along North Walk, and walk along the l. side of the Sluice to reach the Harbour (3). Pass St Julian's Seamen's Church and reach Castle Sq. Take the footpath to the l. round Castle Hill (4). On the far side of the headland is Tenby Museum (5). Continue on the footpath back to Castle Sq. Go forward in the square, then bear r. along Bridge St, and keep l. into Harbour Court. Reach the Tudor Merchant's House (6) and then turn l, climbing the steps up Quay Hill. Turn r. into Tudor Sq, keep forward into the High St, with St Mary's Church (7) on the left. Go through the churchyard and leave by the south gate, cross St George's St and enter St Mary's St. At the end turn r. into Paragon. Turn l. and r, passing the entrance to the Imperial Hotel, and pass through an arch of the town wall, Belmont Archway, to reach St Florence Parade. Turn l. then r. along the Esplanade (8). At the end turn r. into Victoria St, then r. into Southcliffe St, then l. into St Florence Parade to return to the start.

The bustling harbour of Tenby – one of the most delightful Welsh resorts

TRETOWER COURT & CASTLE (AM CADW), Powys

Open daily; between A40 & A479. Map Ref: SO1821

Just north of Crickhowell, this stately home stands in the beautiful Usk Valley. Across a nearby meadow is ruined Tretower Castle, a tall round tower with a short stretch of 13th-century curtain wall and parapet.

VALE OF RHEIDOL LIGHT RAILWAY, Dyfed

Open spring to autumn; off A44 & A4120. Map Ref: SN5881 to SN7376

From Aberystwyth, the diminutive tank engines of this narrow-gauge railway climb 12 miles through woods and forested hillsides, past Aberffrwd Reservoir and into steep gorges before terminating just below the village of Devil's Bridge, nearly 700ft above sea-level. Here the River Mynach meets the River Rheidol in a series of spectacular falls which drop a total of 300ft. Three bridges span the gorge, one above the other, the lowest reputedly built by the Devil. A spectacular and steep footpath past thundering water and through paths wet with spray provides a 45-minute walk to the lowest level down hundreds of steps. Seats are placed at strategic points on the climb, and less energetic trails also exist in the area.

WELSH MINERS' MUSEUM, Cynonville, West Glamorgan
See Afan Argoed Country Park

WELSHPOOL, Powys

Map Ref: SJ2207

Welshpool's half-timbered buildings, rich with carved oak decoration and white plaster, are more characteristic of the upper Severn Valley than of Wales. The excellent Powysland Museum contains much about the ancient princedom of Gwenwynwyn, who granted the town a market charter in 1263.

Powis Castle (NT), 1 mile south, is a stately home that has been continuously inhabited for over 500 years. Visitors can buy shrubs and plants in its 18th-century gardens. Near by, a 7-mile stretch of the Shropshire Union Canal is used by craft specially adapted for use by severely handicapped people. At Llanfair Caereinion, some 7 miles west of Welshpool, are beautiful forested valleys with picnic sites, parking and viewing places.

WHITE CASTLE (AM CADW), Gwent

Open daily; on unclassified road off B4233 7m E Abergavenny. Map Ref: SO3816

The gentle valley of the River Monnow was a weakness in the Welsh border defences between the River Wye cliffs and the Welsh hills, and three castles were built to plug it – the White Castle, and nearby Grosmont (AM Cadw) and Skenfrith (AM Cadw, NT) castles. Started in about 1180 and extended in the 13th century, the White Castle was defended by great towers and a deep moat. Curiously, it was once covered in white plaster, hence its name. In recent times it had an odd historical connection with Rudolph Hess, Hitler's Deputy, who used to feed the swans in the moat on outings from nearby Abergavenny.

WOLVES NEWTON MODEL FARM, Llangwm, Gwent

Open all year; off B4235. Map Ref: ST4599

Housed in 18th-century farm buildings is a museum and craft centre where visitors can watch old skills being demonstrated and explore a Victorian Cottage Bedroom, complete in every detail. Other fascinating exhibits include 'Toys of Yesteryear', an agricultural section and some rather curious (and to say the least painful-looking) medical instruments.

Craft workshops are grouped around the mill courtyard, and the Country Kitchen Restaurant serves good food all day. There is also an audio-visual show giving a humorous insight into Victorian life, including a daunting Victorian pin-up! Picnic areas offer plenty of space to relax and enjoy the magnificent views; from near by Wolves Newton it is possible to see seven counties of England and Wales.

WREXHAM, Clwyd

Map Ref: SJ3349

Wrexham, the most important industrial town in North Wales, is an excellent shopping centre and offers many other attractions. In the lovely Church of St Giles are two monuments by the celebrated early 18th-century French sculptor Roubiliac, plus an altar piece and painting given by Elihu Yale – who gave his name to Yale University and is buried here.

Erddig Hall (NT), a magnificent house in 1,900 acres, has remained undisturbed for centuries and gives a rare insight into the days of the great country residence. Its priceless contents include exquisite mirrors, period furniture, Chinese paintings, magnificent tapestries and a state bed with rare Chinese covers. Out of doors are workshops, stables, old vehicles, penny-farthing cycles and formal gardens restored as near as possible to the original plan laid 250 years ago.

Old skills passed down the generations of Welsh craftspeople are demonstrated in the Wolves Newton Model Farm, housed in 18th-century buildings, in Gwent

INDEX OF SUBJECTS

Acknowledgements

The Automobile Association wishes to thank the following organisations and libraries for their assistance in the compilation of this book.

Ruth Wollen, Blue Chip Illustration 6/7, 14/15, 20, 23, 26/7, 42/3; *British Waterways Board* 29 Narrowboat; *National Trust Photo Library* 25 Textile conservation at Kingston Lacy; *P & O Cruises* 54/5 On board ship; *PPP* 13 Hospital patient; *Saga Scene* 10 Exercise, 36 Scrabble, 39 Jogging; *Sally Line* 48 Boarding the ferry; *Spectrum Colour Library* 9 Lunch tray, 18 Timeshare apartments, Puerto Banus, 25 Village fête, 52 Capri, 53 Limassol, 56 Benidorm; *Swiss National Tourist Office* 50 Grindelwald, 51 Jungfrau railway; *West Country Tourist Board* 72/3 Barge at Cotehele

The following photographs are from the Automobile Association's Picture Library:

M Adelman 134 Lichfield, 135 Lincoln, 181 Dunfermline Abbey, 188/9 Skye, 193 Scourie; *D Austin* 81 Poole; *M Birkitt* 129 Cromford, 130/1 Ely Cathedral, 138/9 Well dressing, 141 Stowmarket; *E A Bowness* 156 Dove Cottage, Grasmere; *P & G Bowater* 167 Ripon, 190/1 Preston Mill; *D Corrance* 44 Golf at Gullane; *R Czaja* 71 Corfe Castle; *R Eames* 202/3 Bodnant Garden; *R Fletcher* 90 Christchurch, 112 Butterfly Farm; *A Grierley* 4/5 Red Wharf Bay, 59 St James's Park, 94/5 Blenheim Palace, 118 Windsor, 198 Llyn Gwynant; *B Johnson* 80 Penzance, 114/5 HMS *Warrior*, 174 Gairloch; *S King* 195 Younger Botanic Garden; *A Lawson* 63 Mousehole, 74 Exeter, 78 Land's End; *B Littlewood* 148/9 Beamish Museum; *S & O Mathews* 31 Bird watchers, 66/7 Bicton, 84/5 Tewkesbury, 86 Wells, 92/3 Bateman's, 96 Brighton rock, 98 Old Weavers' shop, 99 Greyfriars, 100/1 Tapestry, Chichester Cathedral, 146 Aysgarth Lower Falls, 157 Durham, 160 Housesteads Fort, 180 Dumfries; *E Meacher* 68/9 Bowood House; *C Molyneux* 151 Beverley Minster, 199 Nr Cwmystwyth, 201 Aberystwyth, 209 Conwy castle; *R Newton* 64 Avebury, 87 Wilton House, 122 Derwent valley, 132 Ironbridge, 150 Bradford, 153 Castle Howard, 164 North York Moors railway, 166 Rievaulx, 169 York; *C Ridley* 113 Oxford; *P Russell* 205 Caerleon Castle; *Stephen Gibson Photography* 184/5 Pollok House; *R Surman* 123 Snowshill Manor, 124/5 Birmingham, 126/7 Bury St Edmunds, 133 Old Custom House, King's Lynn, 136 Ludlow Castle, 137 Much Wenlock, 142/3 Warwick, 155 Coniston, 159 Lindisfarne, 204 Caernarfon, 208 Conwy; *M Trelawny* 40 Walkers at Cissbury Ring, 91 Alfriston; *R Weir* 176/7 River Dee, 179 Craigievar Castle; *H Williams* 33 Saltram House, 62 Oare, 76/7 Glastonbury Tor, 82/3 Stonehenge, 97 Box Hill, 104/5 Hawk Conservancy, 116/7 Weald & Downland Open-Air Museum, 186 Highland Wildlife Park, 200 Afan Argoed CP, 206 Chepstow, 210/11 Kidwelly, 214/5 St David's Head, 216/7 Tintern Abbey, 220 Wolves Newton; *T Woodcock* 108/9 Royal Naval College